井上雄彦

Takehiko Inoue

I'VE STARTED PRACTICING CALLIGRAPHY. I USE BRUSHES IN MY WORK ALL THE TIME, BUT THIS IS THE FIRST TIME SINCE JUNIOR HIGH THAT I'VE USED A PROPER CALLIGRAPHY BRUSH. I ENJOY IT BECAUSE I HAVE TO PUT PRESSURE ON MYSELF TO FOCUS.

IT WAS HARDER THAN I EXPECTED AT FIRST, PARTICULARLY BECAUSE THE CHARACTER I CHOSE AS MY FIRST WAS SUPPOSED TO BE A GOOD ONE FOR BEGINNERS. AFTER TWO OR THREE TRIES THOUGH, I REALIZED I WAS COMPLETELY FOCUSED ON WHAT I WAS DOING AND I WASN'T THINKING AT ALL ABOUT MY EVERYDAY LIFE. GOTTA LOVE THAT.

Takehiko Inoue's *Slam Dunk* is one of the most popular manga of all time, having sold over 100 million copies worldwide. He followed that series up with two titles lauded by critics and fans alike—*Vagabond*, a fictional account of the life of Miyamoto Musashi, and *Real*, a manga about wheelchair basketball.

SLAM DUNK
Vol. 13: UNSTOPPABLE

SHONEN JUMP Manga Edition

STORY AND ART BY TAKEHIKO INOUE

English Adaptation/Kelly Sue DeConnick
Translation/Joe Yamazaki
Touch-up Art & Lettering/James Gaubatz
Cover and Graphic Design/Sean Lee, Matt Hinrichs
Editors/Kit Fox, Mike Montesa

Printed in Canada

Published by VIZ Media, LLC
P.O. Box 77010
San Francisco, CA 94107

10 9 8 7 6 5 4 3 2 1
First printing, December 2010

SLAM DUNK

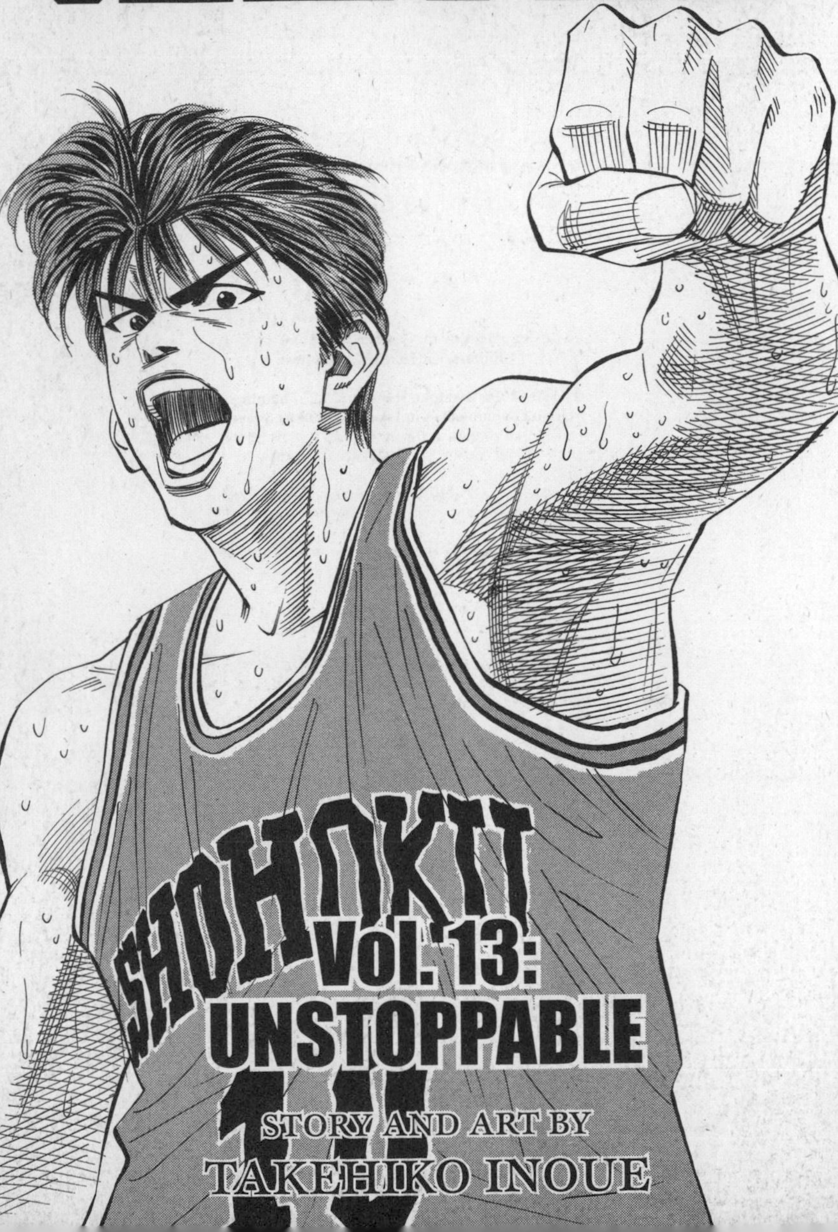
SHOHOKU

Vol. 13: UNSTOPPABLE

STORY AND ART BY

TAKEHIKO INOUE

Character Introduction

Hanamichi Sakuragi
A first-year at Shohoku High School, Sakuragi is in love with Haruko Akagi.

Haruko Akagi
Also a first-year at Shohoku, Takenori Akagi's little sister has a crush on Kaede Rukawa.

Takenori Akagi
A third-year and the basketball team's captain, Akagi has an intense passion for his sport.

Kaede Rukawa
The object of Haruko's affection (and that of many of Shohoku's female students!), this first-year has been a star player since junior high.

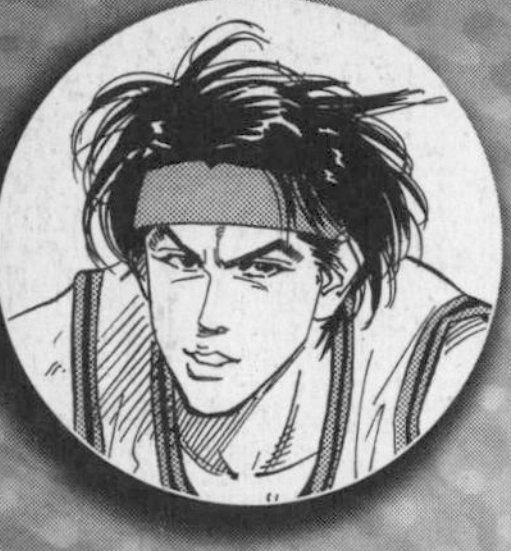

Kiyota

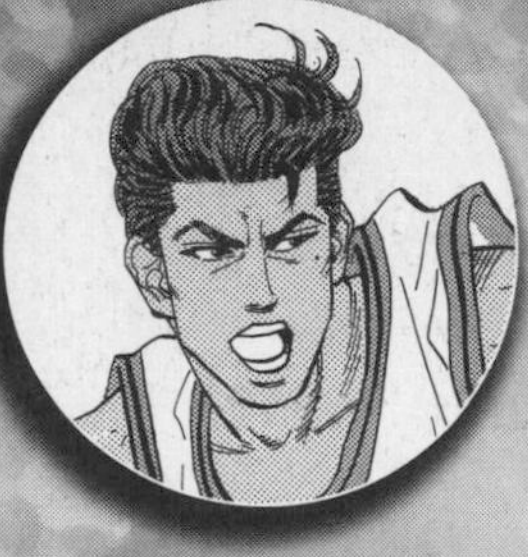

Maki

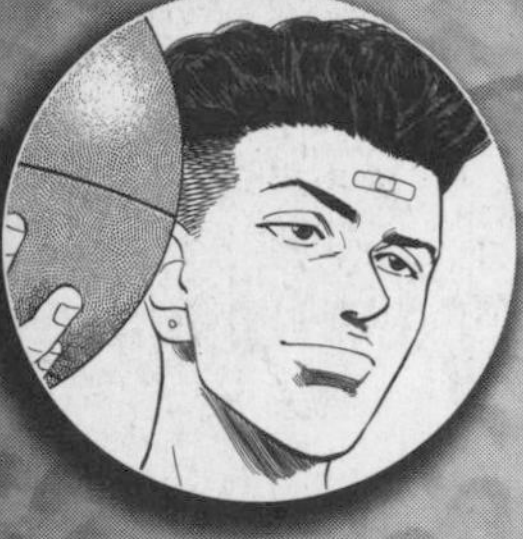

Ryota Miyagi
A problem child with a thing for Ayako.

Ayako
Basketball Team Manager

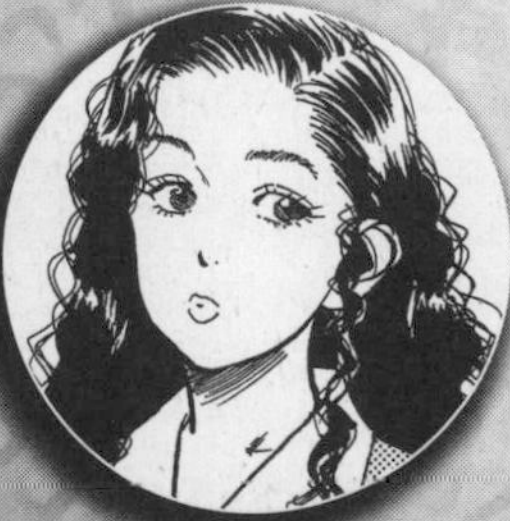

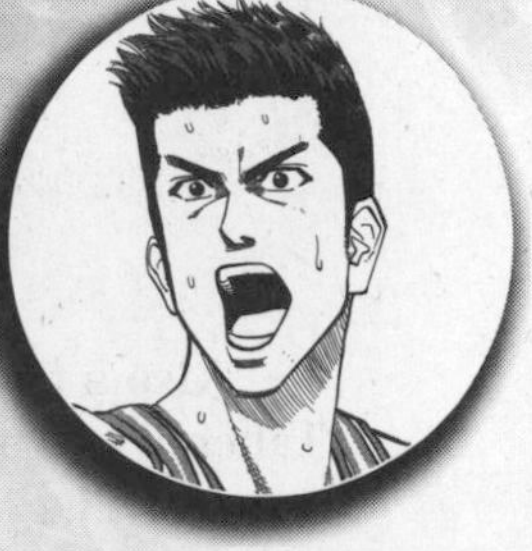

Hisashi Mitsui
An MVP during junior high.

Our Story Thus Far

Hanamichi Sakuragi is rejected by close to 50 girls during his three years in junior high. In high school, he joins the basketball team in order to get closer to his beloved Haruko, whose brother is the team captain. However, the endless fundamental drills do not suit his personality, and he and Captain Akagi frequently butt heads.

After a good showing at their first exhibition, the team has its sights set on Nationals when ex-problem-child Ryota Miyagi reclaims his position as Point Guard. Not long after Miyagi, Hisashi Mitsui—a junior-high-MVP-turned-gang-thug—finds he too misses the game and rejoins the team.

Shohoku's new lineup advances through Prefecturals to face Shoyo, and amazingly, Mitsui and Rukawa lead the boys to a two-point victory. In their first game against Kainan, "King" Kainan's Coach Takato uncovers Sakuragi's weakness and Shohoku finds itself in a pinch...

Vol. 13:
UNSTOPPABLE

Table of Contents

#108
SUPER POWERFUL REBOUND MACHINE

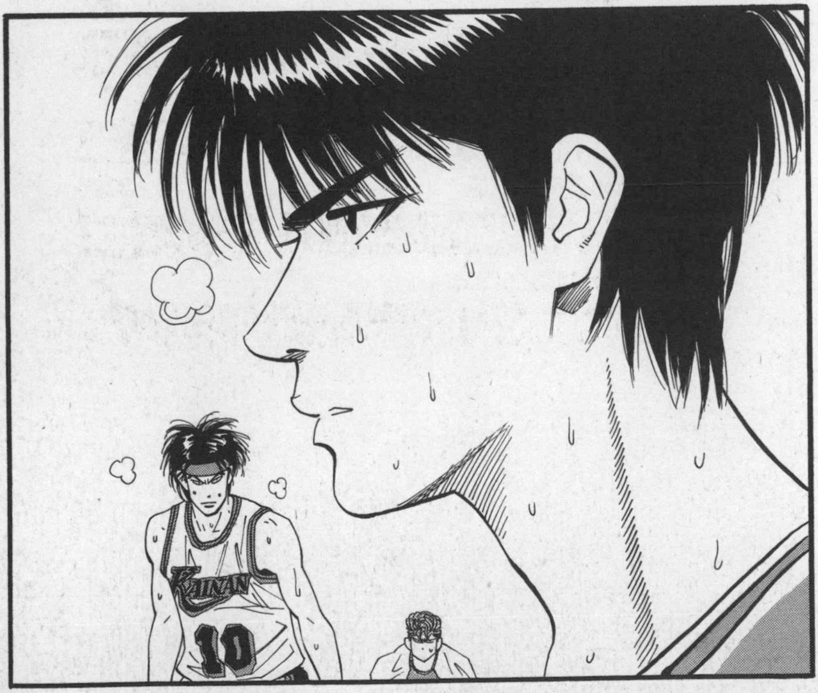
KAINAN
10

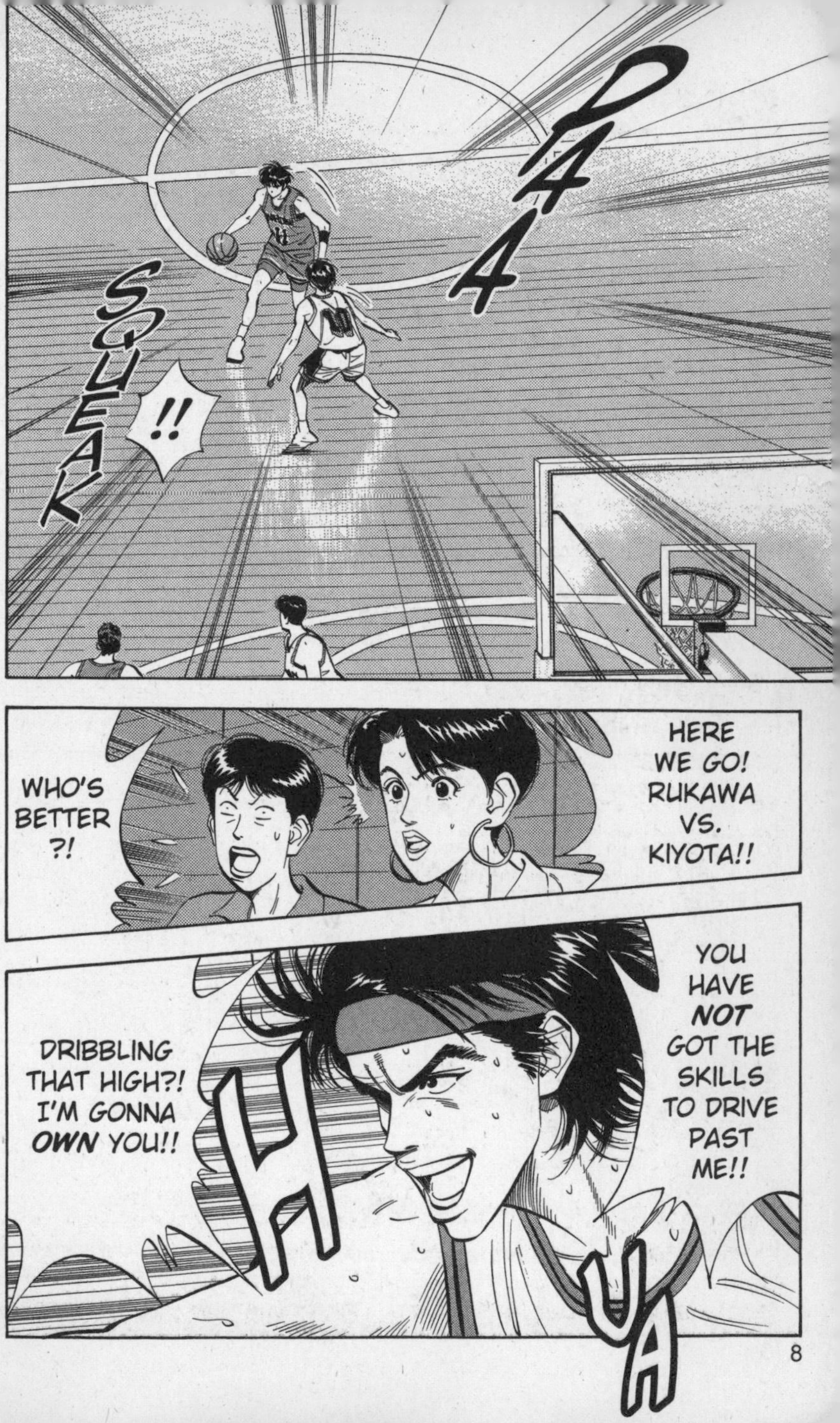
SQUEAK
!!
HERE WE GO! RUKAWA VS. KIYOTA!!
WHO'S BETTER ?!
YOU HAVE **NOT** GOT THE SKILLS TO DRIVE PAST ME!!
DRIBBLING THAT HIGH?! I'M GONNA **OWN** YOU!!
HUA

READ THIS WAY

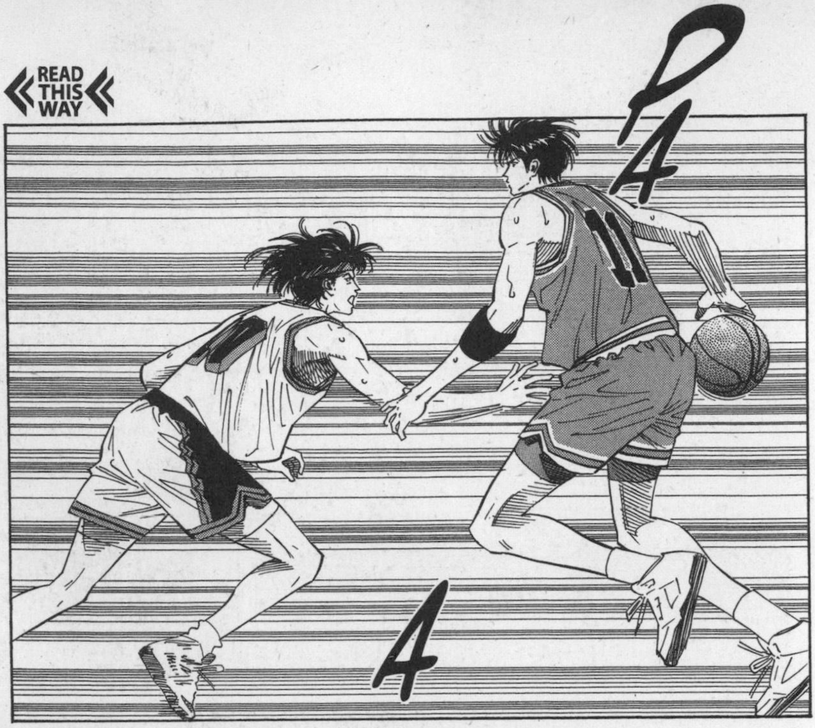

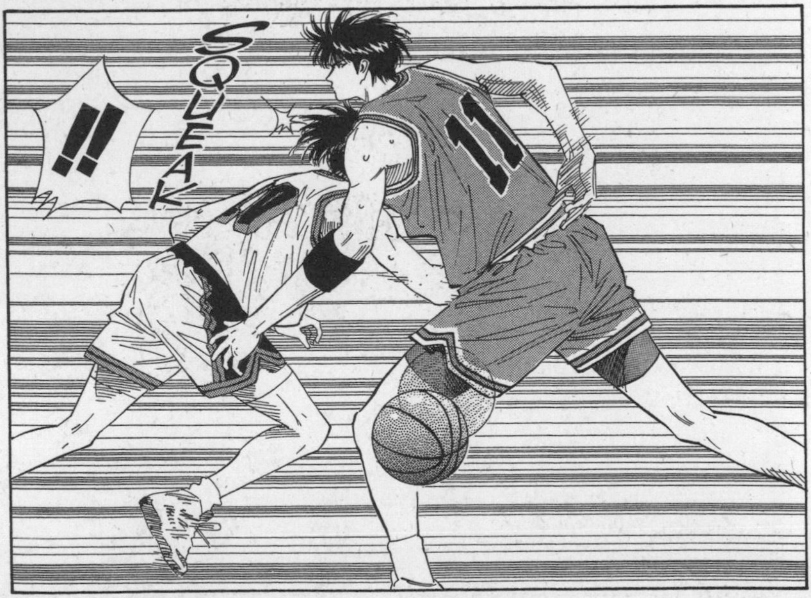
SQUEAK
!!

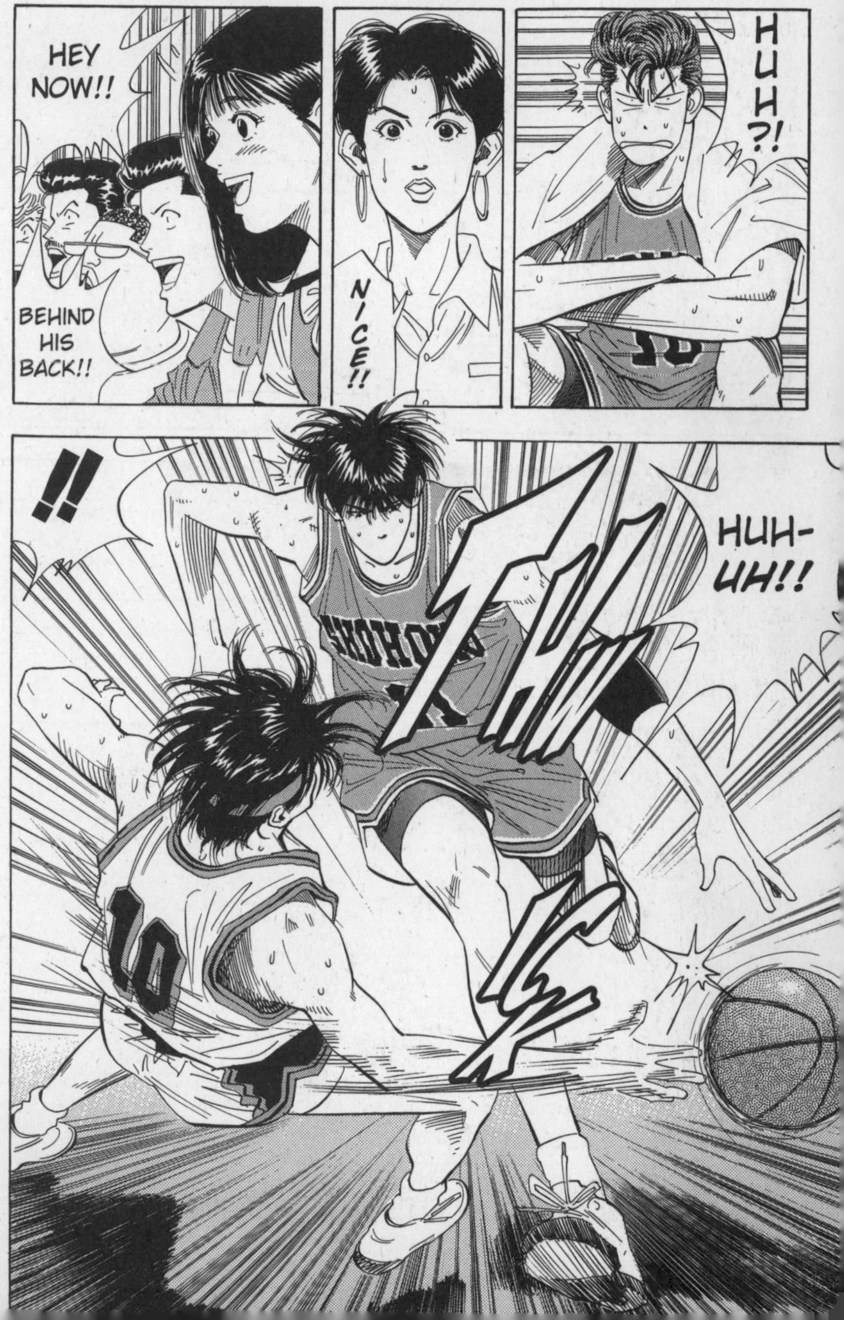
HUH?!
NICE!!
HEY NOW!!
BEHIND HIS BACK!!
HUH-UH!!
!!

READ THIS WAY

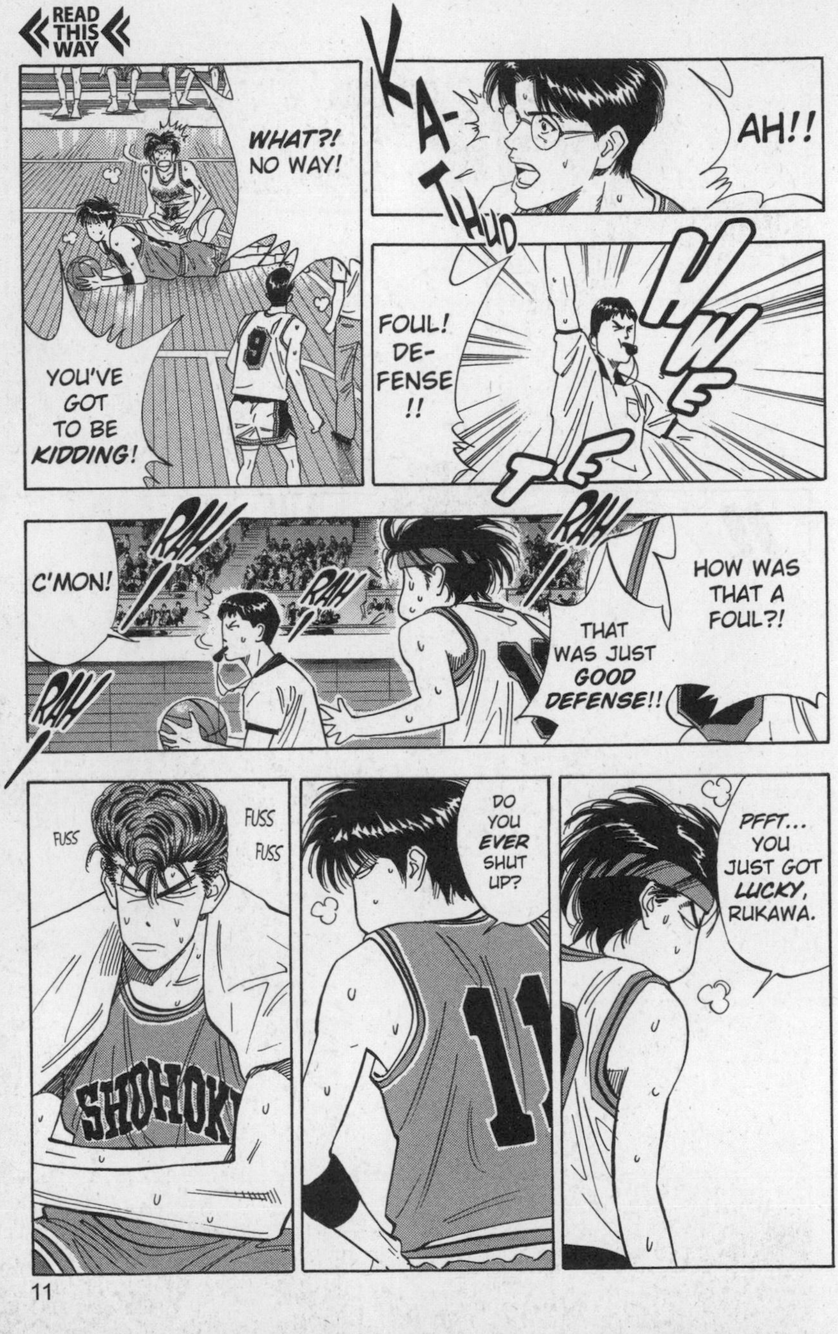
KA-THUD
AH!!
HWEET
FOUL! DE-FENSE!!
WHAT?! NO WAY!
YOU'VE GOT TO BE KIDDING!
HOW WAS THAT A FOUL?!
THAT WAS JUST GOOD DEFENSE!!
RAH
RAH
C'MON!
RAH
RAH
PFFT... YOU JUST GOT LUCKY, RUKAWA.
DO YOU EVER SHUT UP?
FUSS
FUSS
FUSS

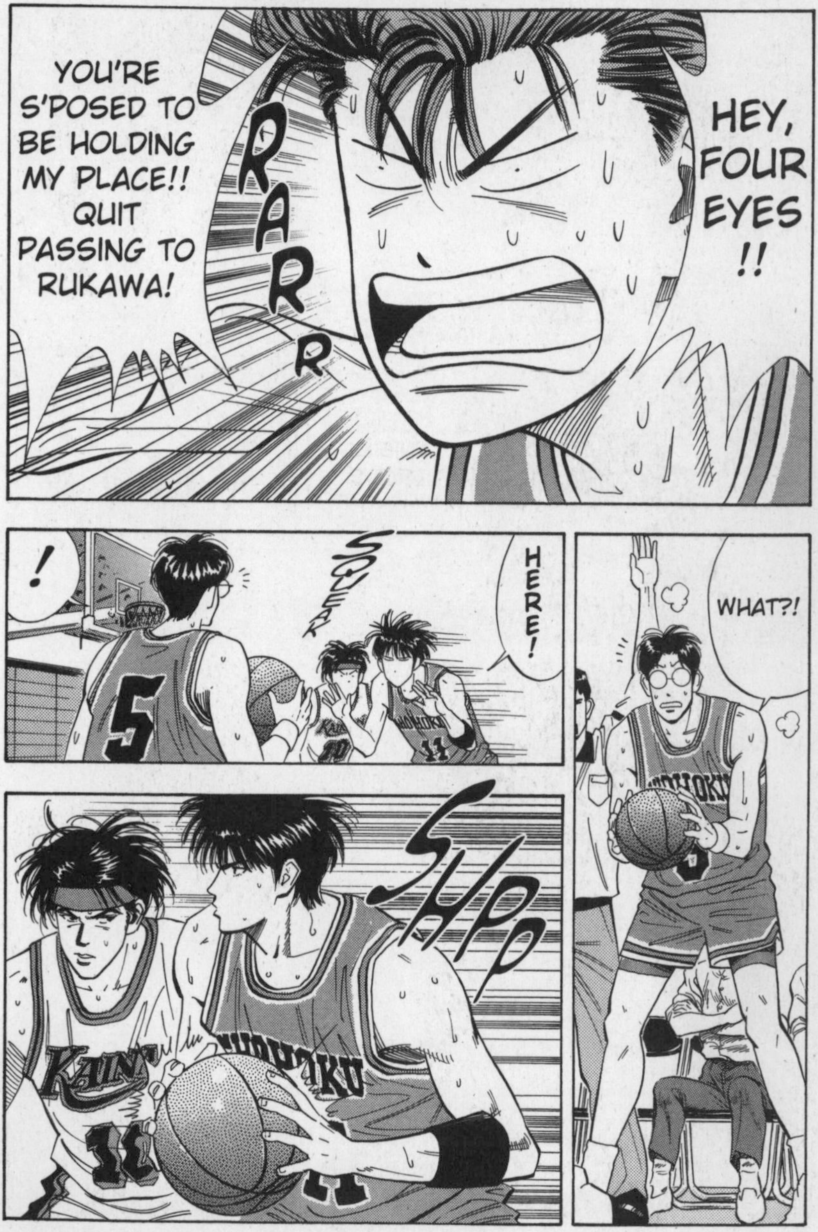
HEY, FOUR EYES!!
YOU'RE S'POSED TO BE HOLDING MY PLACE!! QUIT PASSING TO RUKAWA!
RARR
WHAT?!
HERE!
SQUEAK
!
SHPP

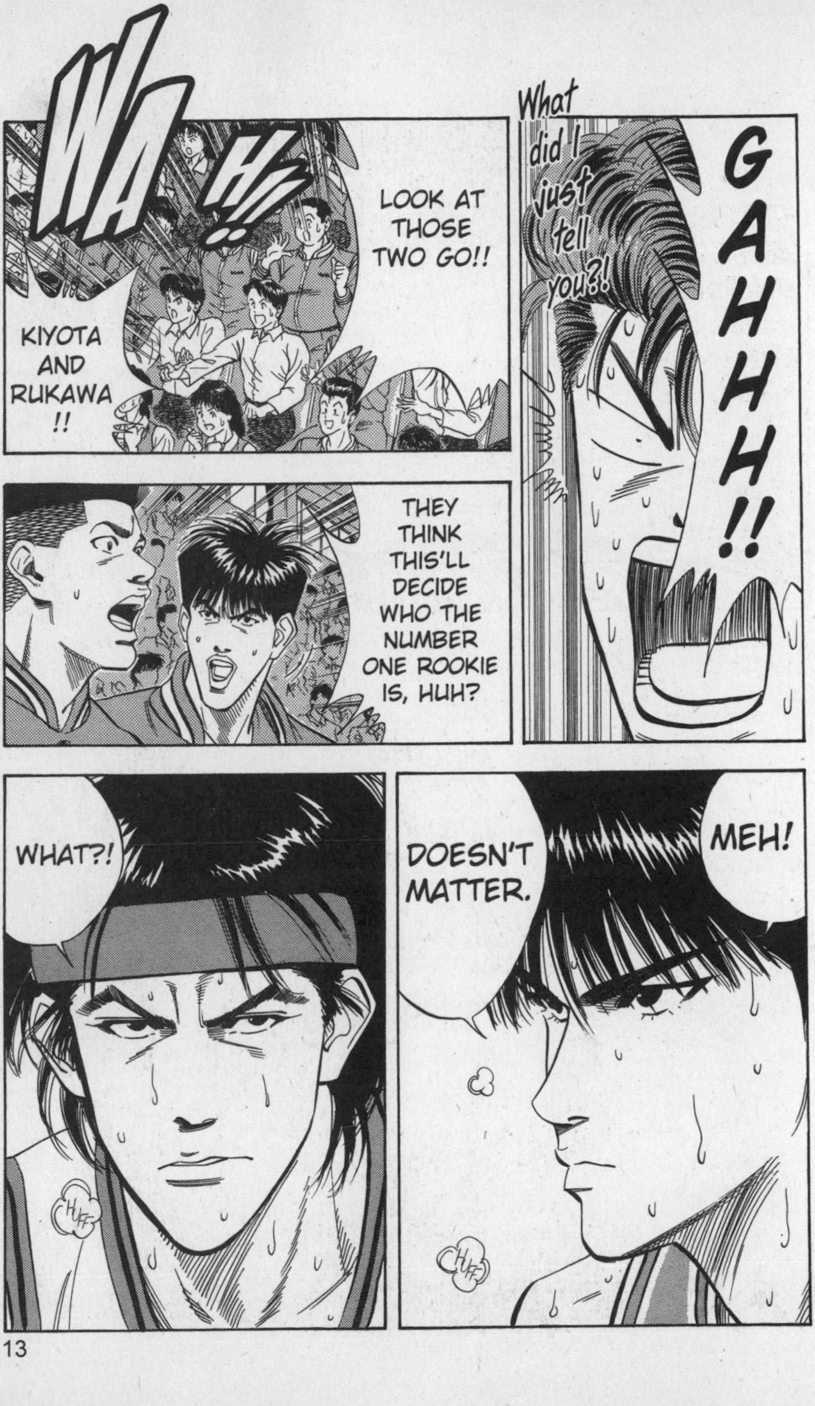
What did I just tell you?!
GAHHH!!
WAH!!
LOOK AT THOSE TWO GO!!
KIYOTA AND RUKAWA!!
THEY THINK THIS'LL DECIDE WHO THE NUMBER ONE ROOKIE IS, HUH?
MEH!
DOESN'T MATTER.
HUFF
WHAT?!
HUFF

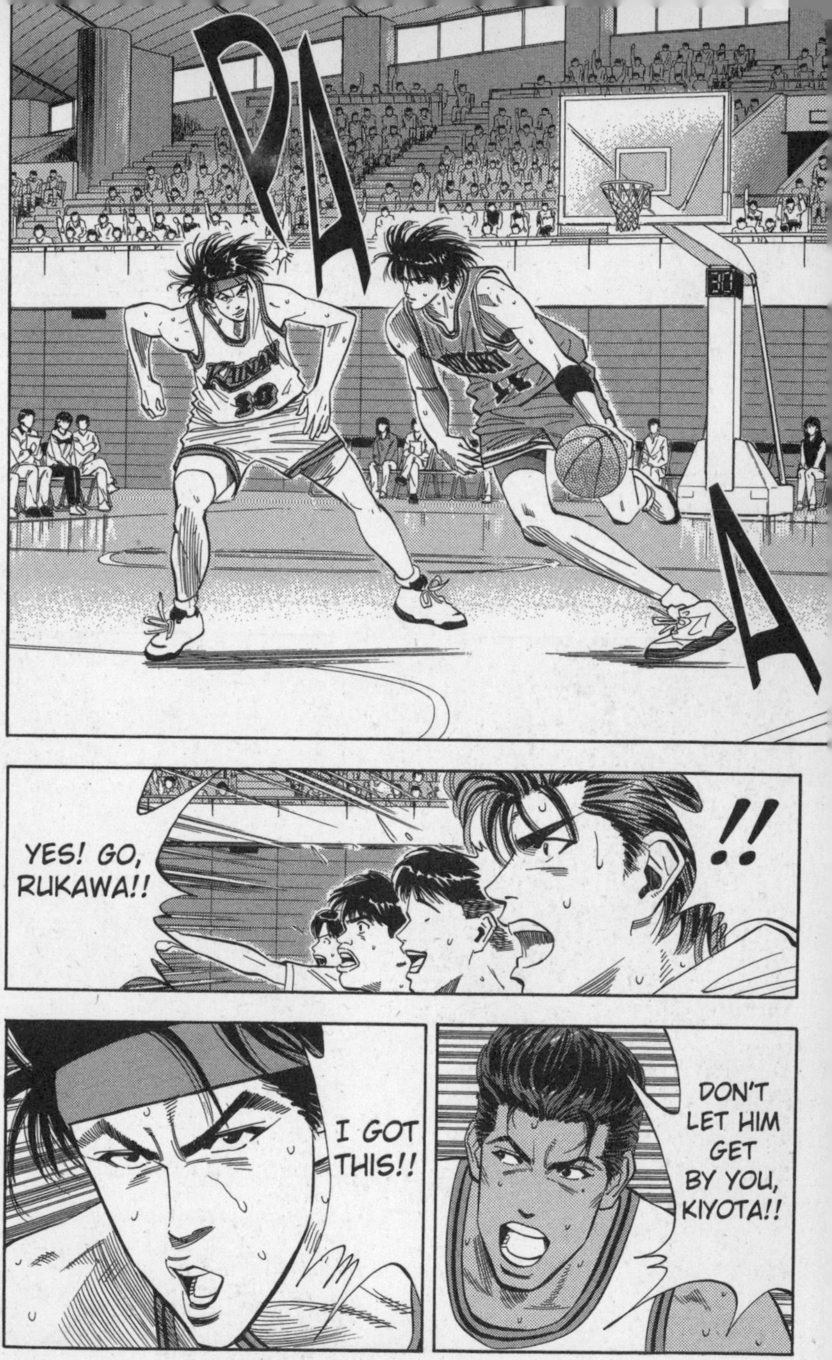
DA
A
!!
YES! GO, RUKAWA!!
DON'T LET HIM GET BY YOU, KIYOTA!!
I GOT THIS!!

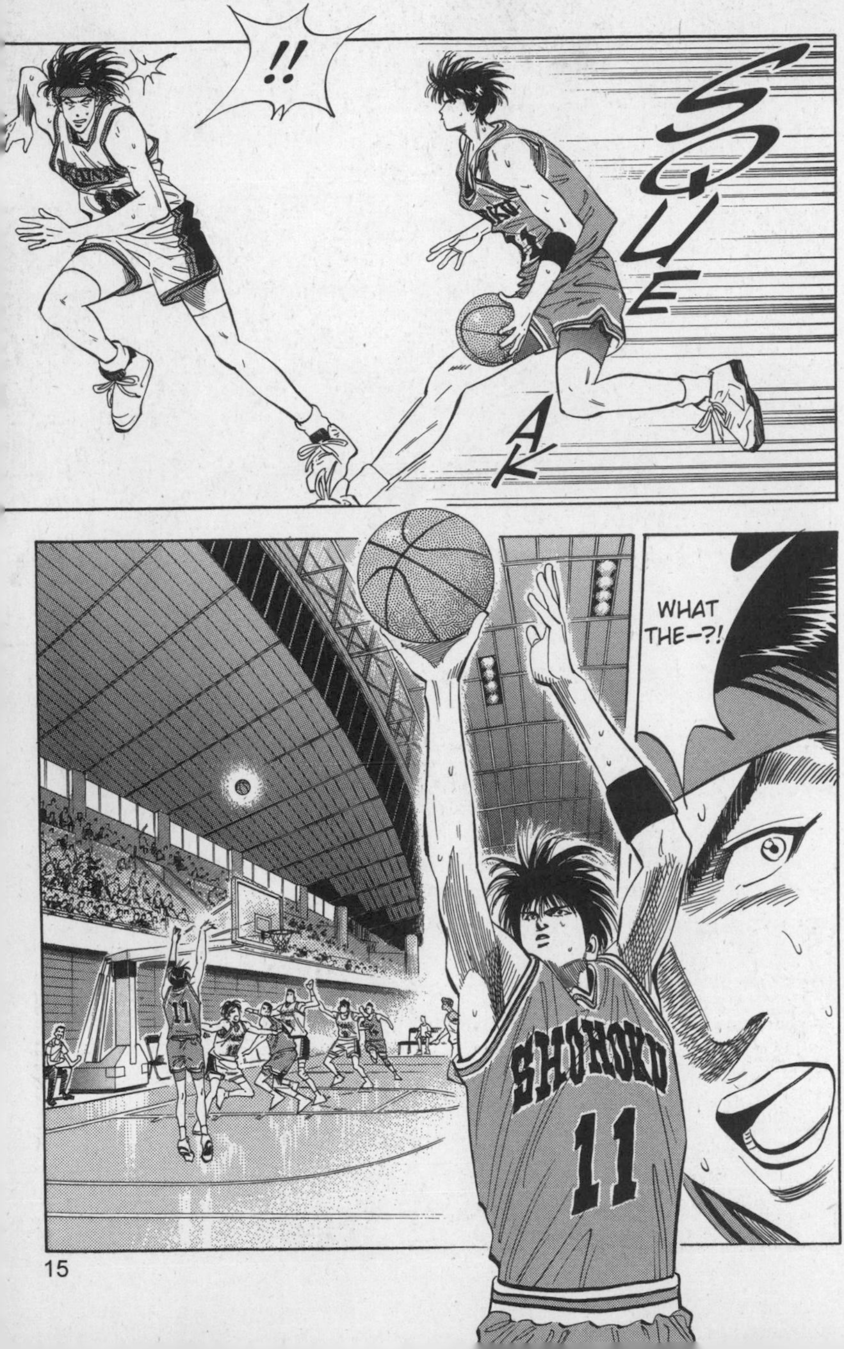
SQUEAK
!!
WHAT THE–?!
SHOHOKU
11

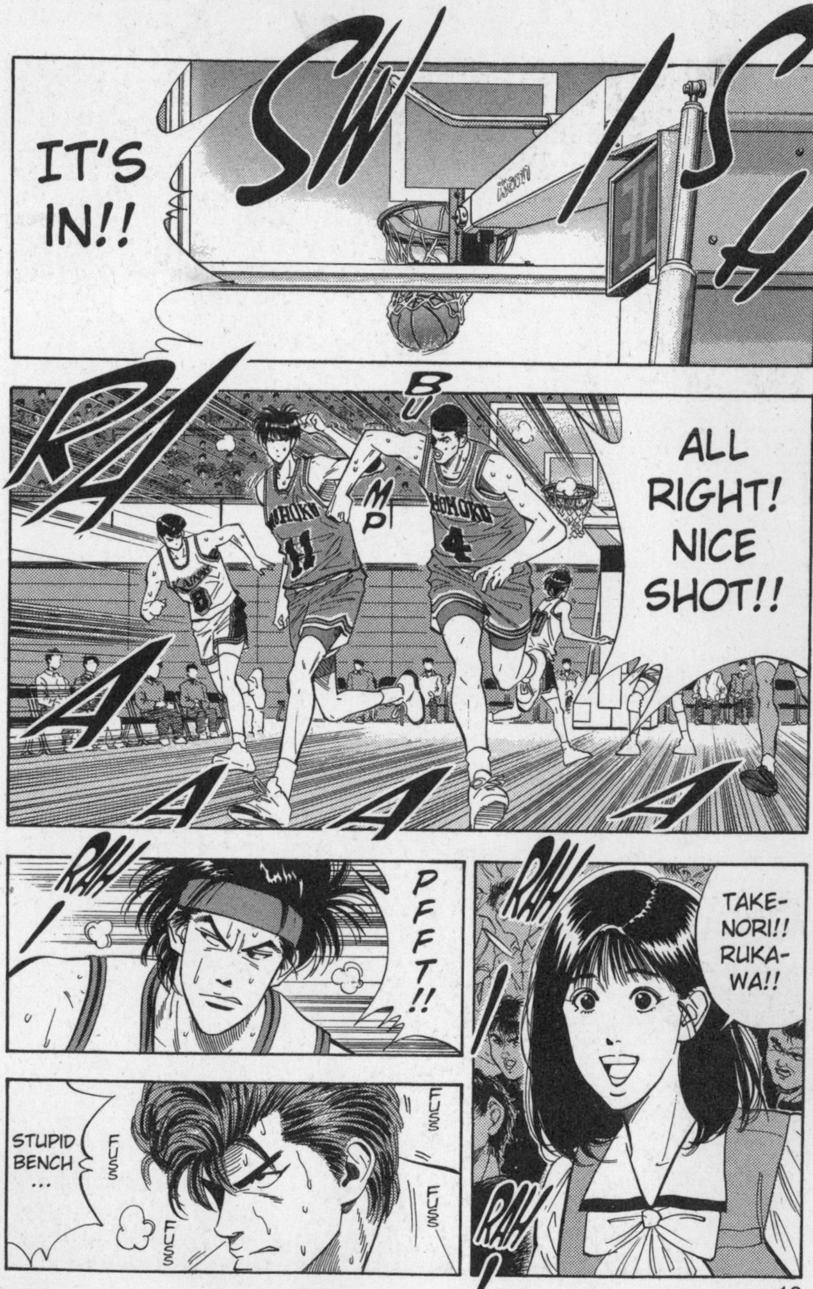
SWISH
IT'S IN!!
KRAAAAA
BUMP
ALL RIGHT! NICE SHOT!!
RAH!
TAKE-NORI!! RUKAWA!!
RAH!
RAH!
PFFT!!
FUSS
FUSS
STUPID BENCH ...
FUSS
FUSS

READ THIS WAY

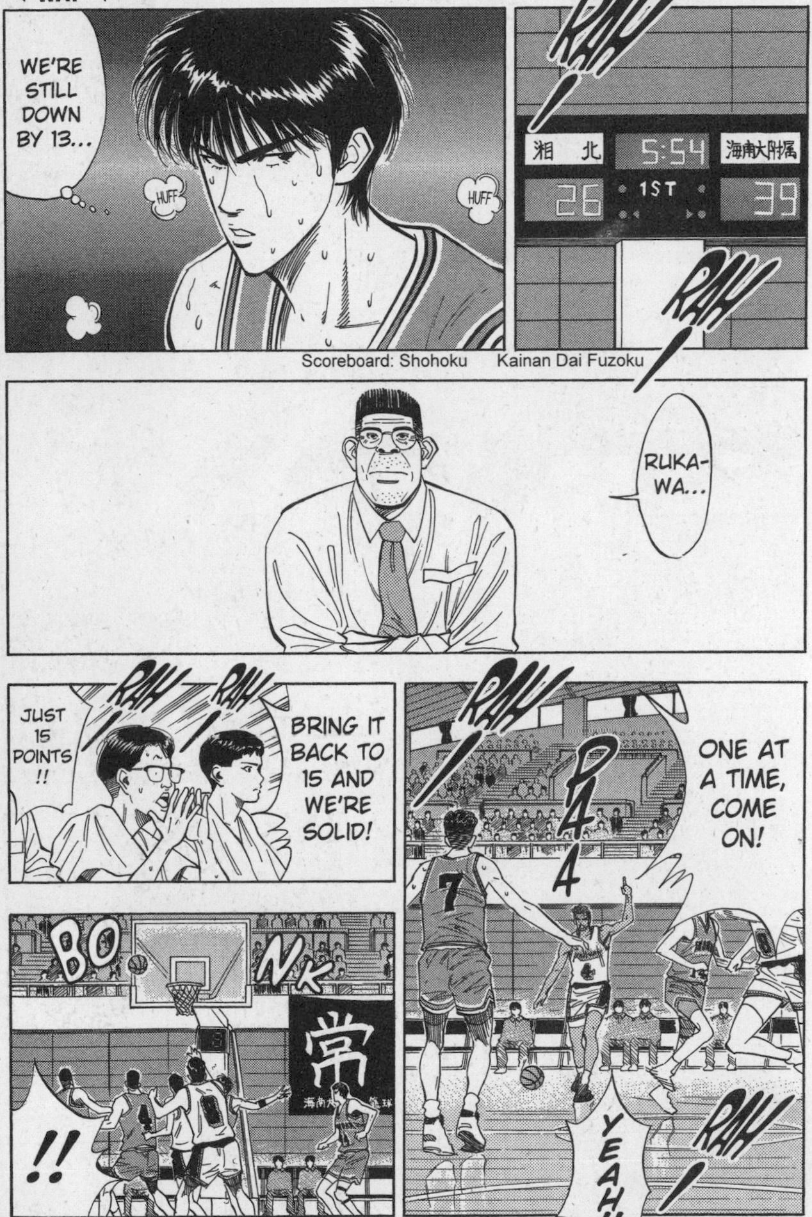
RAH
湘北
5:54
海南大附属
26
1ST
39
RAH
WE'RE STILL DOWN BY 13...
HUFF
HUFF
Scoreboard: Shohoku Kainan Dai Fuzoku
RUKAWA...
RAH
ONE AT A TIME, COME ON!
YEAH!!
RAH
RAH
RAH
BRING IT BACK TO 15 AND WE'RE SOLID!
JUST 15 POINTS !!
BONK
常
!!

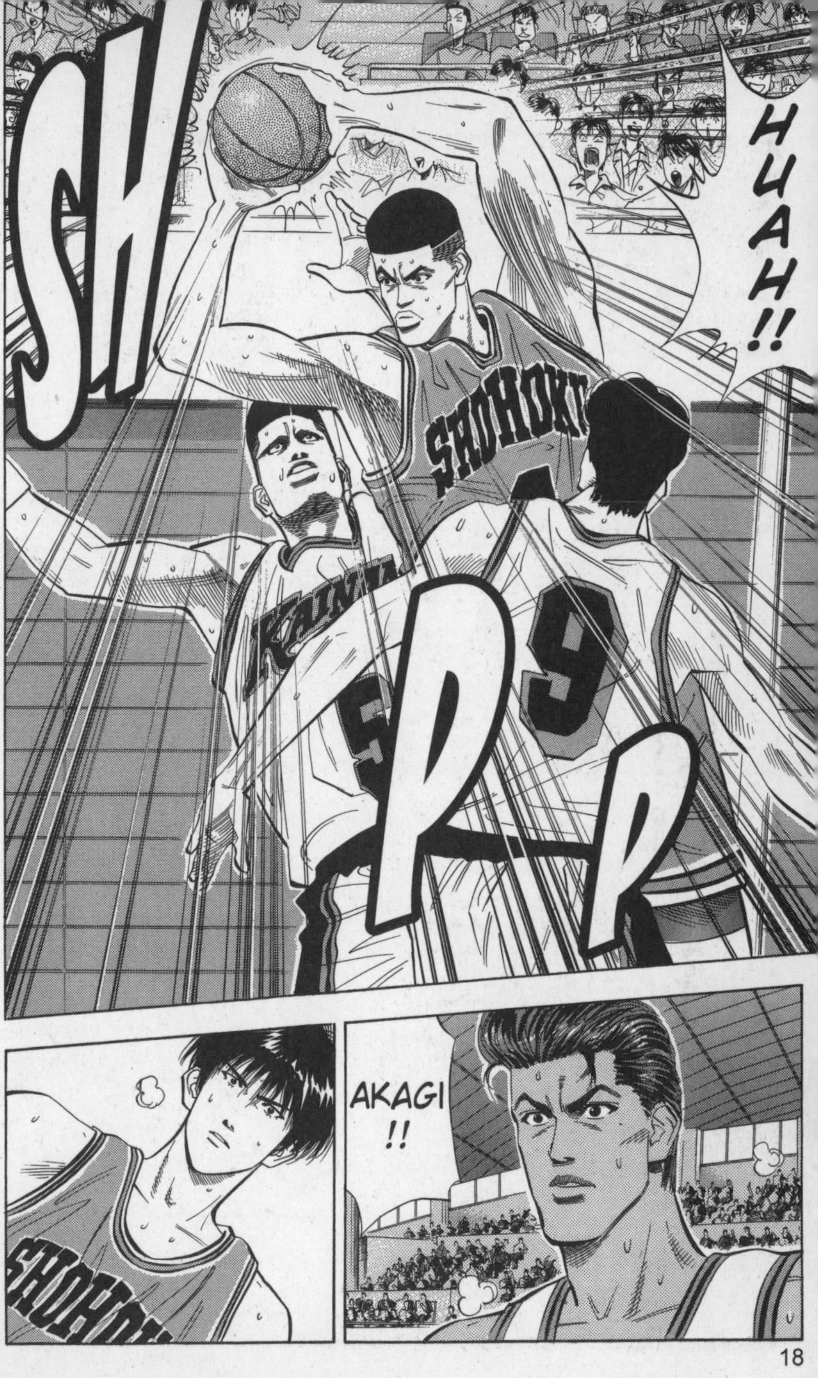
HUAH!!
SHPP
AKAGI !!

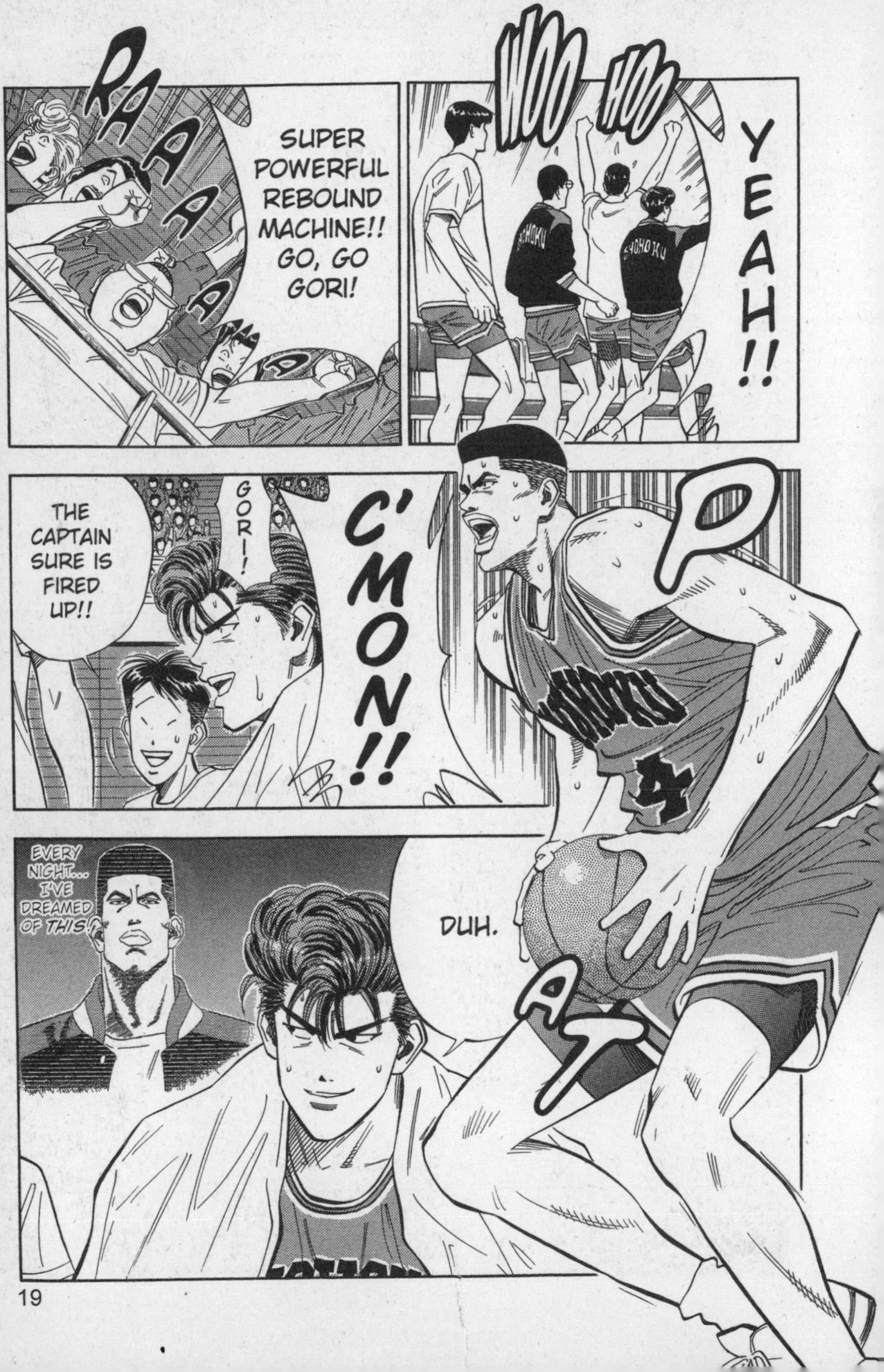
WOO HOO
YEAH!!
RAAAAA
SUPER POWERFUL REBOUND MACHINE!! GO, GO GORI!
C'MON!!
PAT
GORI!
THE CAPTAIN SURE IS FIRED UP!!
DUH.
EVERY NIGHT... I'VE DREAMED OF THIS!

Banner: *Josho* (ever victorious)
Kainan Dai Fuzoku High School Basketball Team

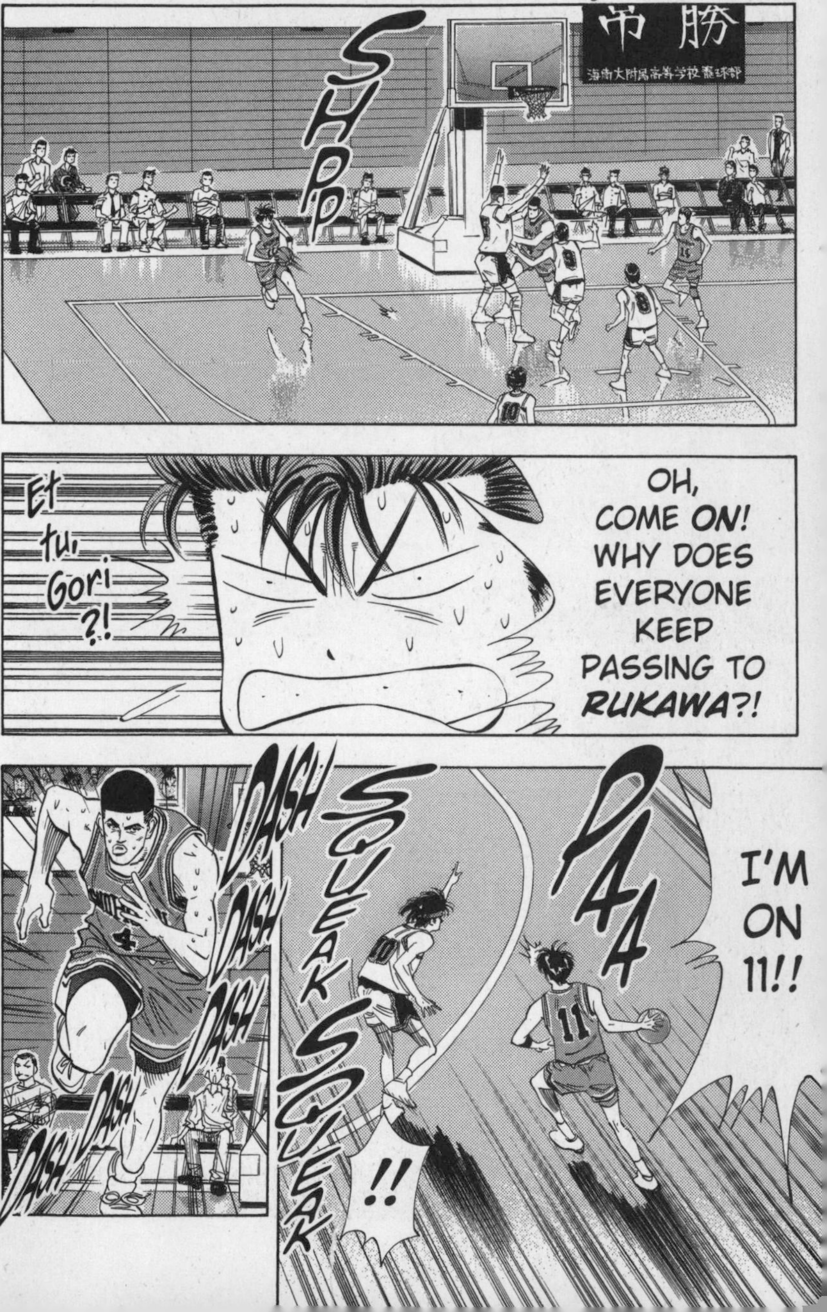
SHPP
OH, COME ON! WHY DOES EVERYONE KEEP PASSING TO RUKAWA?!
Et tu, Gori?!
I'M ON 11!!
PAA
!!
SQUEAK SQUEAK
DASH DASH DASH DASH DASH DASH DASH

READ THIS WAY

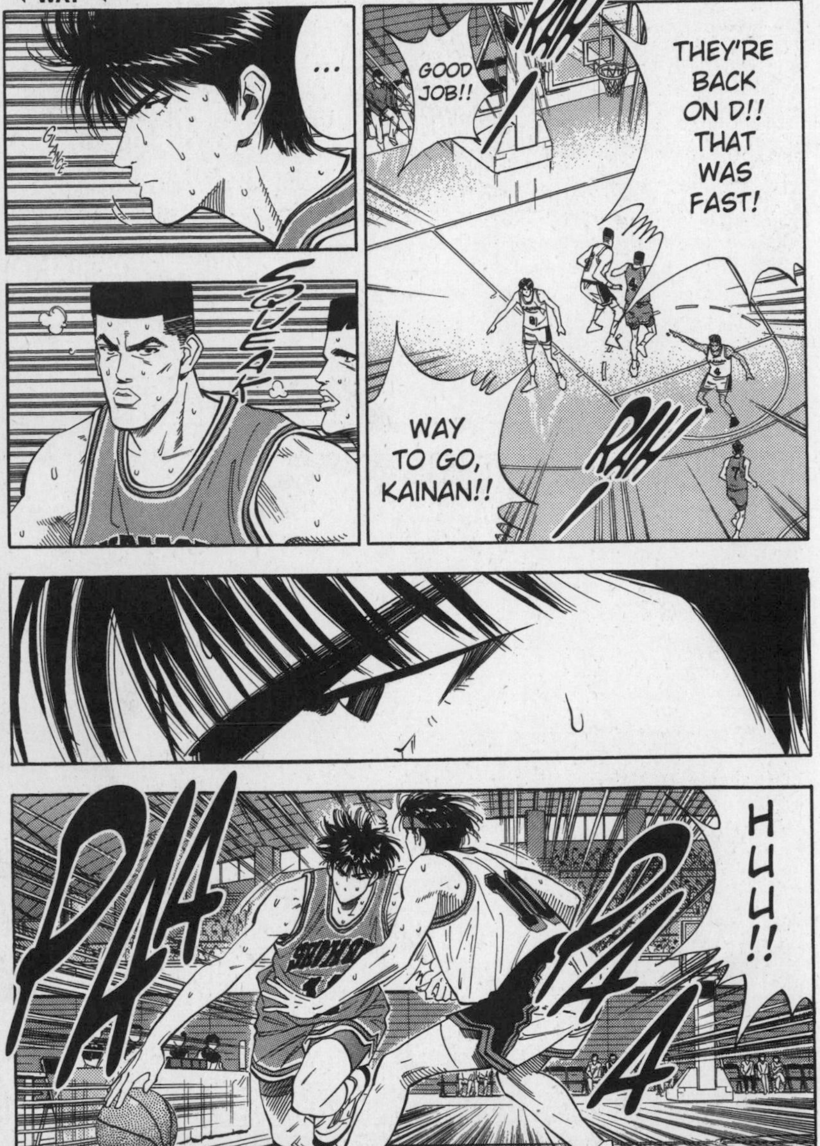
RAH
GOOD JOB!!
THEY'RE BACK ON D!! THAT WAS FAST!
WAY TO GO, KAINAN!!
RAH
...
GLANCE
SQUEAK
HUU!!

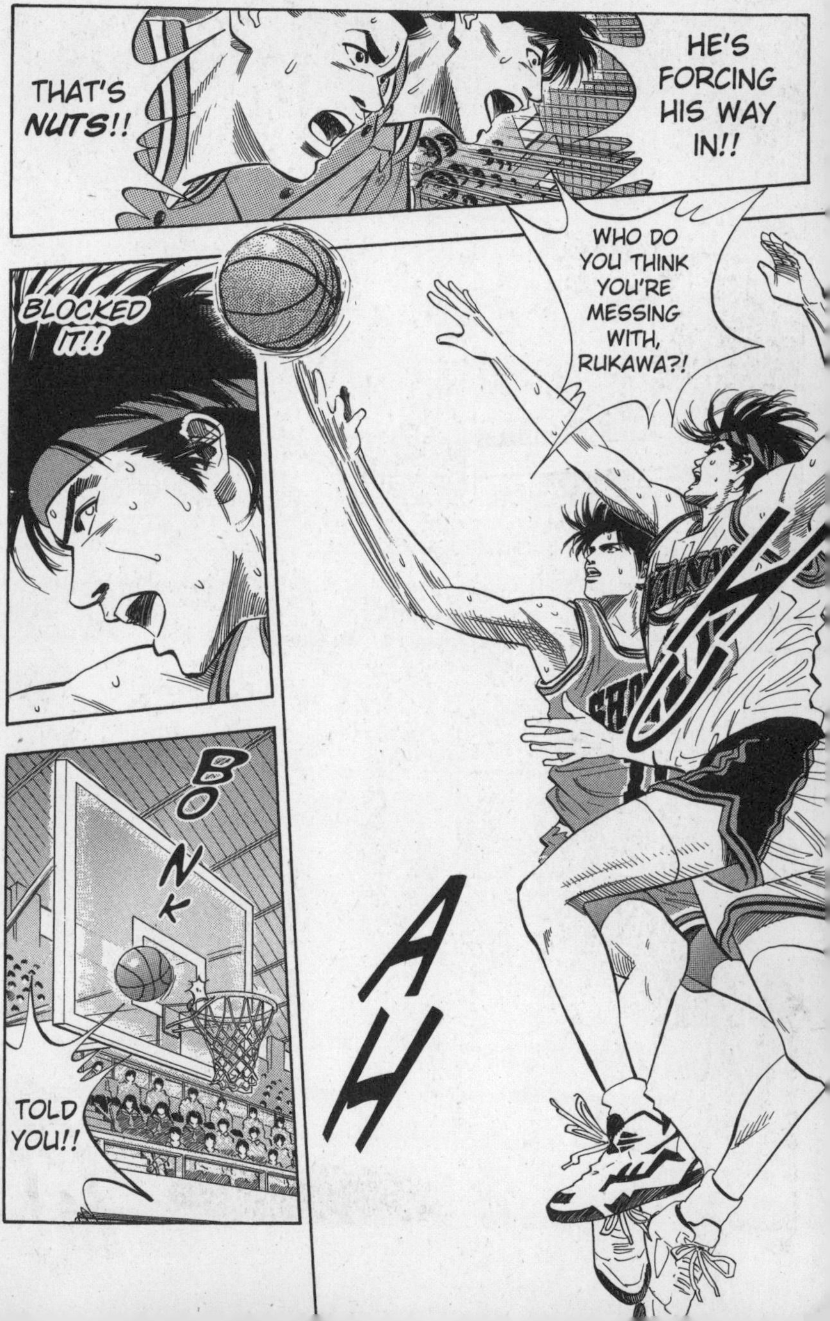
HE'S FORCING HIS WAY IN!!
THAT'S NUTS!!
WHO DO YOU THINK YOU'RE MESSING WITH, RUKAWA?!
AH
BLOCKED IT!!
BONK
TOLD YOU!!

READ THIS WAY

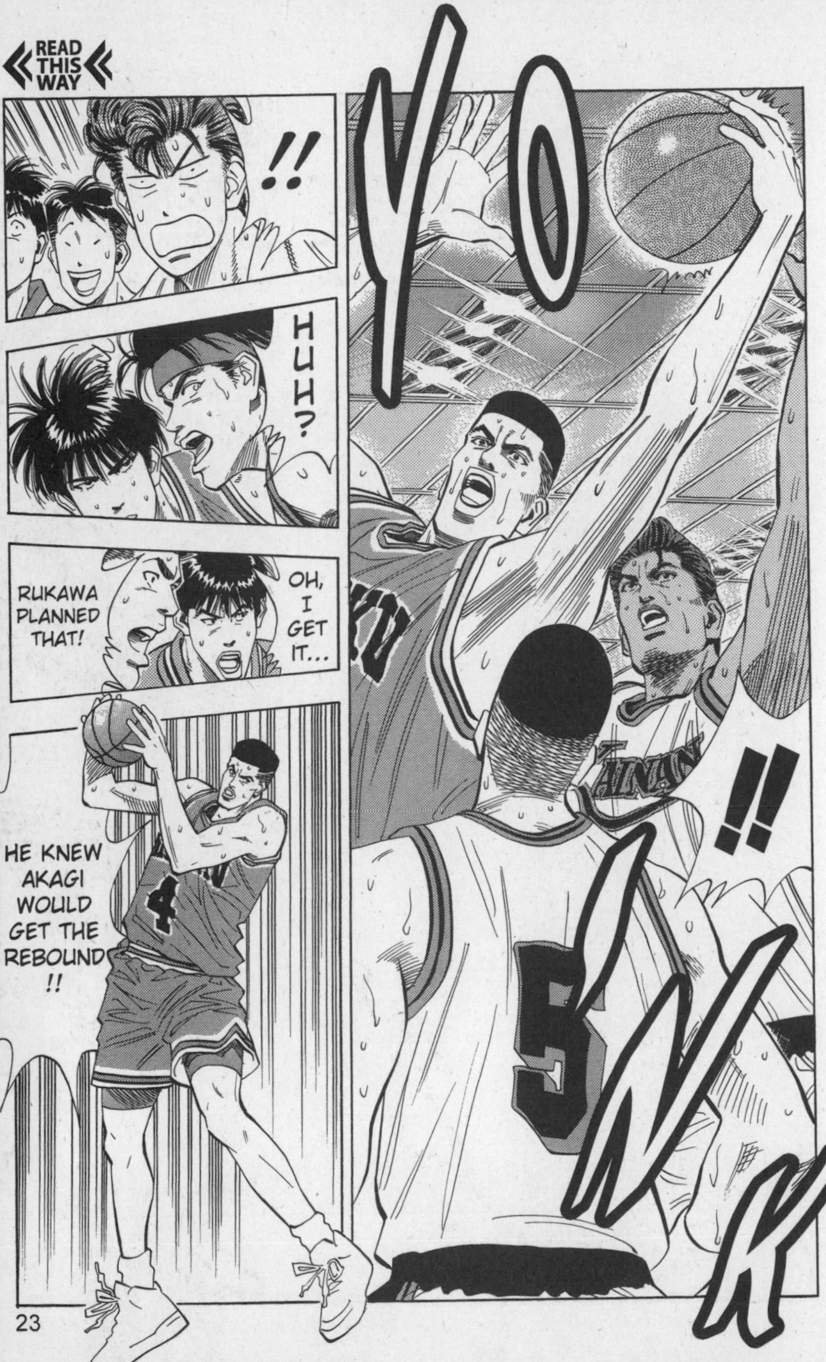

YO
!!
NK
!!
HUH?
OH, I GET IT...
RUKAWA PLANNED THAT!
HE KNEW AKAGI WOULD GET THE REBOUND!!

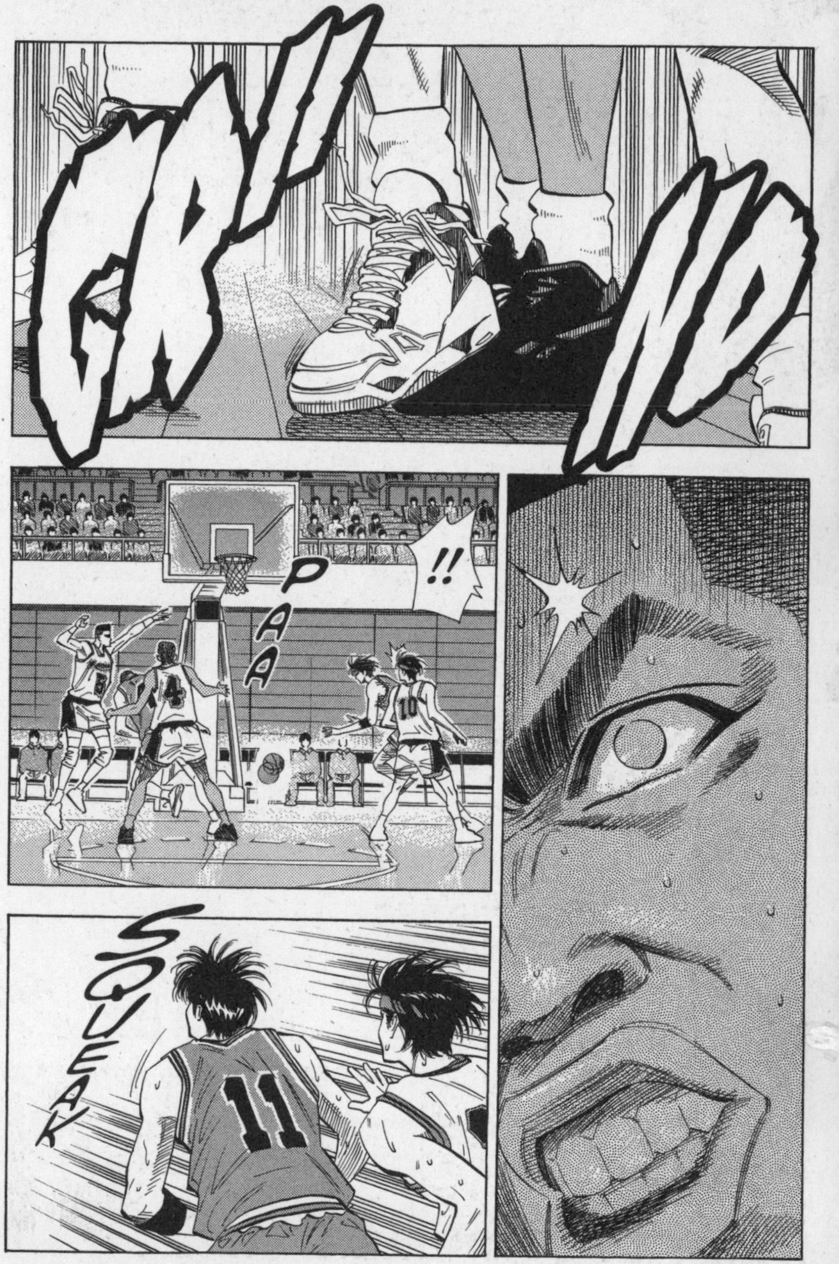
GRIND
!!
PAAA
SQUEAK

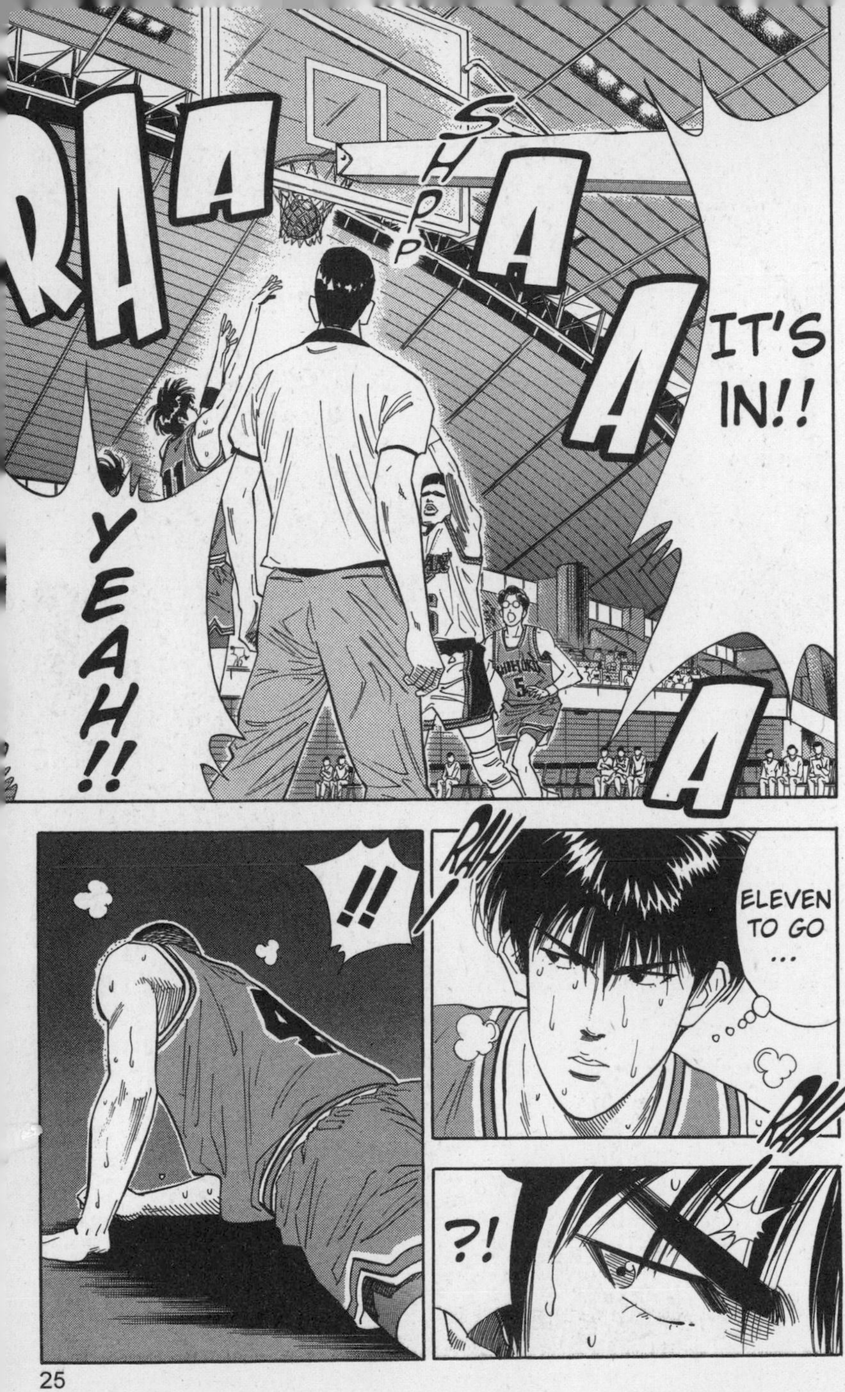
RAAAAAAA
SHPP
IT'S IN!!
YEAH!!
RAH
ELEVEN TO GO ...
!!
RAH
?!

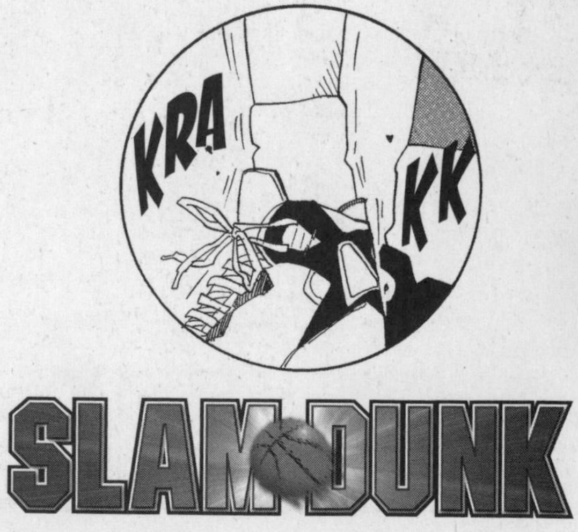
KRA KK

SLAM DUNK

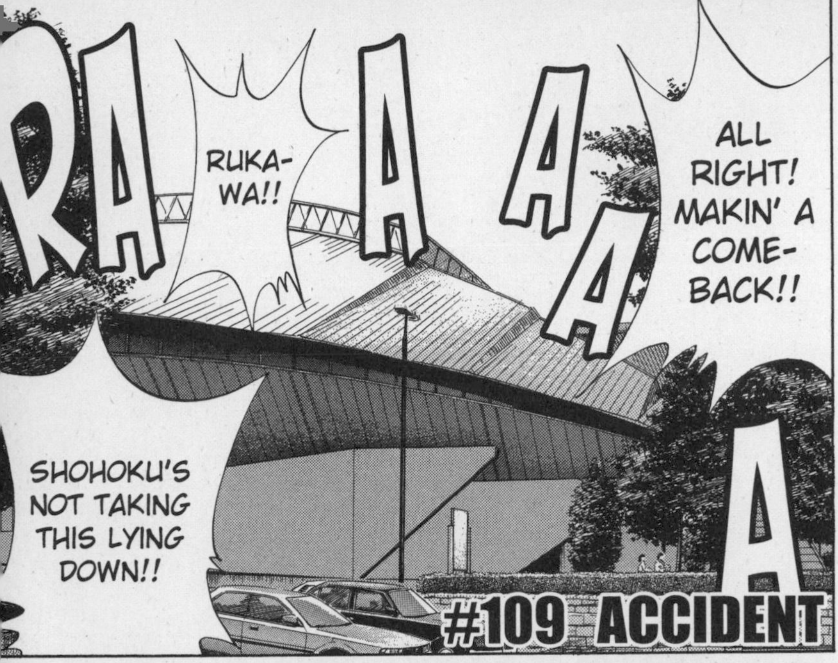
RAAAAA
ALL RIGHT! MAKIN' A COME-BACK!!
RUKA-WA!!
SHOHOKU'S NOT TAKING THIS LYING DOWN!!

#109 ACCIDENT

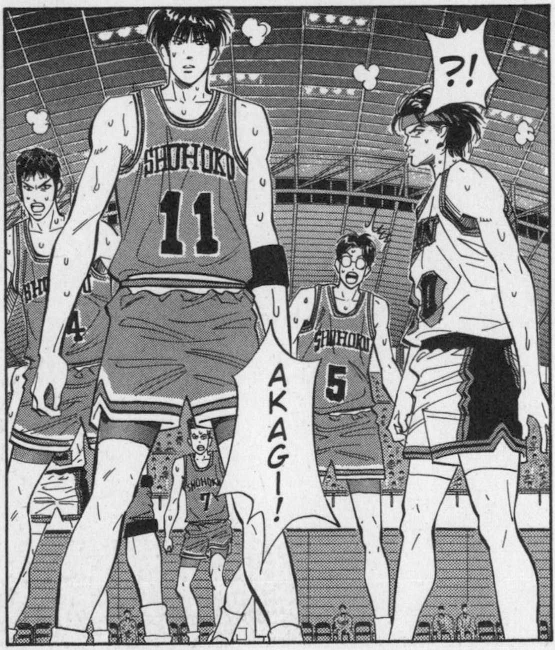
?!
AKAGI!

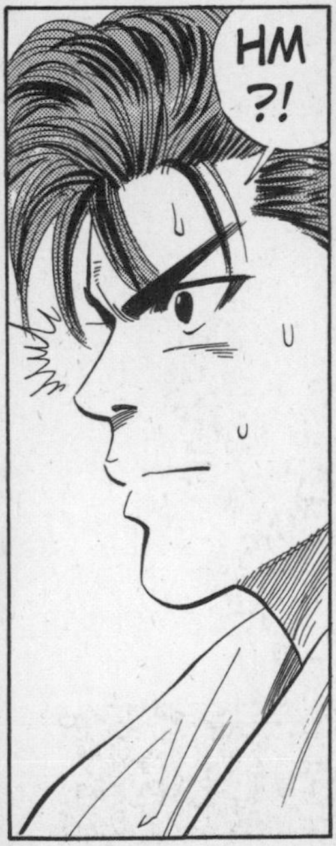
HM ?!

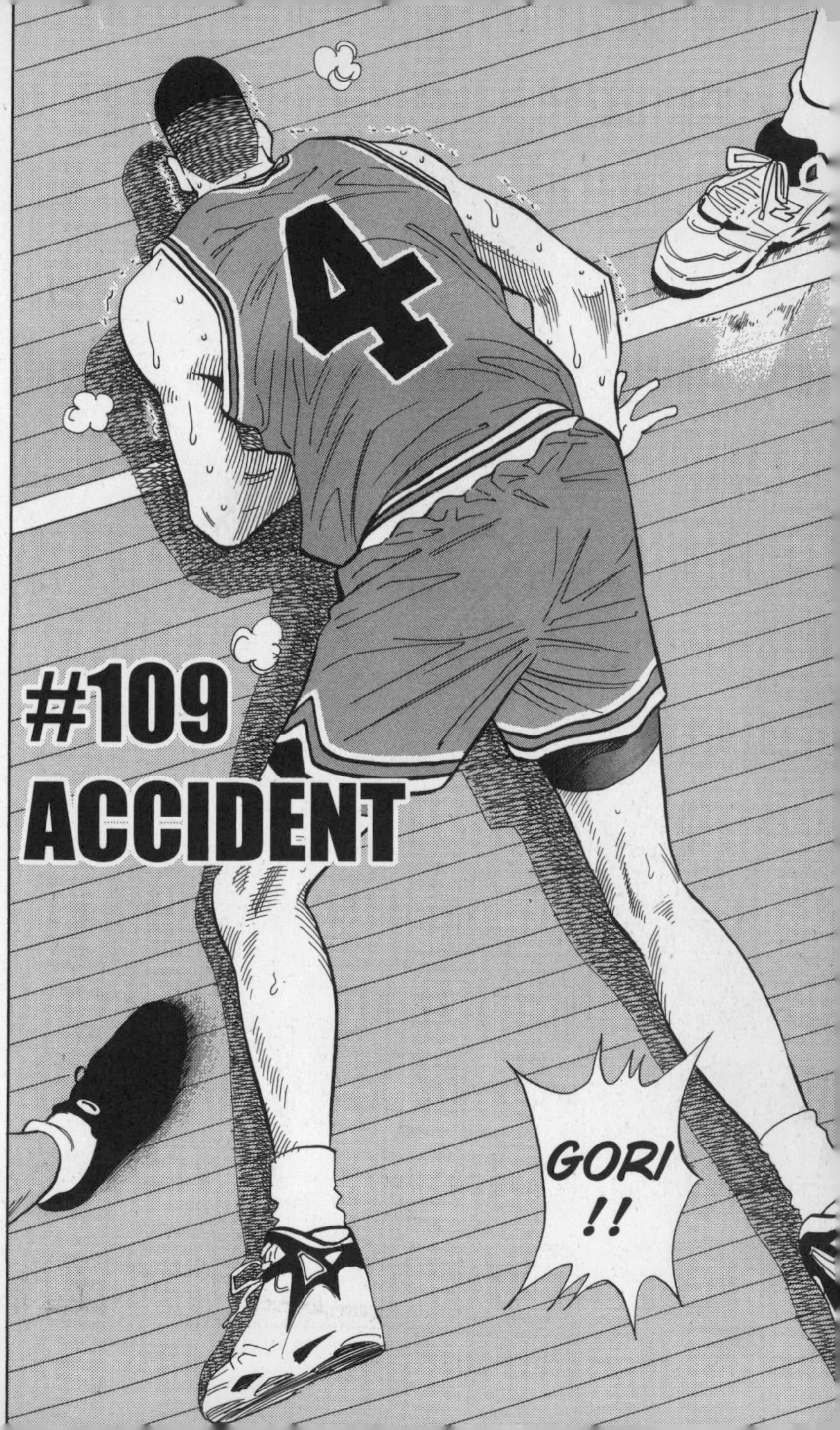
#109
ACCIDENT
GORI
!!

READ THIS WAY

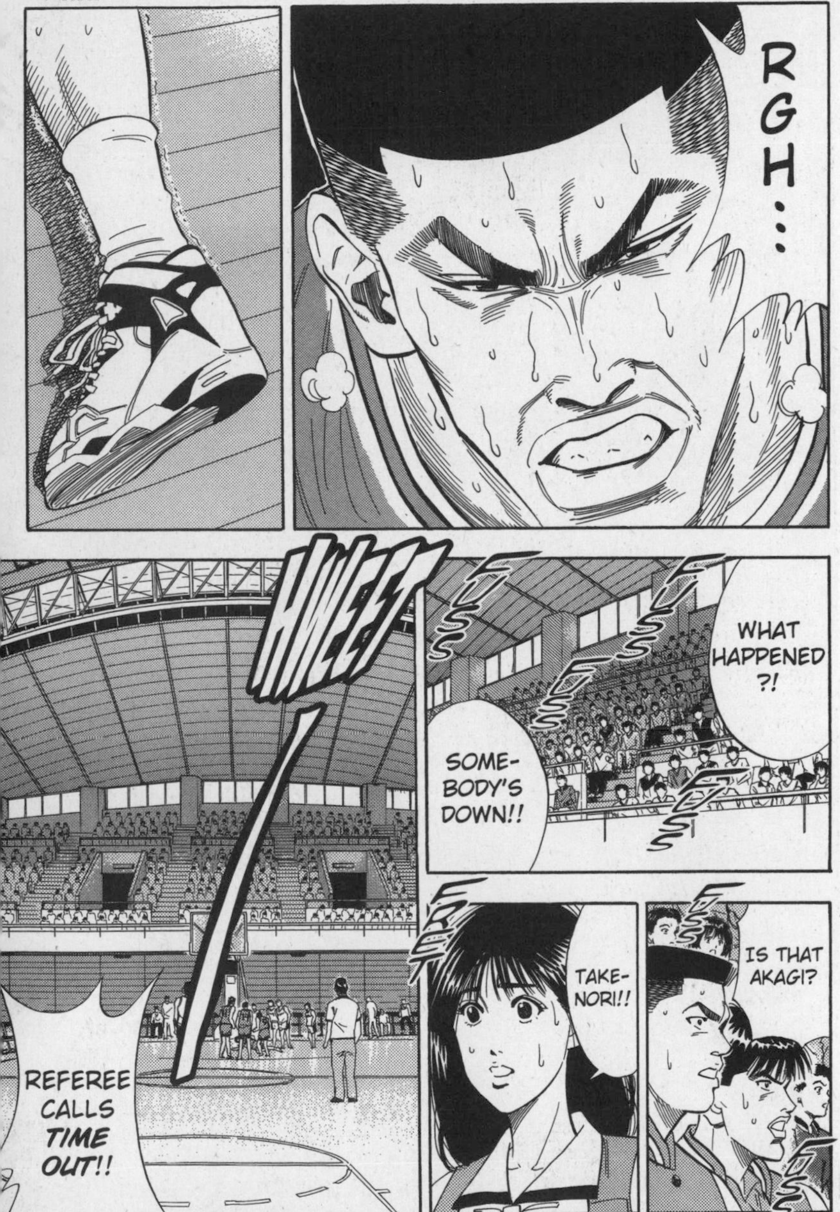
RGH...
WHAT HAPPENED ?!
SOME-BODY'S DOWN!!
FUSS
IS THAT AKAGI?
TAKE-NORI!!
HWEEE
REFEREE CALLS TIME OUT!!

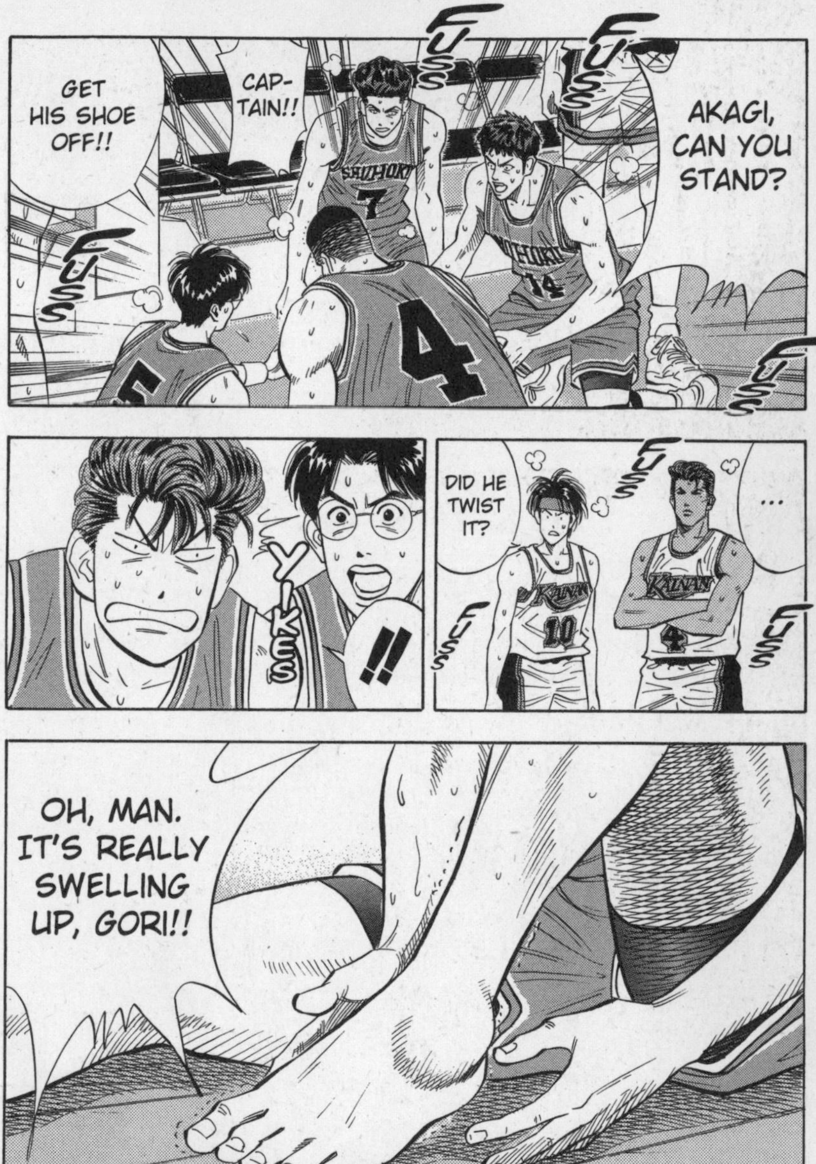
FUSS
FUSS
AKAGI, CAN YOU STAND?
CAP-TAIN!!
GET HIS SHOE OFF!!
FUSS
FUSS
FUSS
...
FUSS
DID HE TWIST IT?
FUSS
!!
YIKES
OH, MAN. IT'S REALLY SWELLING UP, GORI!!

READ THIS WAY

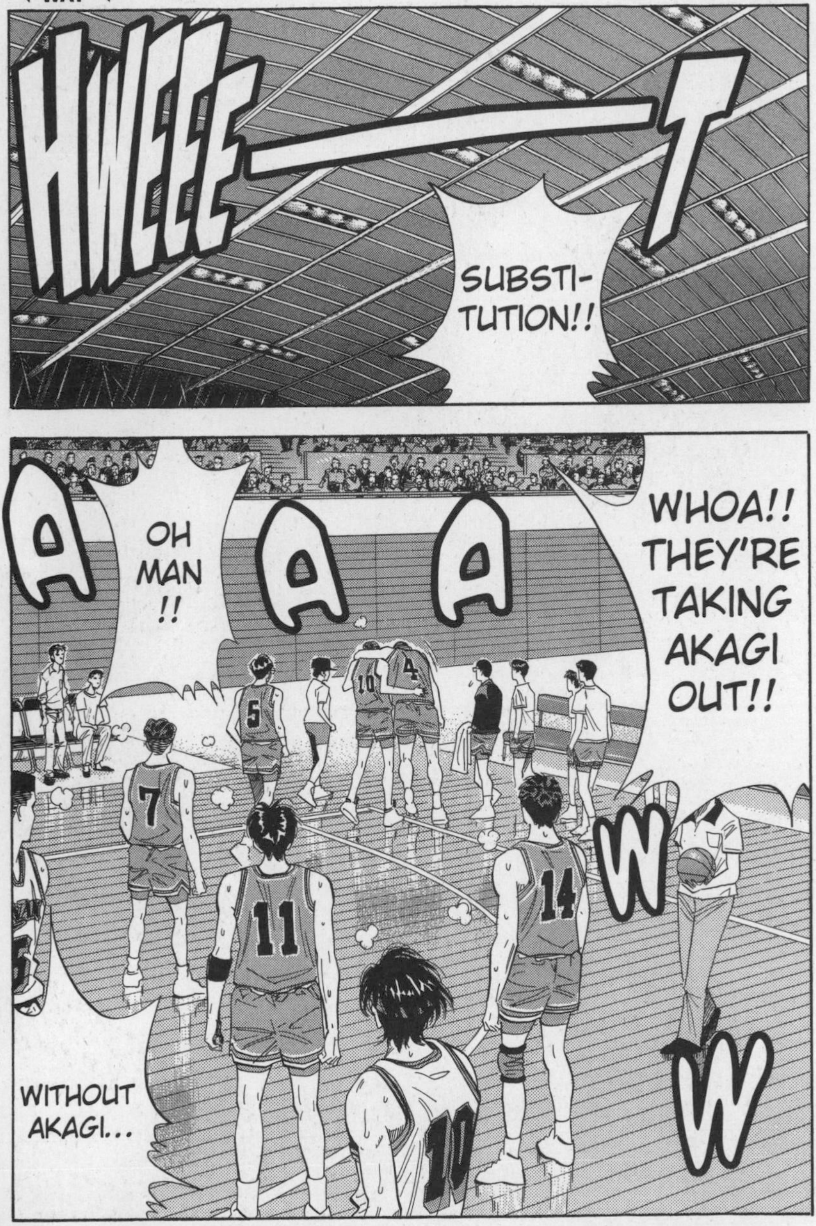
HWEEE—T
SUBSTI-TUTION!!
WHOA!! THEY'RE TAKING AKAGI OUT!!
A
A
OH MAN !!
A
W
W
WITHOUT AKAGI...

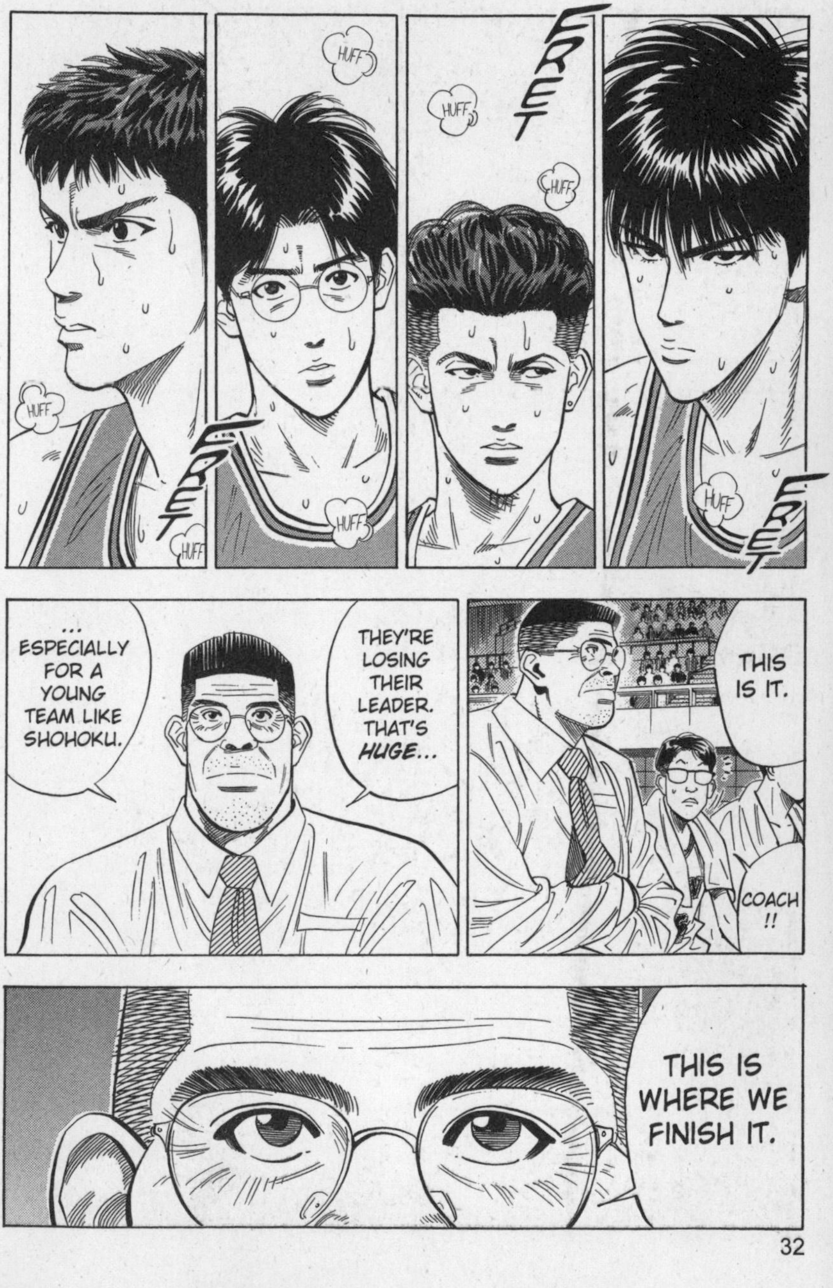
HUFF
FRET
HUFF
HUFF
FRET
HUFF
HUFF
FRET
HUFF
HUFF
THIS IS IT.
COACH !!
THEY'RE LOSING THEIR LEADER. THAT'S *HUGE...*
... ESPECIALLY FOR A YOUNG TEAM LIKE SHOHOKU.
THIS IS WHERE WE FINISH IT.

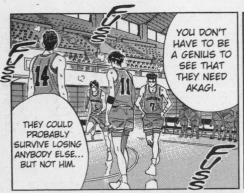

FUSS
SHOHOKU'S THROUGH...
FUSS
FUSS
FUSS
FUSS
YOU DON'T HAVE TO BE A GENIUS TO SEE THAT THEY NEED AKAGI.
THEY COULD PROBABLY SURVIVE LOSING ANYBODY ELSE... BUT NOT HIM.
FUSS
I SUSPECT YOU'RE NOT ALONE IN THAT ASSESSMENT, NAKAMURA...
CHATTER
!!
CHATTER
...

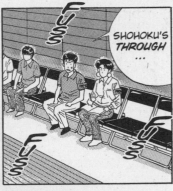

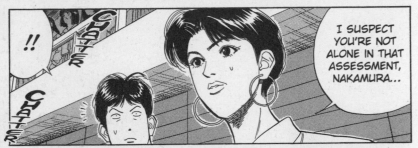

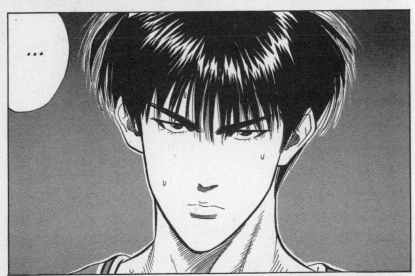

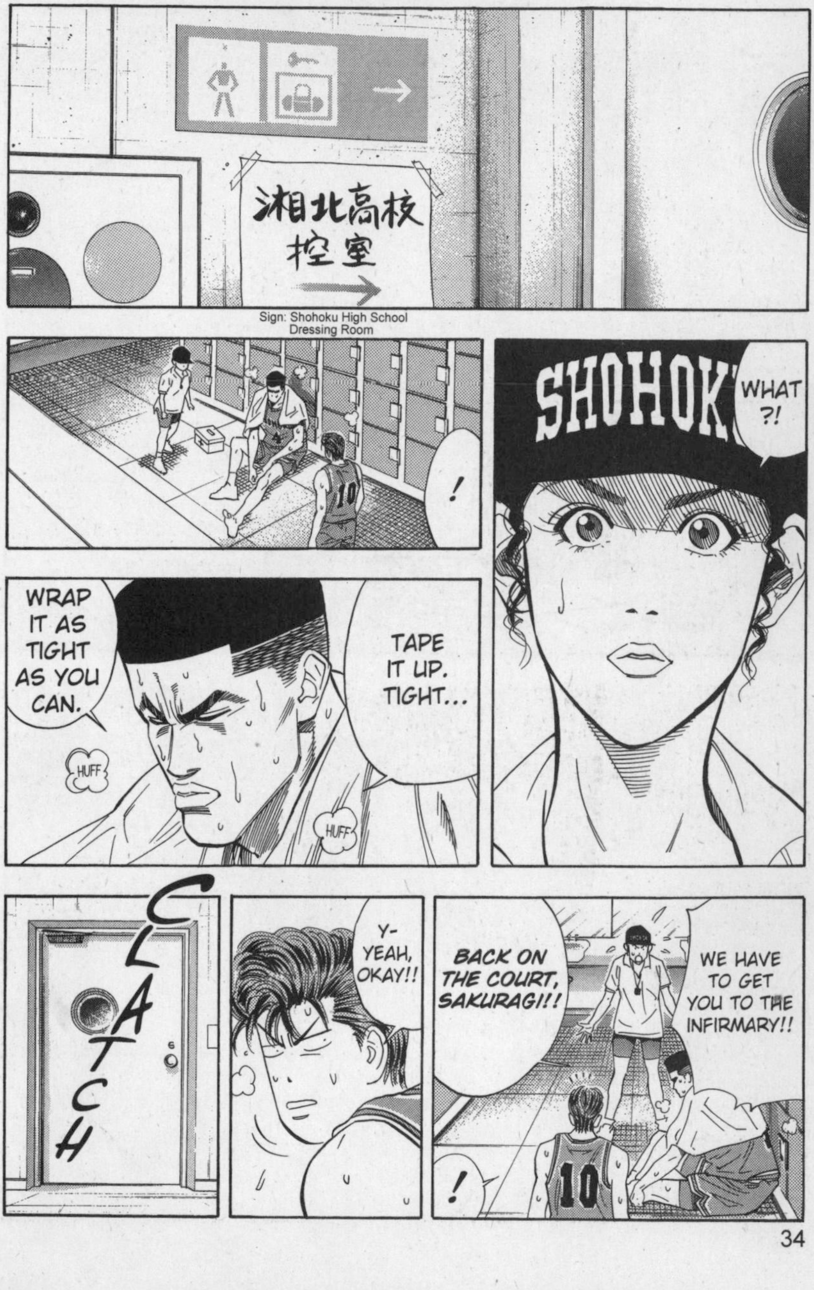
湘北高校
控室
WHAT ?!
!
TAPE IT UP. TIGHT...
HUFF
WRAP IT AS TIGHT AS YOU CAN.
HUFF
WE HAVE TO GET YOU TO THE INFIRMARY!!
BACK ON THE COURT, SAKURAGI!!
!
Y- YEAH, OKAY!!
CLATCH
Sign: Shohoku High School Dressing Room

READ THIS WAY

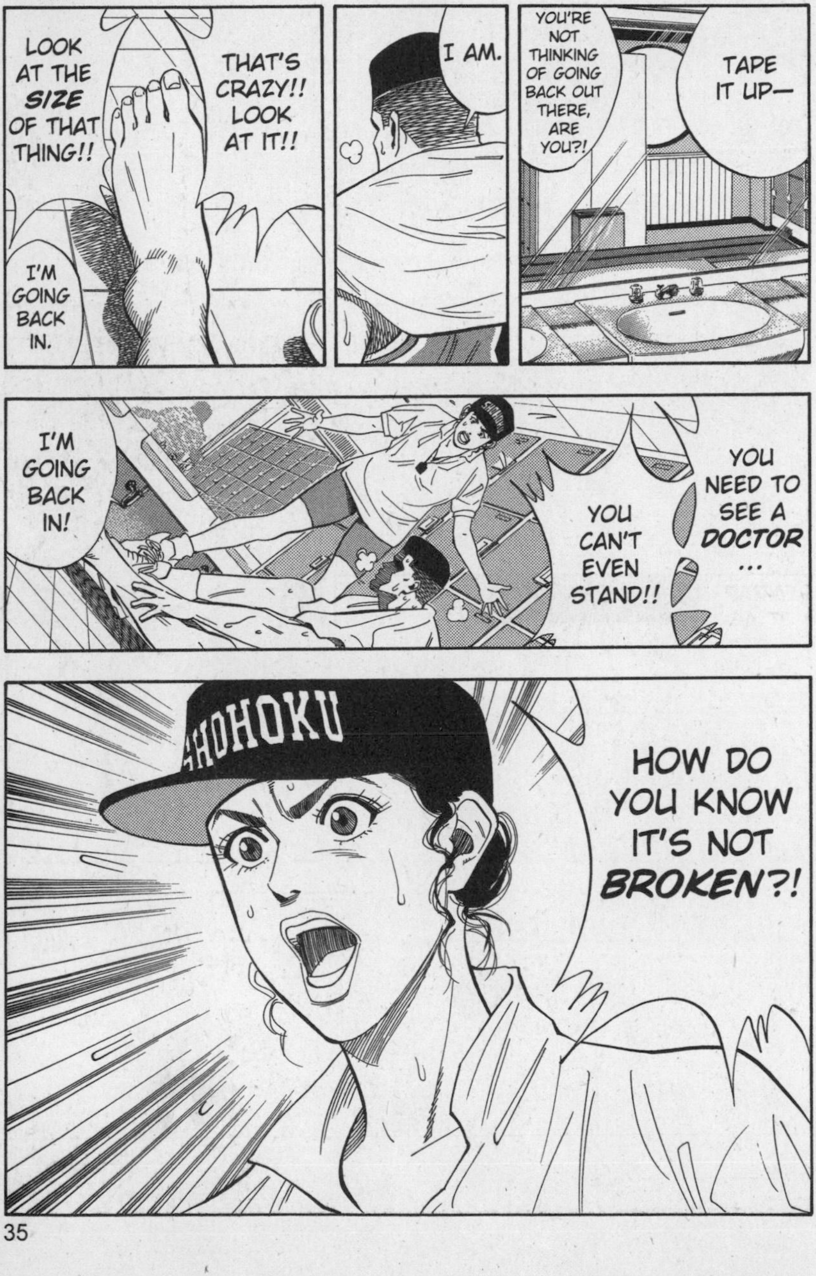

TAPE IT UP—
YOU'RE NOT THINKING OF GOING BACK OUT THERE, ARE YOU?!
I AM.
THAT'S CRAZY!! LOOK AT IT!!
LOOK AT THE *SIZE* OF THAT THING!!
I'M GOING BACK IN.
YOU NEED TO SEE A *DOCTOR* ...
YOU CAN'T EVEN STAND!!
I'M GOING BACK IN!
HOW DO YOU KNOW IT'S NOT *BROKEN*?!

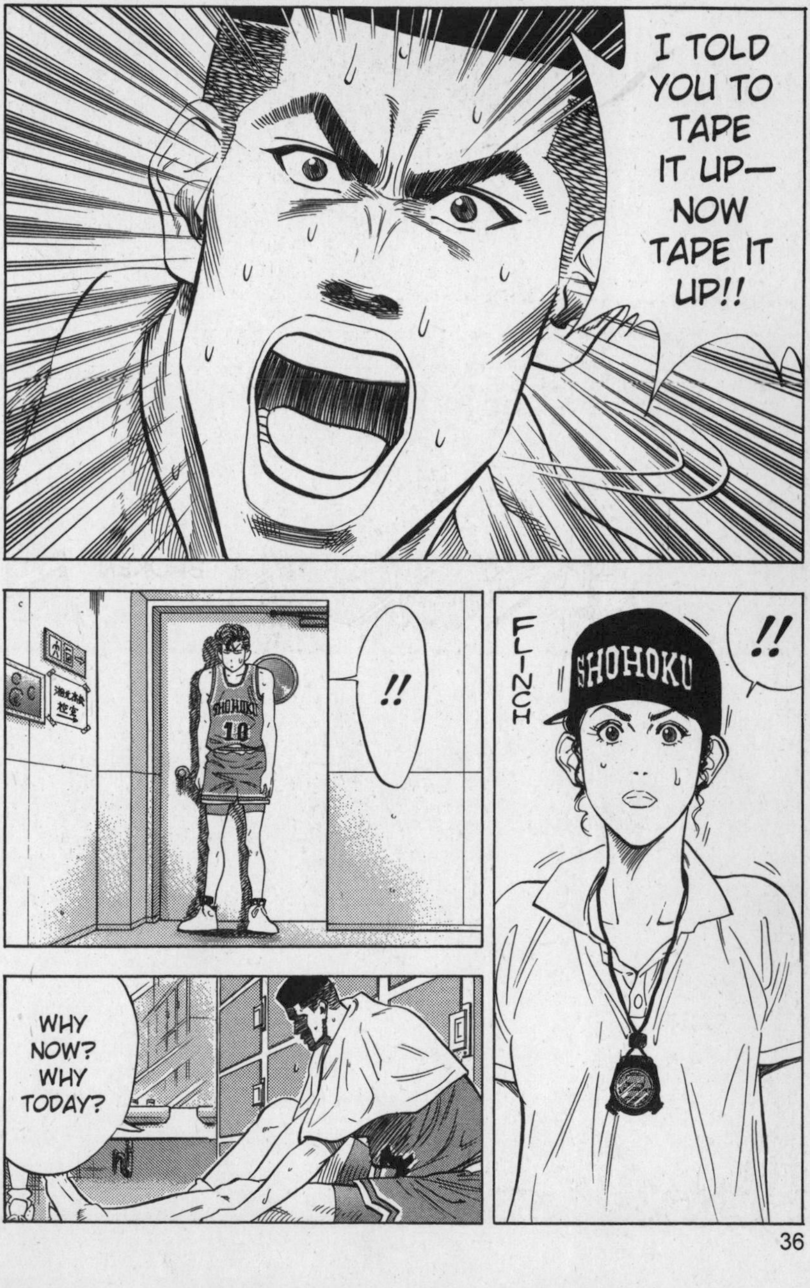
I TOLD YOU TO TAPE IT UP— NOW TAPE IT UP!!
FLINCH
SHOHOKU
!!
SHOHOKU 10
!!
WHY NOW? WHY TODAY?

READ THIS WAY

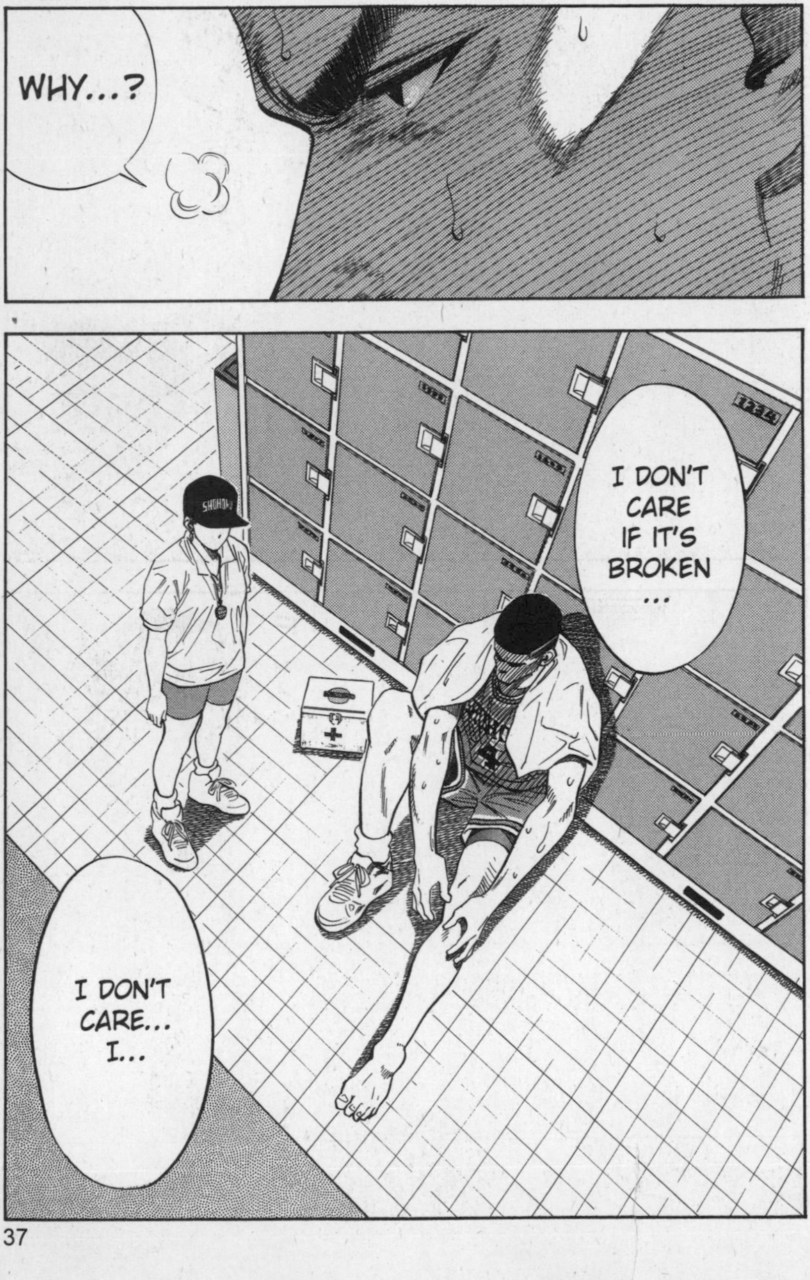
WHY...?
I DON'T CARE IF IT'S BROKEN ...
I DON'T CARE... I...

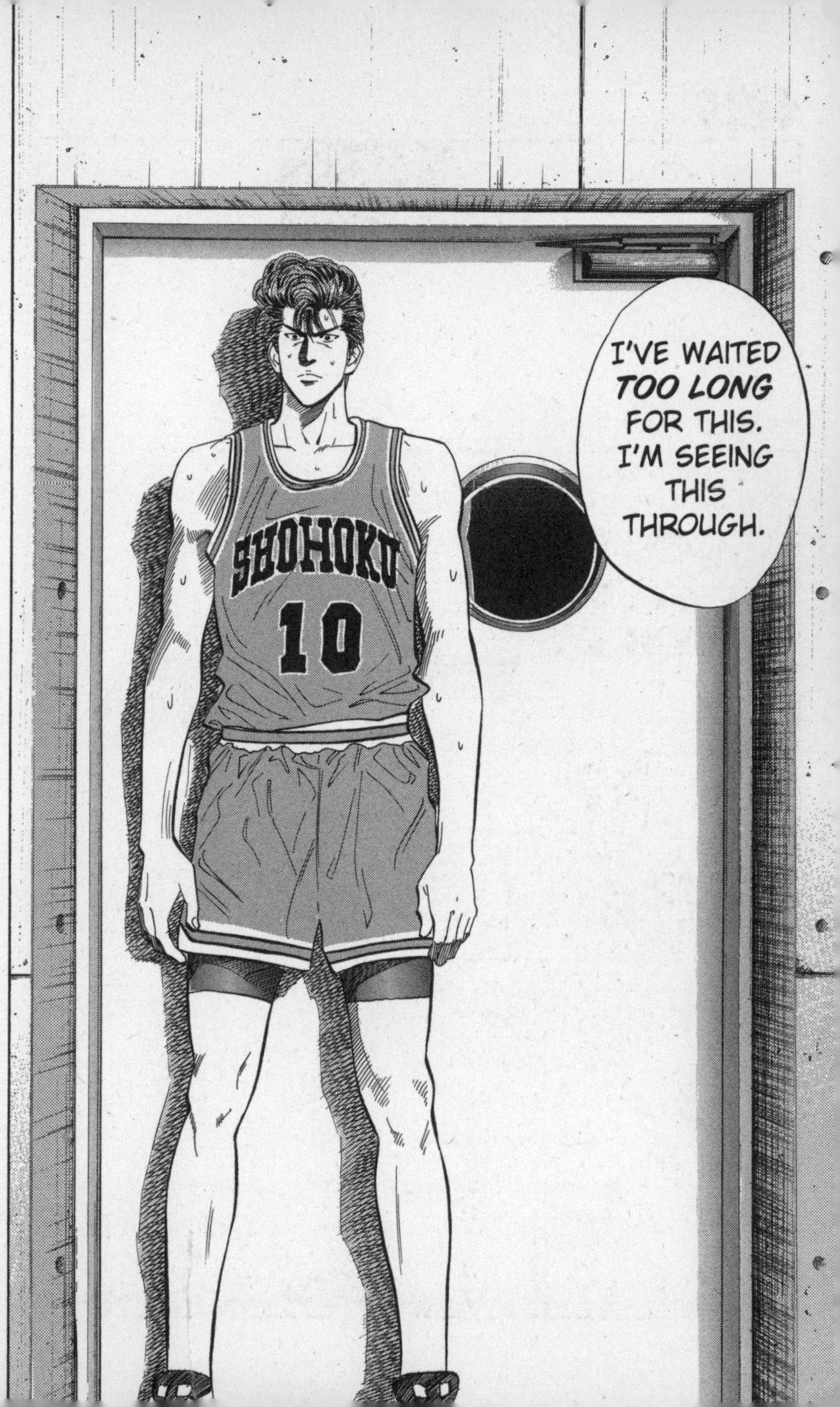
I'VE WAITED *TOO LONG* FOR THIS. I'M SEEING THIS THROUGH.
SHOHOKU
10

READ THIS WAY

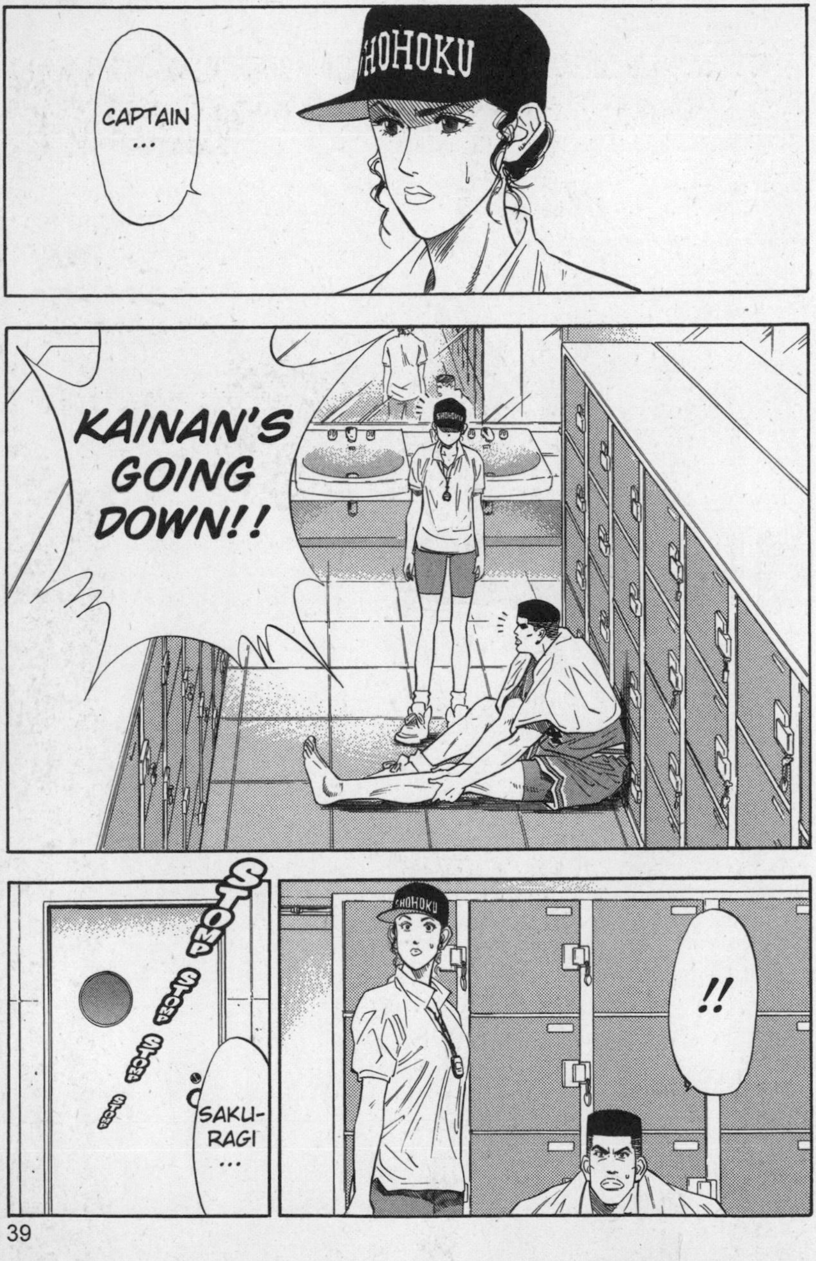
CAPTAIN ...
SHOHOKU
KAINAN'S GOING DOWN!!
!!
STOMP STOMP STOMP STOMP
SAKU-RAGI ...

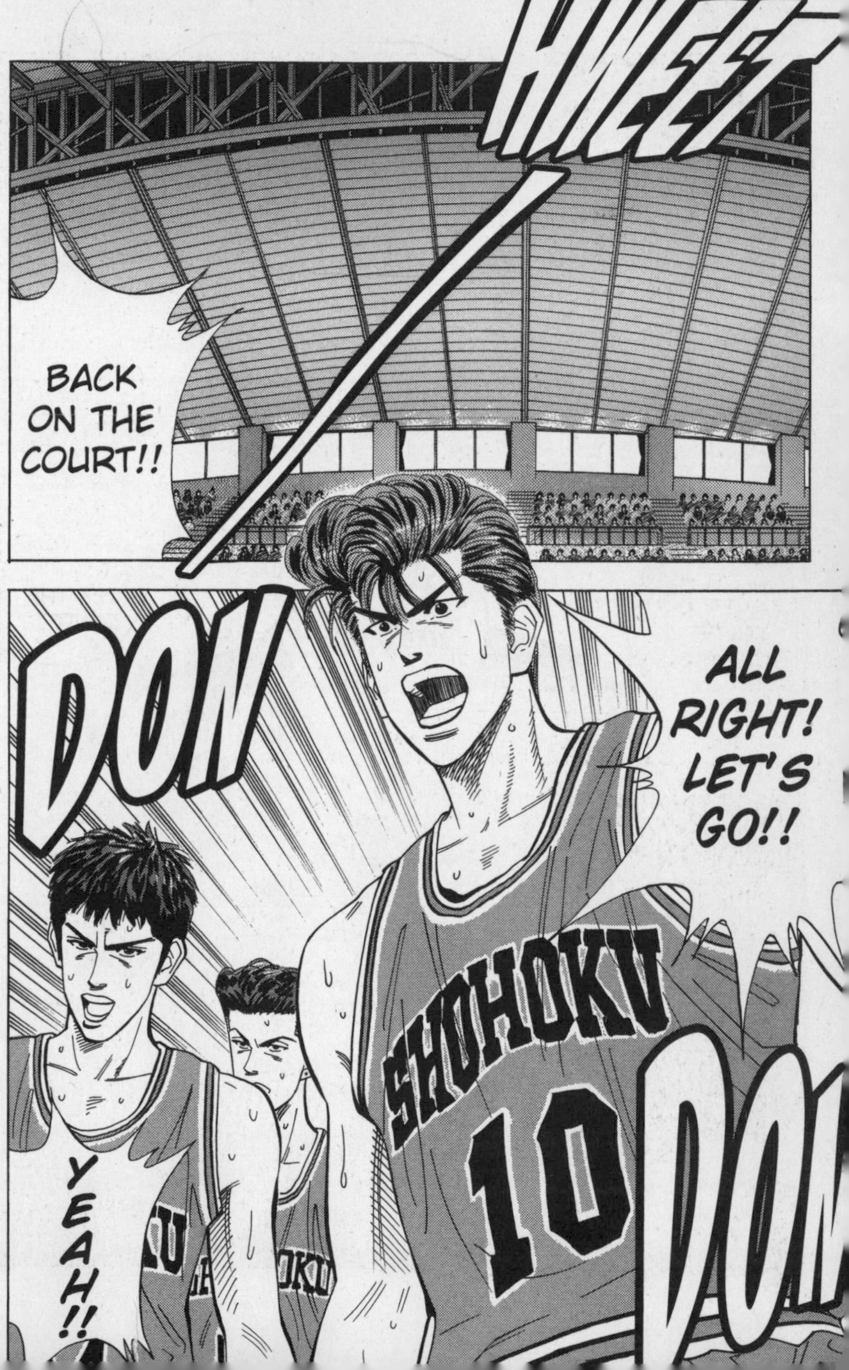
HWEET
BACK ON THE COURT!!
ALL RIGHT! LET'S GO!!
DON
YEAH!!

READ THIS WAY

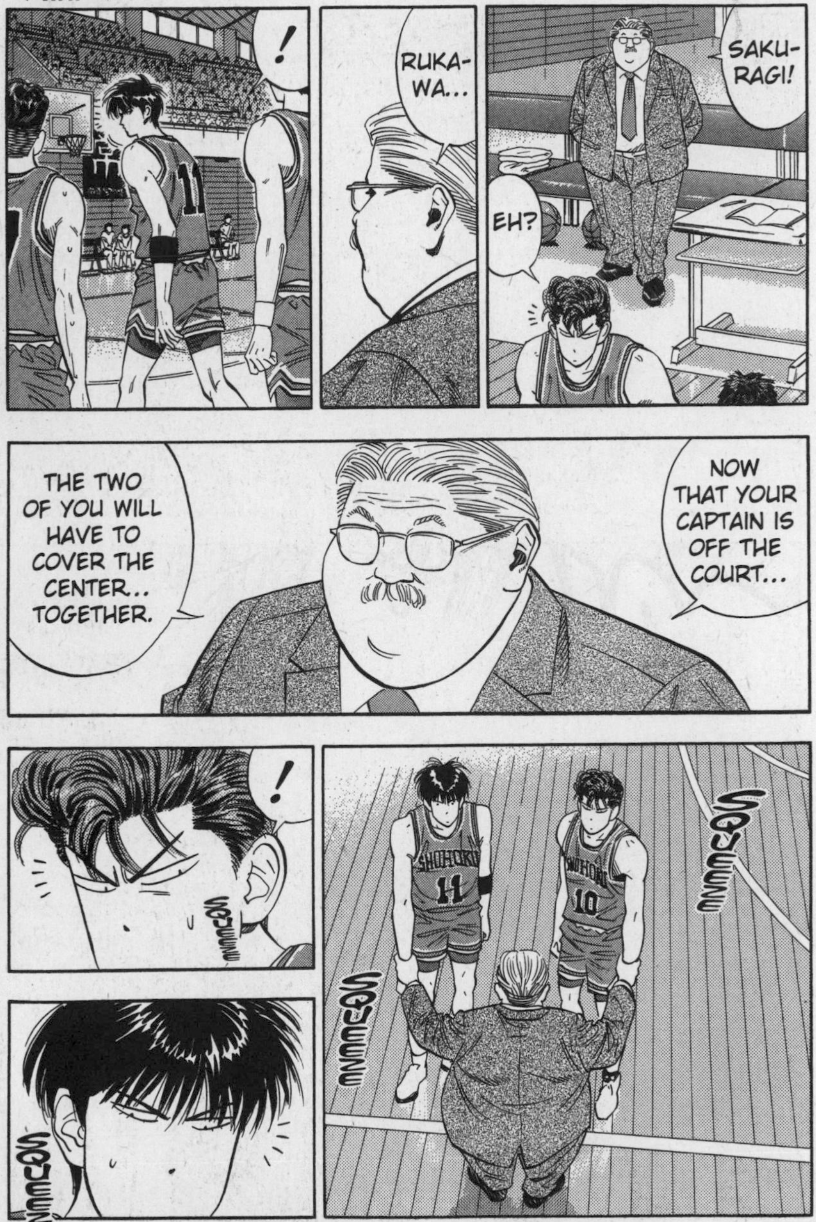
SAKU-RAGI!
EH?
RUKA-WA...
!
NOW THAT YOUR CAPTAIN IS OFF THE COURT...
THE TWO OF YOU WILL HAVE TO COVER THE CENTER... TOGETHER.
SQUEEEE
SQUEEEE
!
SQUEEEE
SQUEEEE

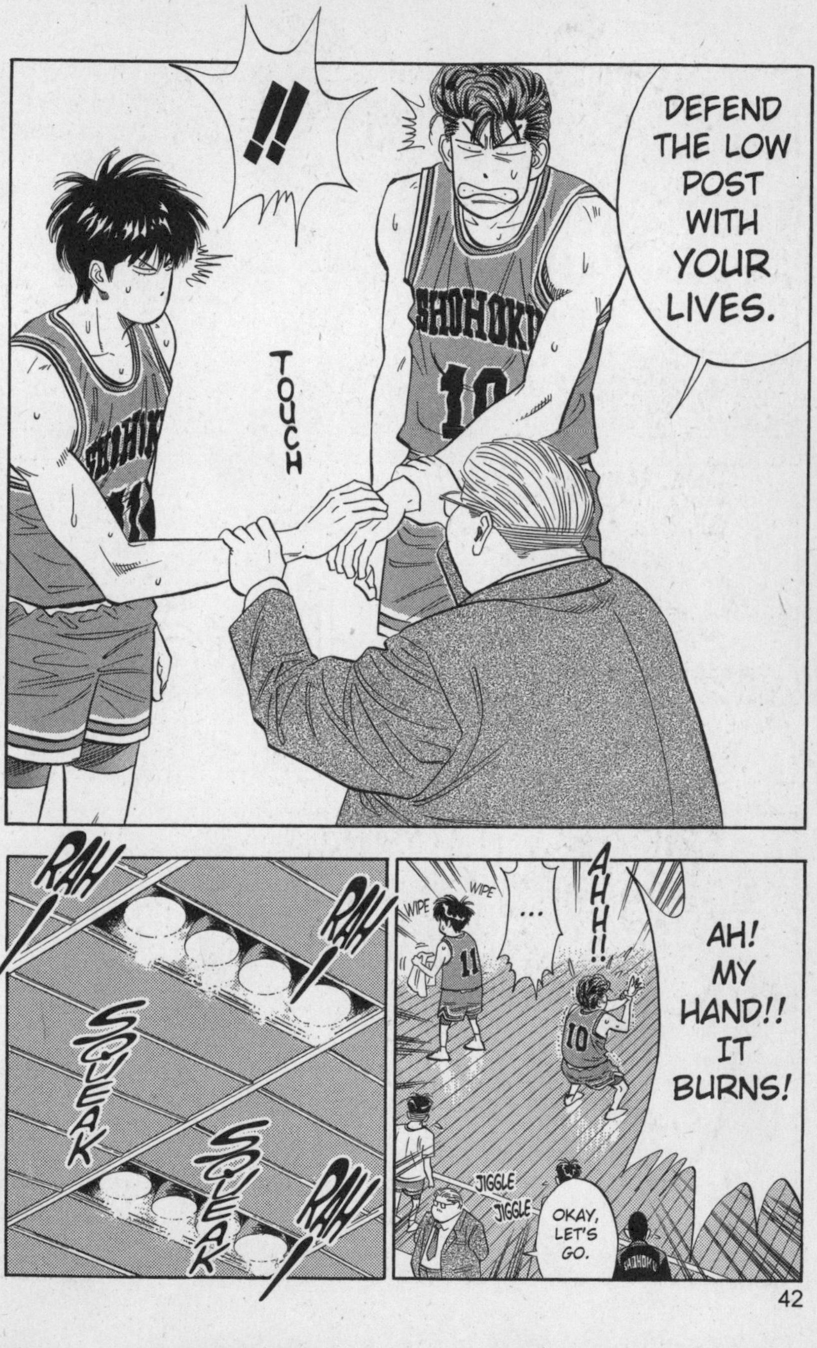
DEFEND THE LOW POST WITH YOUR LIVES.
!!
TOUCH
AH! MY HAND!! IT BURNS!
AHH!!
WIPE
...
WIPE
JIGGLE
JIGGLE
OKAY, LET'S GO.
RAH!
RAH!
SQUEAK
SQUEAK
RAH!

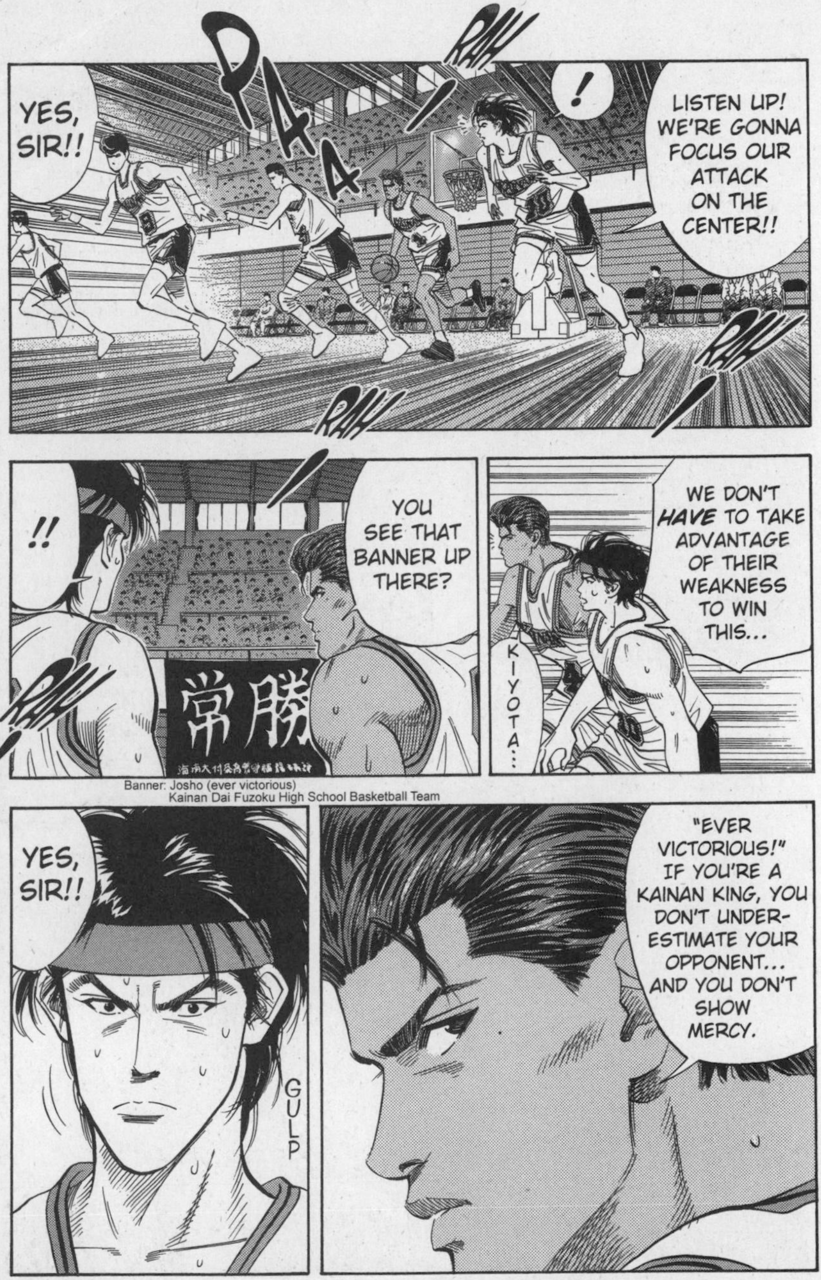
LISTEN UP! WE'RE GONNA FOCUS OUR ATTACK ON THE CENTER!!
!
RAH
PAA
YES, SIR!!
RAH
RAH
WE DON'T *HAVE* TO TAKE ADVANTAGE OF THEIR WEAKNESS TO WIN THIS...
KIYOTA...
RAH
YOU SEE THAT BANNER UP THERE?
!!
RAH
"EVER VICTORIOUS!" IF YOU'RE A KAINAN KING, YOU DON'T UNDER-ESTIMATE YOUR OPPONENT... AND YOU DON'T SHOW MERCY.
YES, SIR!!
GULP
Banner: Josho (ever victorious)
Kainan Dai Fuzoku High School Basketball Team

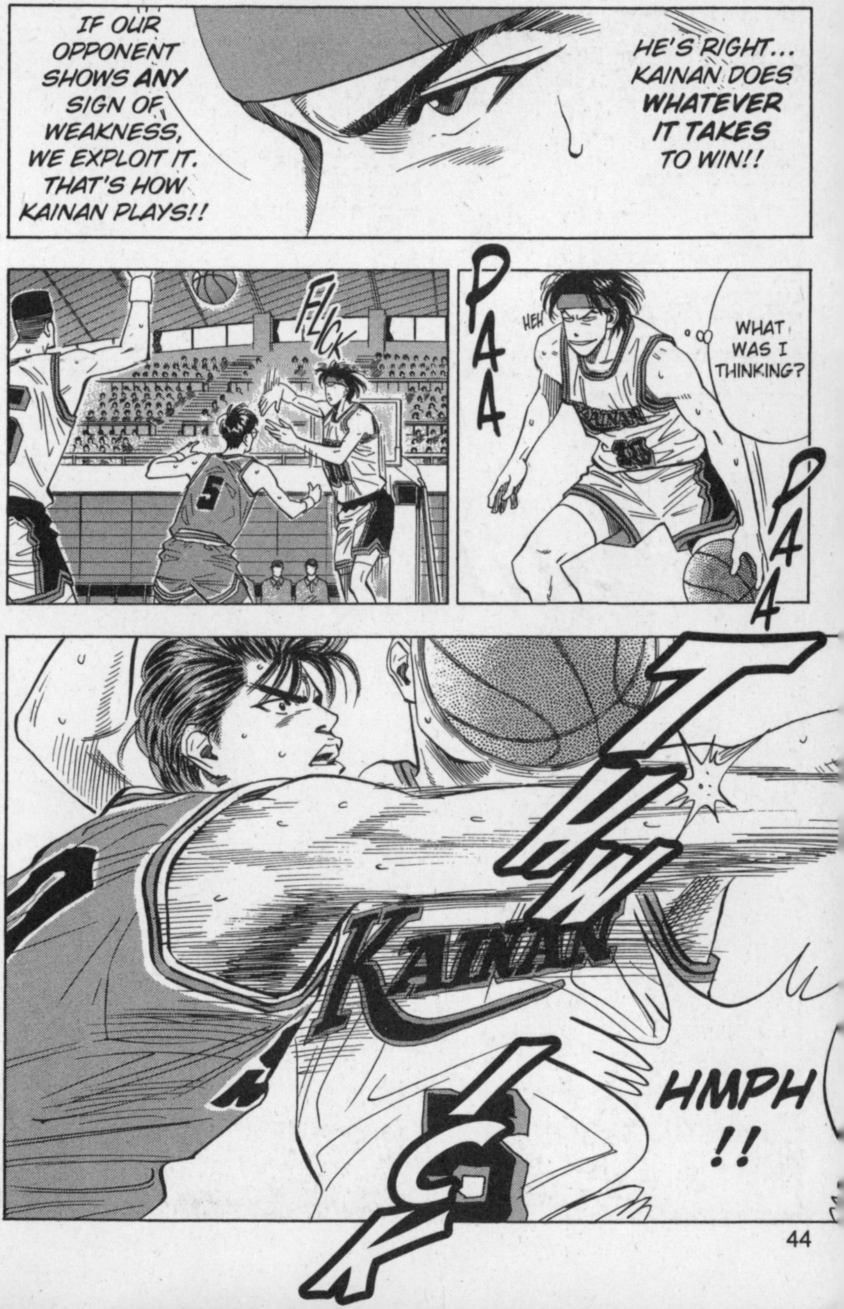
IF OUR OPPONENT SHOWS ANY SIGN OF WEAKNESS, WE EXPLOIT IT. THAT'S HOW KAINAN PLAYS!!
HE'S RIGHT... KAINAN DOES WHATEVER IT TAKES TO WIN!!
PAA
HEH
WHAT WAS I THINKING?
PAA
FLICK
HMPH !!

READ THIS WAY

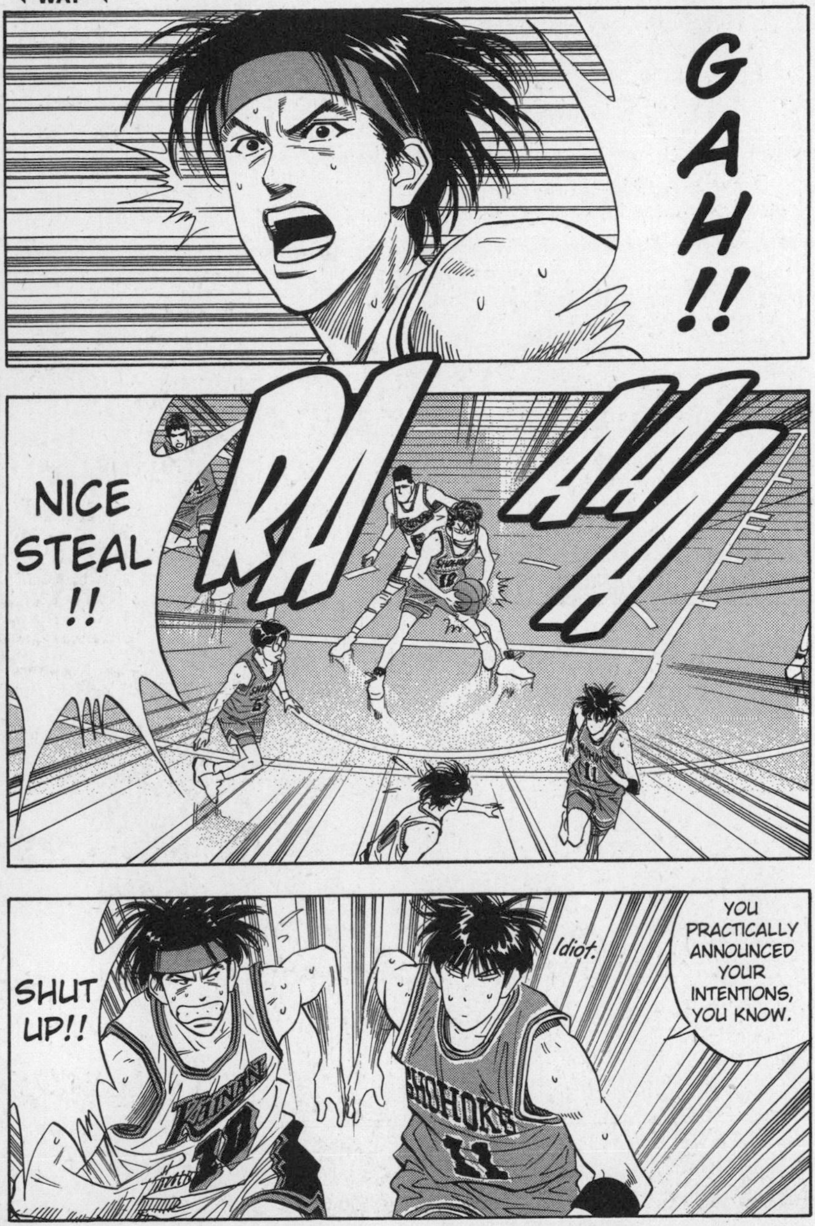
GAH!!
BAM
NICE STEAL!!
YOU PRACTICALLY ANNOUNCED YOUR INTENTIONS, YOU KNOW.
Idiot.
SHUT UP!!

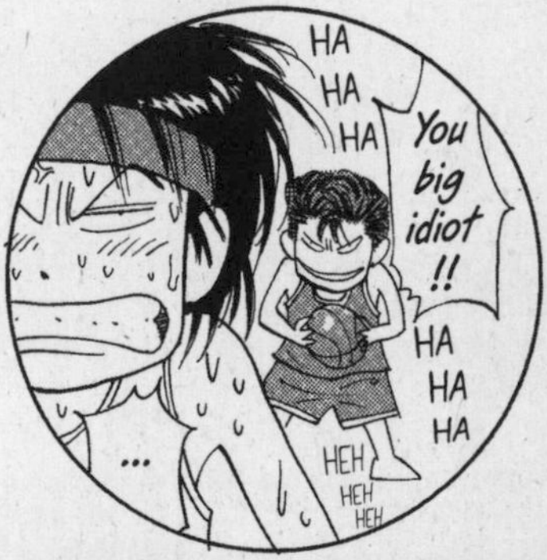
You big idiot!!
HA
HA
HA
HA
HA
HA
HEH
HEH
HEH
...

SLAM DUNK

#110 GORI'S SHOES

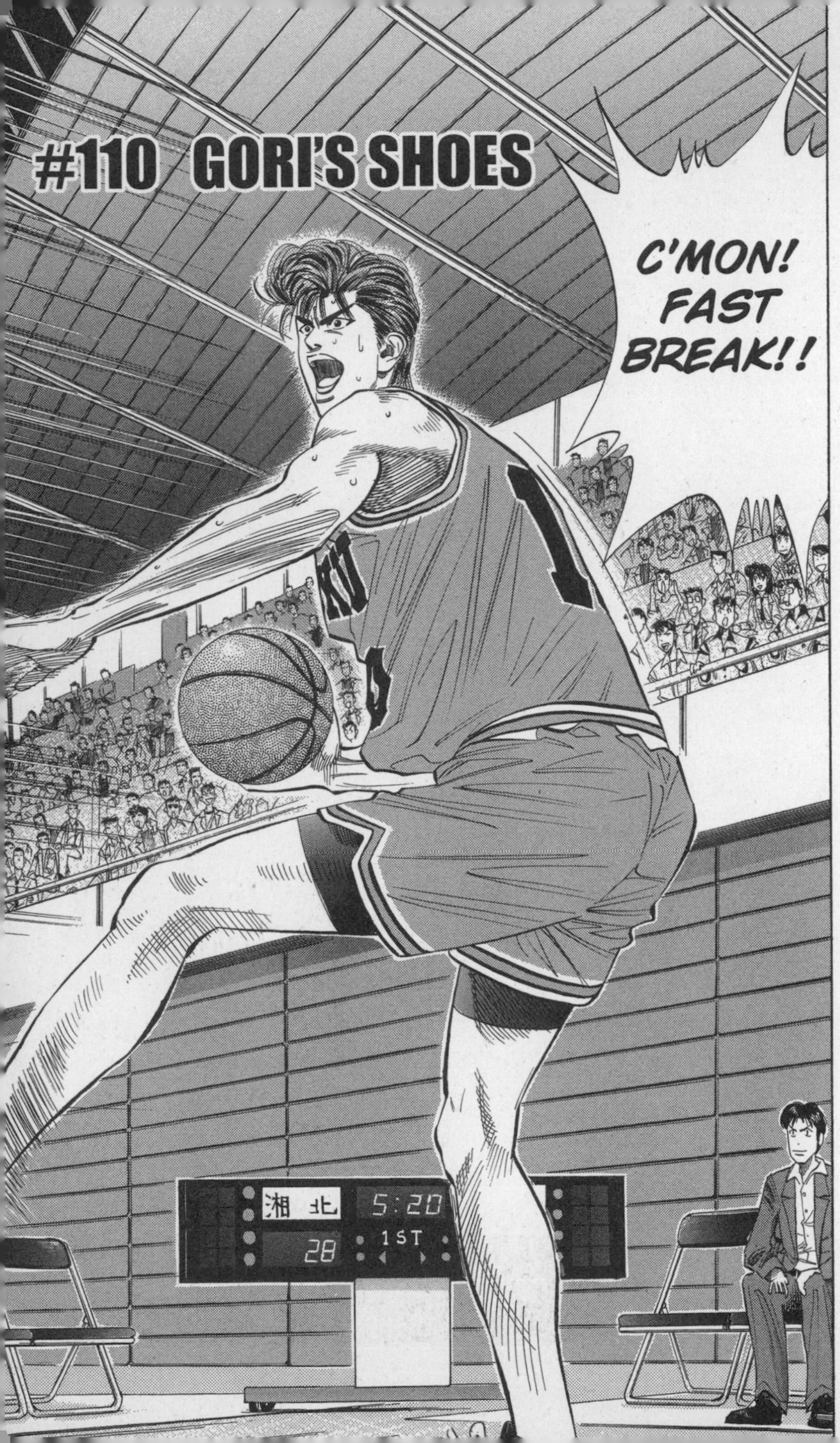
C'MON! FAST BREAK!!
湘北
5:20
28
1ST

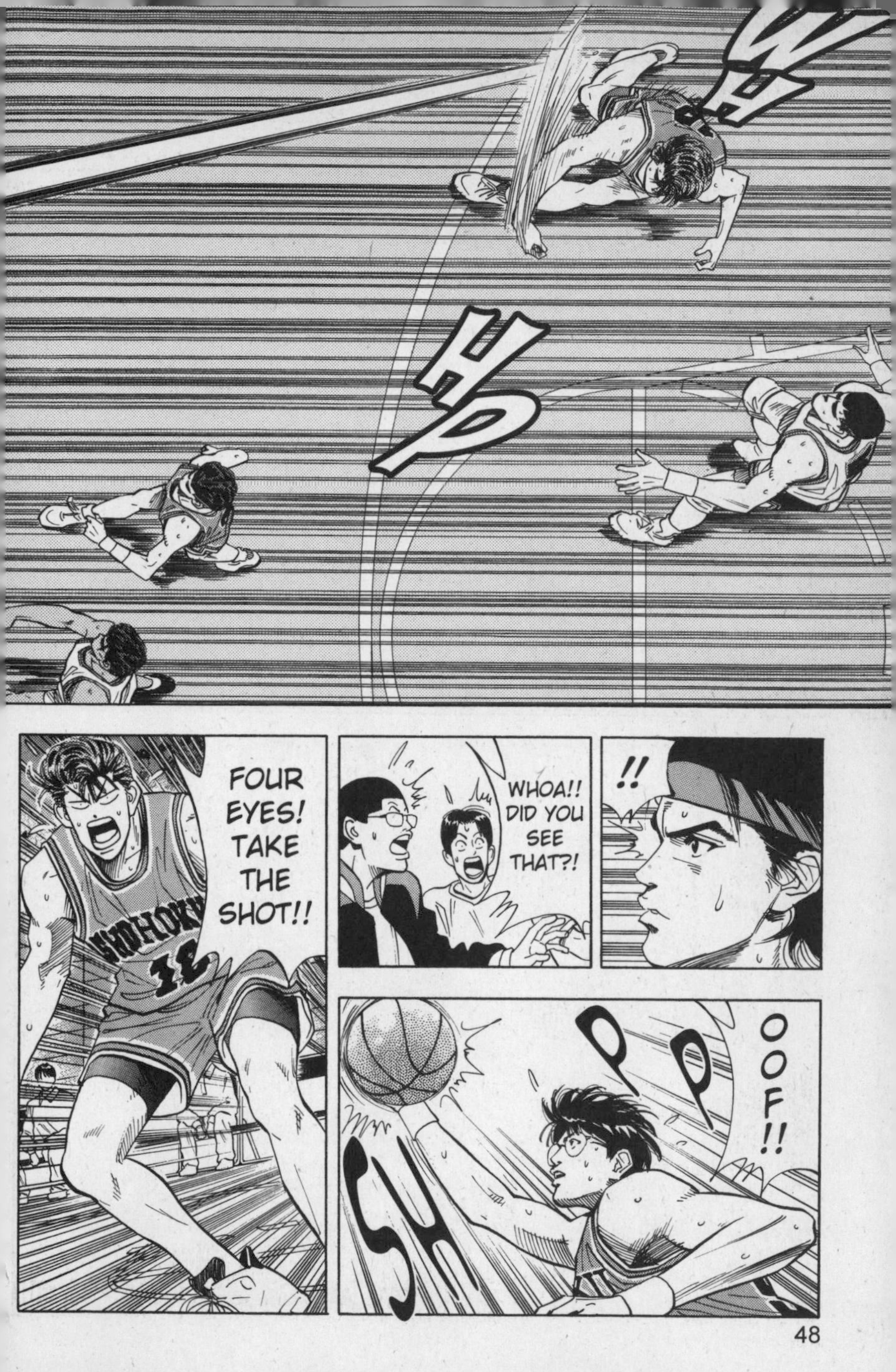
!!
WHOA!! DID YOU SEE THAT?!
OOF!!
SH
FOUR EYES! TAKE THE SHOT!!

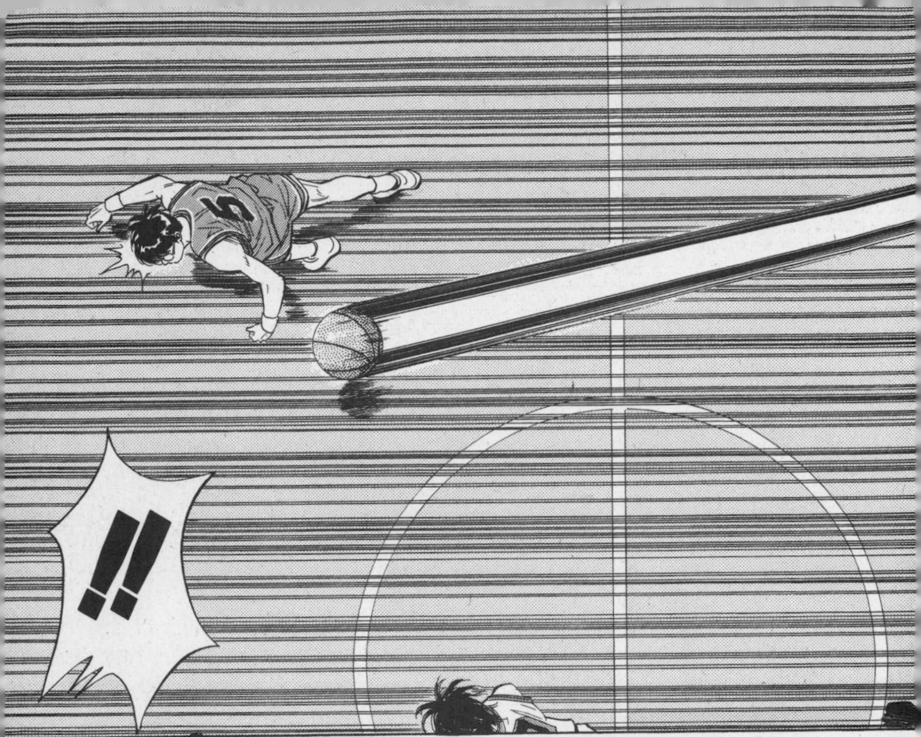
!!

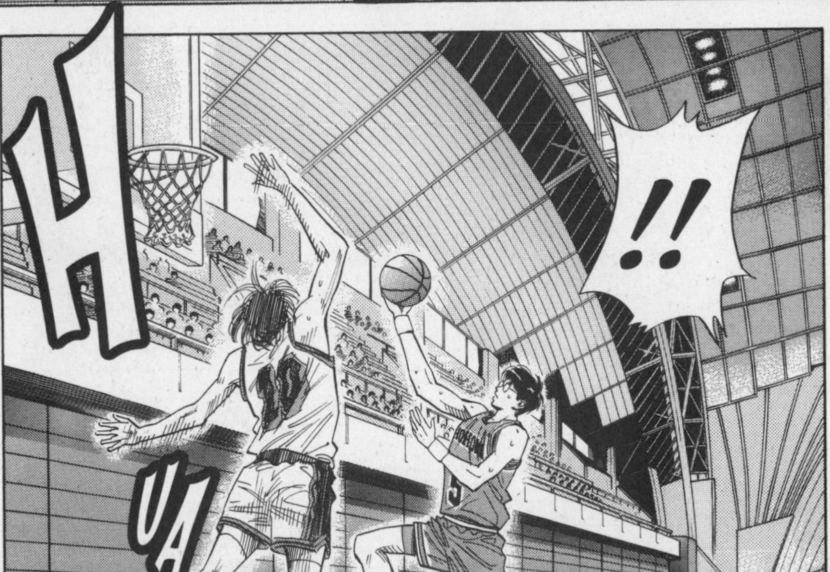
!!
H
UA

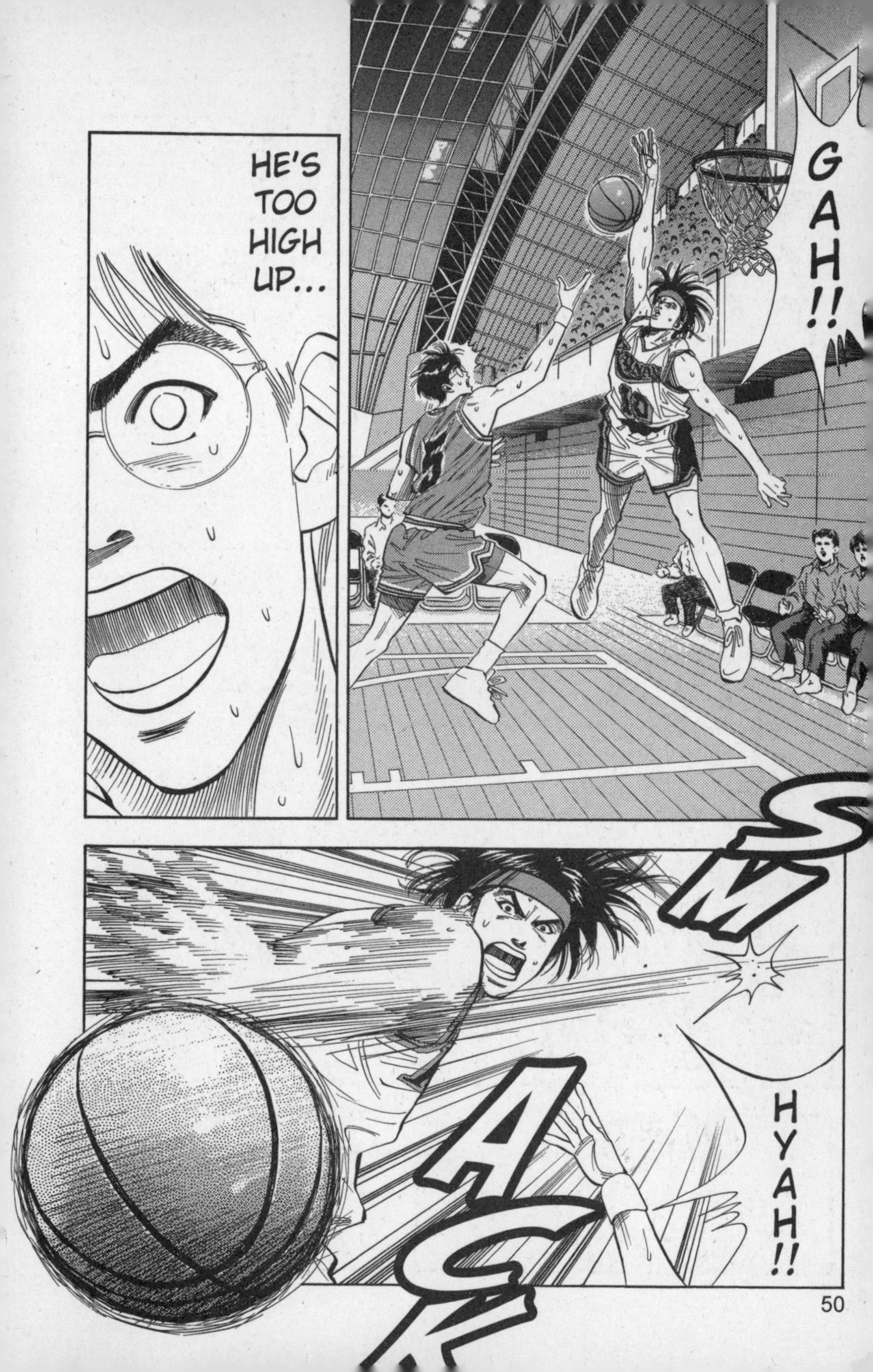
GAH!!
HE'S TOO HIGH UP...
SMAC
HYAH!!

READ THIS WAY

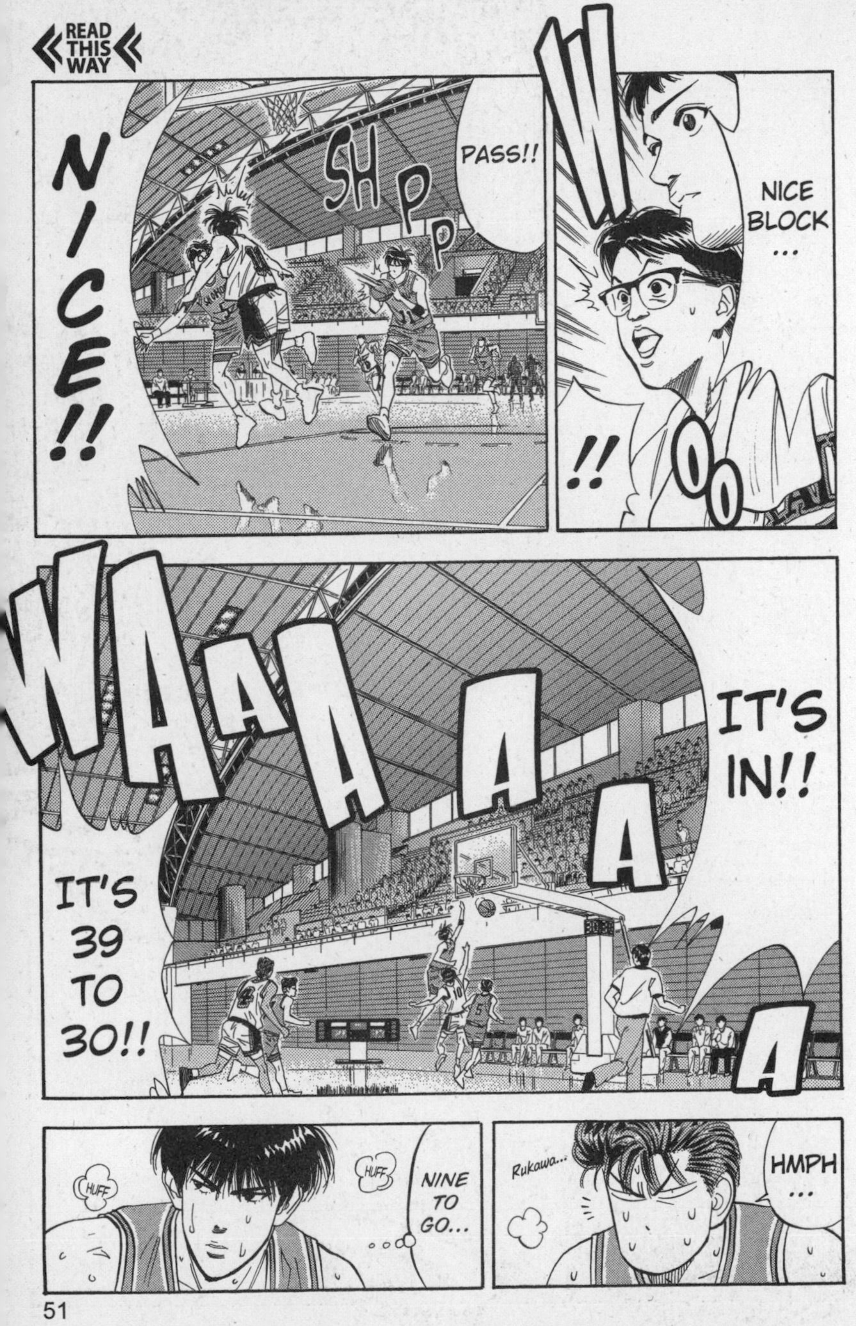
WO
NICE BLOCK...
!!
OO
PASS!!
SHPP
NICE!!
WAAAAAA
IT'S IN!!
IT'S 39 TO 30!!
HMPH...
Rukawa...
NINE TO GO...
HUFF
HUFF

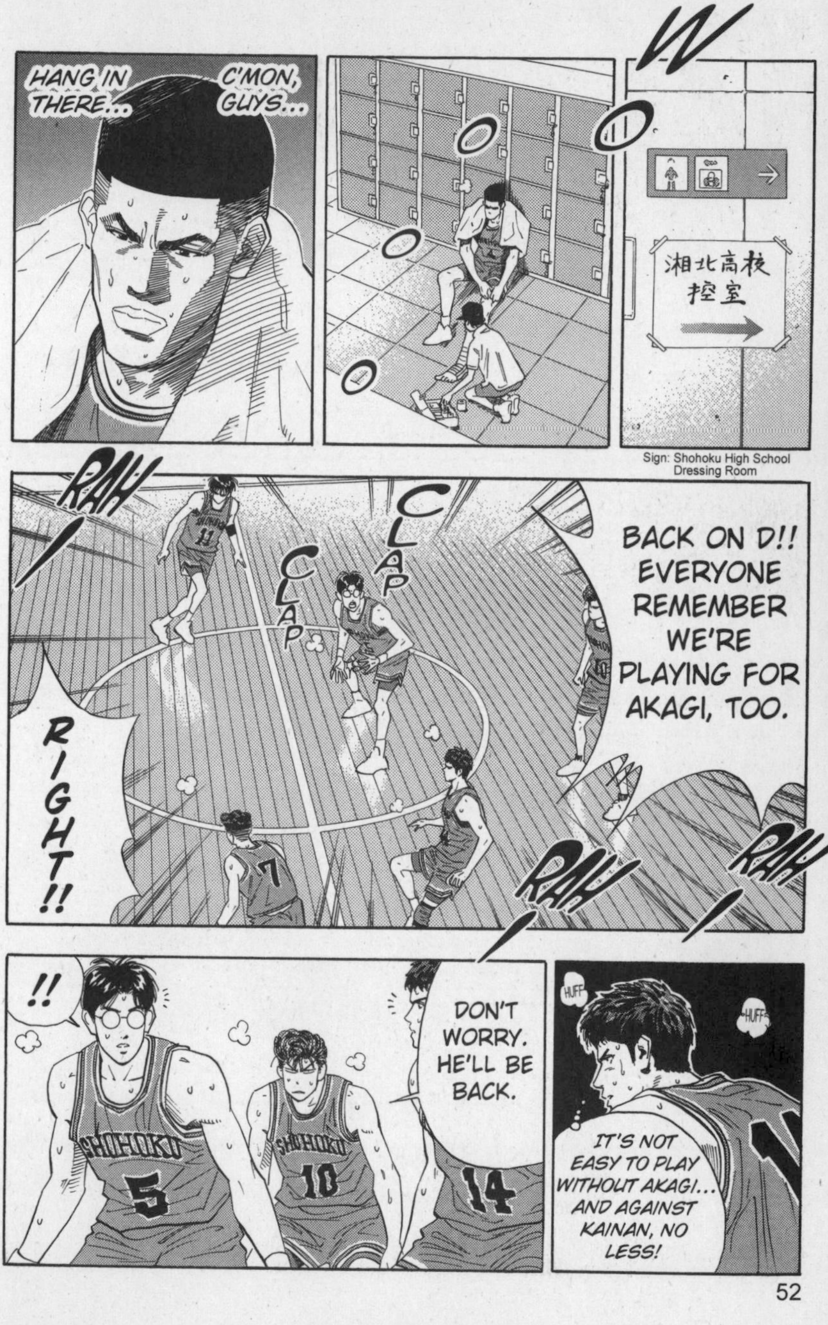
WOOOO
湘北高校
控室
Sign: Shohoku High School Dressing Room
C'MON, GUYS...
HANG IN THERE...
RAH
CLAP
CLAP
BACK ON D!! EVERYONE REMEMBER WE'RE PLAYING FOR AKAGI, TOO.
RIGHT!!
RAH
RAH
HUFF
HUFF
IT'S NOT EASY TO PLAY WITHOUT AKAGI... AND AGAINST KAINAN, NO LESS!
DON'T WORRY. HE'LL BE BACK.
!!

READ THIS WAY

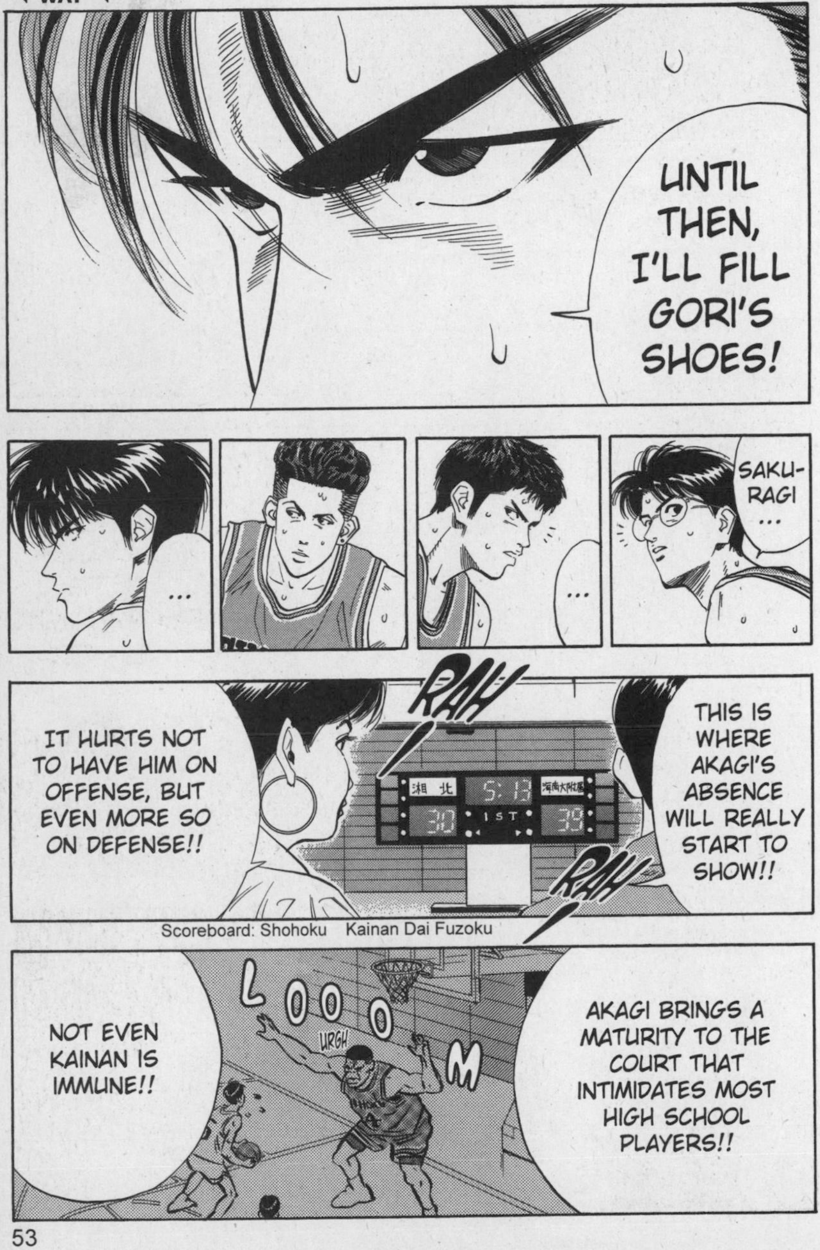

UNTIL THEN, I'LL FILL GORI'S SHOES!
SAKU-RAGI ...
...
...
THIS IS WHERE AKAGI'S ABSENCE WILL REALLY START TO SHOW!!
RAH
RAH
IT HURTS NOT TO HAVE HIM ON OFFENSE, BUT EVEN MORE SO ON DEFENSE!!
Scoreboard: Shohoku Kainan Dai Fuzoku
AKAGI BRINGS A MATURITY TO THE COURT THAT INTIMIDATES MOST HIGH SCHOOL PLAYERS!!
LOOOM
URGH
NOT EVEN KAINAN IS IMMUNE!!

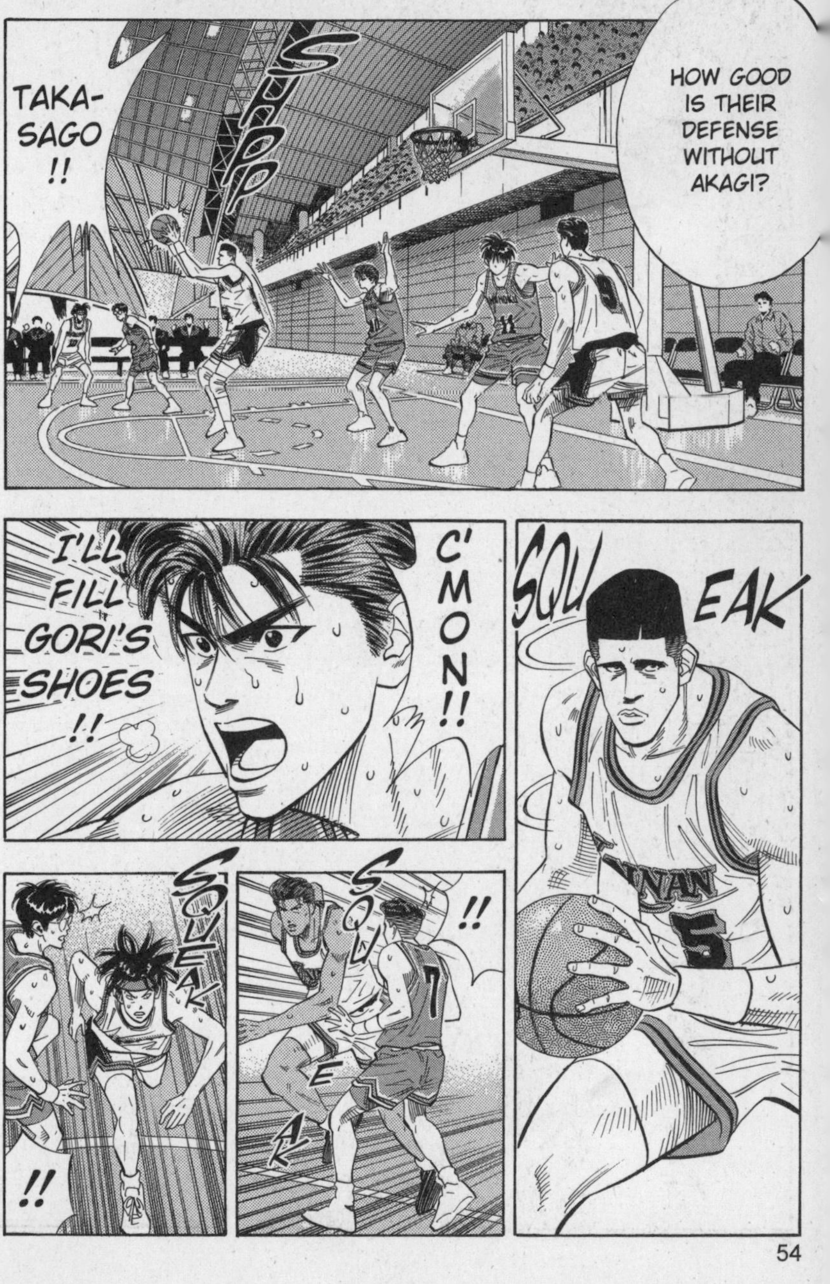
HOW GOOD IS THEIR DEFENSE WITHOUT AKAGI?
SHUPP
TAKA-SAGO!!
SQUEAK
C'MON!!
I'LL FILL GORI'S SHOES!!
!!
SQUEAK
SQUEAK
!!

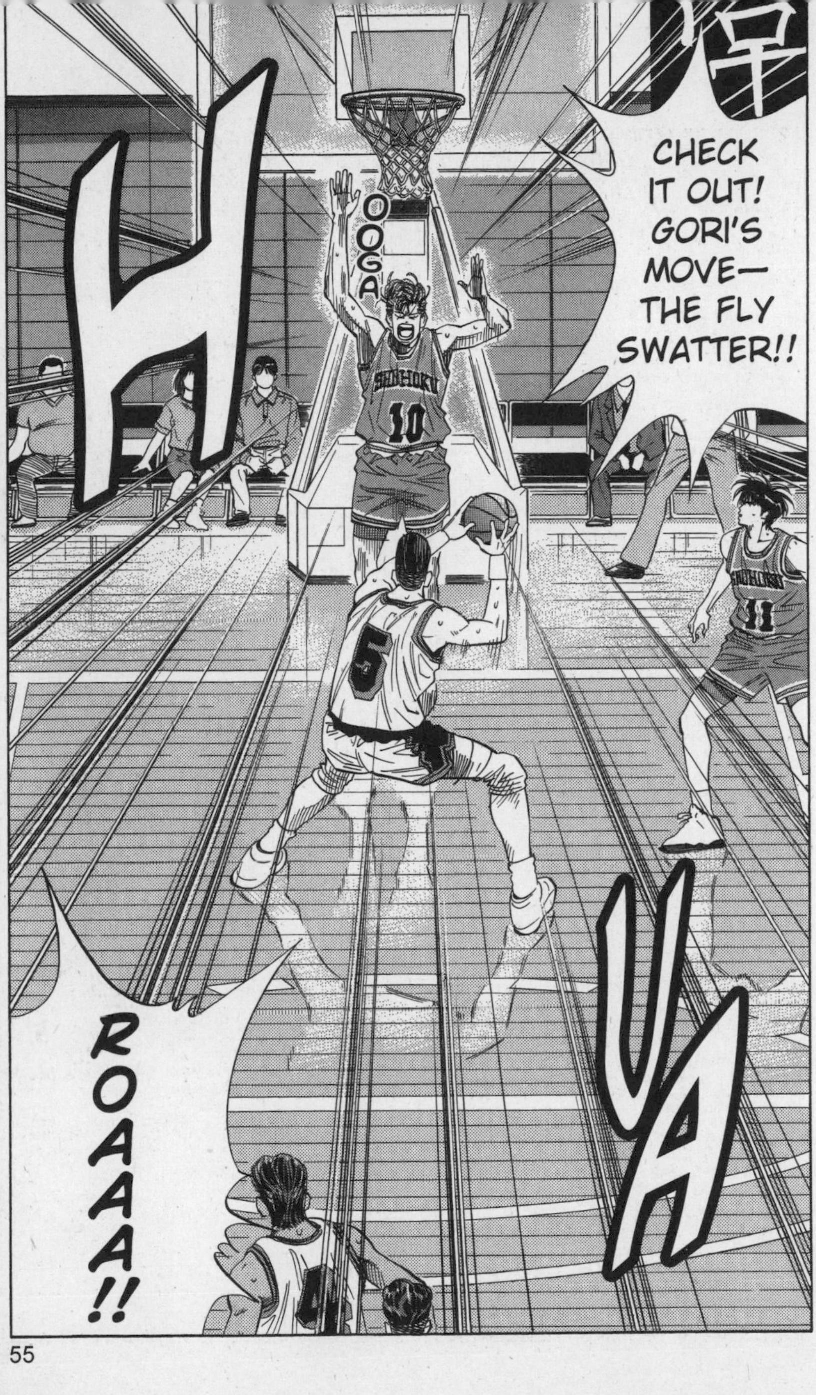
CHECK IT OUT! GORI'S MOVE— THE FLY SWATTER!!
OOGA
H
YA
ROAAAA!!

READ THIS WAY

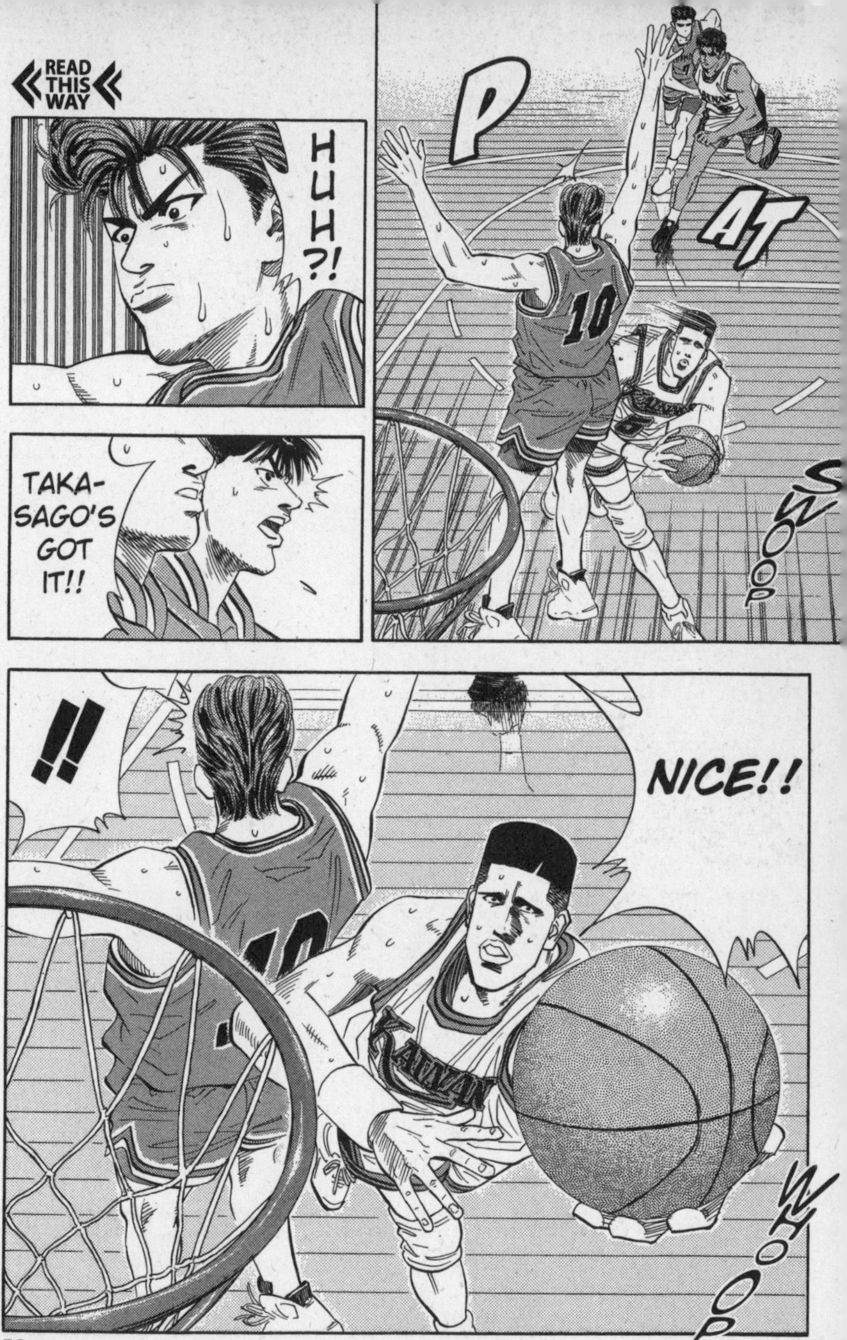
P
AT
SWOOP
HUH?!
TAKA-SAGO'S GOT IT!!
NICE!!
!!
WHOOP

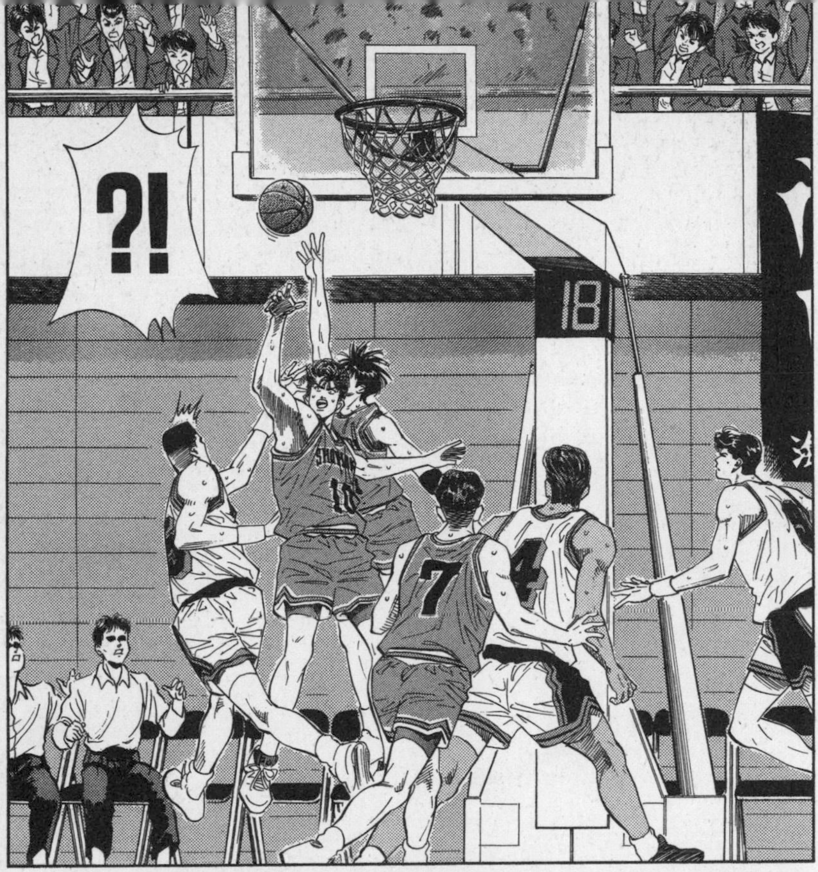
?!
18

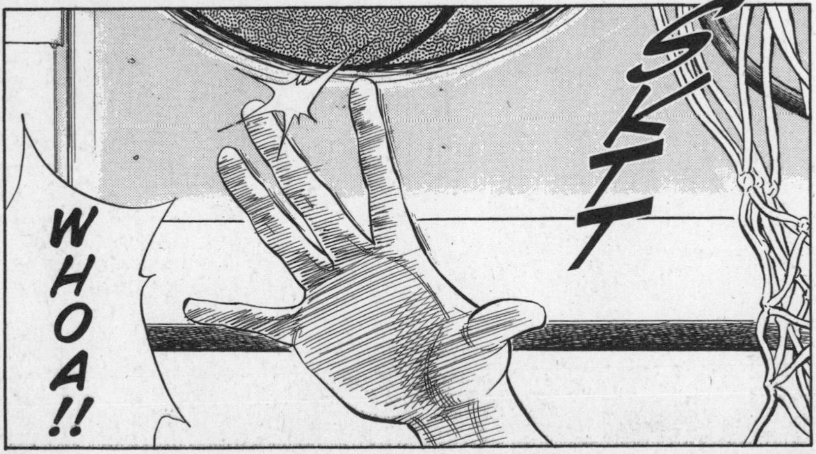
SKTT
WHOA!!

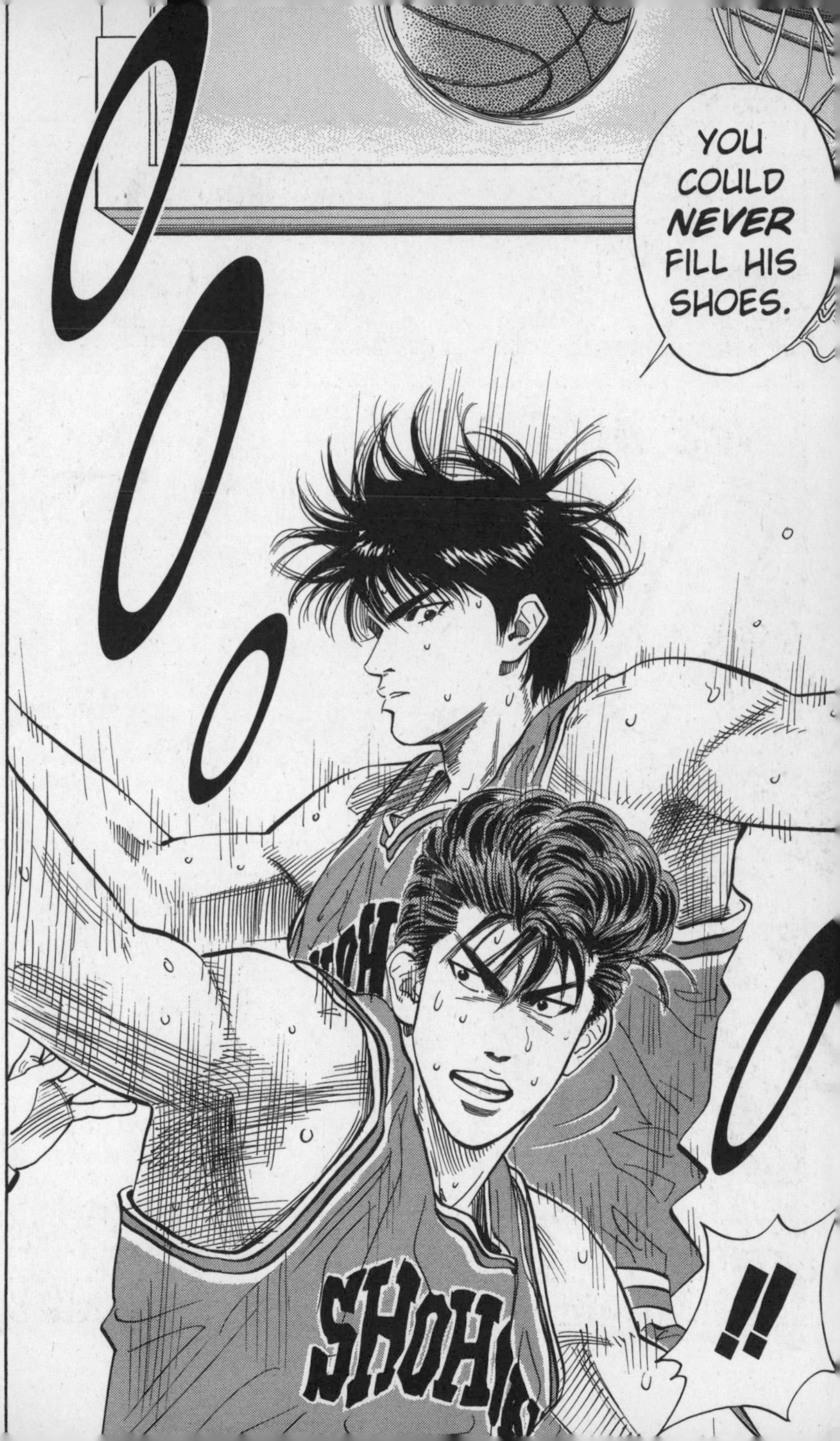
YOU COULD NEVER FILL HIS SHOES.
!!

READ THIS WAY

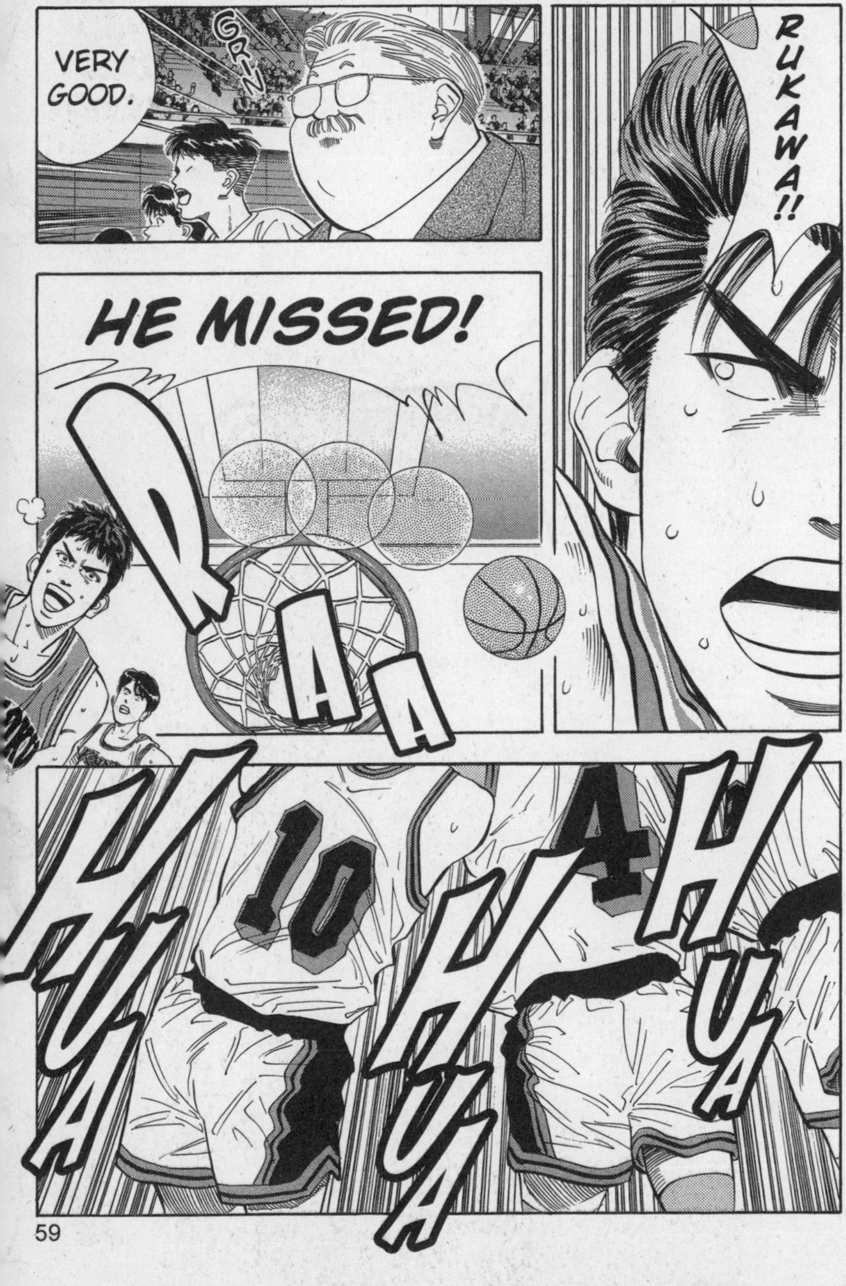
RUKAWA!!
VERY GOOD.
GRIN
HE MISSED!
RAA
HUA
HUA

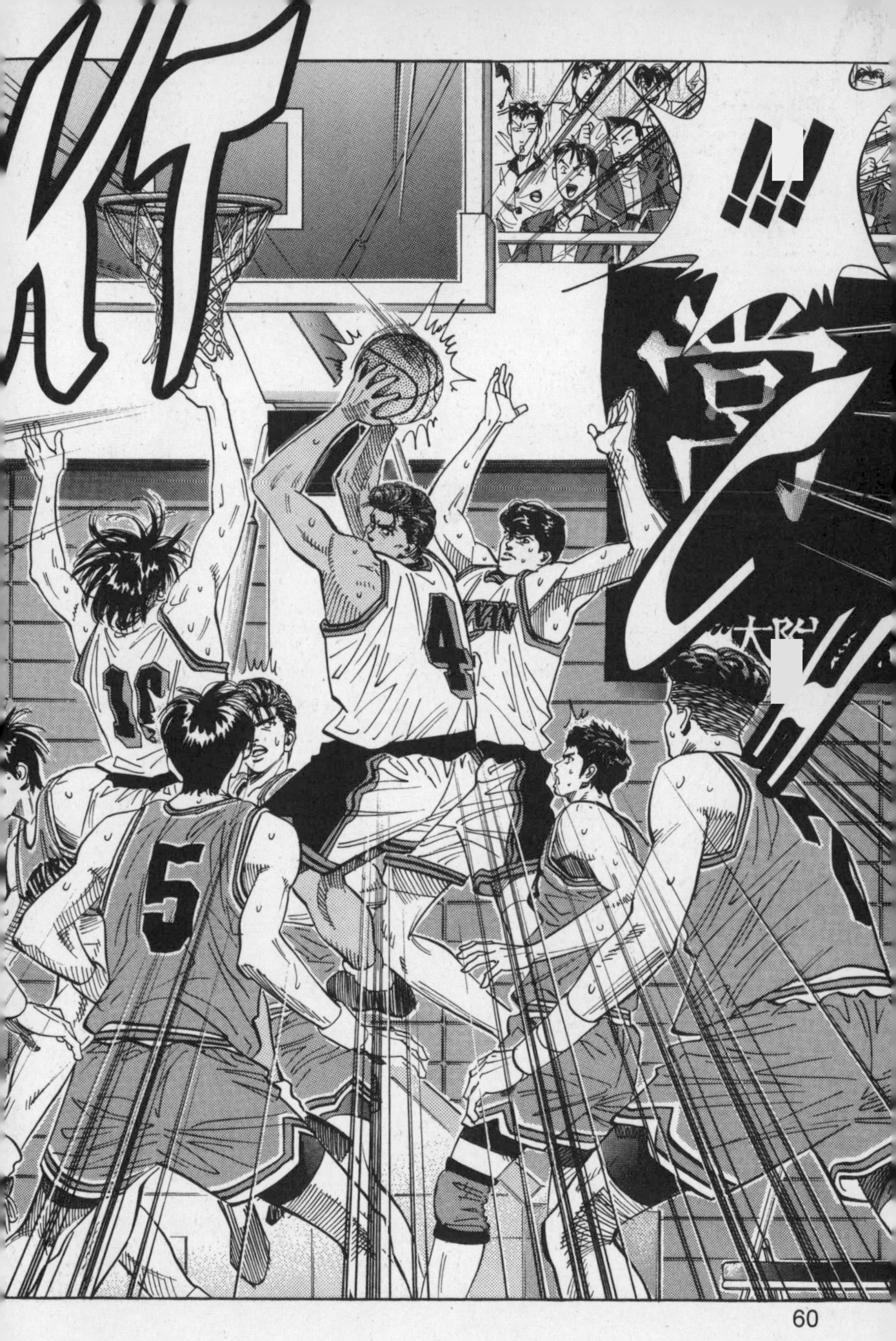
!!!

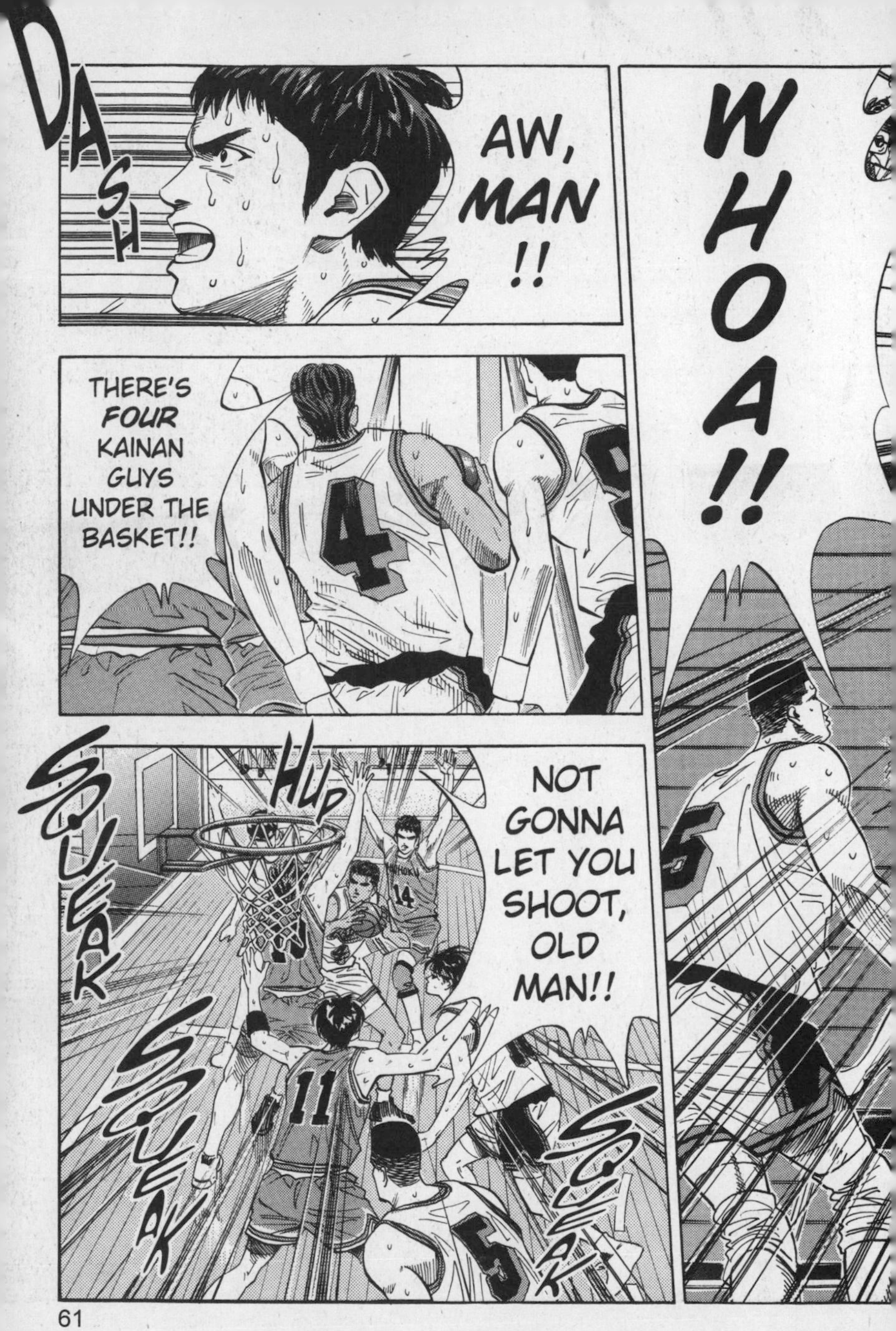
WHOA!!
DASH
AW, MAN!!
THERE'S *FOUR* KAINAN GUYS UNDER THE BASKET!!
HUP
NOT GONNA LET YOU SHOOT, OLD MAN!!
SQUEAK
SQUEAK
SQUEAK

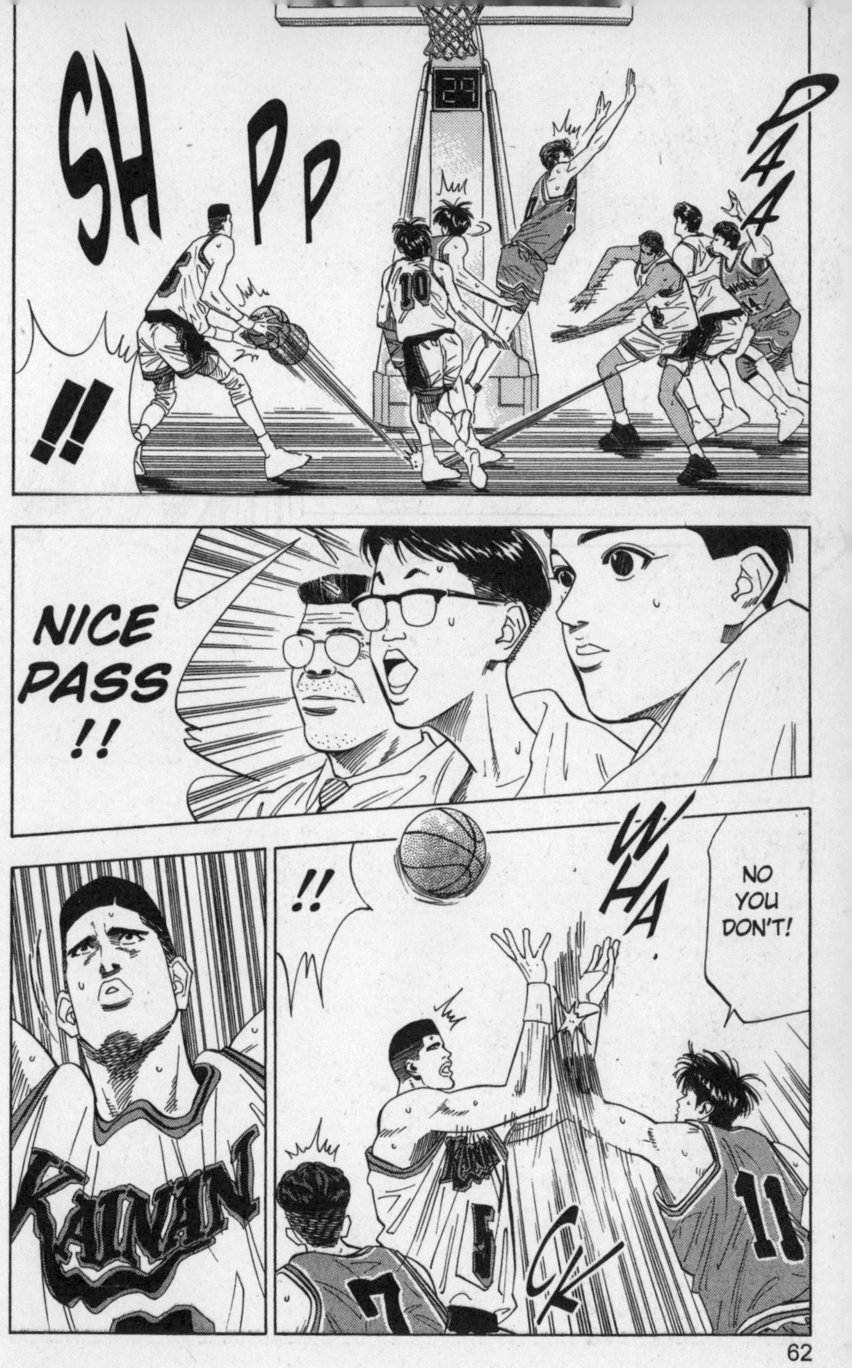
PAA
SH PP
!!
NICE PASS !!
NO YOU DON'T!
WHA
!!
CK
KAINAN

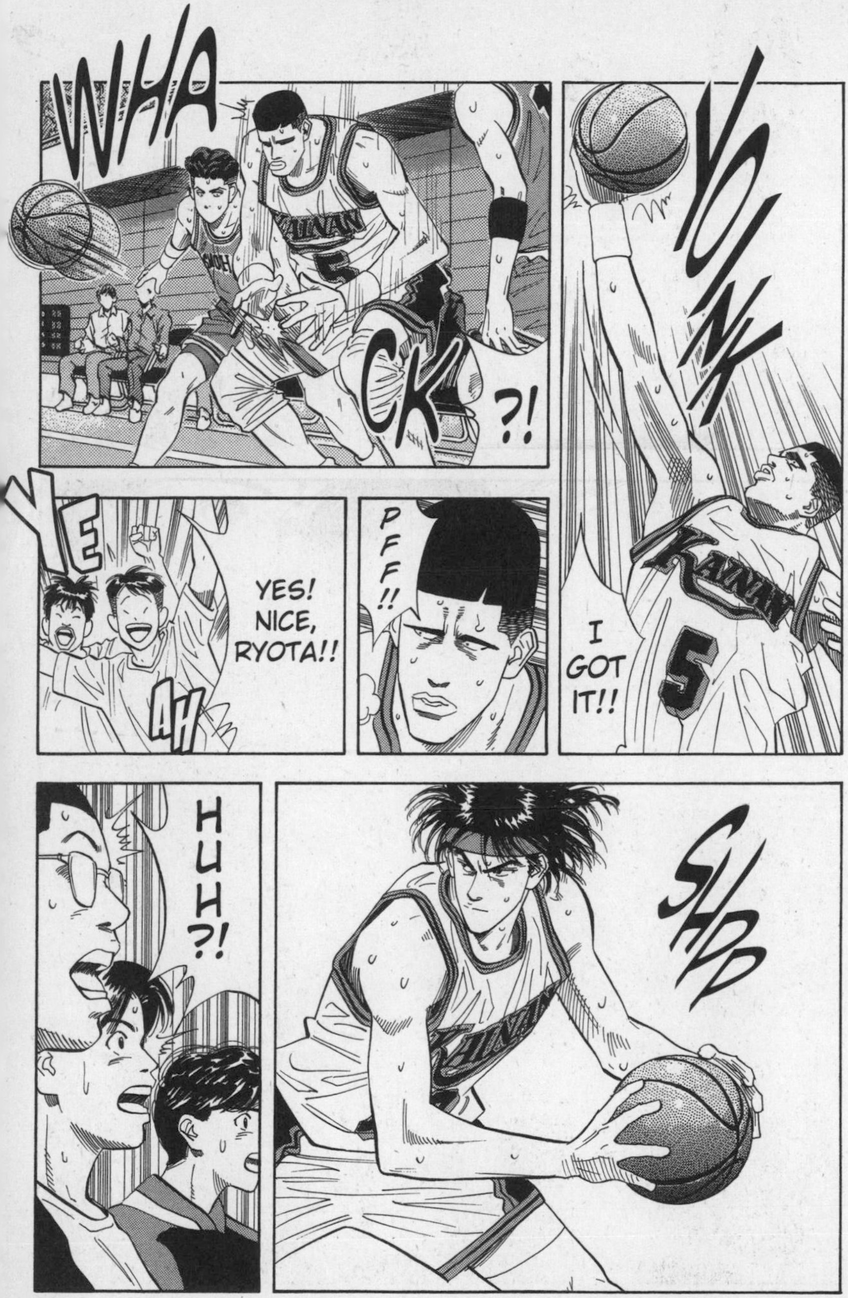
YOINK
I GOT IT!!
WHA
CK
?!
PFF!!
YE
YES! NICE, RYOTA!!
AH
SHOOP
HUH?!

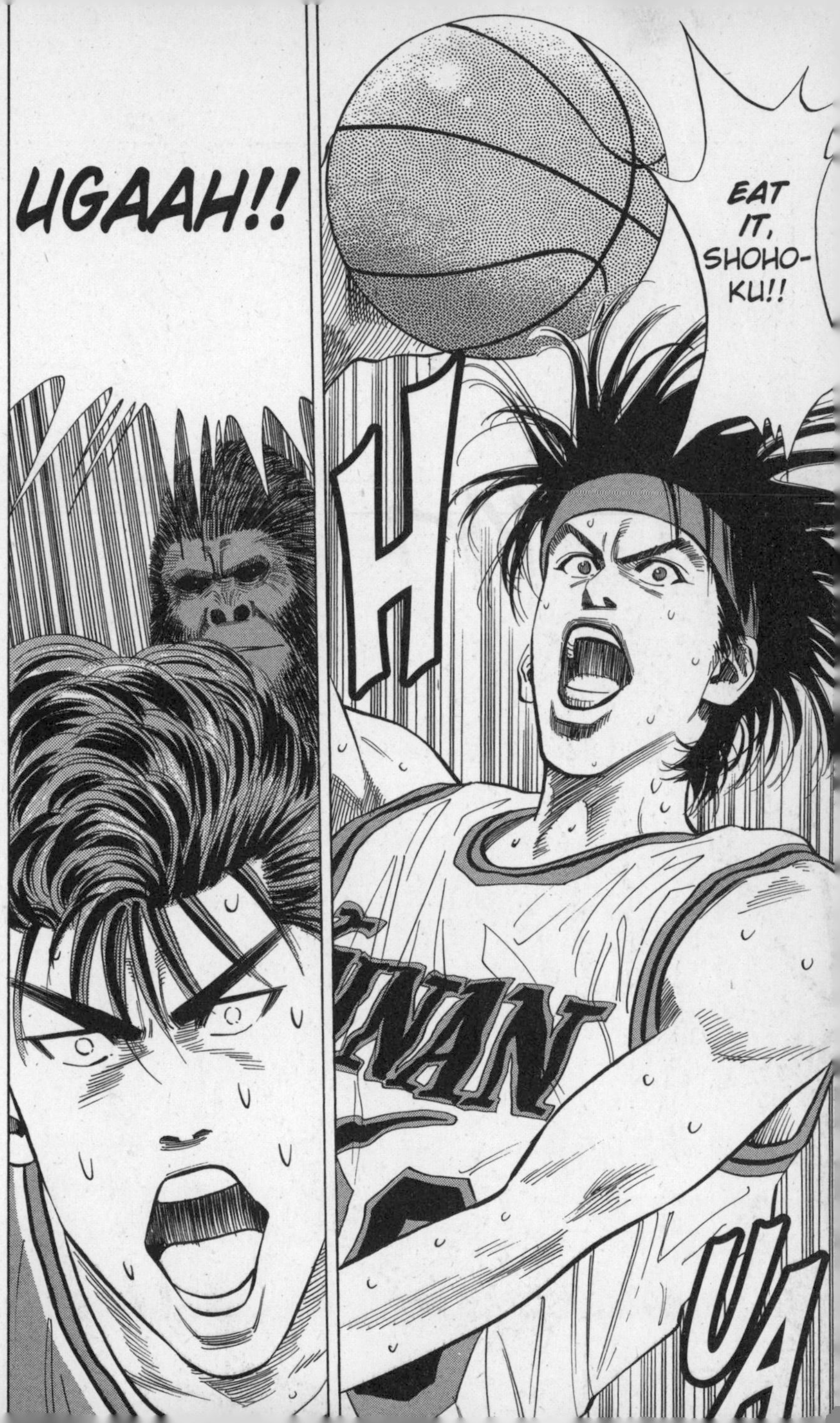
EAT IT, SHOHOKU!!
UGAAH!!

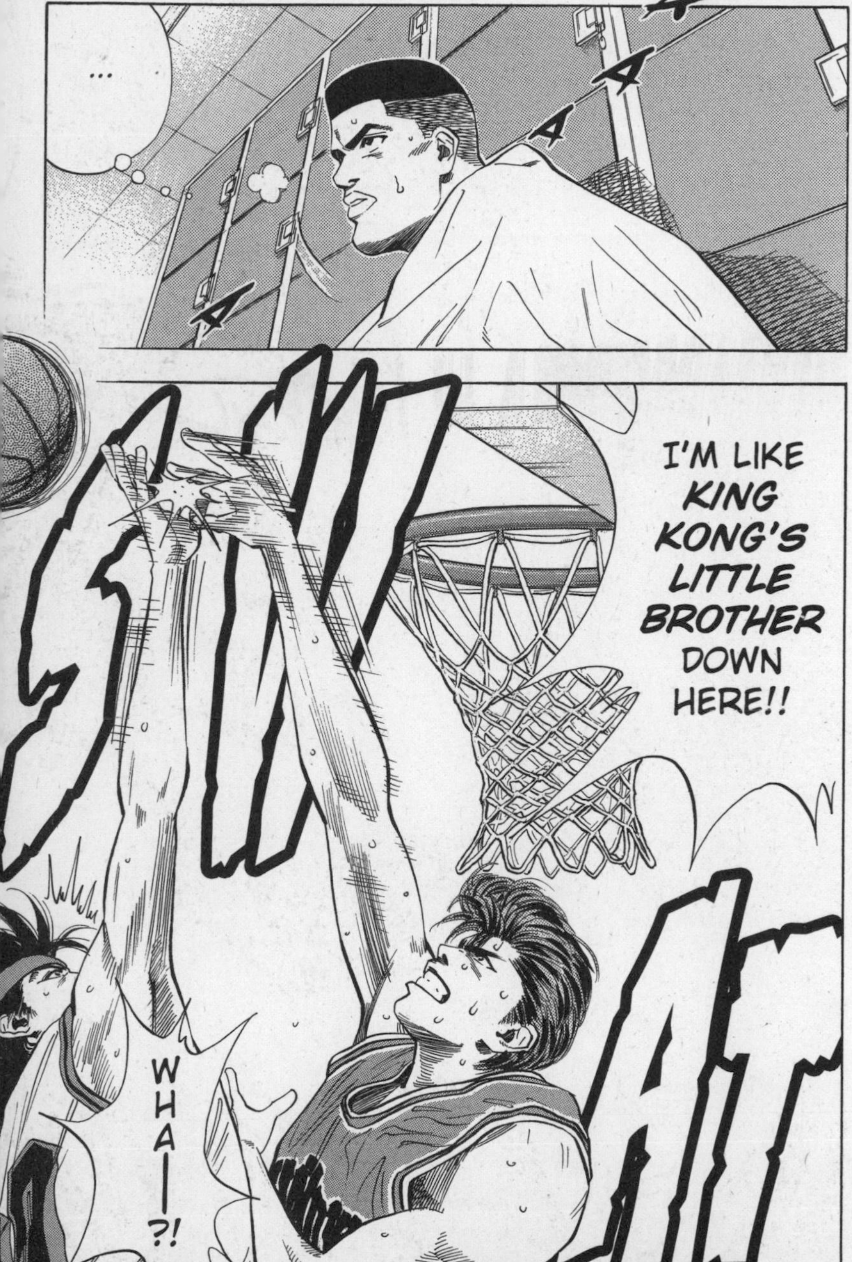
...
I'M LIKE KING KONG'S LITTLE BROTHER DOWN HERE!!
SWAT
WHA--?!

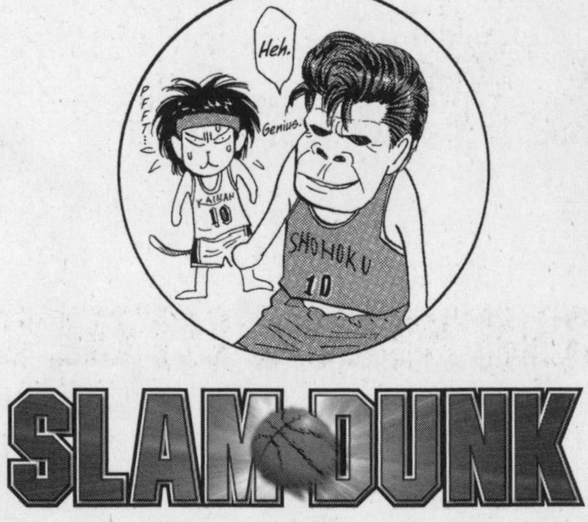
Heh.
PFFT...
Genius.
KAINAN
10
SHOHOKU
10

SLAM DUNK

#111

KING KONG'S LITTLE BROTHER

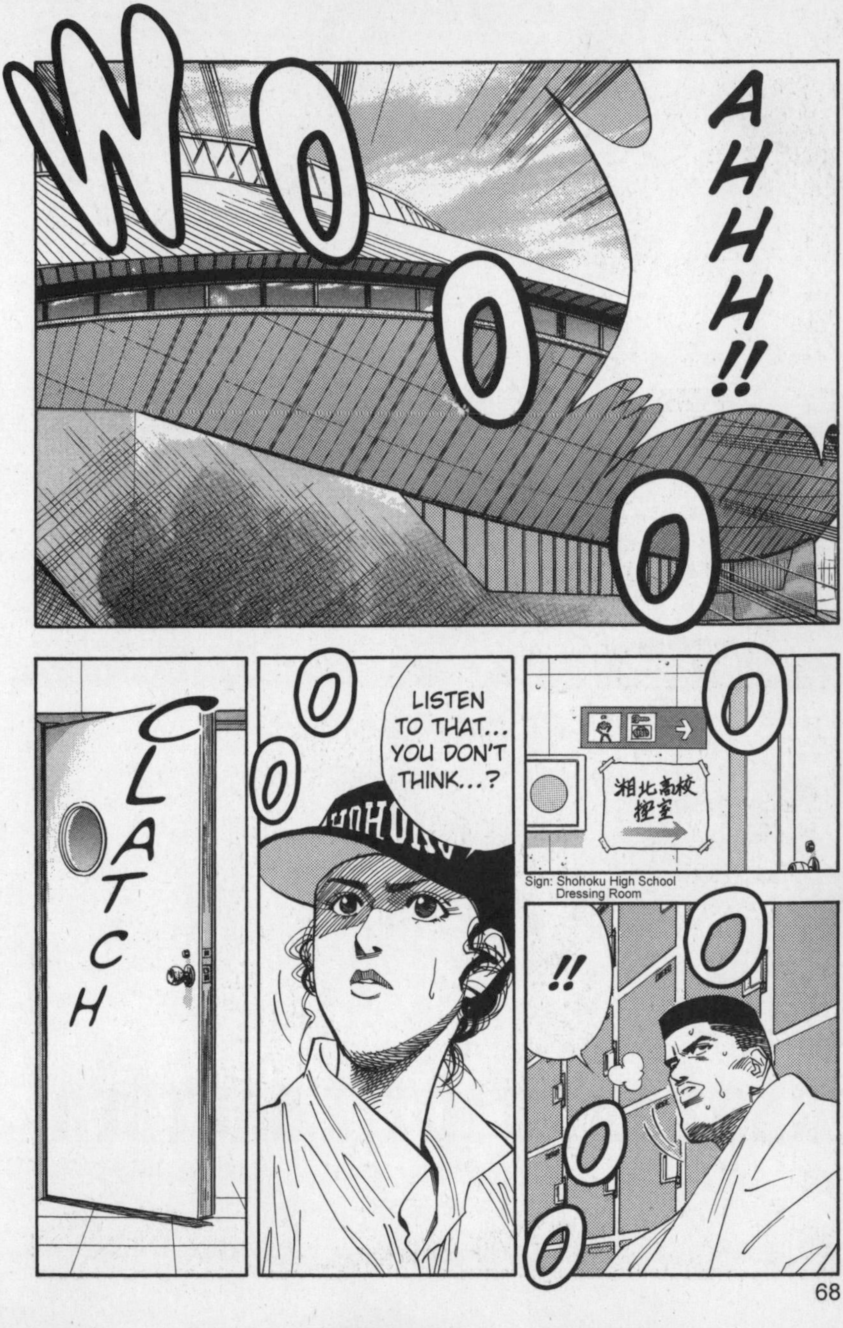
WOOOO
AHHH!!
湘北高校
控室
Sign: Shohoku High School Dressing Room
!!
LISTEN TO THAT... YOU DON'T THINK...?
CLATCH

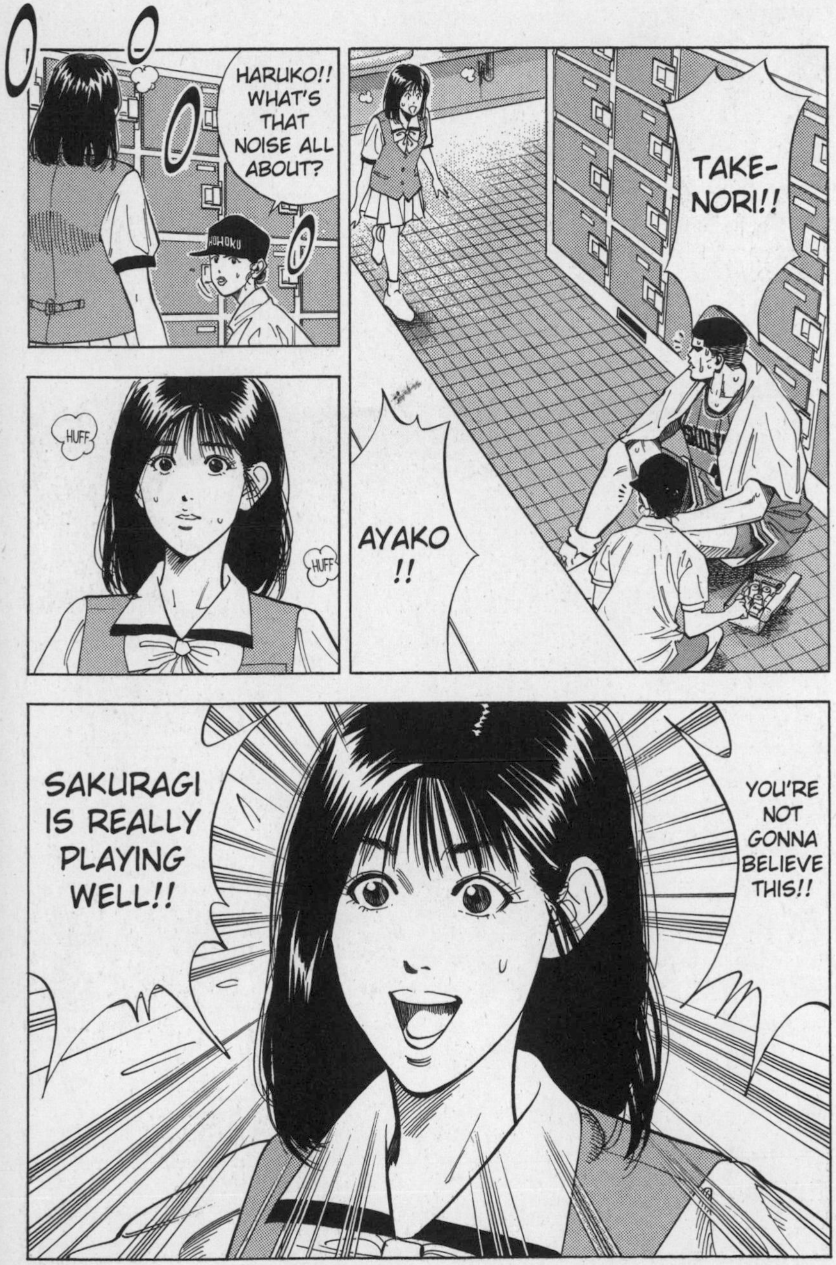
TAKE-NORI!!
AYAKO!!
HARUKO!! WHAT'S THAT NOISE ALL ABOUT?
HUFF
HUFF
YOU'RE NOT GONNA BELIEVE THIS!!
SAKURAGI IS REALLY PLAYING WELL!!

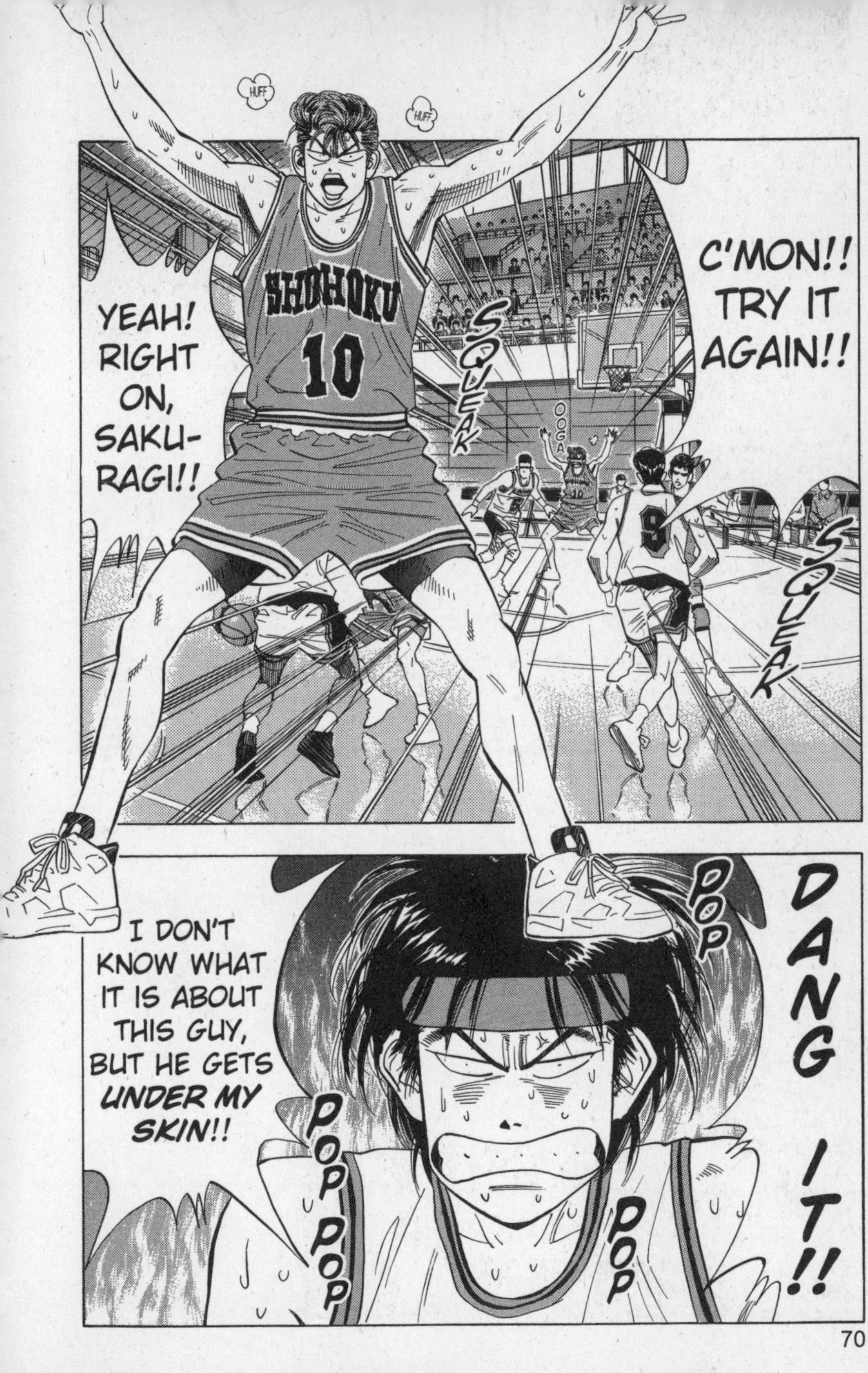
HUFF
HUFF
C'MON!! TRY IT AGAIN!!
SQUEAK
SQUEAK
OOGA
YEAH! RIGHT ON, SAKU-RAGI!!
DANG IT!!
POP POP
POP POP
I DON'T KNOW WHAT IT IS ABOUT THIS GUY, BUT HE GETS *UNDER MY SKIN!!*
POP POP

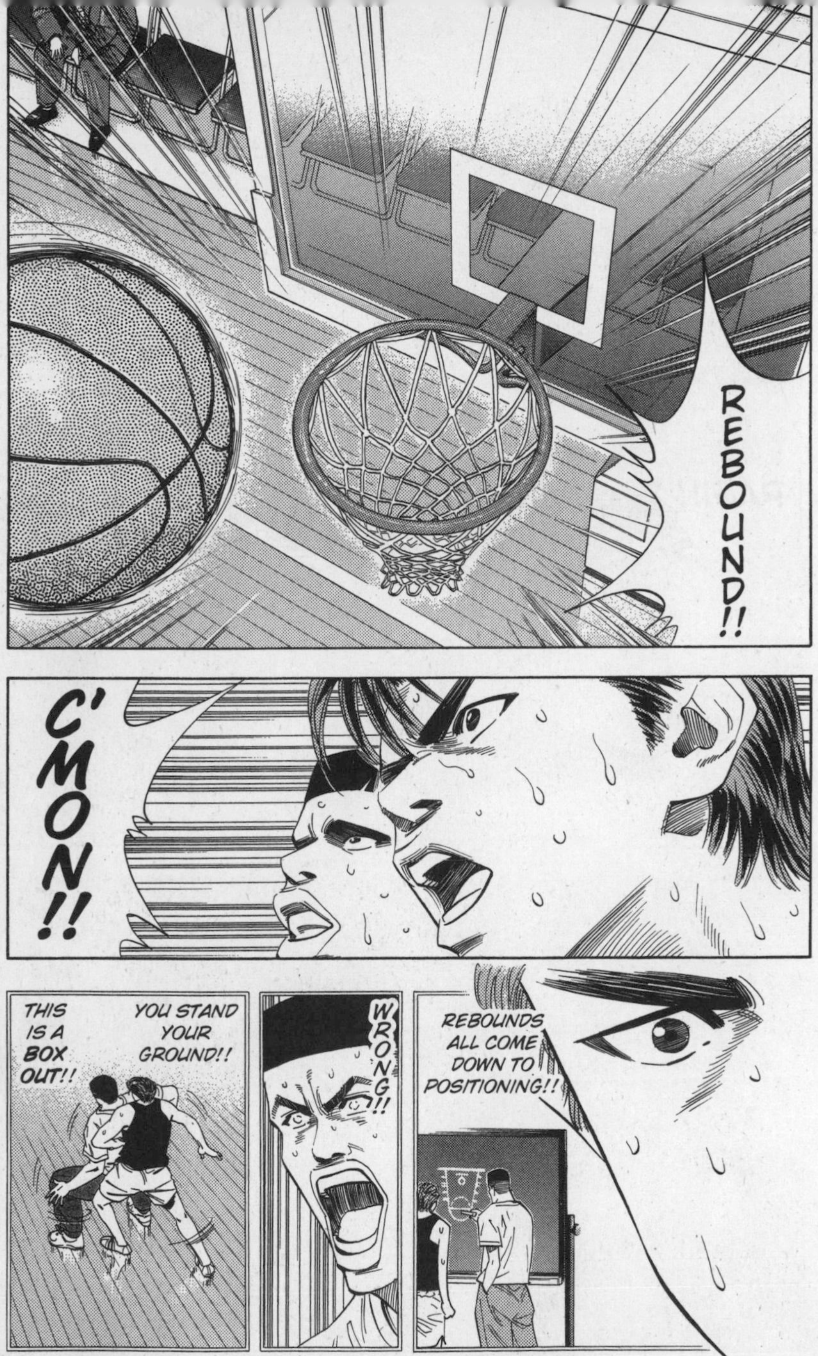
REBOUND!!
C'MON!!
REBOUNDS ALL COME DOWN TO POSITIONING!!
WRONG!!
YOU STAND YOUR GROUND!!
THIS IS A BOX OUT!!

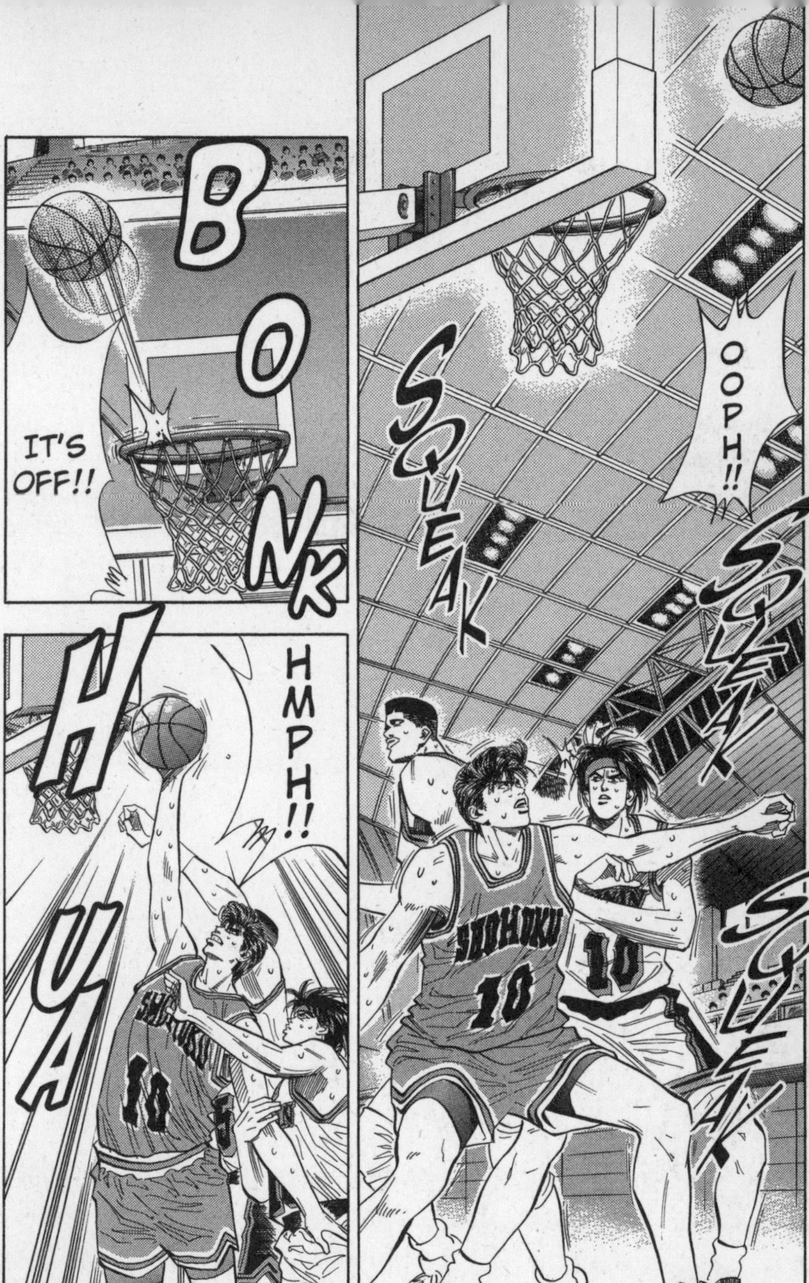
OOPH!!
SQUEAK
SQUEAK
SQUEAK
BONK
IT'S OFF!!
HMMPH!!
HUUA

READ THIS WAY

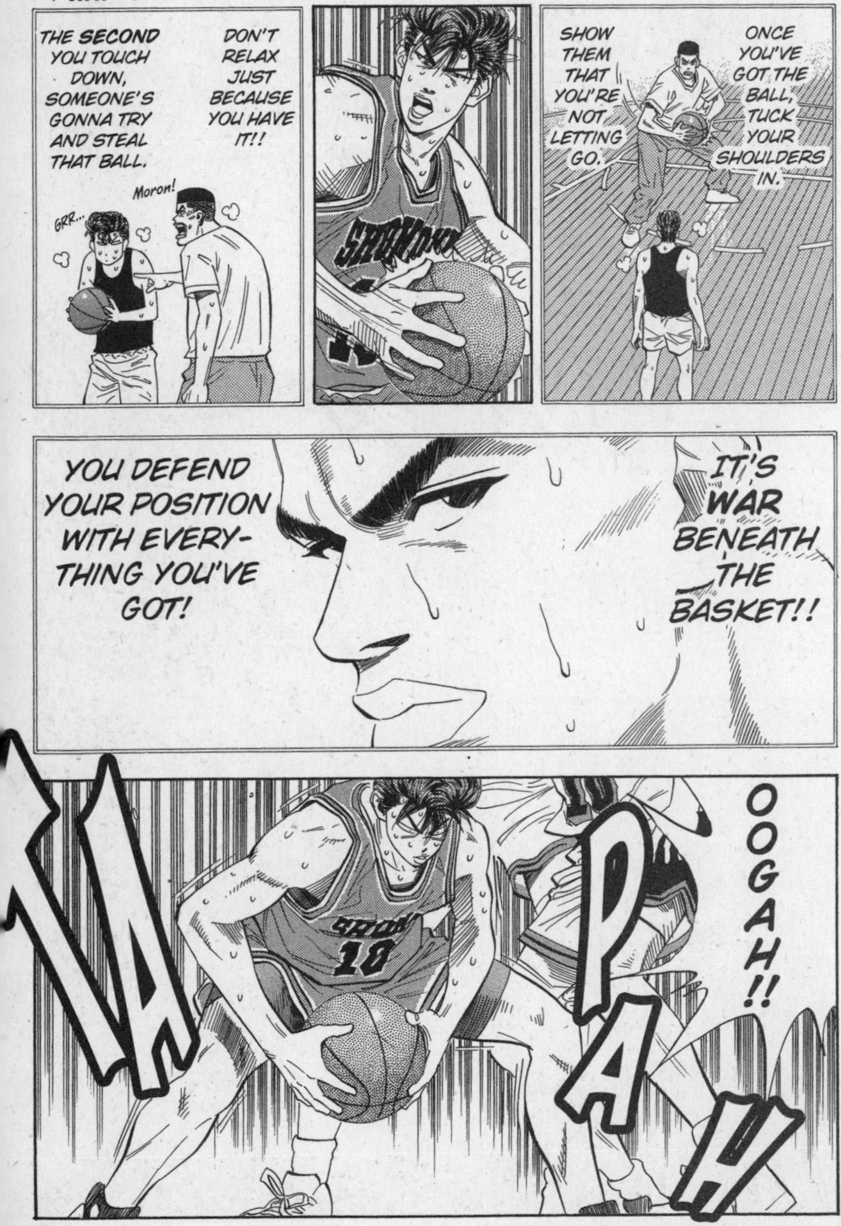
ONCE YOU'VE GOT THE BALL, TUCK YOUR SHOULDERS IN.
SHOW THEM THAT YOU'RE NOT LETTING GO.
DON'T RELAX JUST BECAUSE YOU HAVE IT!!
THE SECOND YOU TOUCH DOWN, SOMEONE'S GONNA TRY AND STEAL THAT BALL.
Moron!
GRR...
IT'S WAR BENEATH THE BASKET!!
YOU DEFEND YOUR POSITION WITH EVERY-THING YOU'VE GOT!
OOGAH!!
PAH

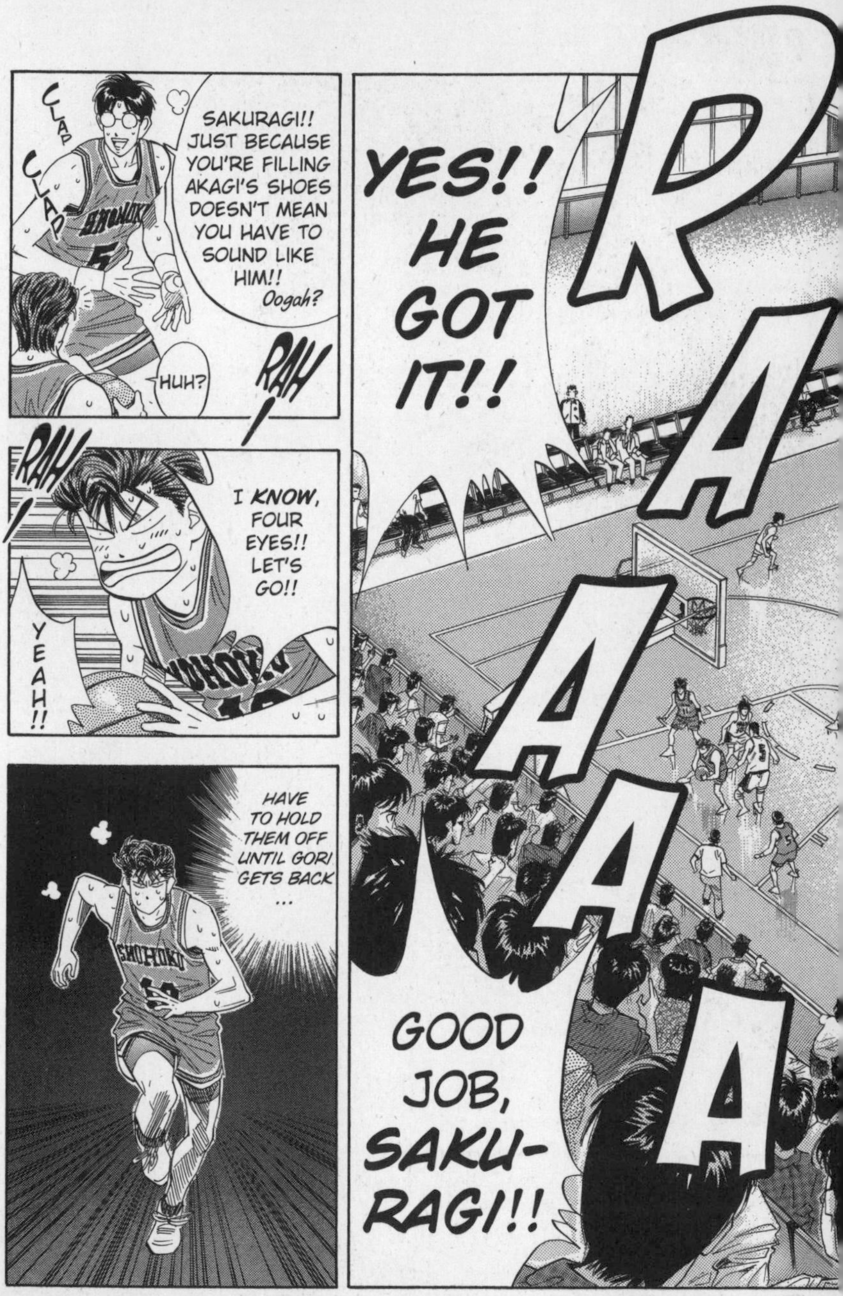
YES!! HE GOT IT!!
RAAAA
GOOD JOB, SAKURAGI!!
CLAP CLAP
SAKURAGI!! JUST BECAUSE YOU'RE FILLING AKAGI'S SHOES DOESN'T MEAN YOU HAVE TO SOUND LIKE HIM!!
Oogah?
HUH?
RAH
RAH
I KNOW, FOUR EYES!! LET'S GO!!
YEAH!!
HAVE TO HOLD THEM OFF UNTIL GORI GETS BACK ...

READ THIS WAY

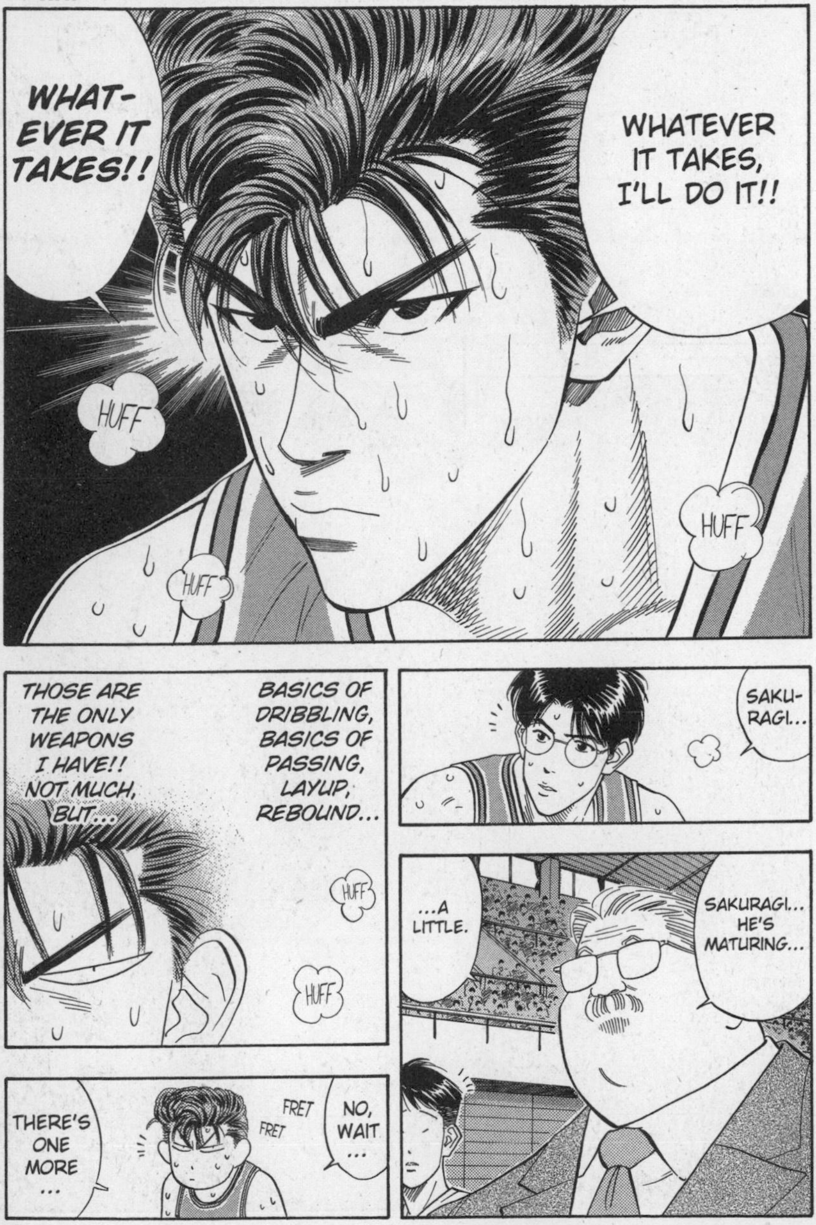
WHATEVER IT TAKES, I'LL DO IT!!
HUFF
WHAT-EVER IT TAKES!!
HUFF
HUFF
SAKU-RAGI...
SAKURAGI... HE'S MATURING...
...A LITTLE.
BASICS OF DRIBBLING, BASICS OF PASSING, LAYUP, REBOUND...
THOSE ARE THE ONLY WEAPONS I HAVE!! NOT MUCH, BUT...
HUFF
HUFF
NO, WAIT ...
FRET
FRET
THERE'S ONE MORE ...

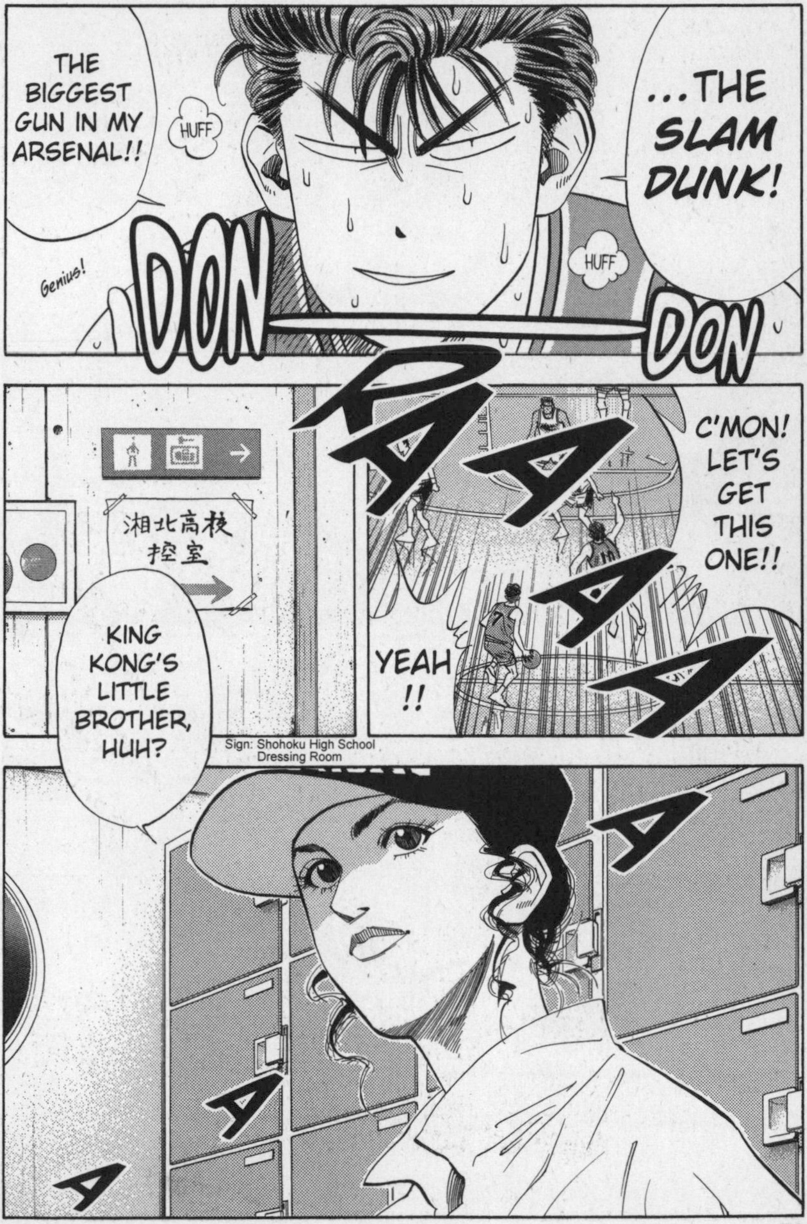
...THE SLAM DUNK!
HUFF
THE BIGGEST GUN IN MY ARSENAL!!
HUFF
Genius!
DON
DON
C'MON! LET'S GET THIS ONE!!
RAAAAA
YEAH!!
湘北高校
控室
KING KONG'S LITTLE BROTHER, HUH?
Sign: Shohoku High School Dressing Room
A
A
A

READ THIS WAY

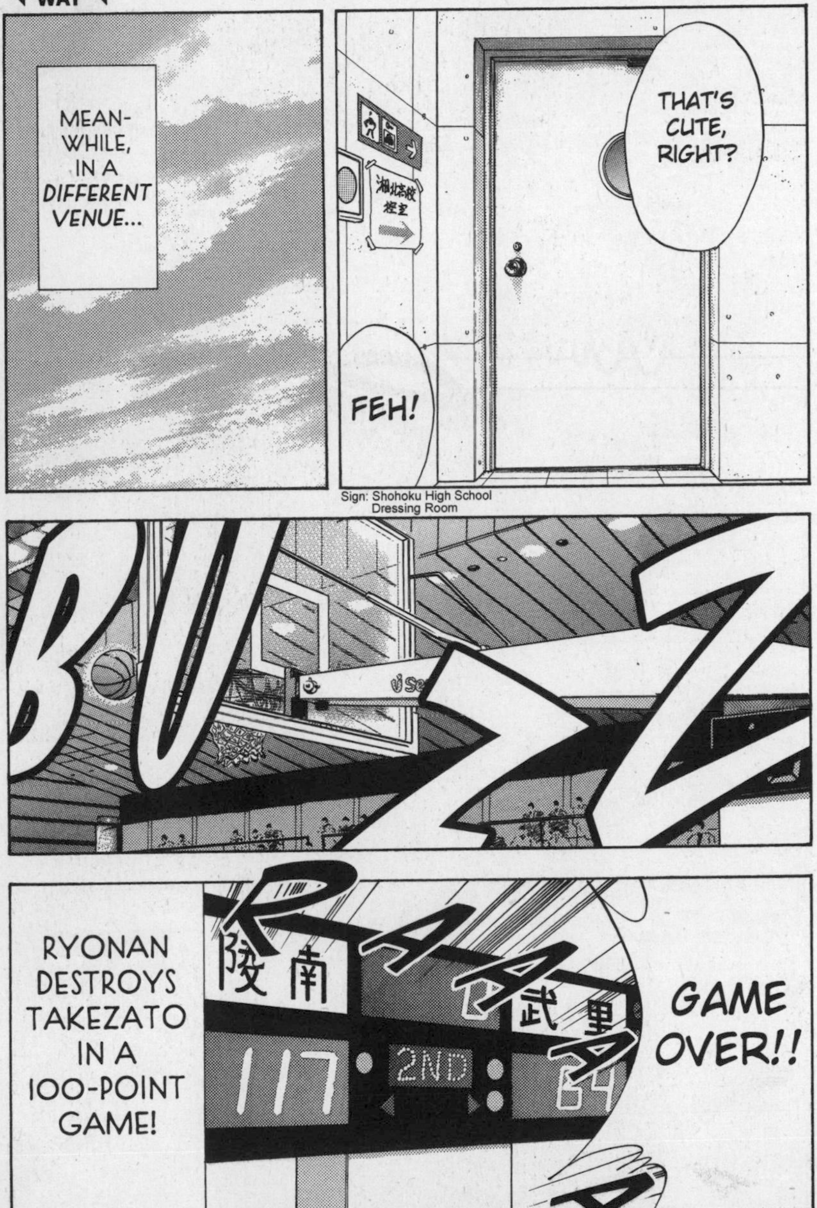
THAT'S CUTE, RIGHT?
FEH!
湘北高校 控室
MEAN-WHILE, IN A DIFFERENT VENUE...
BUZZ
GAME OVER!!
RAAAAA
陵南
武里
117
2ND
64
RYONAN DESTROYS TAKEZATO IN A 100-POINT GAME!
Sign: Shohoku High School Dressing Room

Scoreboard: Ryonan Takezato

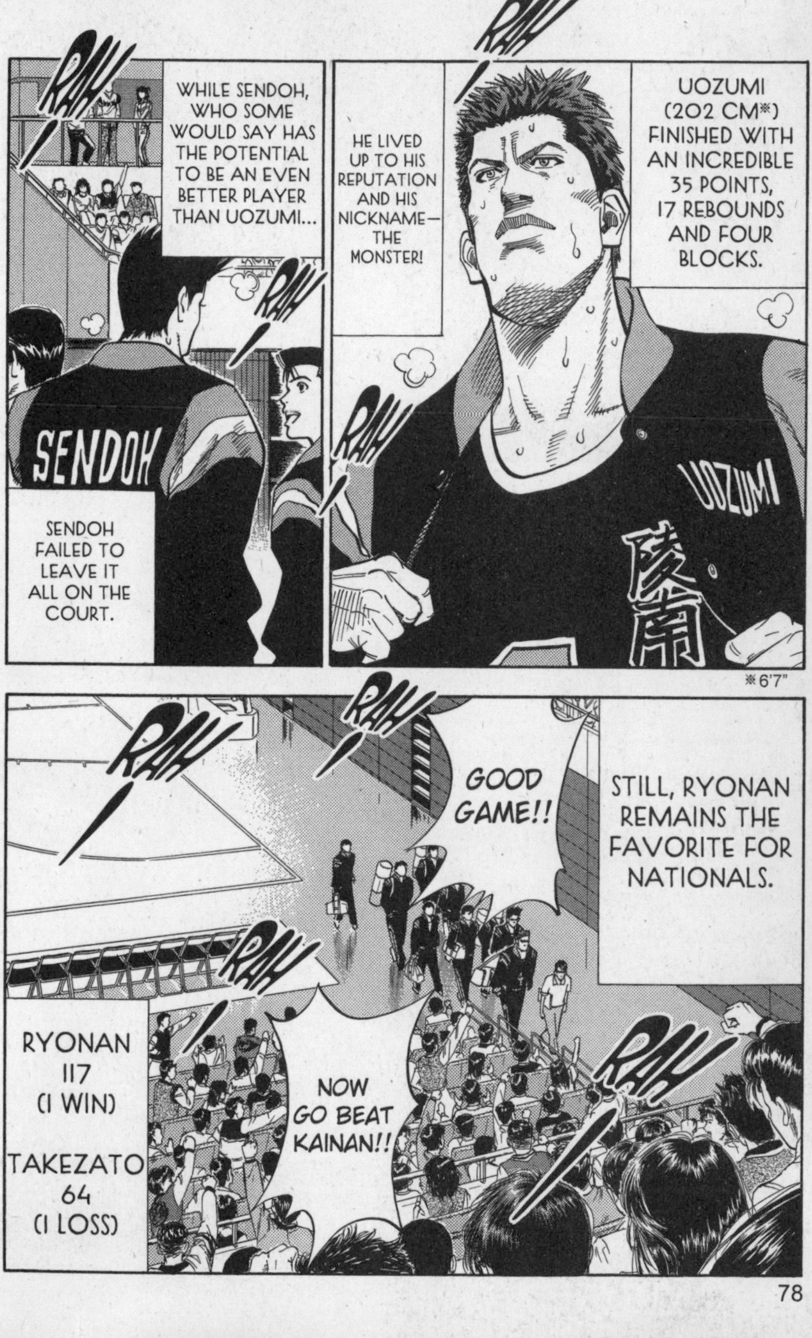

RAH
UOZUMI (202 CM※) FINISHED WITH AN INCREDIBLE 35 POINTS, 17 REBOUNDS AND FOUR BLOCKS.
HE LIVED UP TO HIS REPUTATION AND HIS NICKNAME—THE MONSTER!
RAH
WHILE SENDOH, WHO SOME WOULD SAY HAS THE POTENTIAL TO BE AN EVEN BETTER PLAYER THAN UOZUMI...
RAH
RAH
SENDOH
UOZUMI
SENDOH FAILED TO LEAVE IT ALL ON THE COURT.
※6'7"
RAH
STILL, RYONAN REMAINS THE FAVORITE FOR NATIONALS.
GOOD GAME!!
RAH
RAH
RAH
NOW GO BEAT KAINAN!!
RYONAN 117 (1 WIN)
TAKEZATO 64 (1 LOSS)

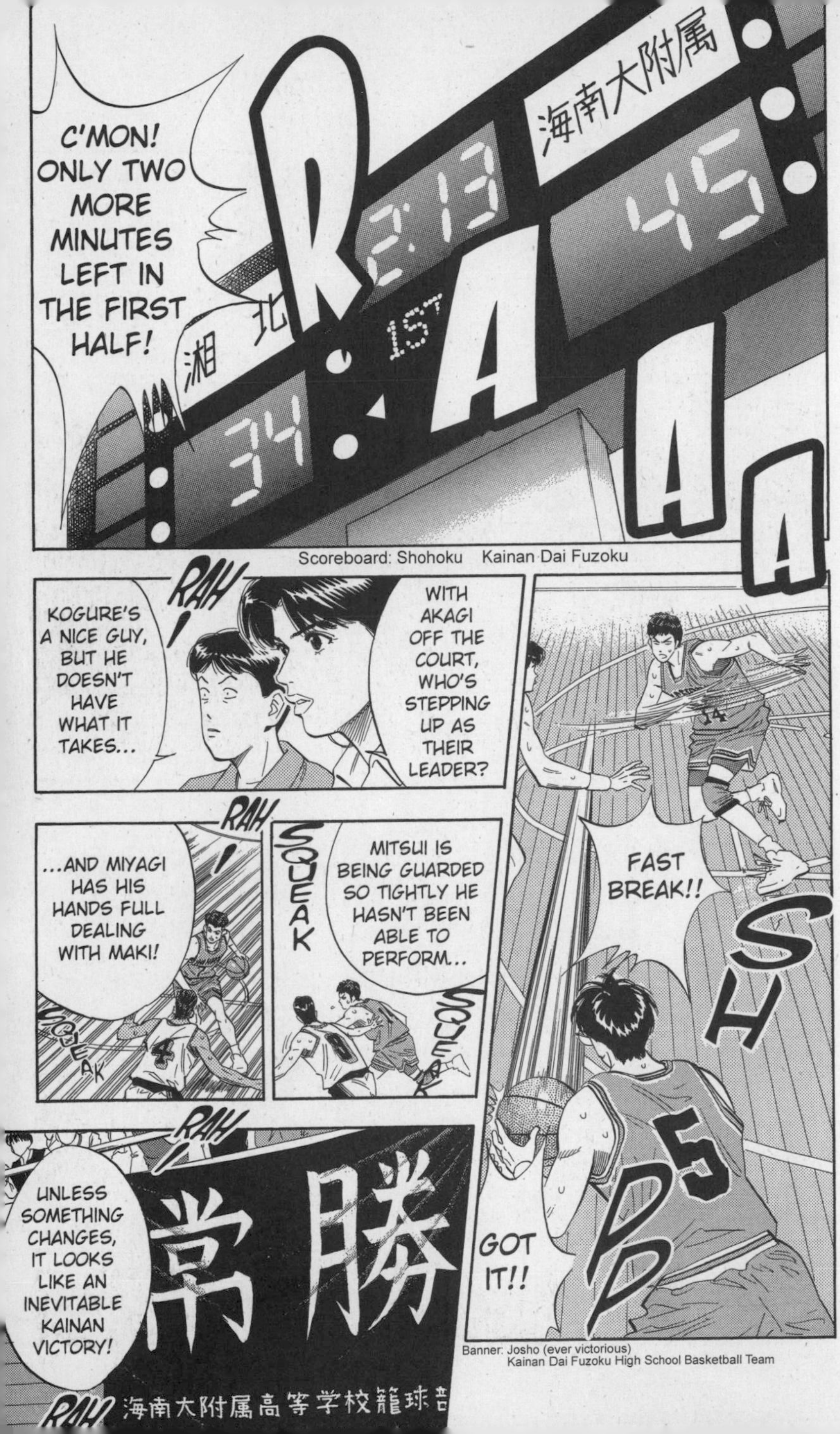
RAAAAA
C'MON! ONLY TWO MORE MINUTES LEFT IN THE FIRST HALF!
海南大附属
45
2:13
1ST
湘北
34
FAST BREAK!!
SHH
GOT IT!!
PP
WITH AKAGI OFF THE COURT, WHO'S STEPPING UP AS THEIR LEADER?
RAH!
KOGURE'S A NICE GUY, BUT HE DOESN'T HAVE WHAT IT TAKES...
SQUEAK
MITSUI IS BEING GUARDED SO TIGHTLY HE HASN'T BEEN ABLE TO PERFORM...
SQUEAK
RAH!
...AND MIYAGI HAS HIS HANDS FULL DEALING WITH MAKI!
SQUEAK
RAH!
UNLESS SOMETHING CHANGES, IT LOOKS LIKE AN INEVITABLE KAINAN VICTORY!
常勝
海南大附属高等学校籠球部
RAH

Scoreboard: Shohoku Kainan Dai Fuzoku

Banner: Josho (ever victorious)
Kainan Dai Fuzoku High School Basketball Team

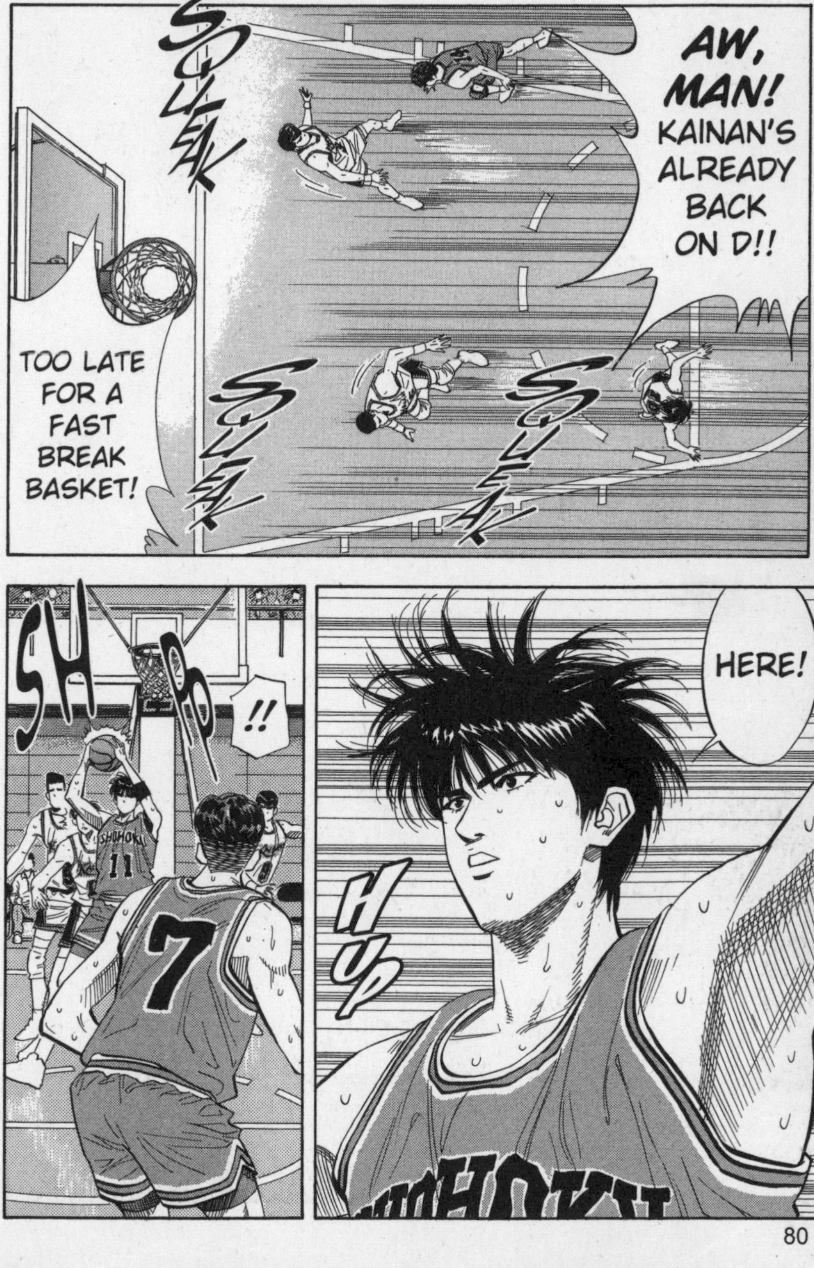
AW, MAN! KAINAN'S ALREADY BACK ON D!!
SQUEAK
SQUEAK
SQUEAK
TOO LATE FOR A FAST BREAK BASKET!
HERE!
HUP
!!
SHPP

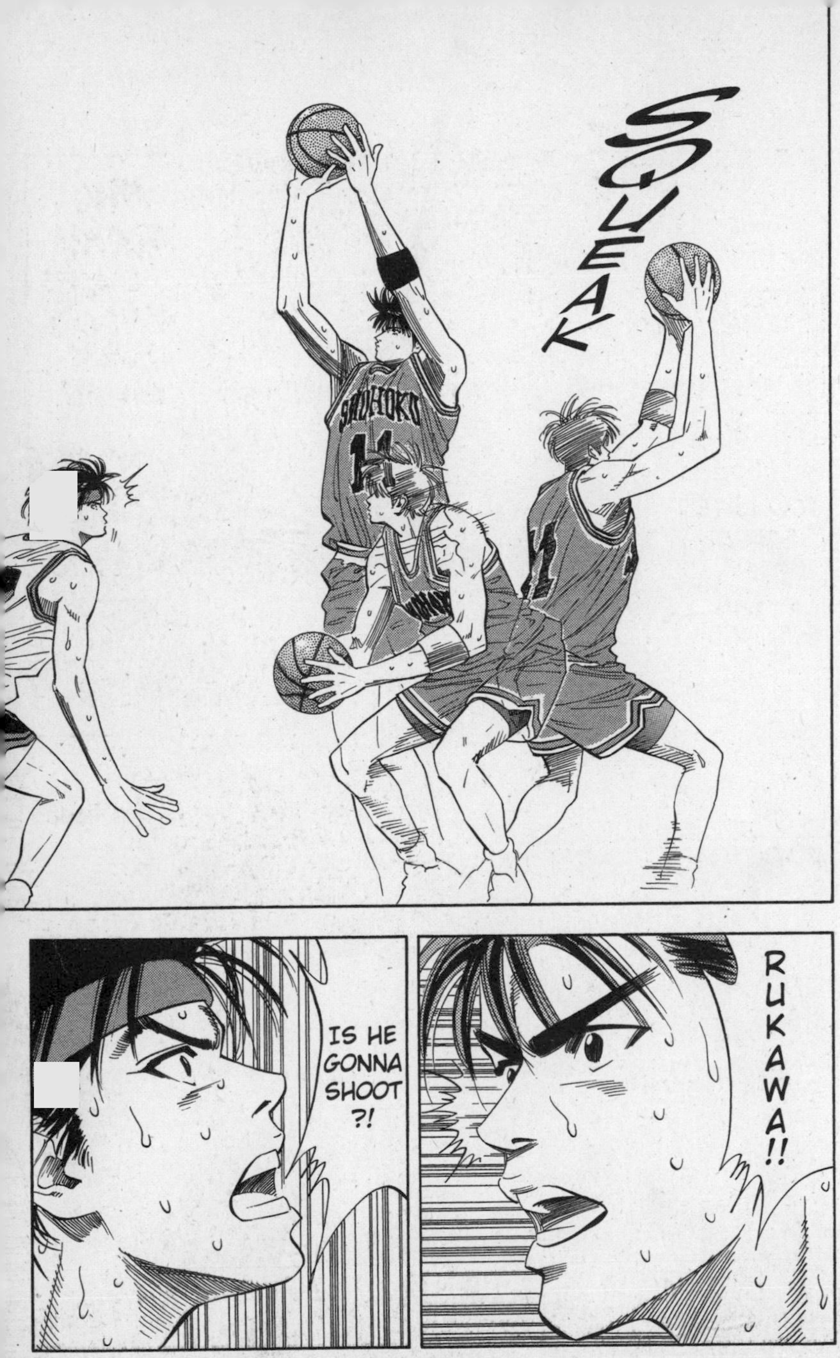
SQUEAK
RUKAWA!!
IS HE GONNA SHOOT?!

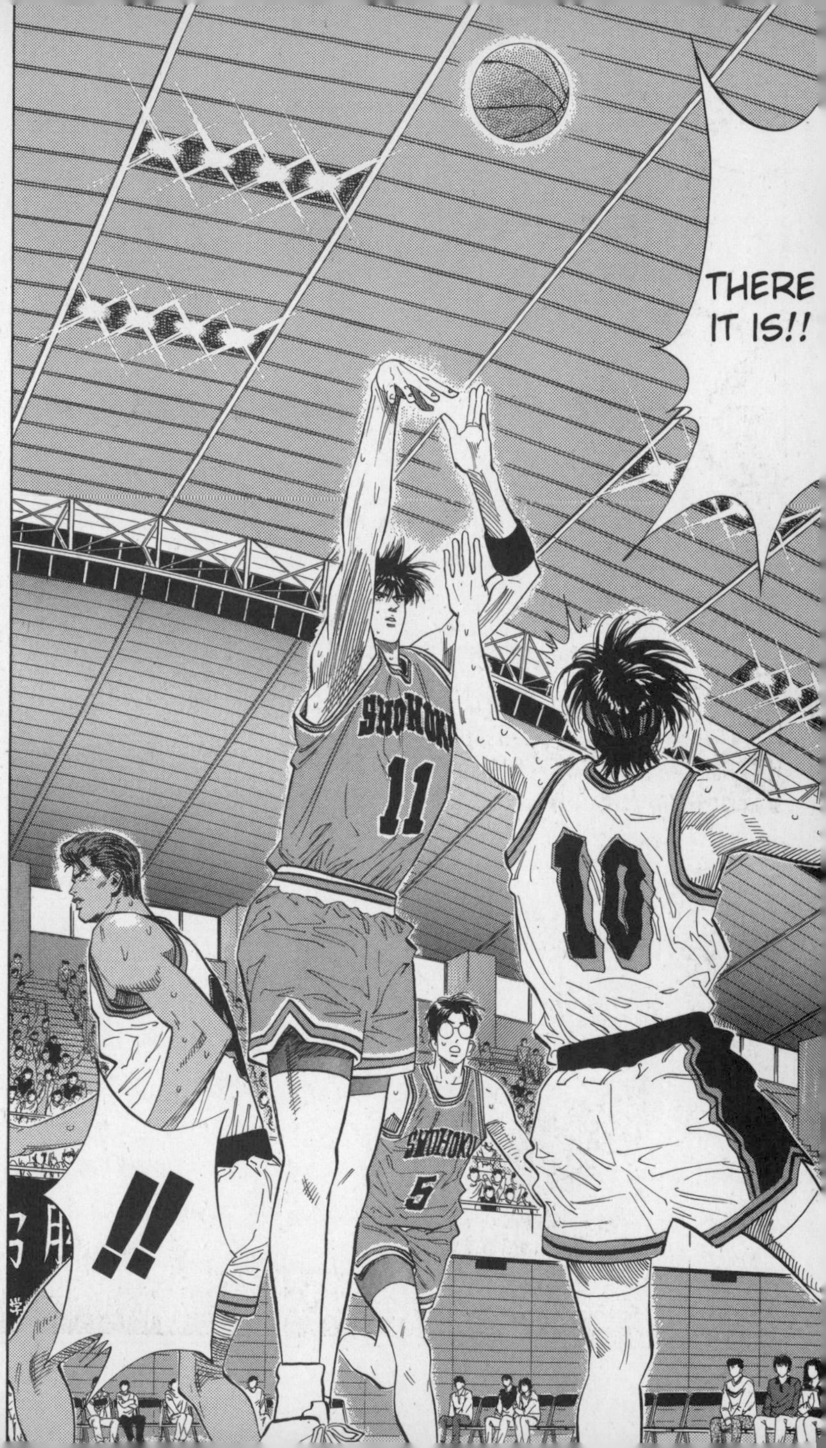
THERE IT IS!!
!!

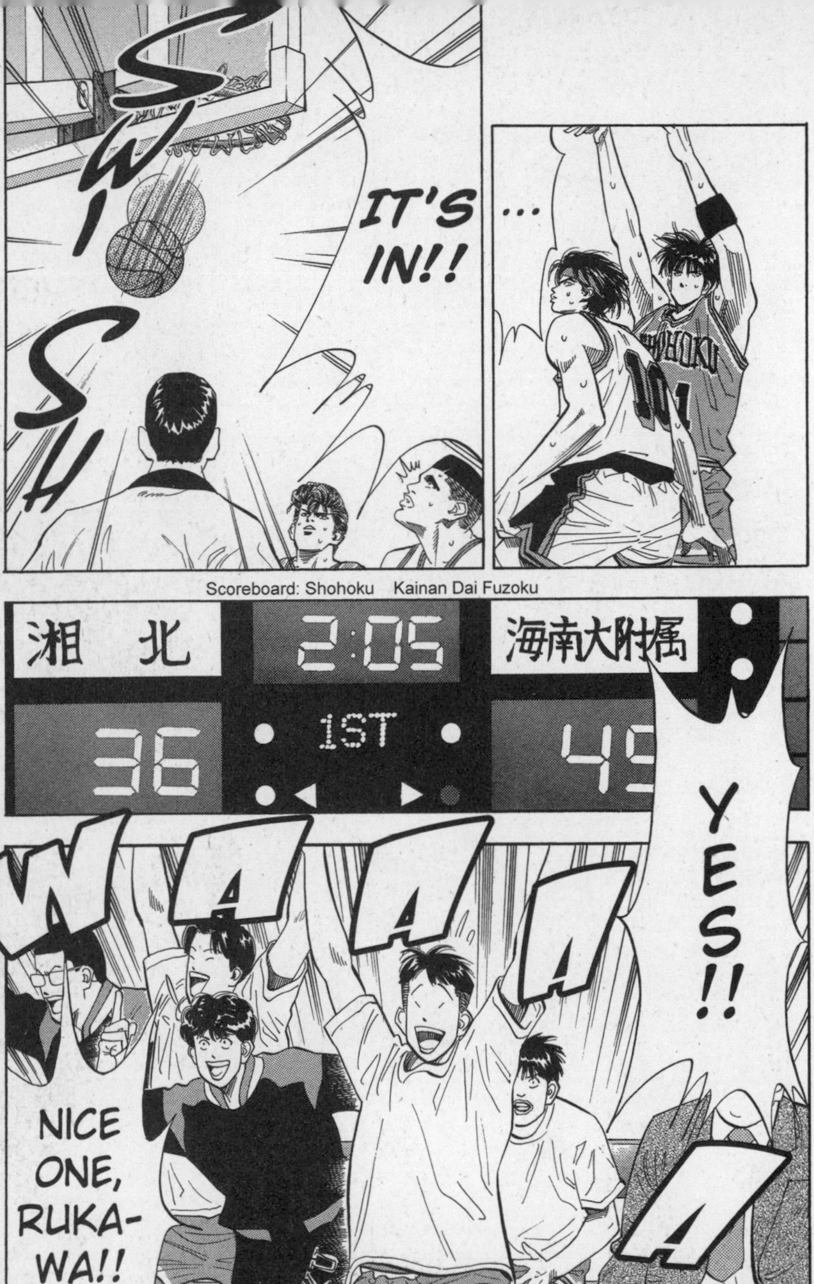
...
SWISH
IT'S IN!!
Scoreboard: Shohoku Kainan Dai Fuzoku
湘北
2:05
海南大附属
36
1ST
YES!!
WAAA
NICE ONE, RUKAWA!!

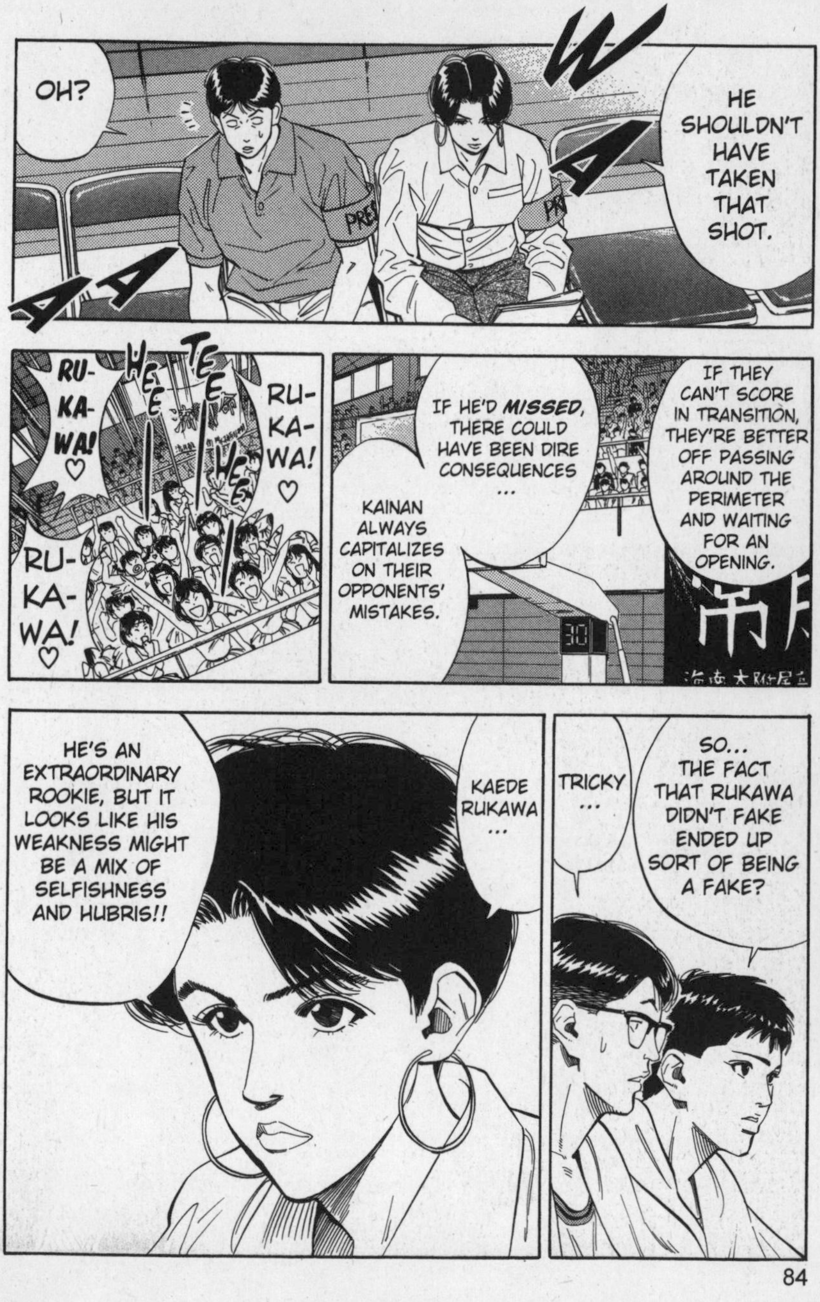
HE SHOULDN'T HAVE TAKEN THAT SHOT.
OH?
WAAAA
IF THEY CAN'T SCORE IN TRANSITION, THEY'RE BETTER OFF PASSING AROUND THE PERIMETER AND WAITING FOR AN OPENING.
IF HE'D ***MISSED***, THERE COULD HAVE BEEN DIRE CONSEQUENCES...
KAINAN ALWAYS CAPITALIZES ON THEIR OPPONENTS' MISTAKES.
RU-KA-WA! ♡
TEE HEE
RU-KA-WA! ♡
HEE HEE
RU-KA-WA! ♡
SO... THE FACT THAT RUKAWA DIDN'T FAKE ENDED UP SORT OF BEING A FAKE?
TRICKY...
KAEDE RUKAWA...
HE'S AN EXTRAORDINARY ROOKIE, BUT IT LOOKS LIKE HIS WEAKNESS MIGHT BE A MIX OF SELFISHNESS AND HUBRIS!!

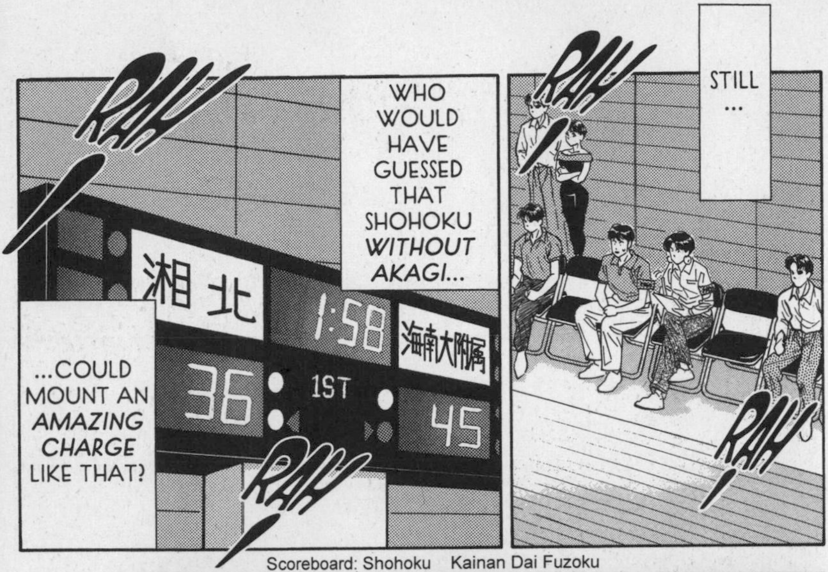
RAH
STILL ...
RAH
WHO WOULD HAVE GUESSED THAT SHOHOKU WITHOUT AKAGI...
RAH
...COULD MOUNT AN AMAZING CHARGE LIKE THAT?
湘北
1:58
海南大附属
36
1ST
45
RAH
Scoreboard: Shohoku Kainan Dai Fuzoku

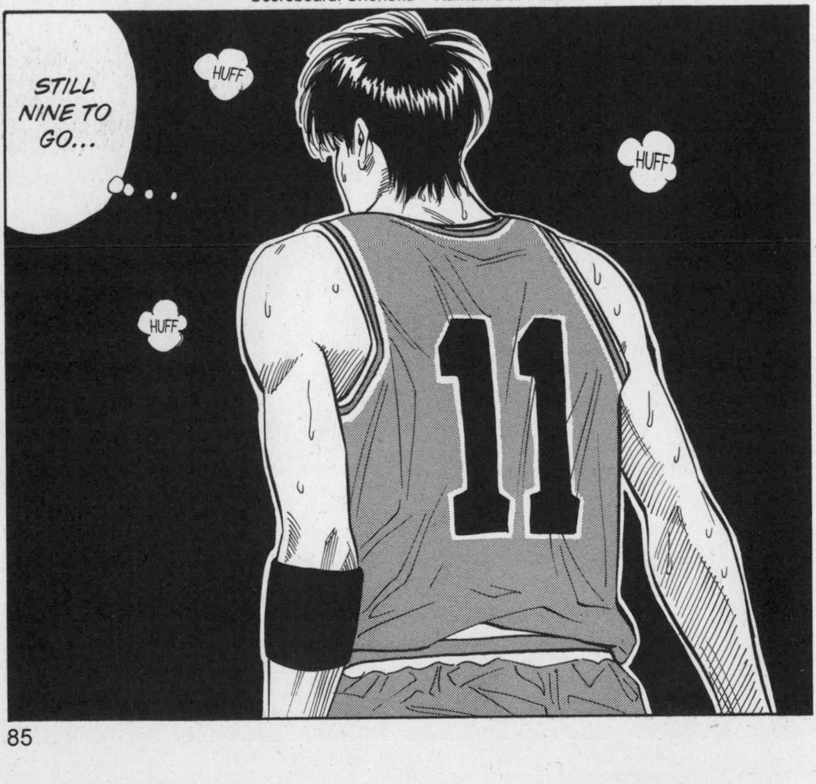
HUFF
STILL NINE TO GO...
HUFF
HUFF

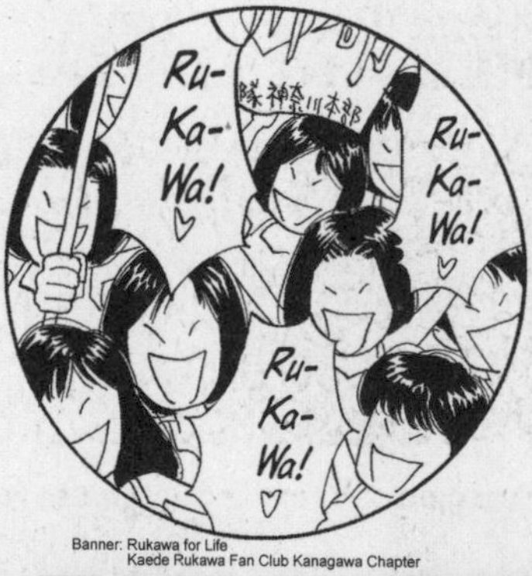
Ru-Ka-Wa!
Ru-Ka-Wa!
Ru-Ka-Wa!
Banner: Rukawa for Life
Kaede Rukawa Fan Club Kanagawa Chapter

SLAM DUNK

READ THIS WAY

#112 SELFISH

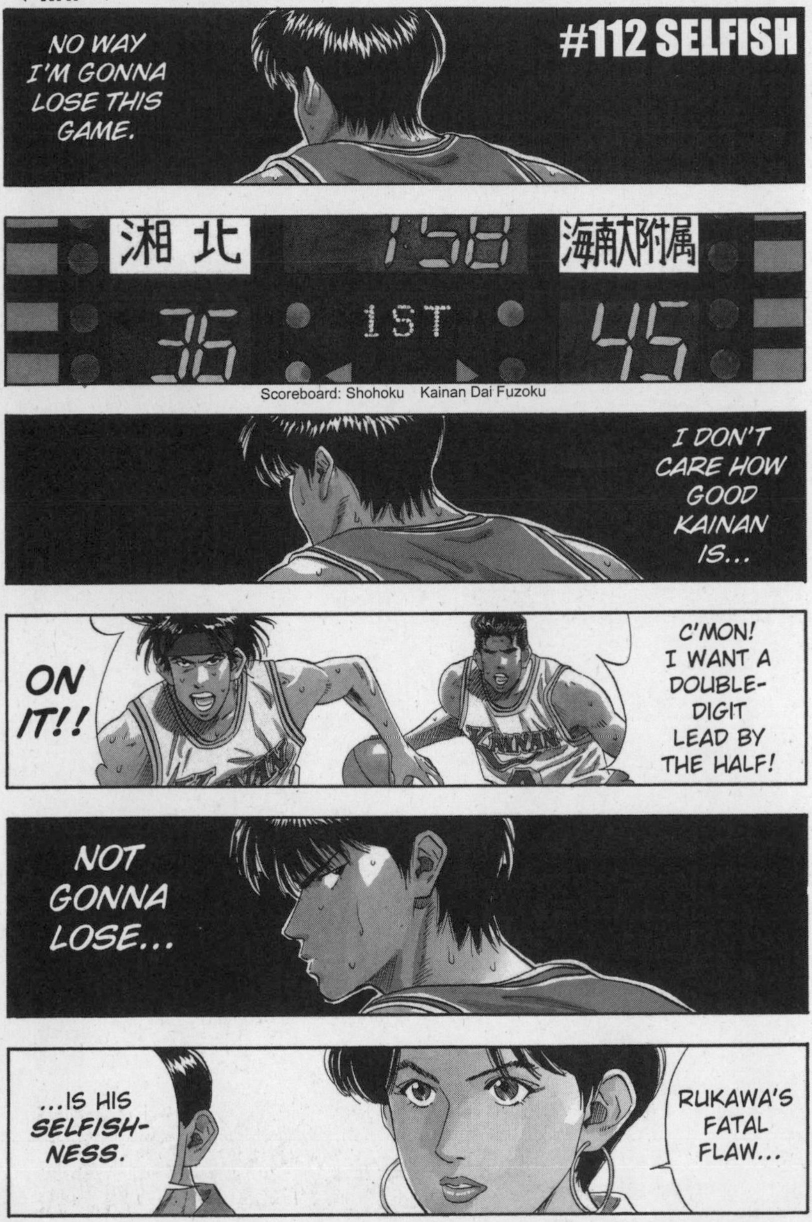
NO WAY I'M GONNA LOSE THIS GAME.
海南大附属
1:58
湘北
45
1ST
36
Scoreboard: Shohoku Kainan Dai Fuzoku
I DON'T CARE HOW GOOD KAINAN IS...
C'MON! I WANT A DOUBLE-DIGIT LEAD BY THE HALF!
ON IT!!
NOT GONNA LOSE...
RUKAWA'S FATAL FLAW...
...IS HIS SELFISHNESS.

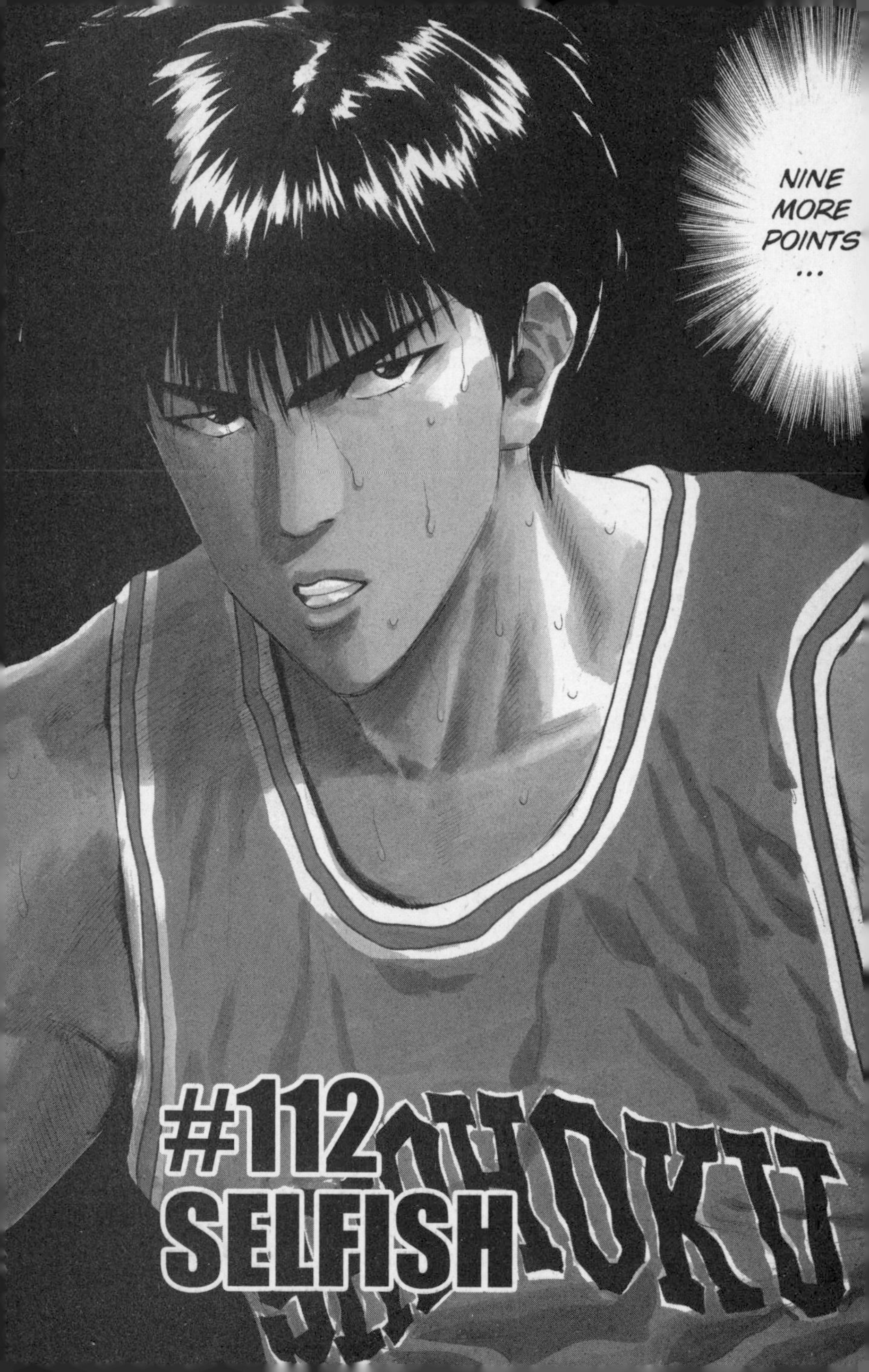
NINE MORE POINTS ...
#112 SELFISH

READ THIS WAY

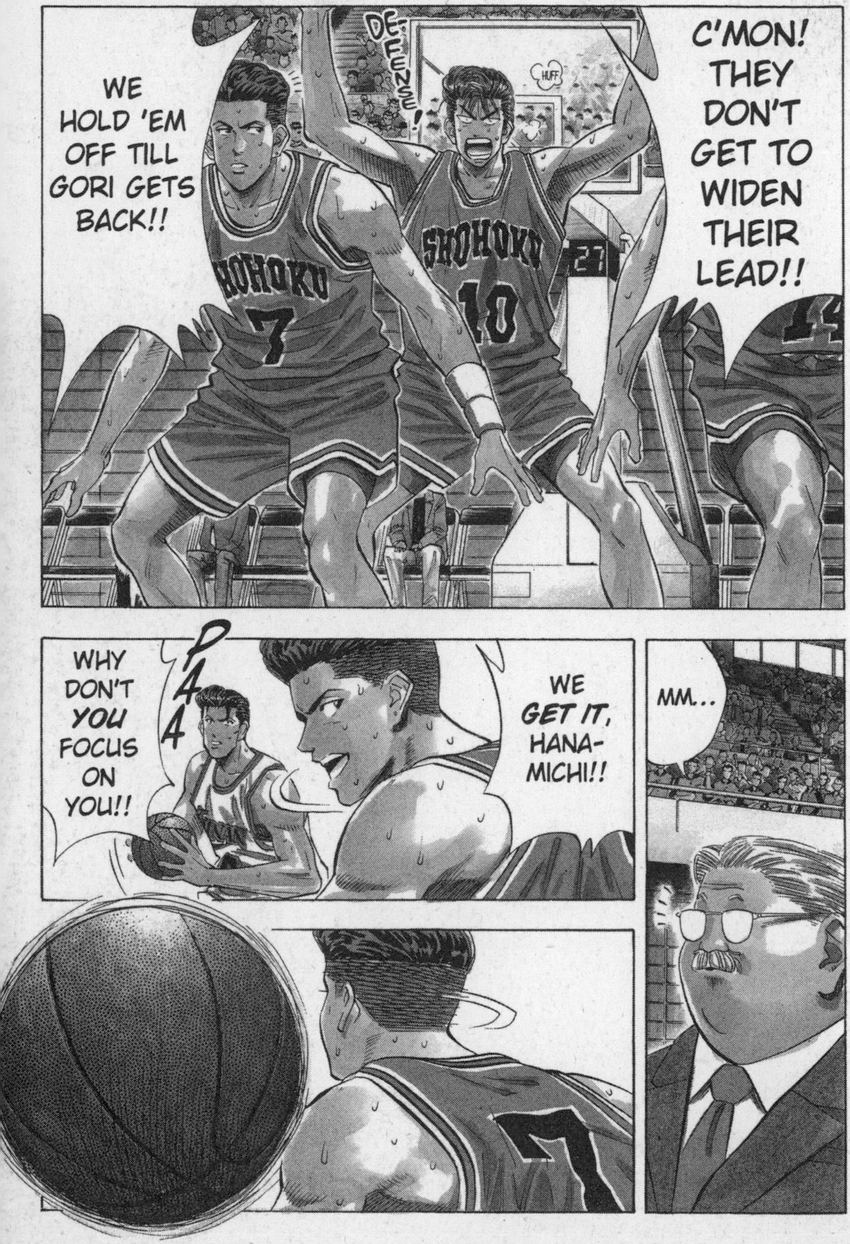
C'MON! THEY DON'T GET TO WIDEN THEIR LEAD!!
DE-FENSE!
HUFF
WE HOLD 'EM OFF TILL GORI GETS BACK!!
MM...
WE GET IT, HANA-MICHI!!
WHY DON'T YOU FOCUS ON YOU!!

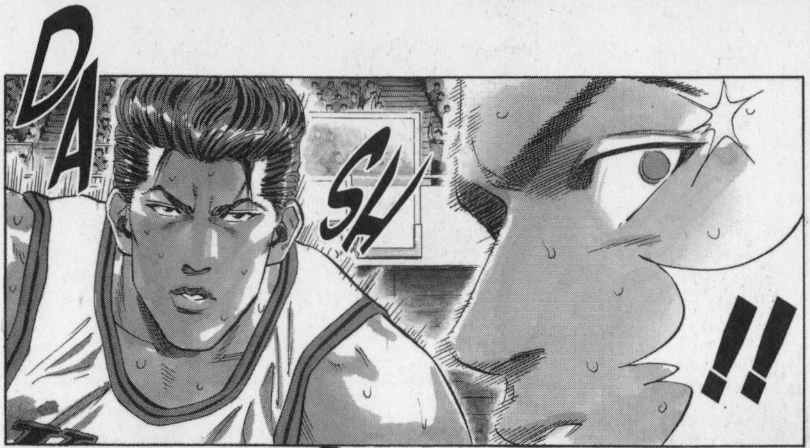
DA
SH
!!
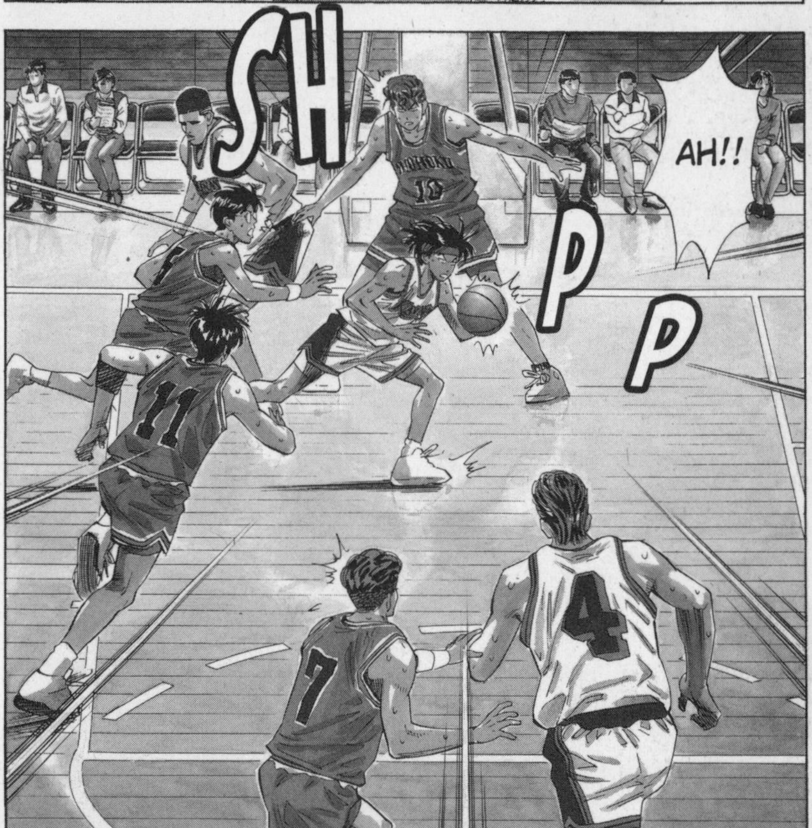
AH!!
SH
P
P

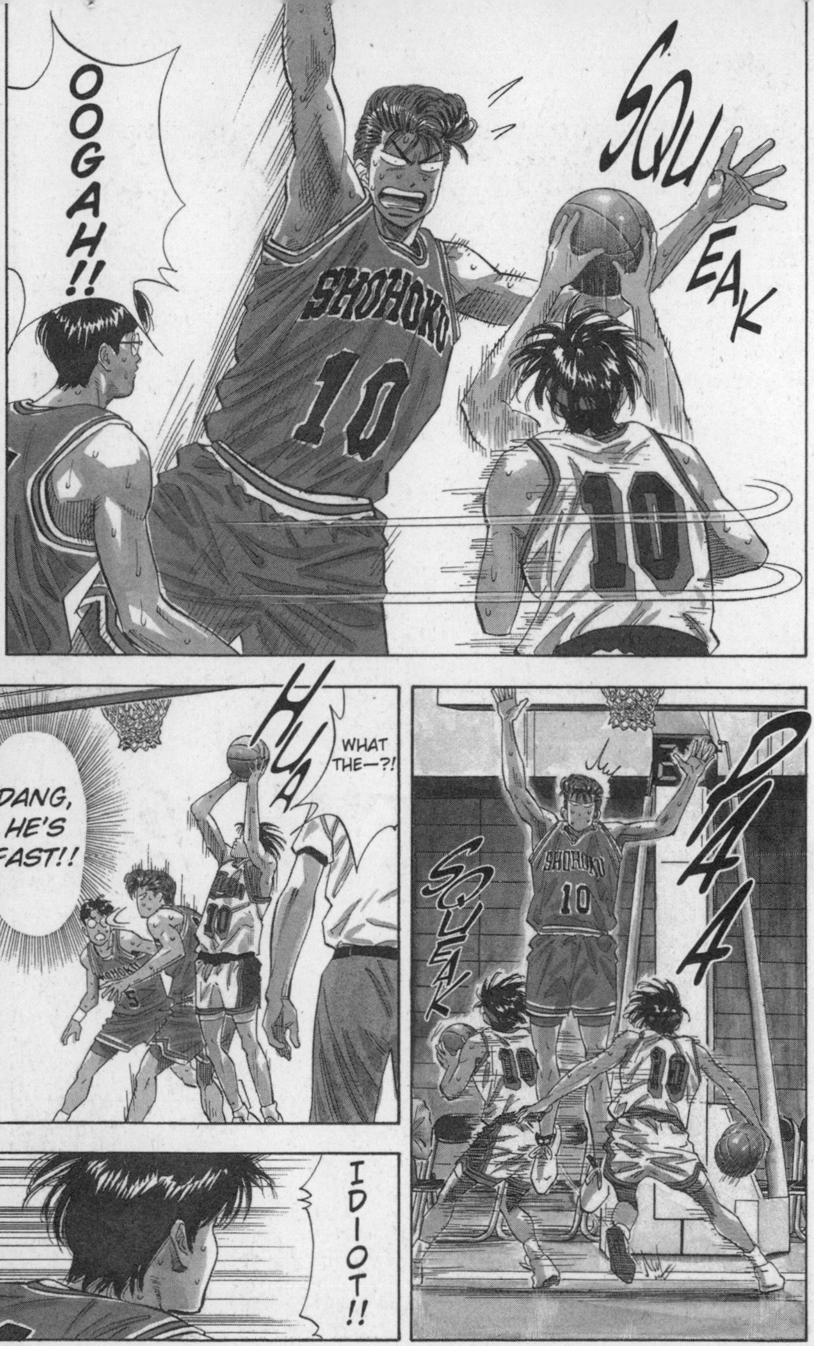
SQUEAK
OOGAH!!
SQUEAK
WHAT THE—?!
HUA
DANG, HE'S FAST!!
IDIOT!!

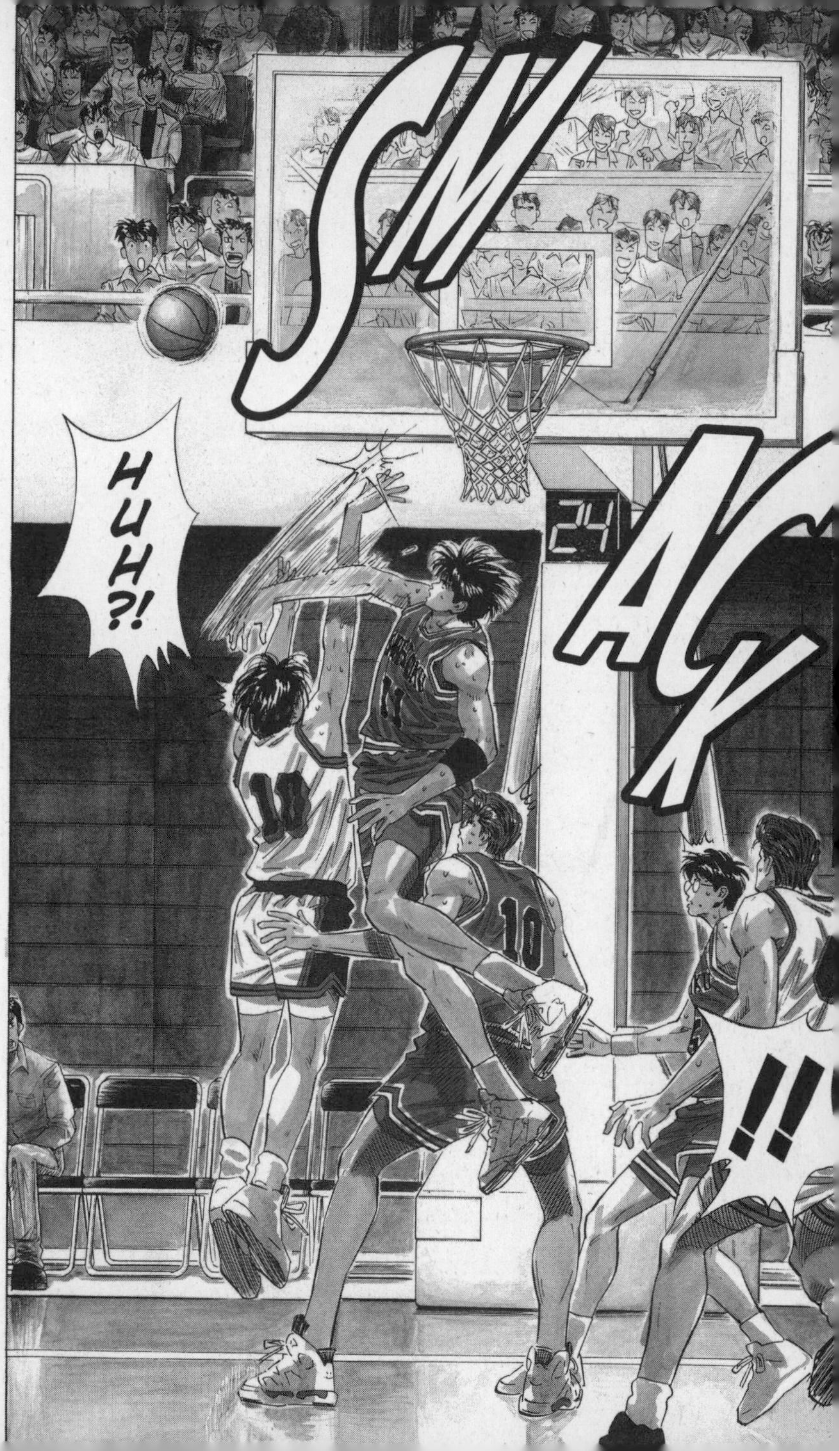
SWACK
HUH?!
!!

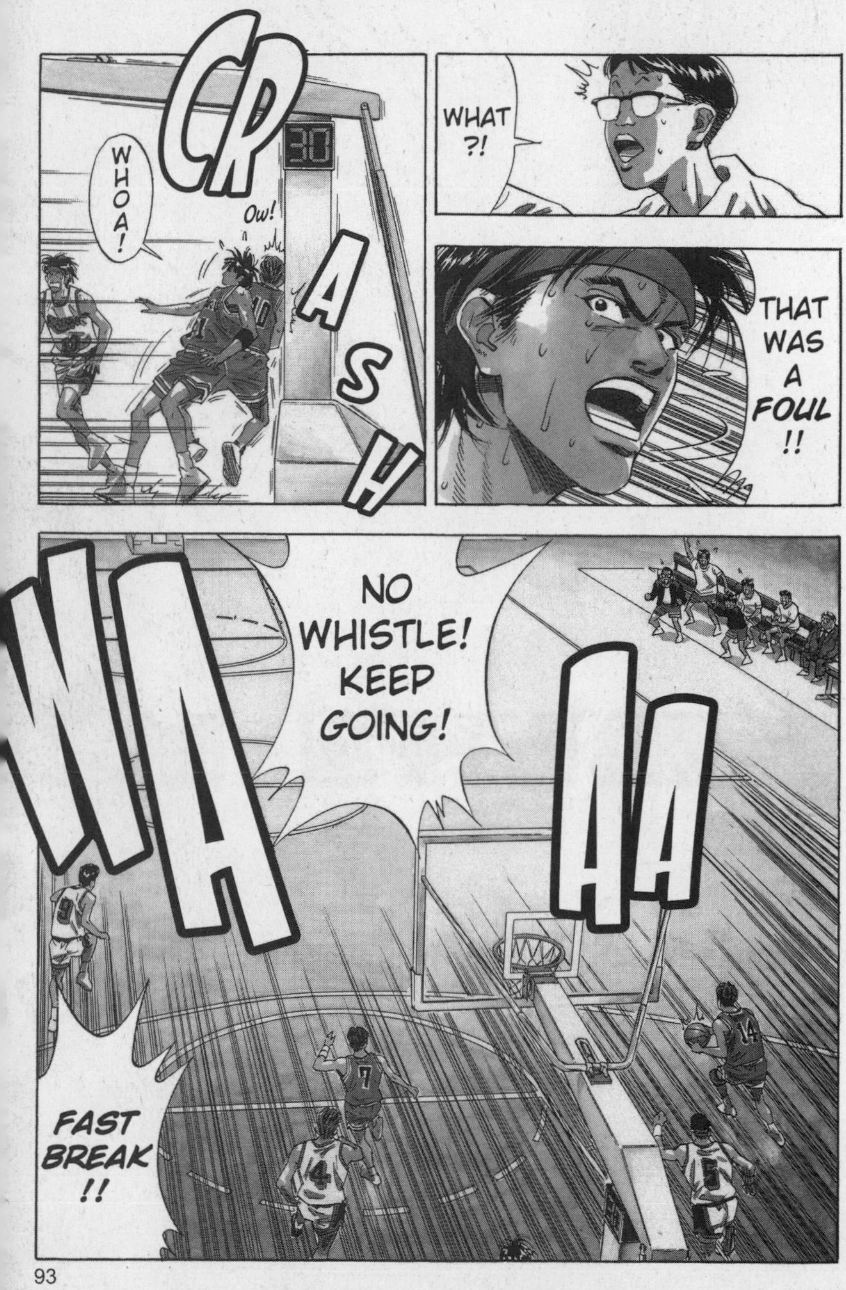
WHAT ?!
THAT WAS A FOUL !!
CRASH
WHOA!
Ow!
WAAA
NO WHISTLE! KEEP GOING!
FAST BREAK !!

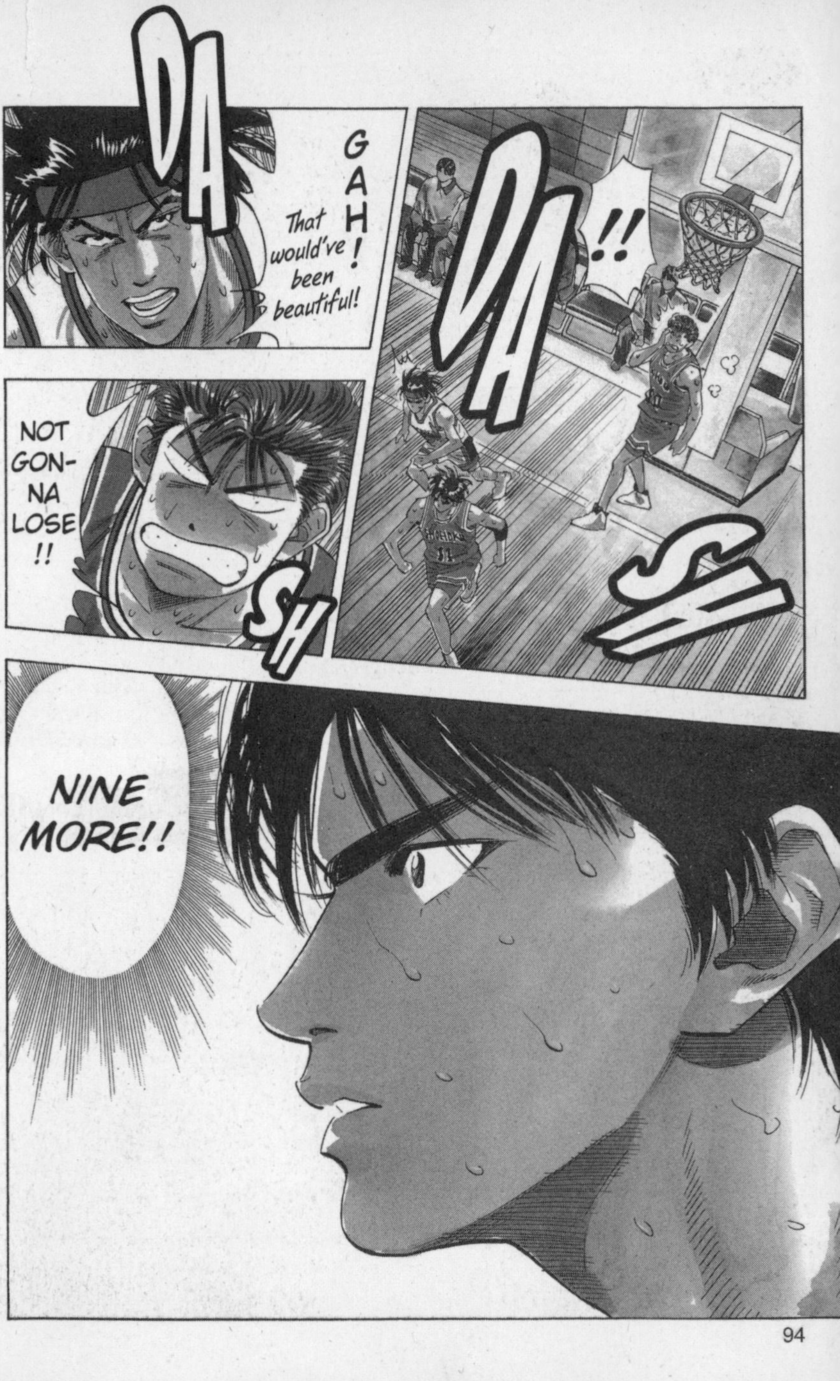
DA
!!
SH
DA
GAH!
That would've been beautiful!
NOT GON-NA LOSE!!
SH
NINE MORE!!

READ THIS WAY

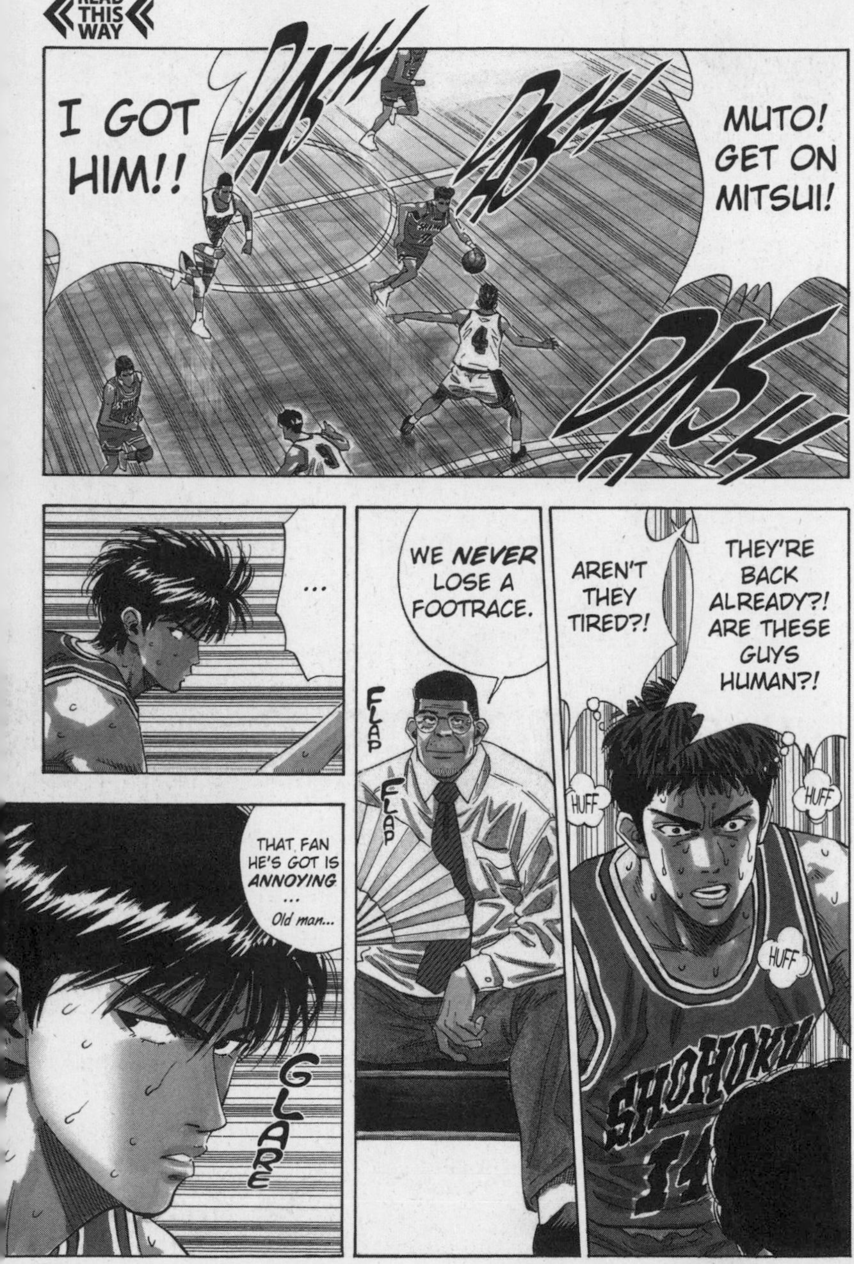
MUTO! GET ON MITSUI!
DASH
DASH
DASH
I GOT HIM!!
THEY'RE BACK ALREADY?! ARE THESE GUYS HUMAN?!
AREN'T THEY TIRED?!
HUFF
HUFF
HUFF
WE NEVER LOSE A FOOTRACE.
FLAP
FLAP
...
THAT FAN HE'S GOT IS ANNOYING ...
Old man...
GLARE

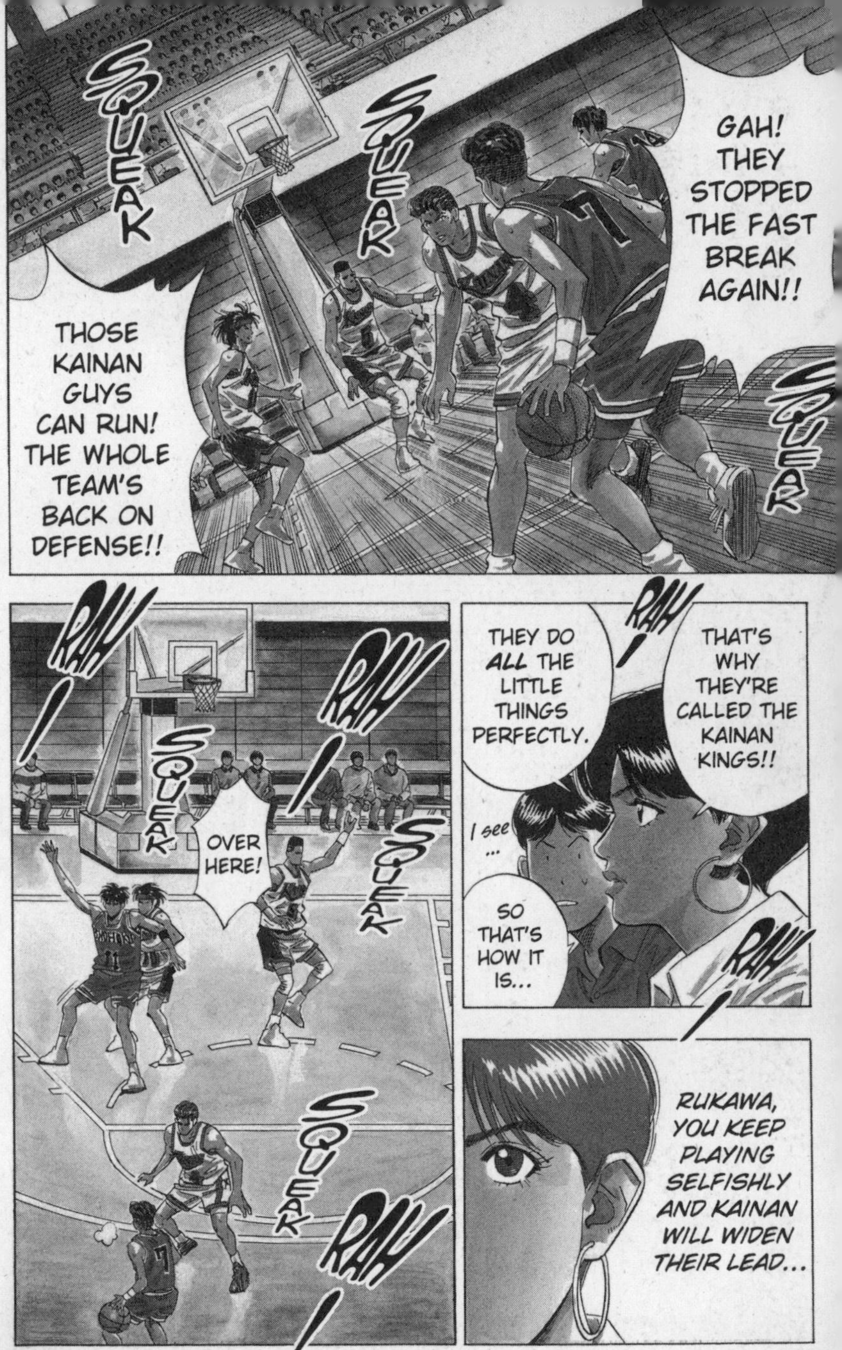
SQUEAK
SQUEAK
GAH! THEY STOPPED THE FAST BREAK AGAIN!!
SQUEAK
THOSE KAINAN GUYS CAN RUN! THE WHOLE TEAM'S BACK ON DEFENSE!!
RAH!
THAT'S WHY THEY'RE CALLED THE KAINAN KINGS!!
THEY DO **ALL** THE LITTLE THINGS PERFECTLY.
I see...
SO THAT'S HOW IT IS...
RAH!
RUKAWA, YOU KEEP PLAYING SELFISHLY AND KAINAN WILL WIDEN THEIR LEAD...
RAH!
RAH!
SQUEAK
OVER HERE!
SQUEAK
SQUEAK
RAH!

READ THIS WAY

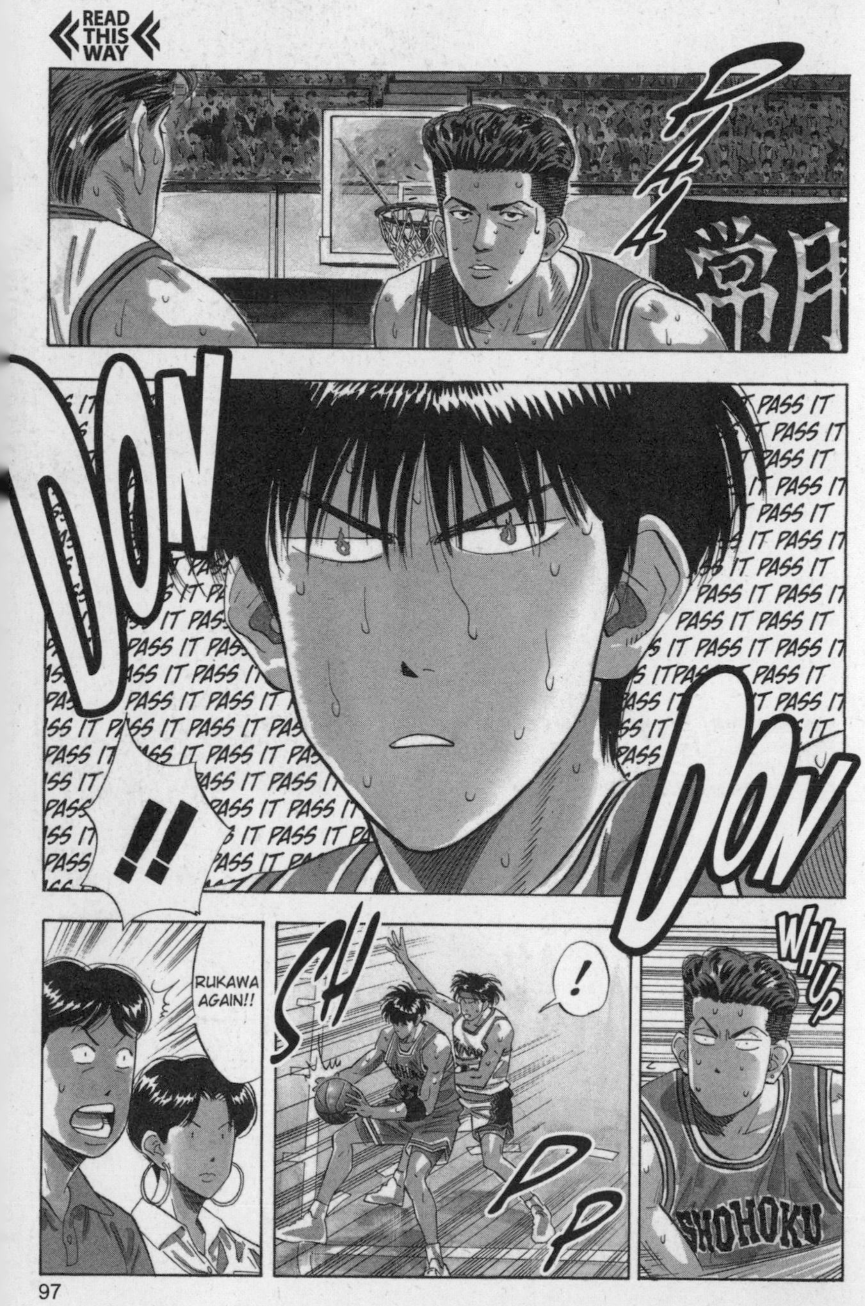
DON
PASS IT PASS IT PASS IT
DON
!!
WHUP
SHOHOKU
!
SH
RUKAWA AGAIN!!

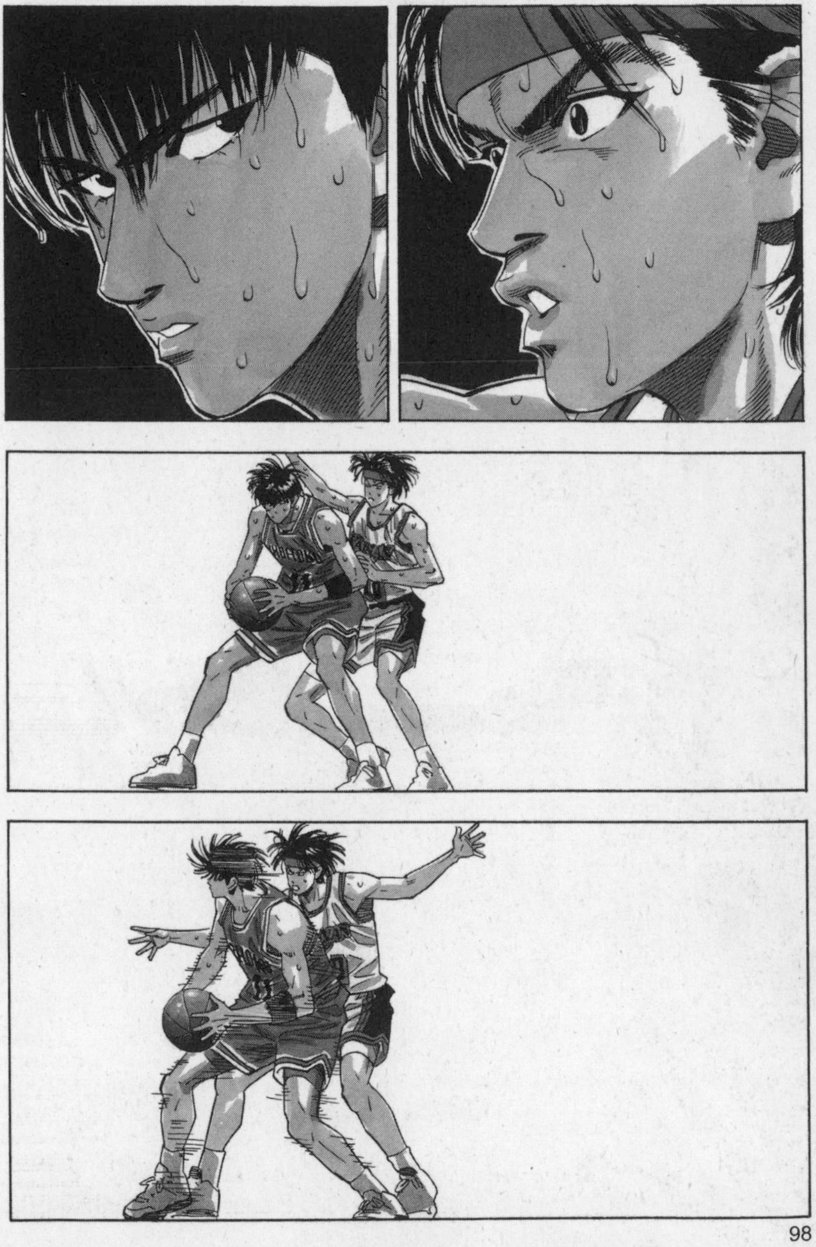

READ THIS WAY

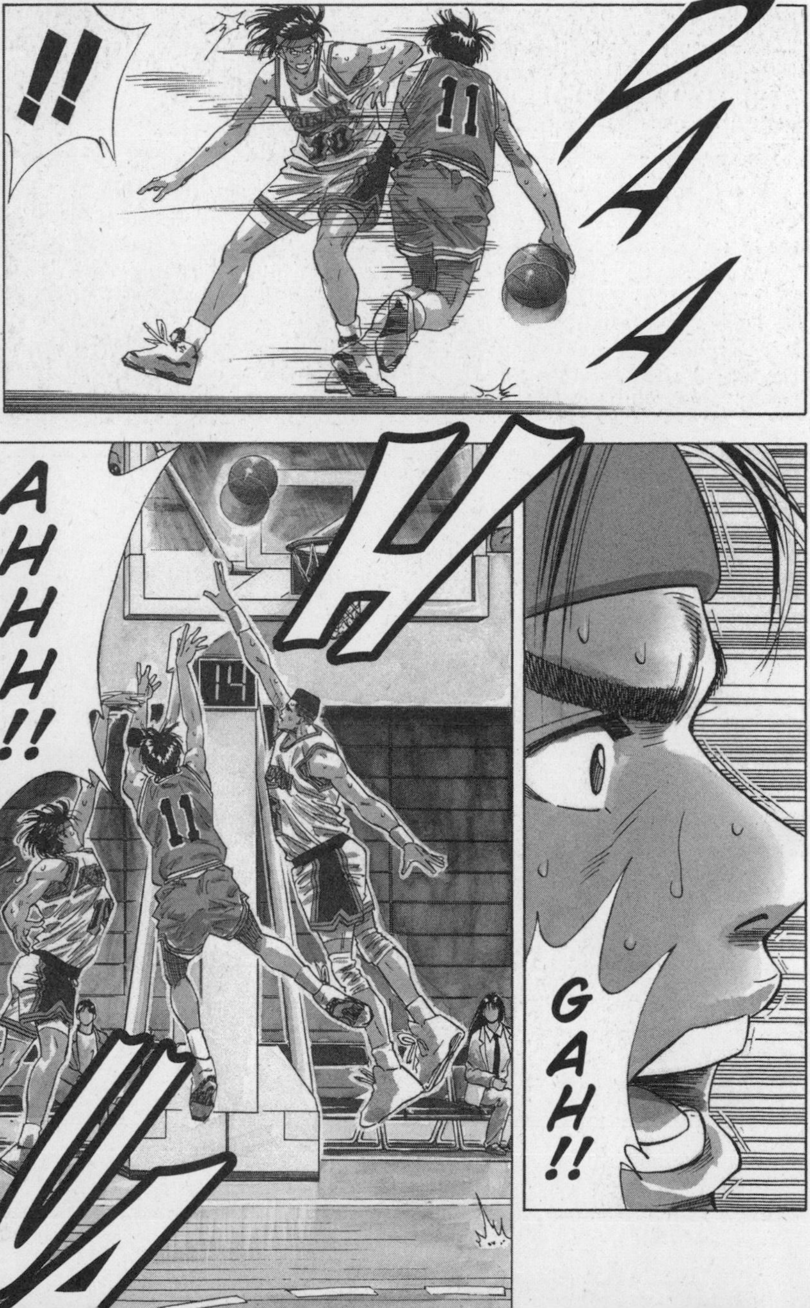
!!
GAH!!
AHHHH!!

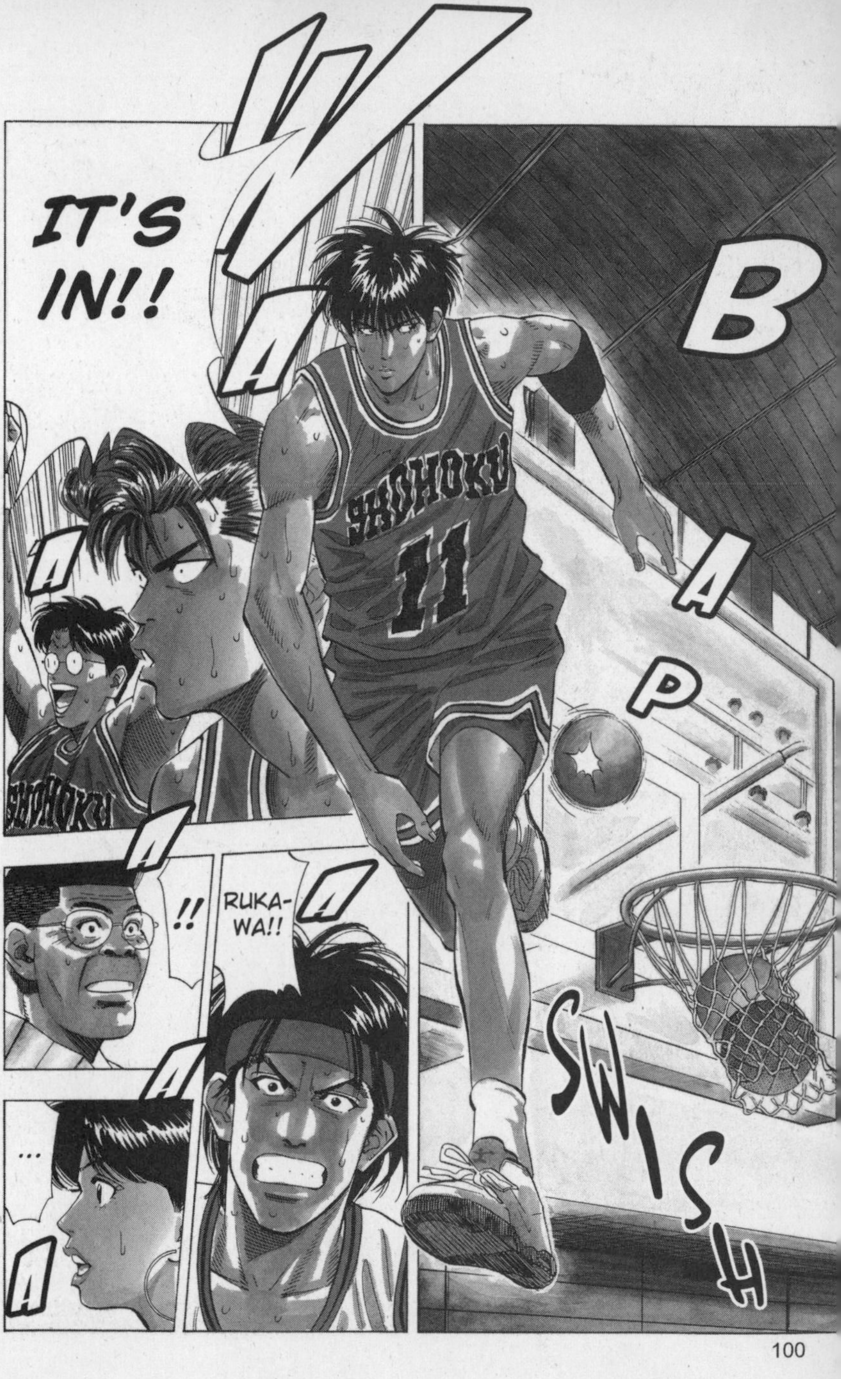

BAP
SWISH
IT'S IN!!
WAAAAAAA
RUKAWA!!
!!
...

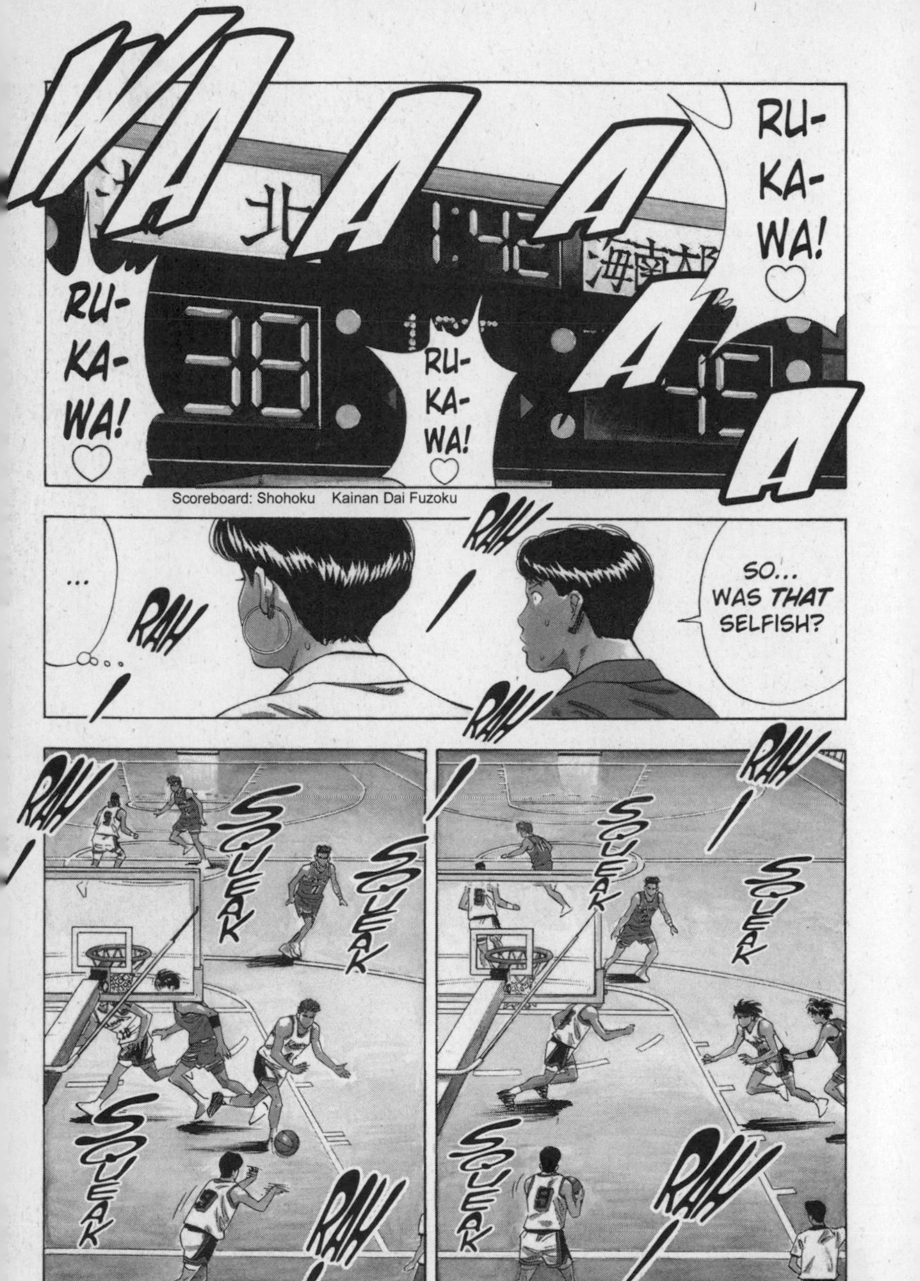
WAAAAA
RU-KAWA! ♡
RU-KAWA! ♡
RU-KAWA! ♡
Scoreboard: Shohoku Kainan Dai Fuzoku
RAH!
SO... WAS THAT SELFISH?
RAH!
...
RAH!
RAH!
SQUEAK
SQUEAK
SQUEAK
RAH!
RAH!
SQUEAK
SQUEAK
SQUEAK
RAH!

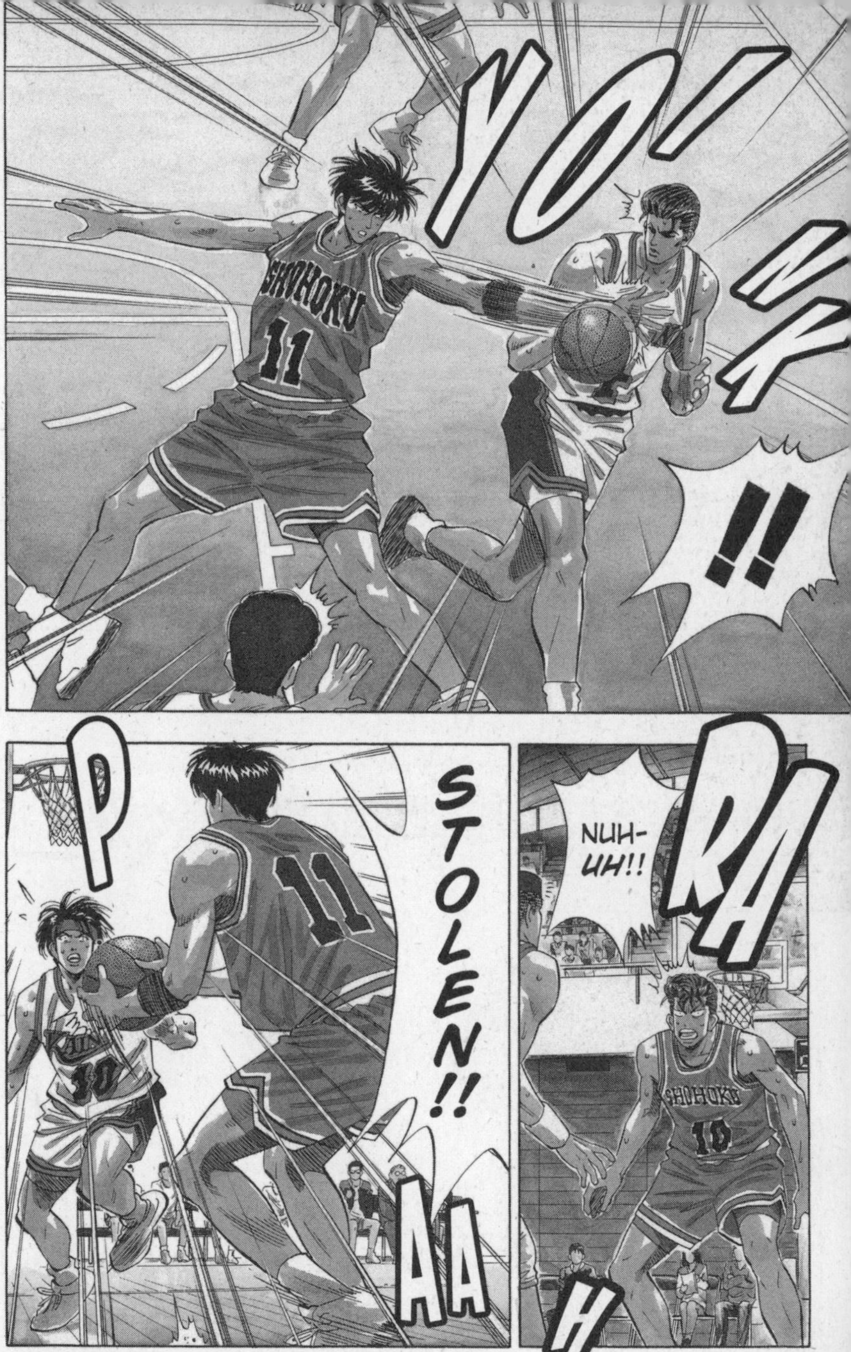
YOINK
!!
RA
NUH-UH!!
H
P
STOLEN!!
AA

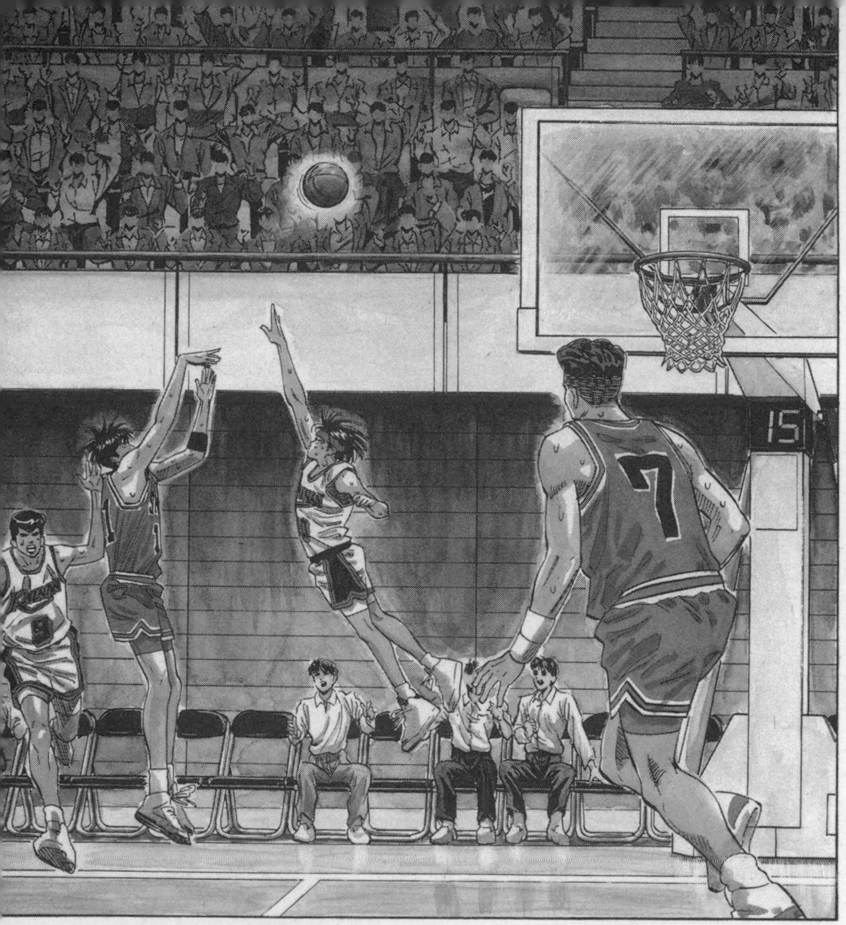
15
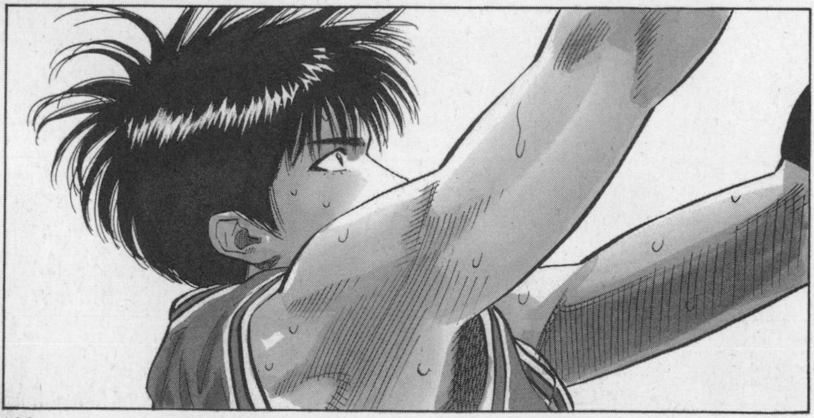

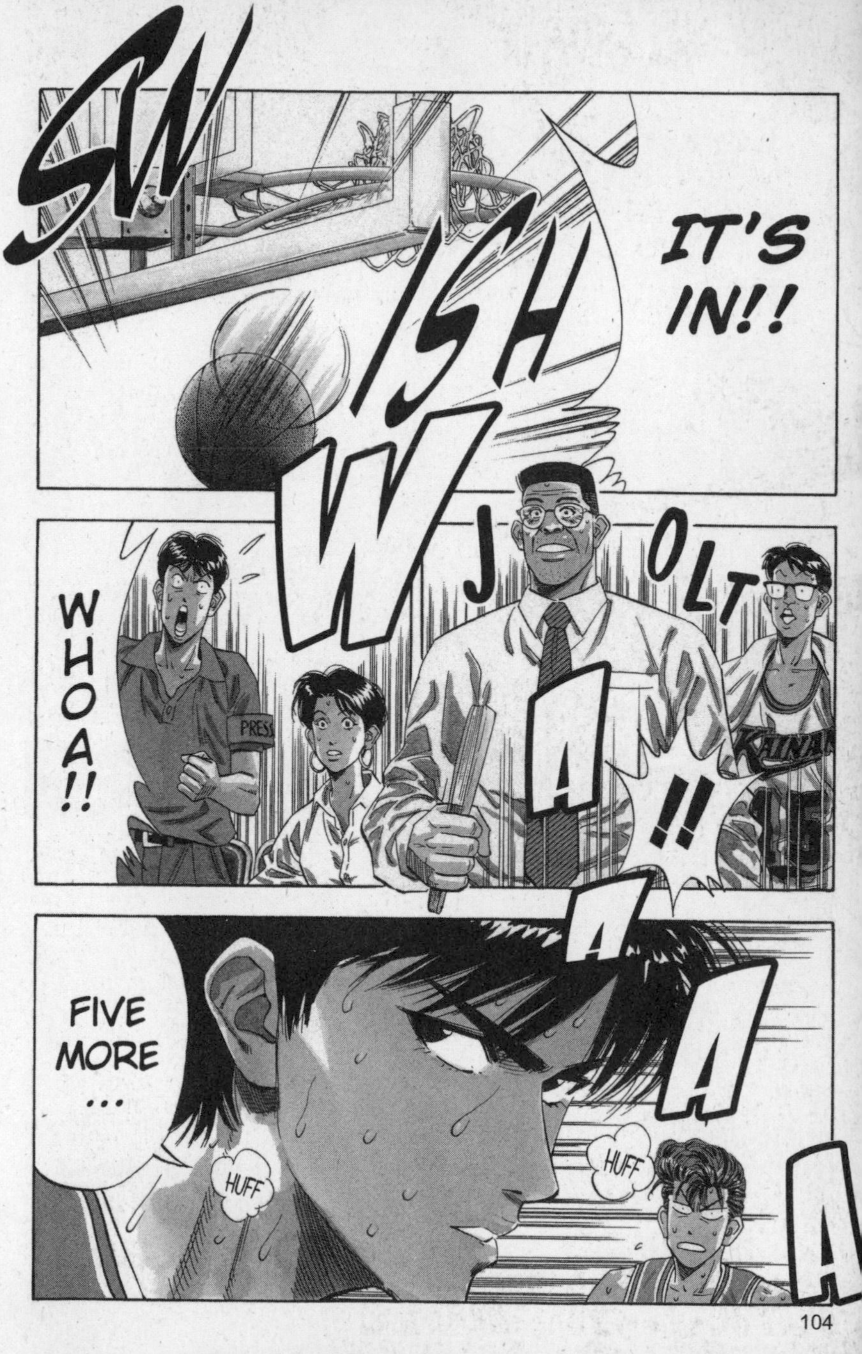
IT'S IN!!
SWISH
JOLT
WHOA!!
WAAAA!!
FIVE MORE ...
HUFF
HUFF
AA

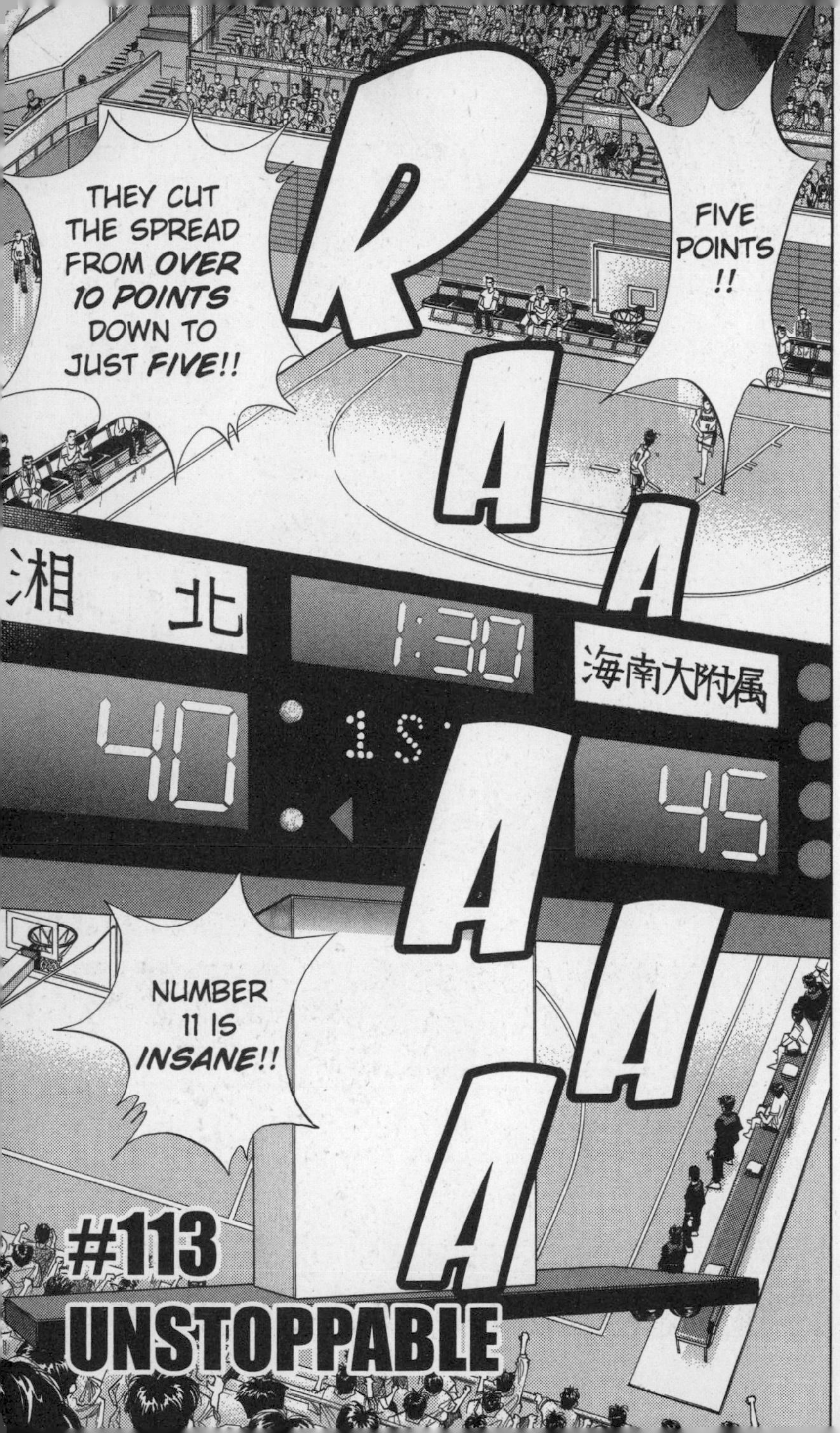
FIVE POINTS!!
THEY CUT THE SPREAD FROM OVER 10 POINTS DOWN TO JUST FIVE!!
RAAAAA
湘北
1:30
海南大附属
40
1S
45
NUMBER 11 IS INSANE!!

#113 UNSTOPPABLE

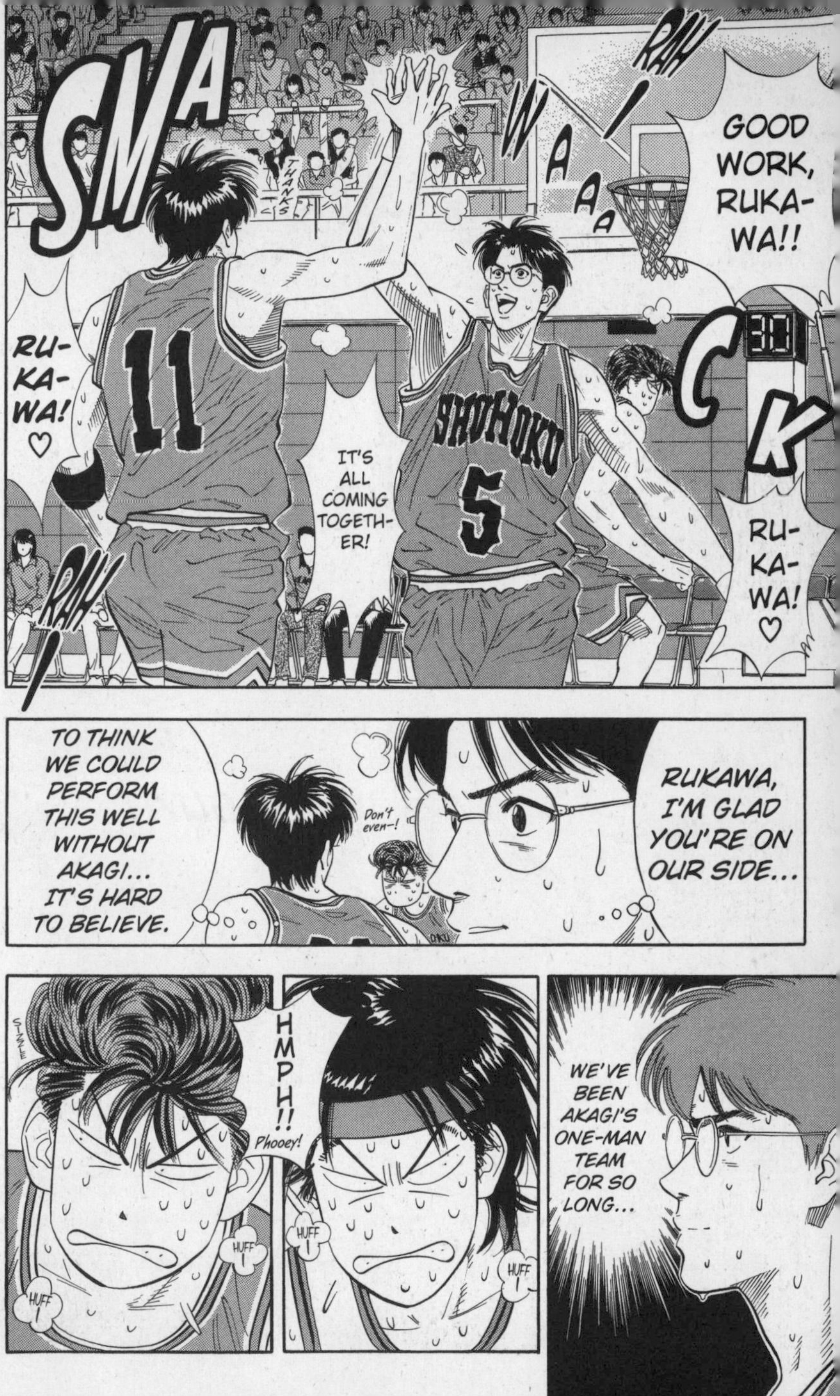
GOOD WORK, RUKAWA!!
WAAAA
RAH
SMACK
RUKAWA! ♡
IT'S ALL COMING TOGETHER!
THANKS
RUKAWA! ♡
RAH
RUKAWA, I'M GLAD YOU'RE ON OUR SIDE...
Don't even-!
TO THINK WE COULD PERFORM THIS WELL WITHOUT AKAGI... IT'S HARD TO BELIEVE.
WE'VE BEEN AKAGI'S ONE-MAN TEAM FOR SO LONG...
HMPH!!
Phooey!
HUFF
HUFF
SIZZLE
HUFF
HUFF

READ THIS WAY

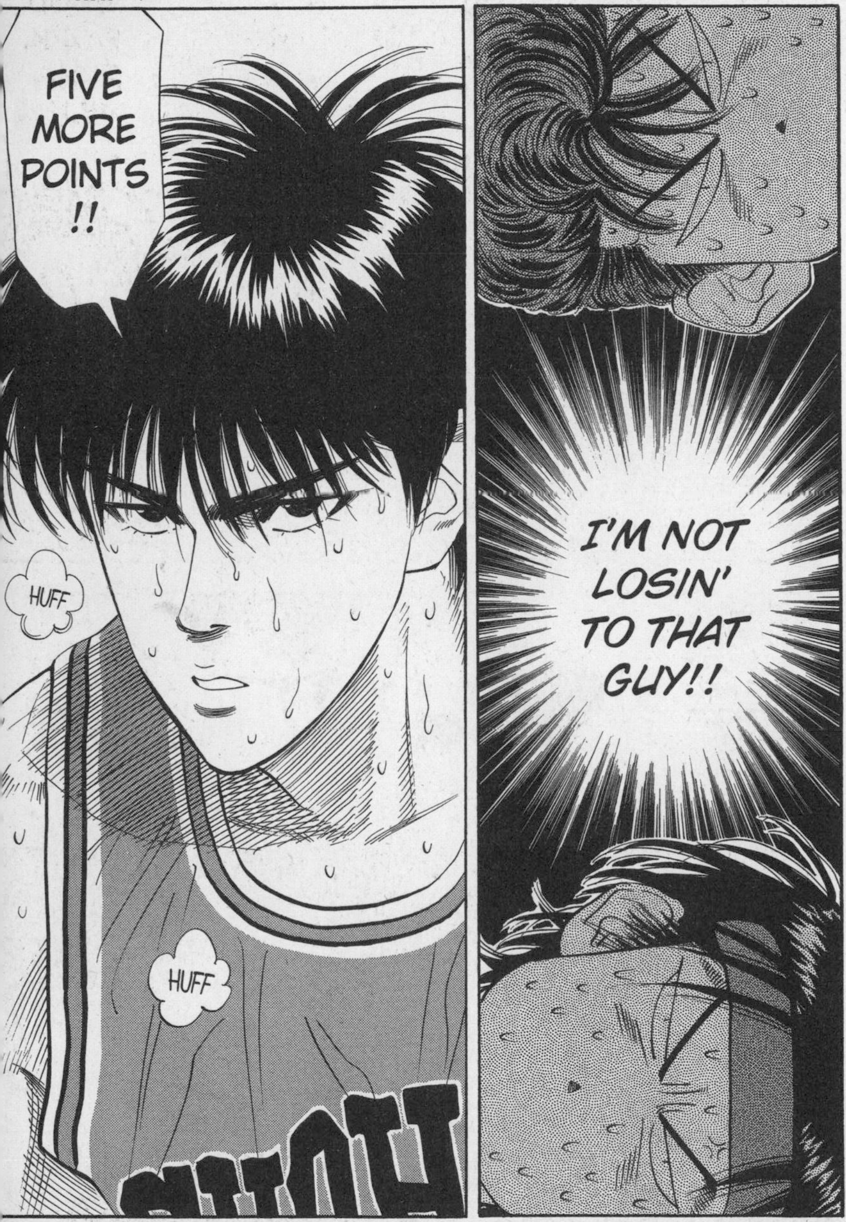
I'M NOT LOSIN' TO THAT GUY!!
FIVE MORE POINTS!!
HUFF
HUFF

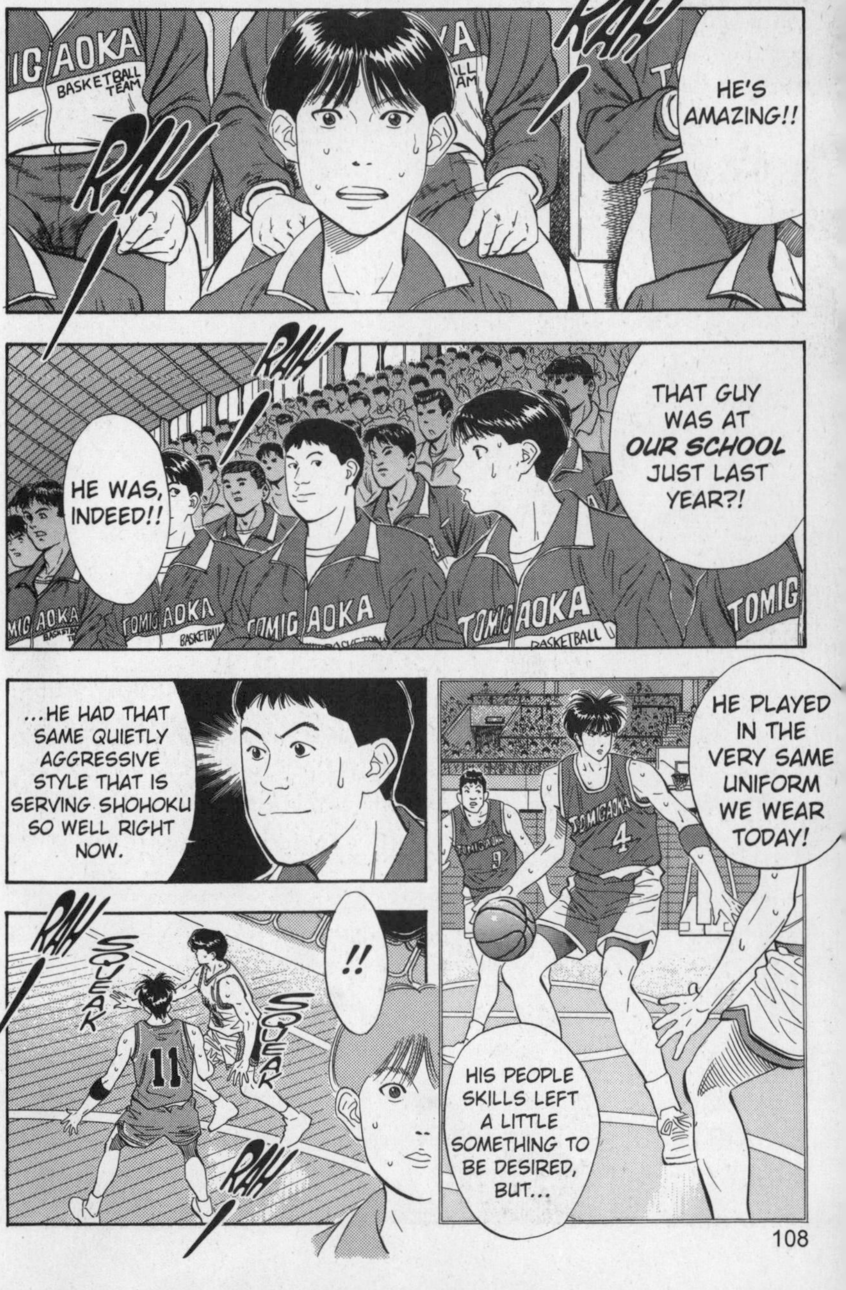
RAH
HE'S AMAZING!!
RAH
THAT GUY WAS AT OUR SCHOOL JUST LAST YEAR?!
RAH
HE WAS, INDEED!!
HE PLAYED IN THE VERY SAME UNIFORM WE WEAR TODAY!
HIS PEOPLE SKILLS LEFT A LITTLE SOMETHING TO BE DESIRED, BUT...
...HE HAD THAT SAME QUIETLY AGGRESSIVE STYLE THAT IS SERVING SHOHOKU SO WELL RIGHT NOW.
!!
SQUEAK
SQUEAK
RAH
RAH

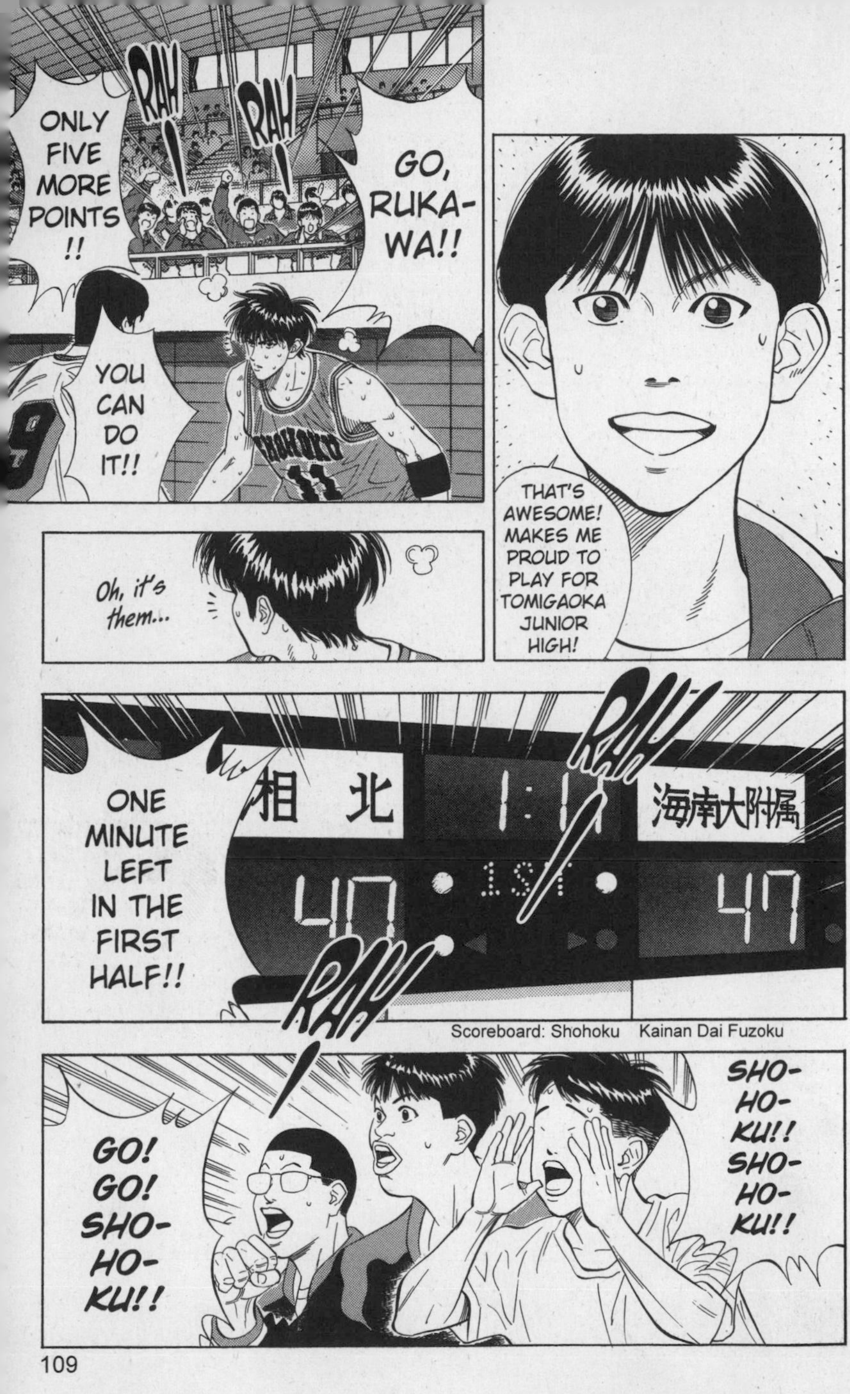
THAT'S AWESOME! MAKES ME PROUD TO PLAY FOR TOMIGAOKA JUNIOR HIGH!
GO, RUKAWA!!
RAH!
RAH!
ONLY FIVE MORE POINTS!!
YOU CAN DO IT!!
Oh, it's them...
RAH!
海南大附属
相 北
1ST
47
40
ONE MINUTE LEFT IN THE FIRST HALF!!
RAH!
SHO-HO-KU!! SHO-HO-KU!!
GO! GO! SHO-HO-KU!!
Scoreboard: Shohoku Kainan Dai Fuzoku

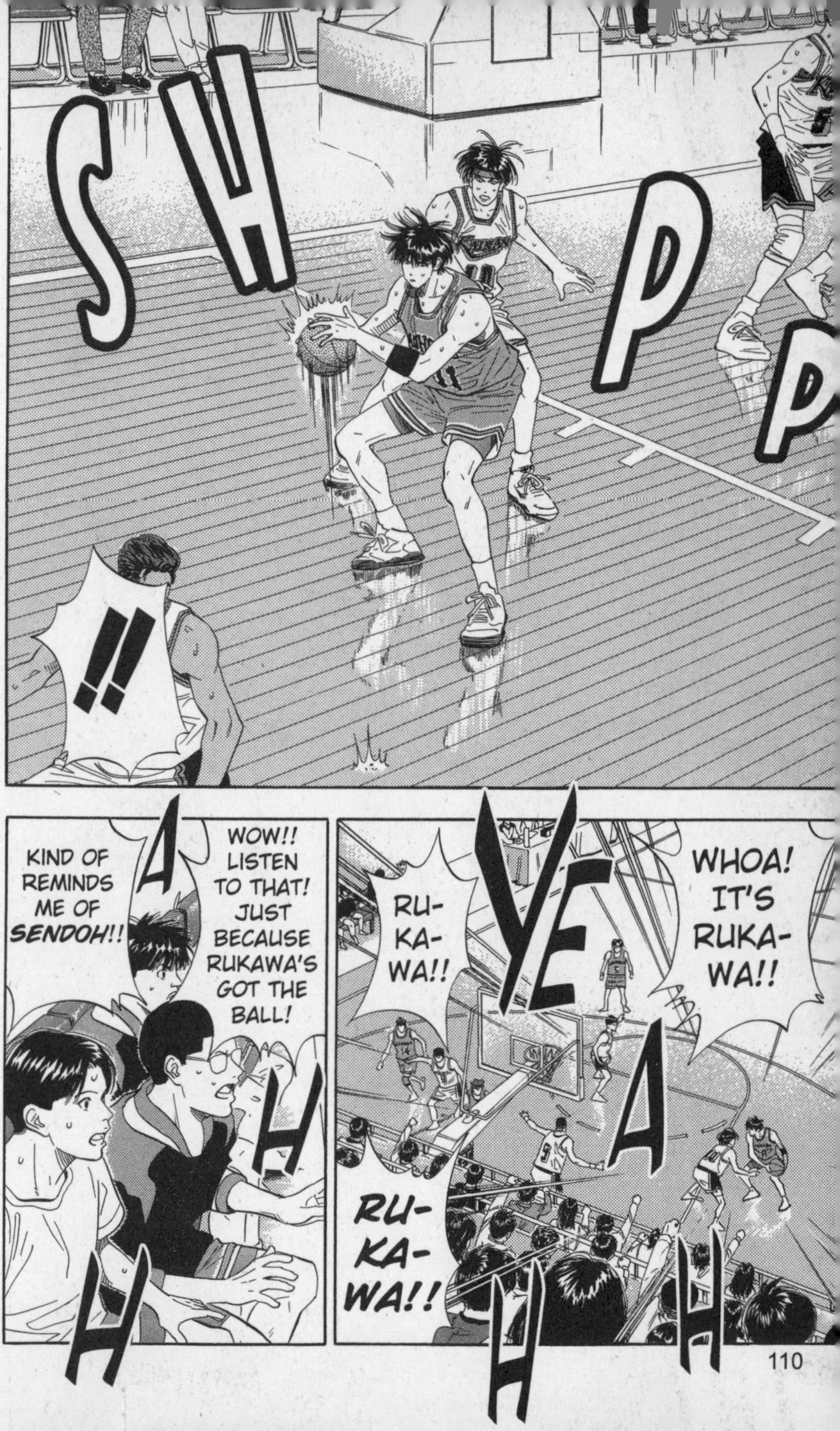
SHPP
!!
WHOA! IT'S RUKAWA!!
RU-KA-WA!!
YEAHHH
RU-KA-WA!!
WOW!! LISTEN TO THAT! JUST BECAUSE RUKAWA'S GOT THE BALL!
KIND OF REMINDS ME OF SENDOH!!
AHH

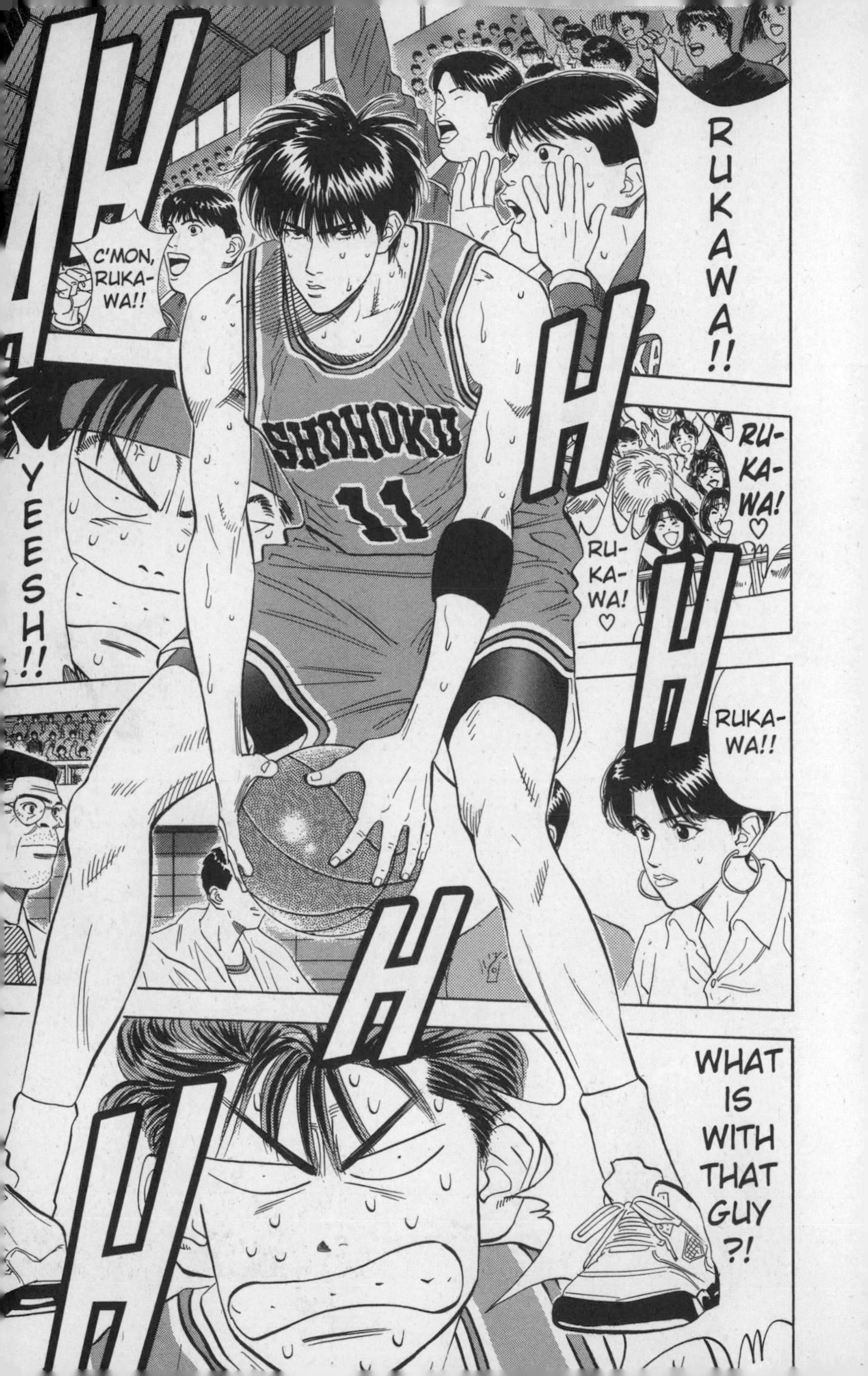
RUKAWA!!
C'MON, RUKAWA!!
RUKAWA! ♥
RUKAWA! ♥
YEESH!!
RUKAWA!!
WHAT IS WITH THAT GUY?!
HHHHHH

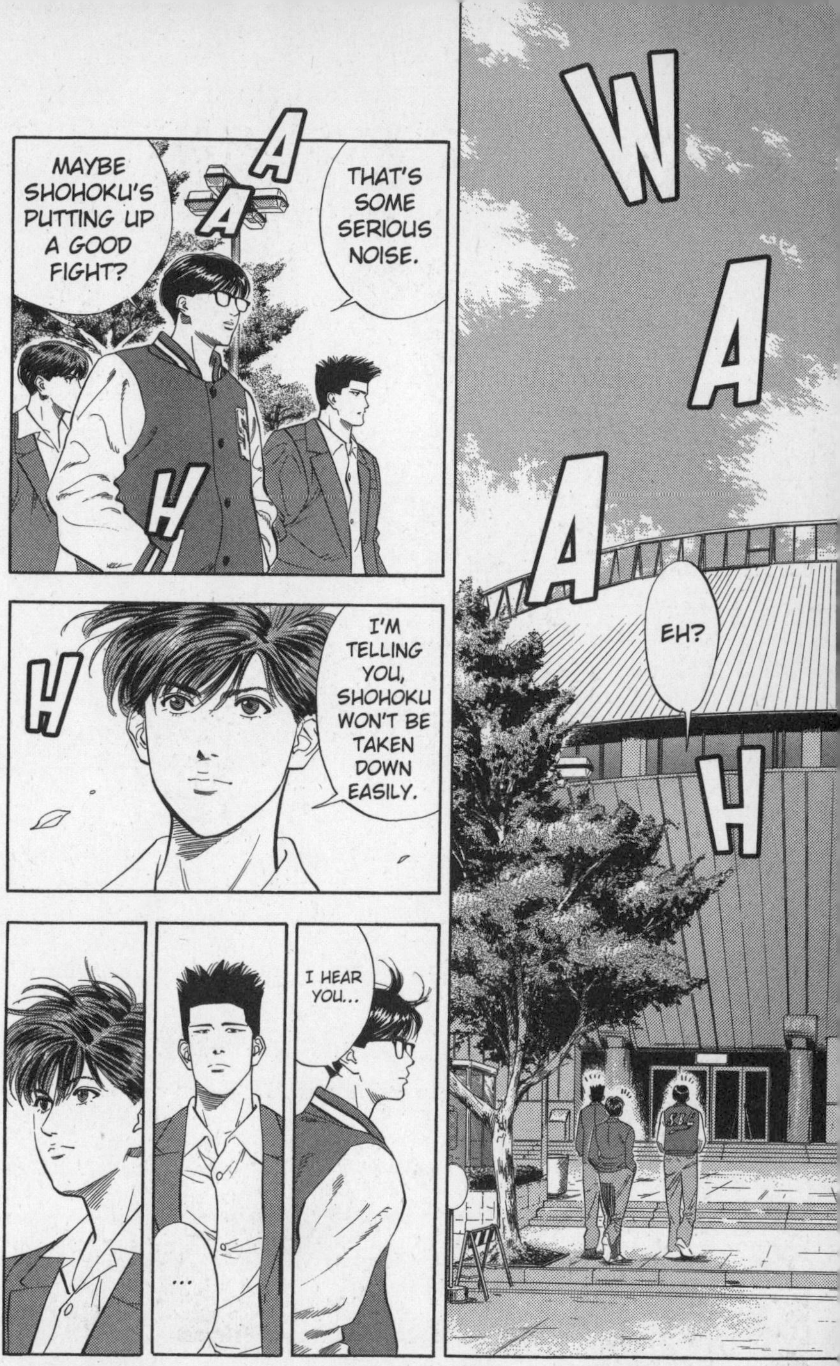
WAAAH
EH?
THAT'S SOME SERIOUS NOISE.
MAYBE SHOHOKU'S PUTTING UP A GOOD FIGHT?
AAH
H
I'M TELLING YOU, SHOHOKU WON'T BE TAKEN DOWN EASILY.
I HEAR YOU...
...

READ THIS WAY

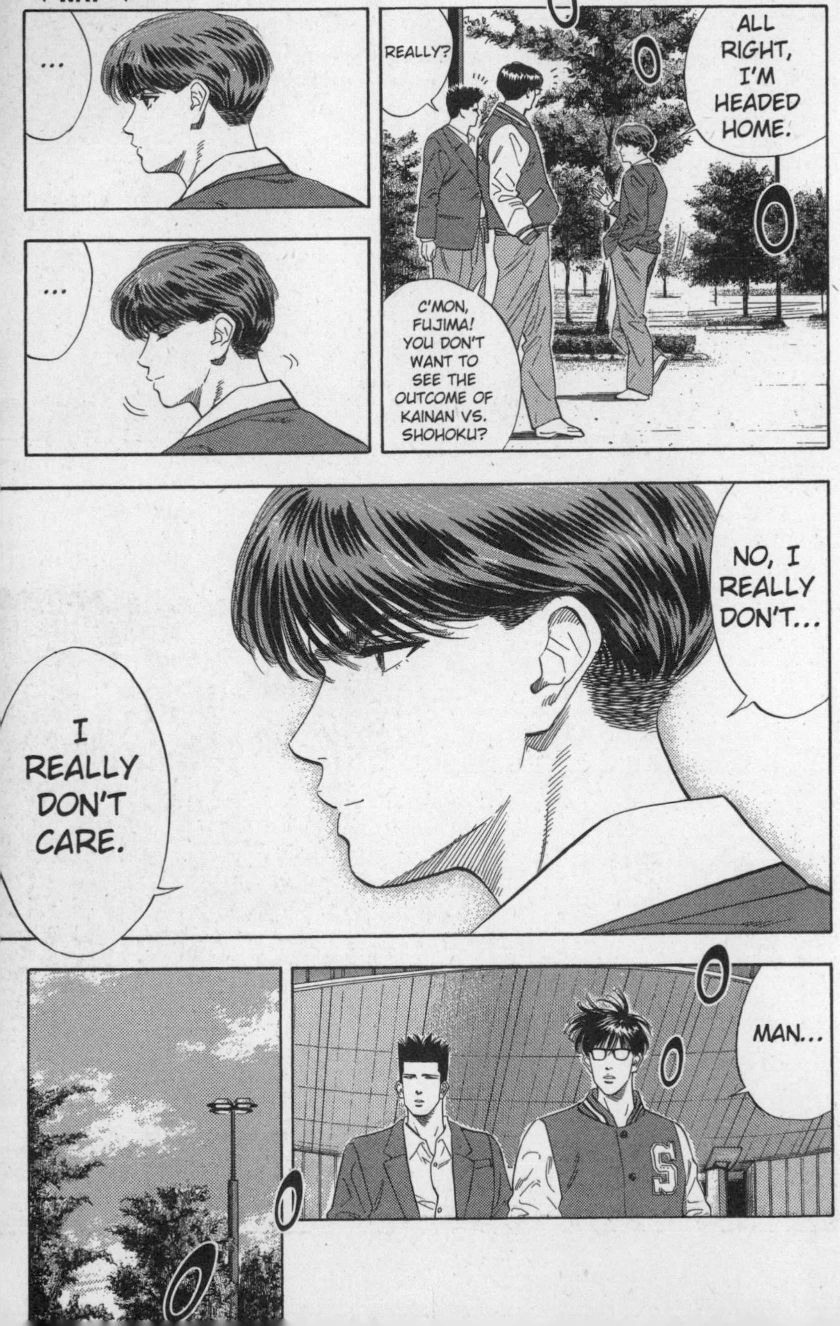

ALL RIGHT, I'M HEADED HOME.
REALLY?
C'MON, FUJIMA! YOU DON'T WANT TO SEE THE OUTCOME OF KAINAN VS. SHOHOKU?
...
...
NO, I REALLY DON'T...
I REALLY DON'T CARE.
MAN...

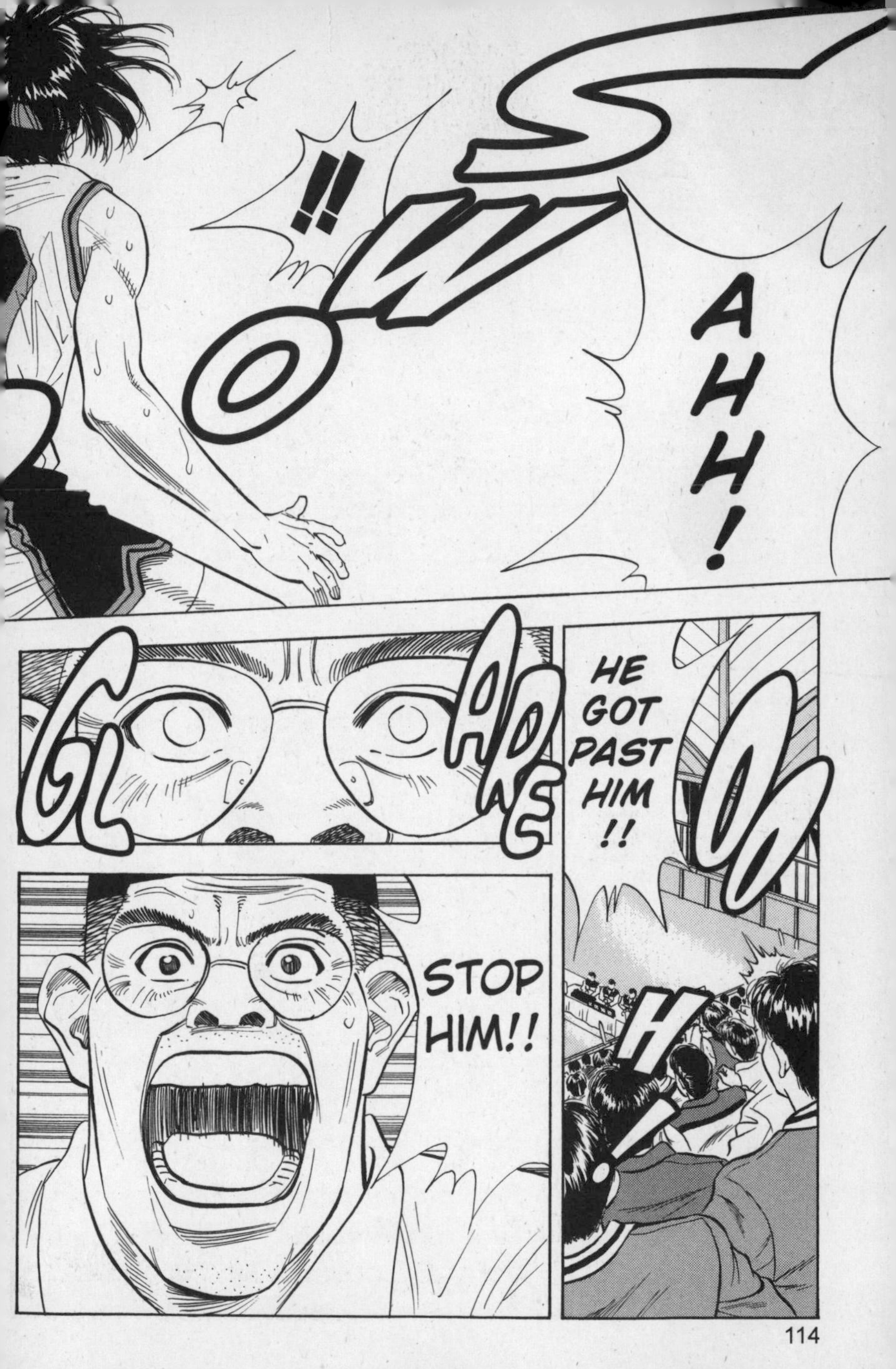
AHH!
HE GOT PAST HIM!!
STOP HIM!!

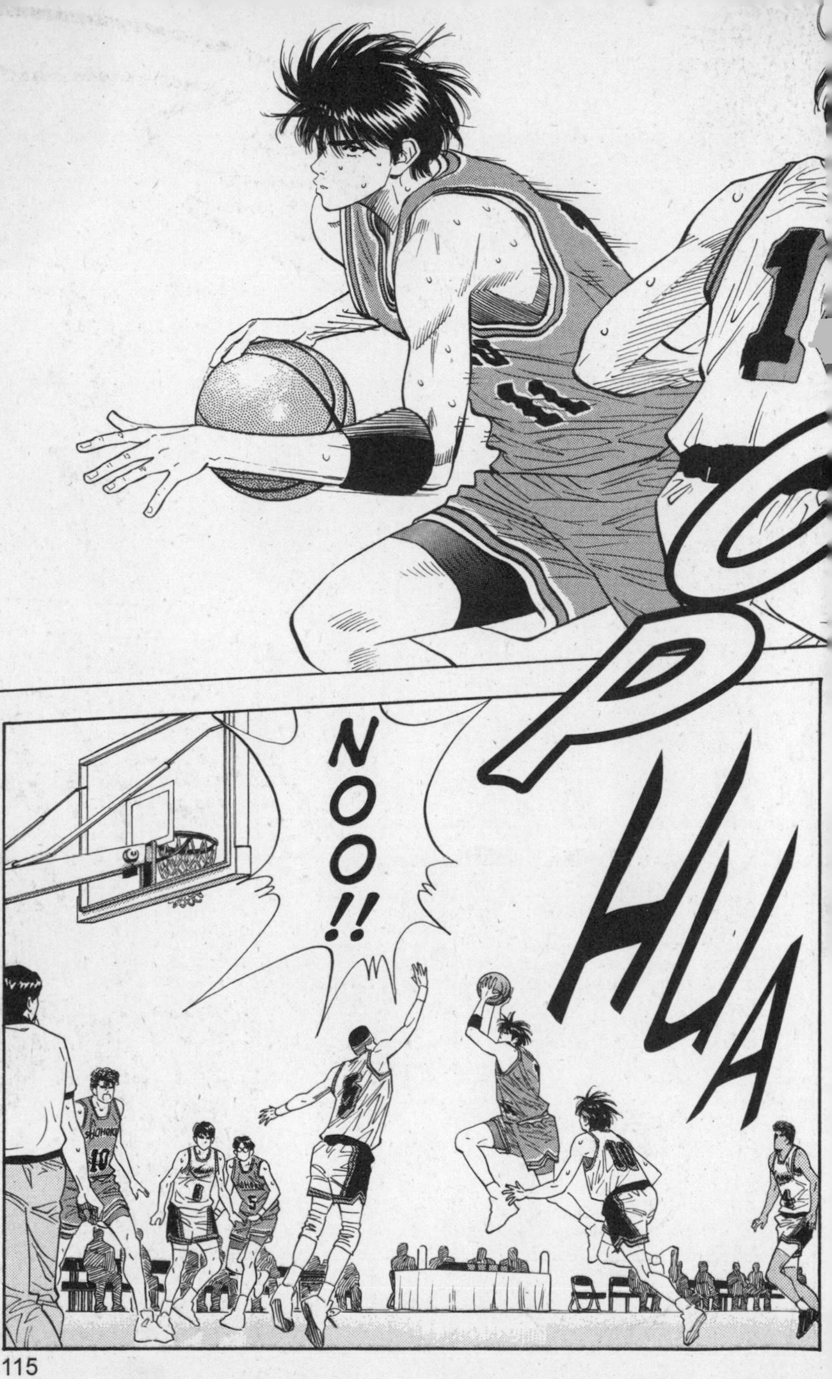
PHUA
NOO!!

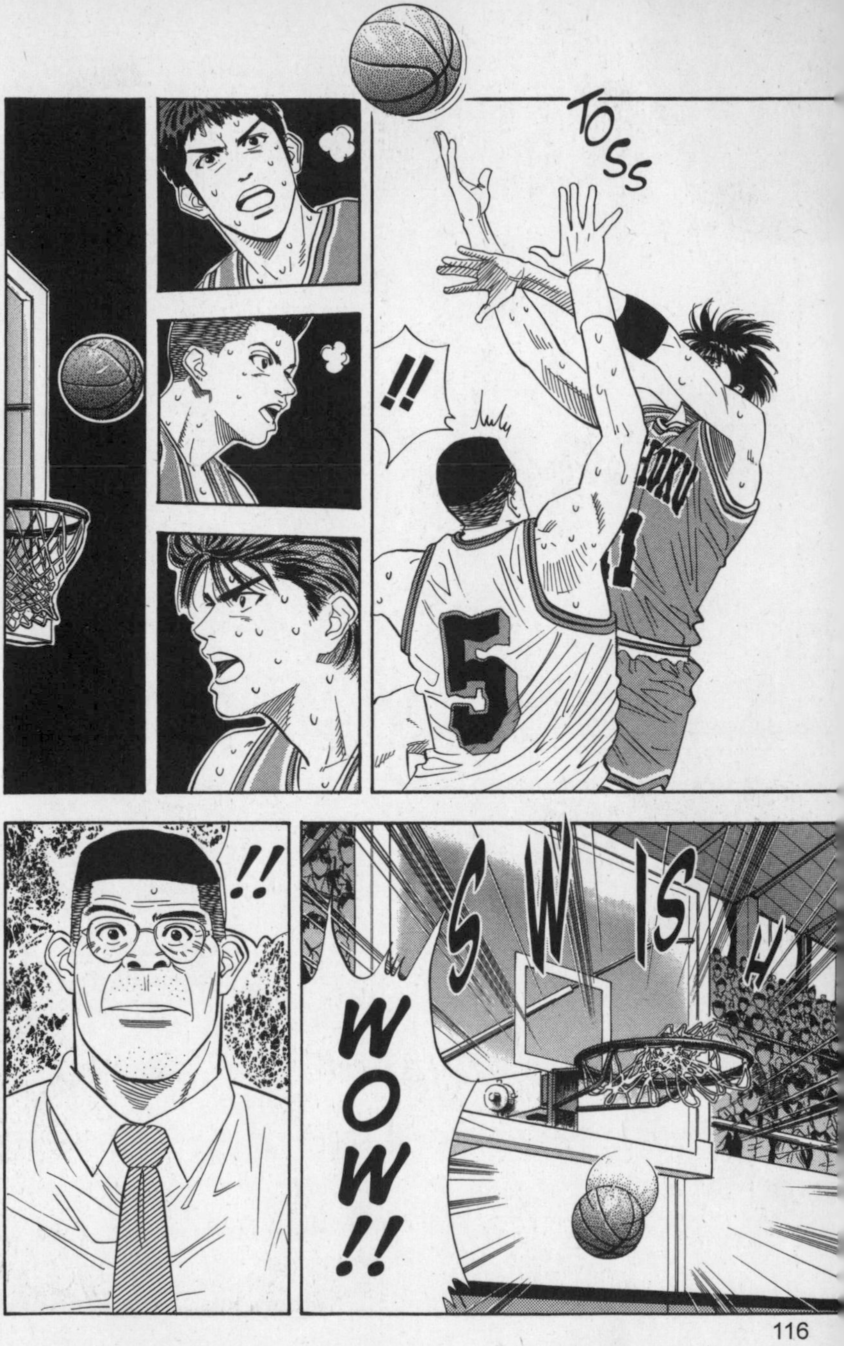
TOSS
!!
SWISH
WOW!!
!!

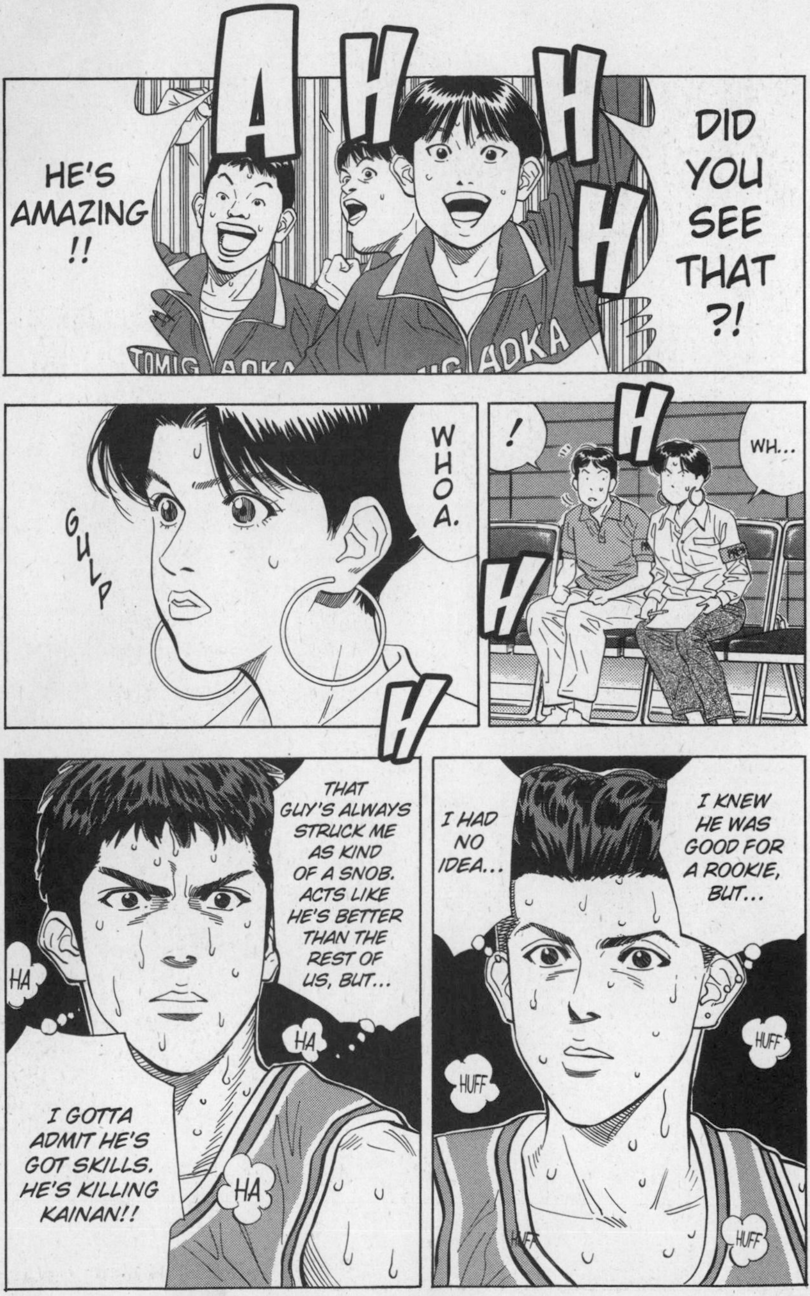
AHHHH
DID YOU SEE THAT?!
HE'S AMAZING!!
WH...
!
H
H
WHOA.
GULP
H
I KNEW HE WAS GOOD FOR A ROOKIE, BUT...
I HAD NO IDEA...
HUFF
HUFF
HUFF
HUFF
THAT GUY'S ALWAYS STRUCK ME AS KIND OF A SNOB. ACTS LIKE HE'S BETTER THAN THE REST OF US, BUT...
HA
HA
I GOTTA ADMIT HE'S GOT SKILLS. HE'S KILLING KAINAN!!
HA

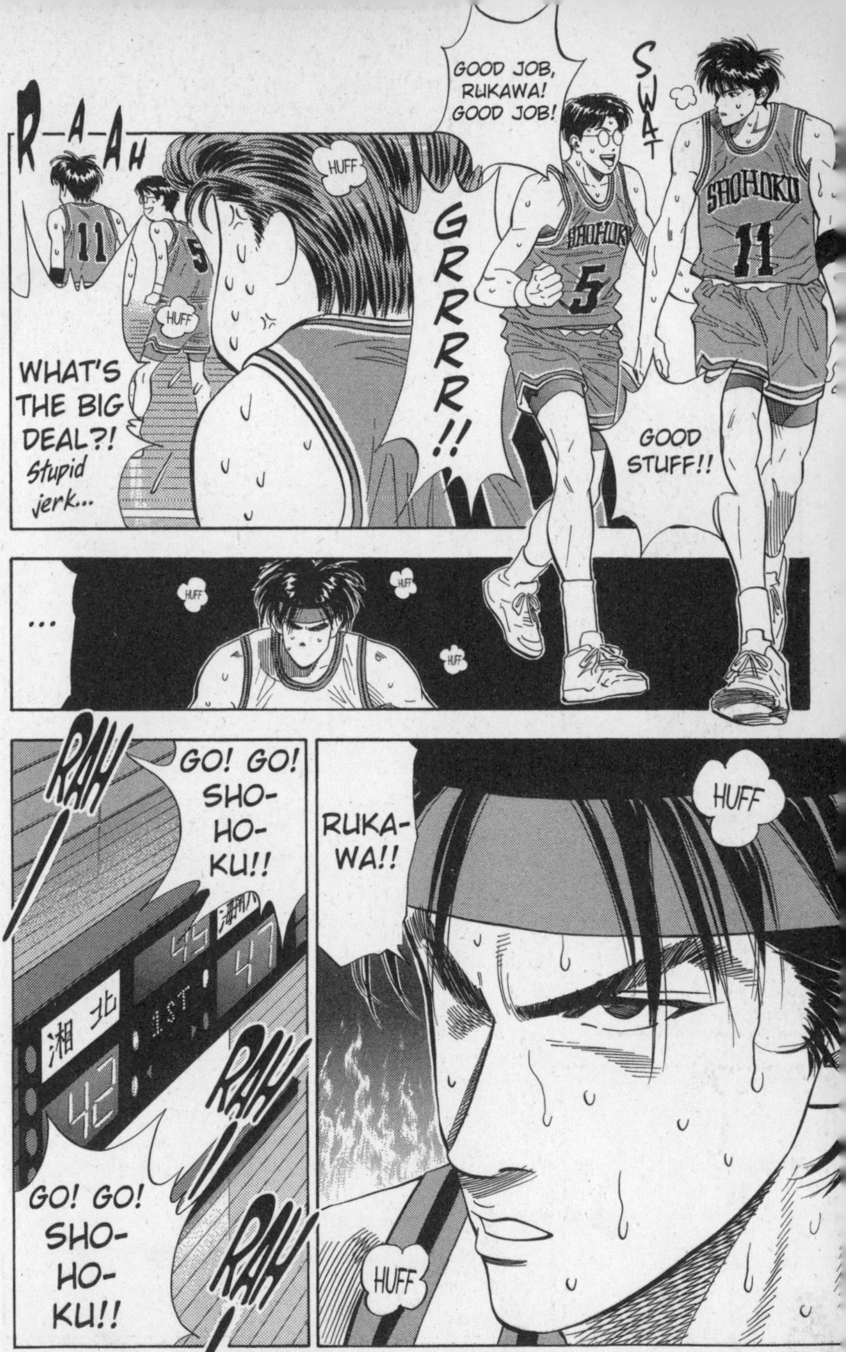
GOOD JOB, RUKAWA! GOOD JOB!
SWAT
GOOD STUFF!!
GRRRR!!
HUFF
HUFF
R-A-AH
WHAT'S THE BIG DEAL?! Stupid jerk...
HUFF
HUFF
HUFF
...
HUFF
RUKA-WA!!
HUFF
RAH
GO! GO! SHO-HO-KU!!
湘北
1ST
RAH
RAH
GO! GO! SHO-HO-KU!!

Scoreboard: Shohoku Kainan Dai Fuzoku

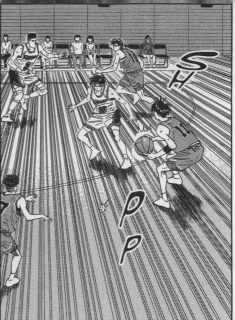

WHA THE —?!

A THREE-POINTER?!

NO WAY!

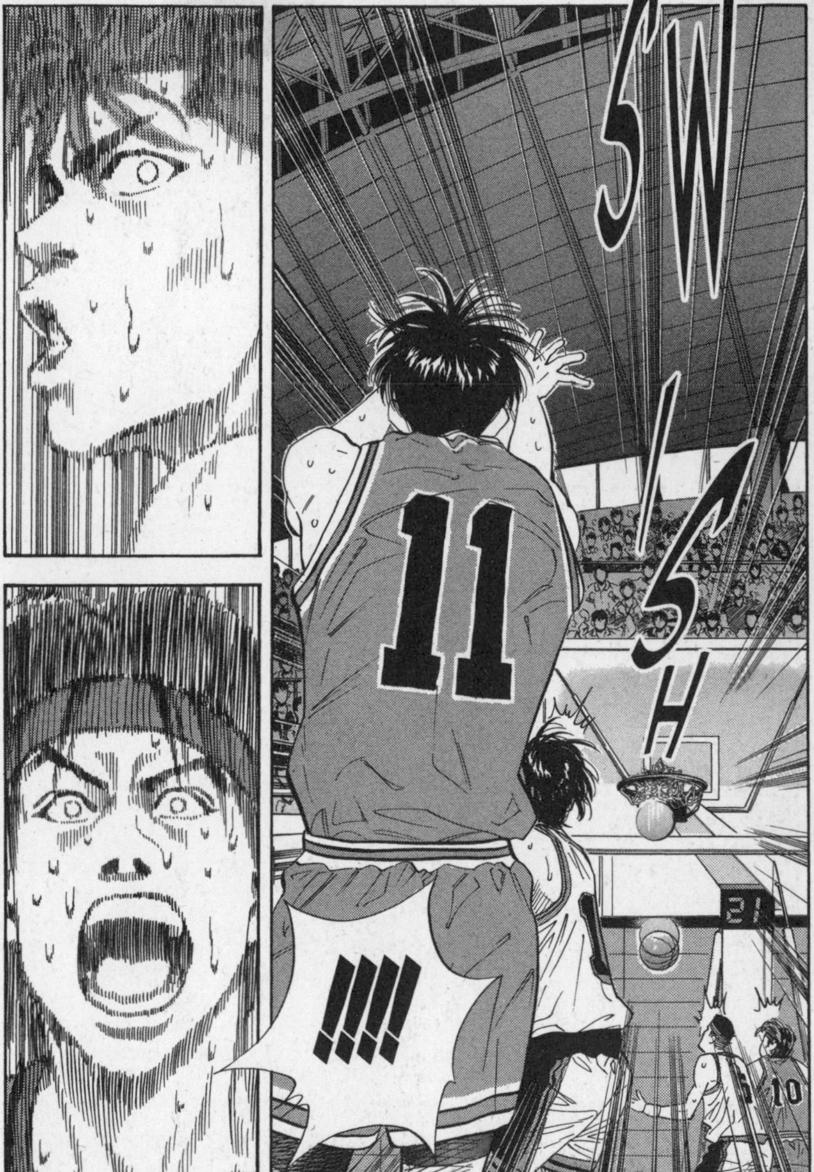
SWISH
!!!!!

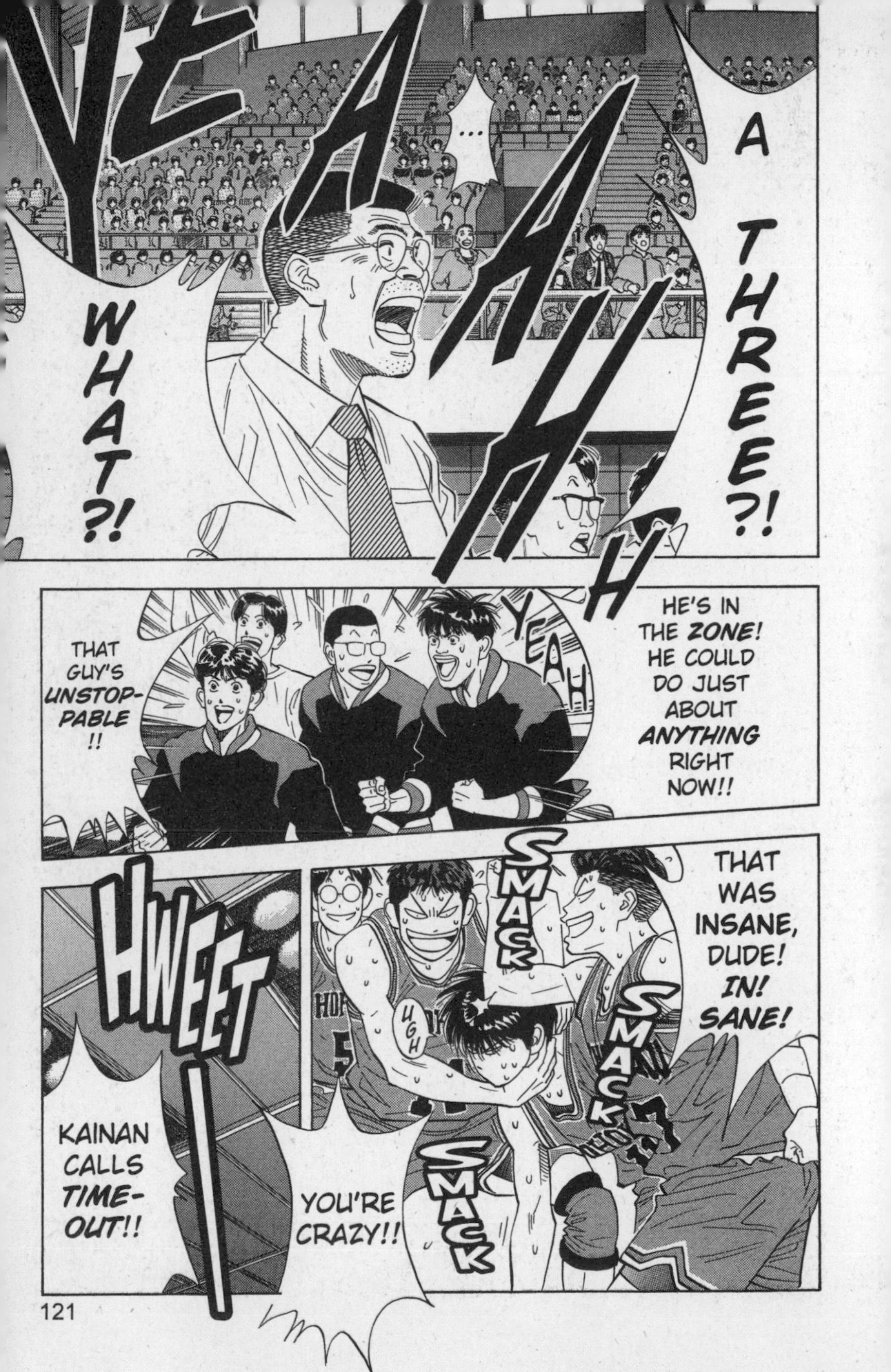
A THREE?!
...
YEAAAHH
WHAT?!
HE'S IN THE *ZONE*! HE COULD DO JUST ABOUT *ANYTHING* RIGHT NOW!!
YEAH
THAT GUY'S *UNSTOPPABLE*!!
THAT WAS INSANE, DUDE! *IN! SANE!*
SMACK
SMACK
UGH
SMACK
YOU'RE CRAZY!!
HWEET
KAINAN CALLS *TIME-OUT*!!

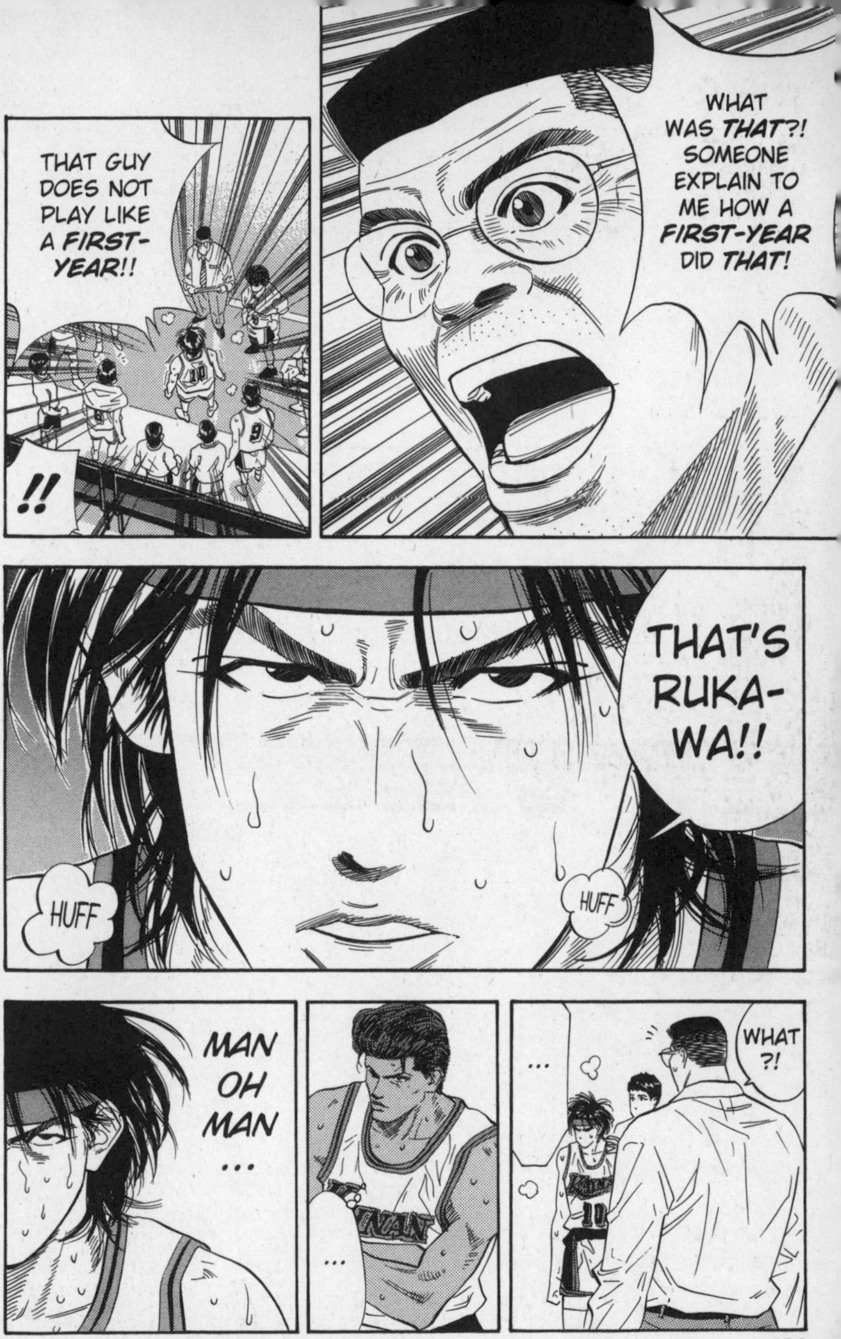
WHAT WAS *THAT*?! SOMEONE EXPLAIN TO ME HOW A *FIRST-YEAR* DID *THAT*!
THAT GUY DOES NOT PLAY LIKE A *FIRST-YEAR*!!
!!
THAT'S RUKAWA!!
HUFF
HUFF
WHAT?!
...
...
MAN OH MAN ...

READ THIS WAY

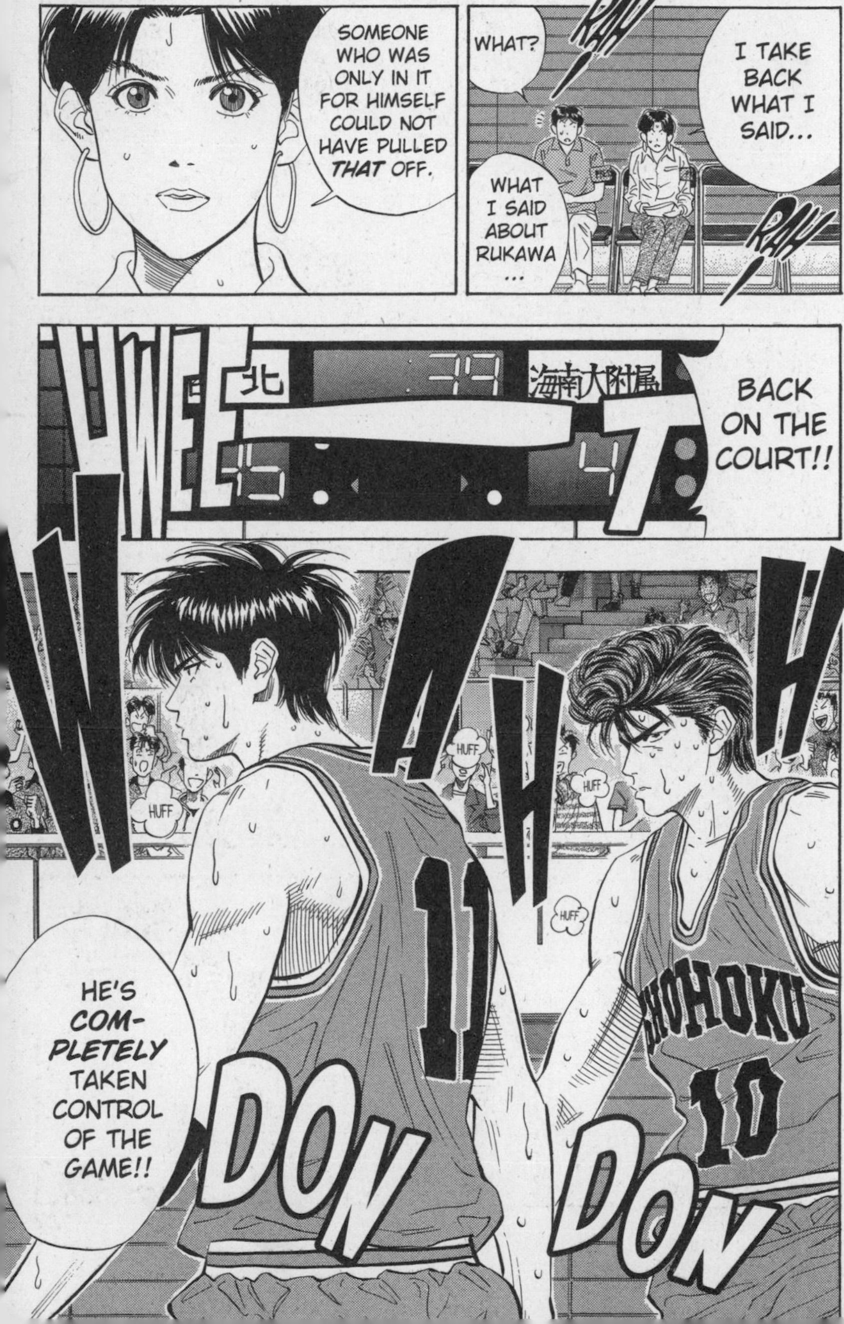
I TAKE BACK WHAT I SAID...
RAH
WHAT?
WHAT I SAID ABOUT RUKAWA ...
RAH
SOMEONE WHO WAS ONLY IN IT FOR HIMSELF COULD NOT HAVE PULLED *THAT* OFF.
BACK ON THE COURT!!
海南大附属
北
WAH
HUFF
HUFF
HUFF
HUFF
11
SHOHOKU
10
HE'S ***COMPLETELY*** TAKEN CONTROL OF THE GAME!!
DON
DON

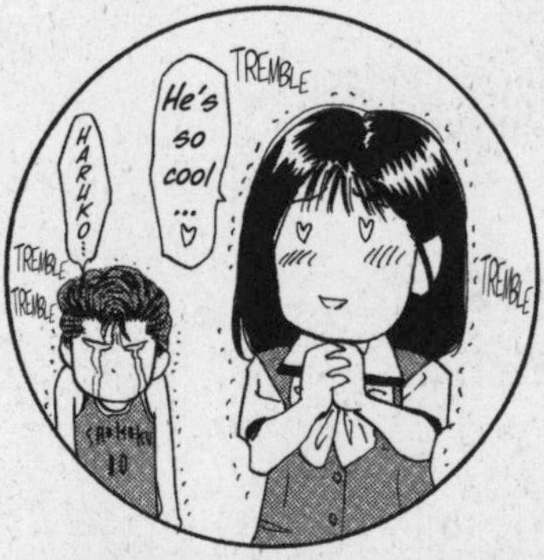
TREMBLE
He's so cool... ♡
TREMBLE
HARUKO...
TREMBLE
TREMBLE

SLAM DUNK

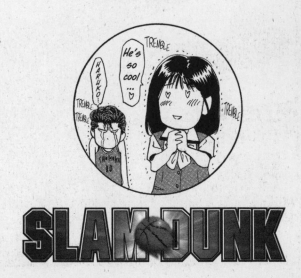

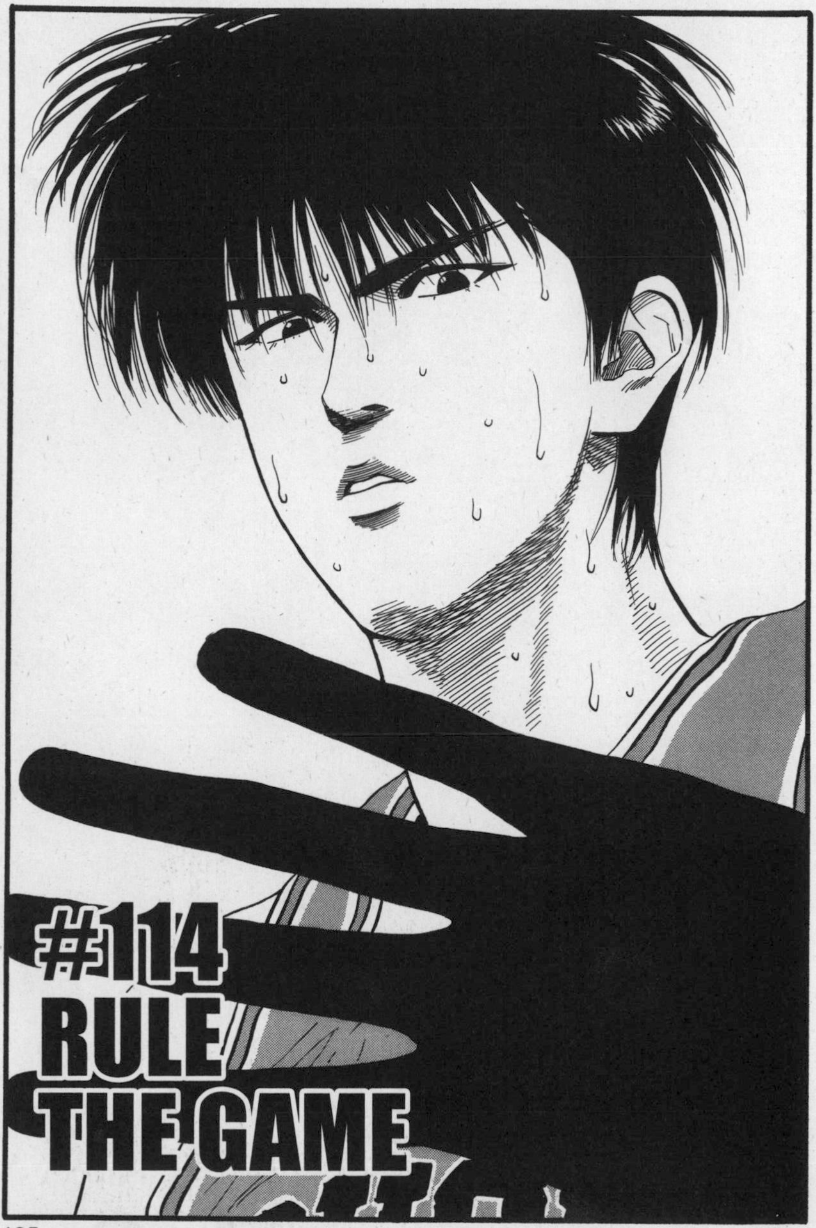
#114
RULE THE GAME

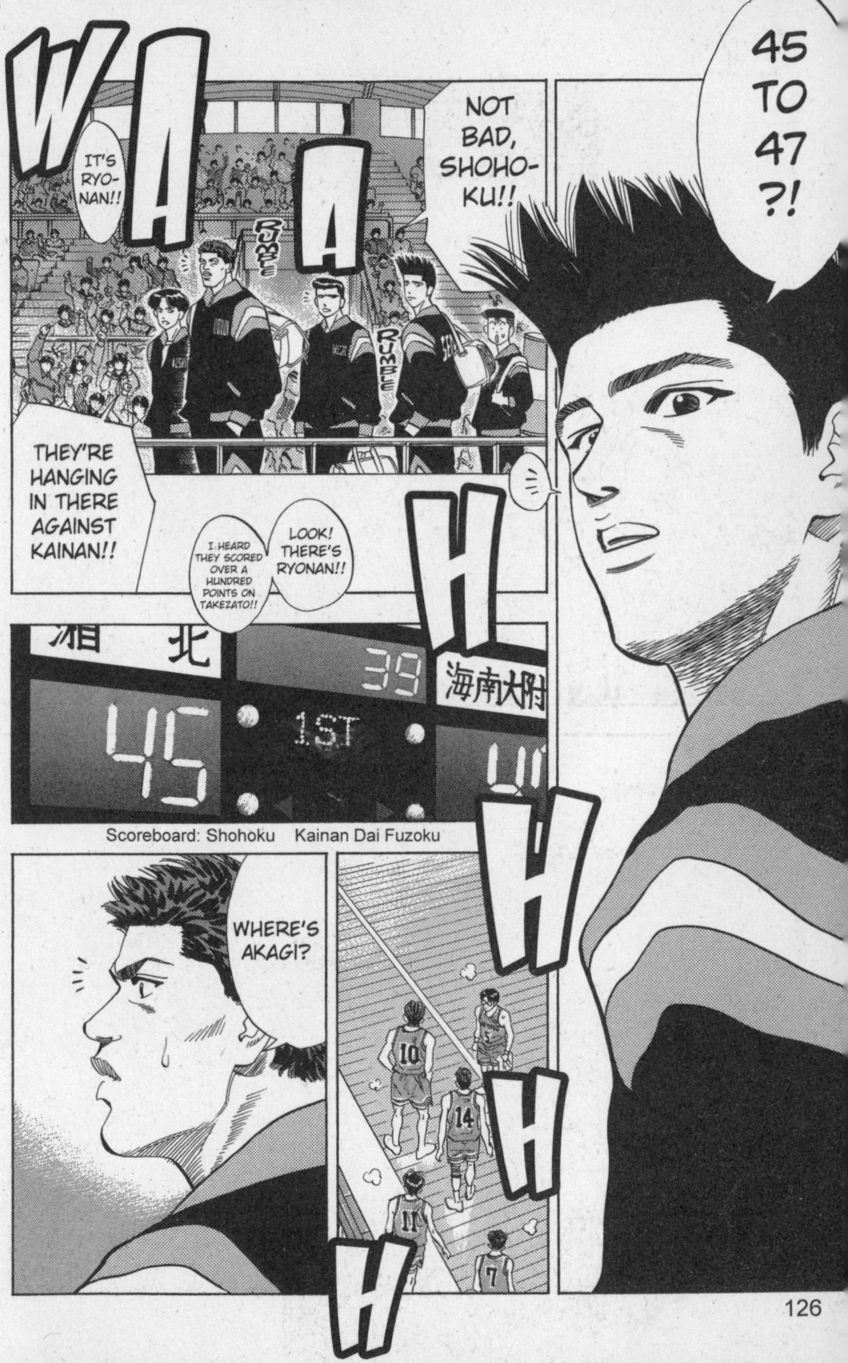

45 TO 47 ?!
WAAHHHHH
NOT BAD, SHOHOKU!!
IT'S RYONAN!!
THEY'RE HANGING IN THERE AGAINST KAINAN!!
LOOK! THERE'S RYONAN!!
I HEARD THEY SCORED OVER A HUNDRED POINTS ON TAKEZATO!!
湘北
39
海南大附
45
1ST
WHERE'S AKAGI?

Scoreboard: Shohoku Kainan Dai Fuzoku

READ THIS WAY

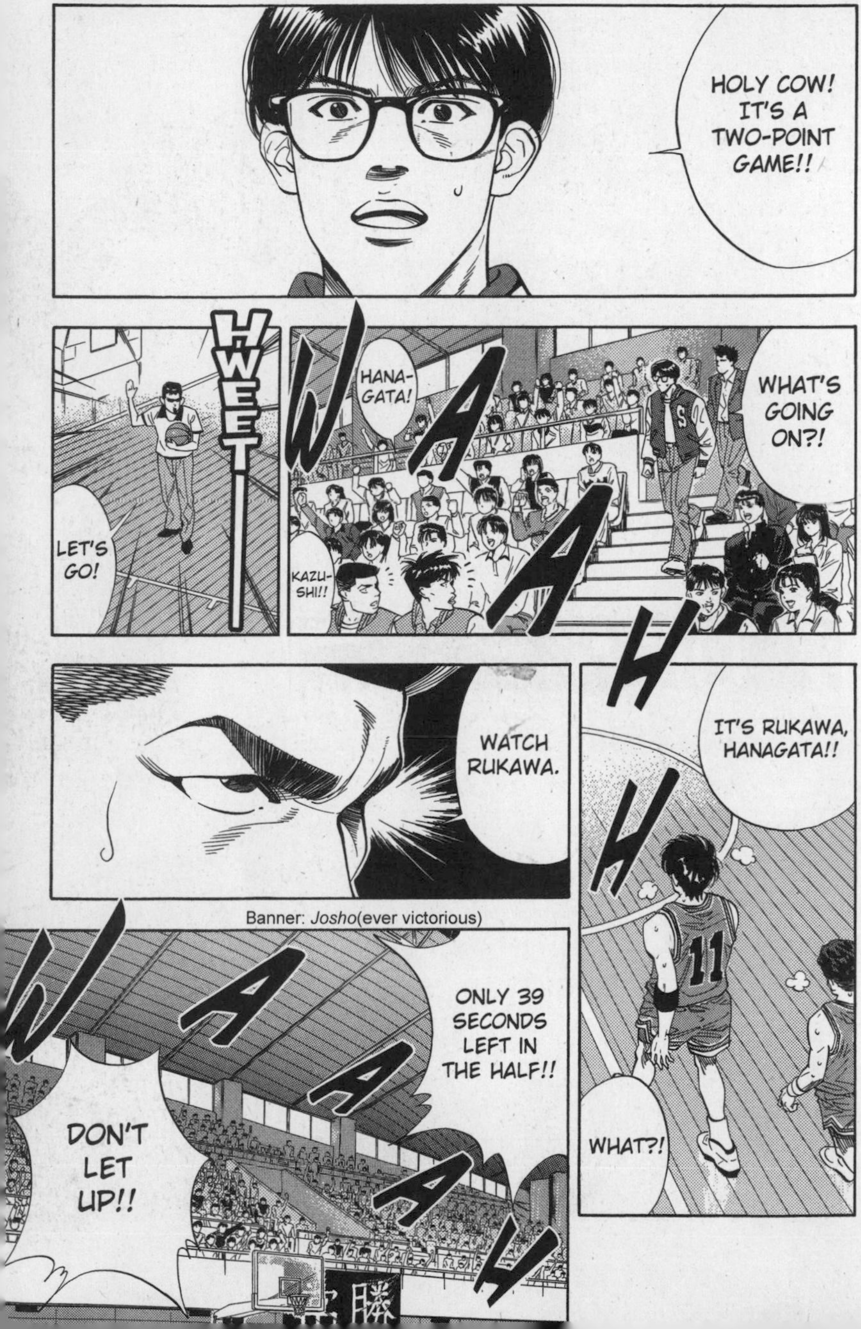
HOLY COW! IT'S A TWO-POINT GAME!!
WHAT'S GOING ON?!
HANA-GATA!
KAZU-SHI!!
WAAAHHH
HWEET
LET'S GO!
IT'S RUKAWA, HANAGATA!!
WHAT?!
WATCH RUKAWA.
ONLY 39 SECONDS LEFT IN THE HALF!!
DON'T LET UP!!
WAAAAAH
Banner: *Josho*(ever victorious)

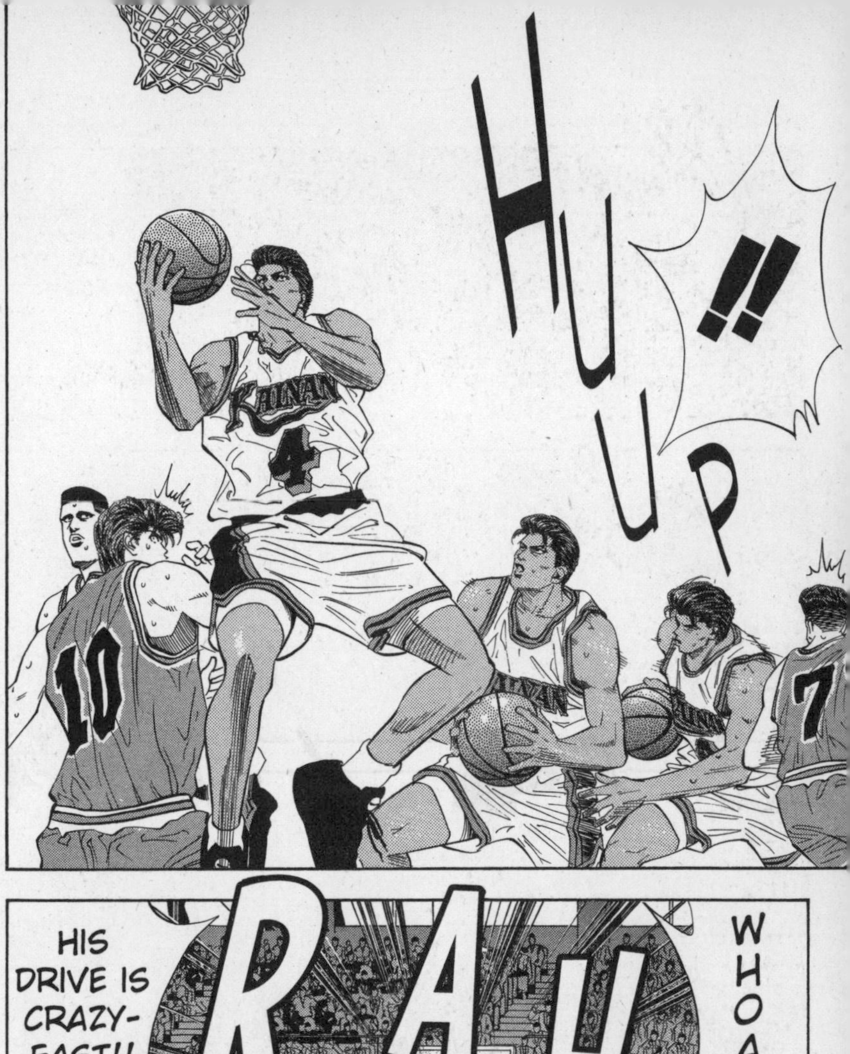
HUUP!!

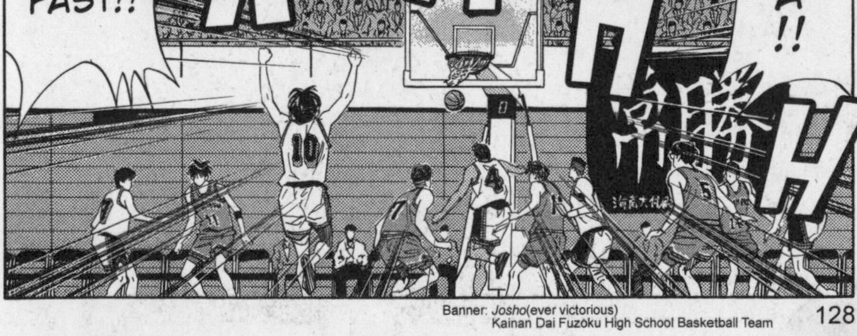
WHOA!!
RAHH
常勝
HIS DRIVE IS CRAZY-FAST!!

Banner: *Josho*(ever victorious)
Kainan Dai Fuzoku High School Basketball Team

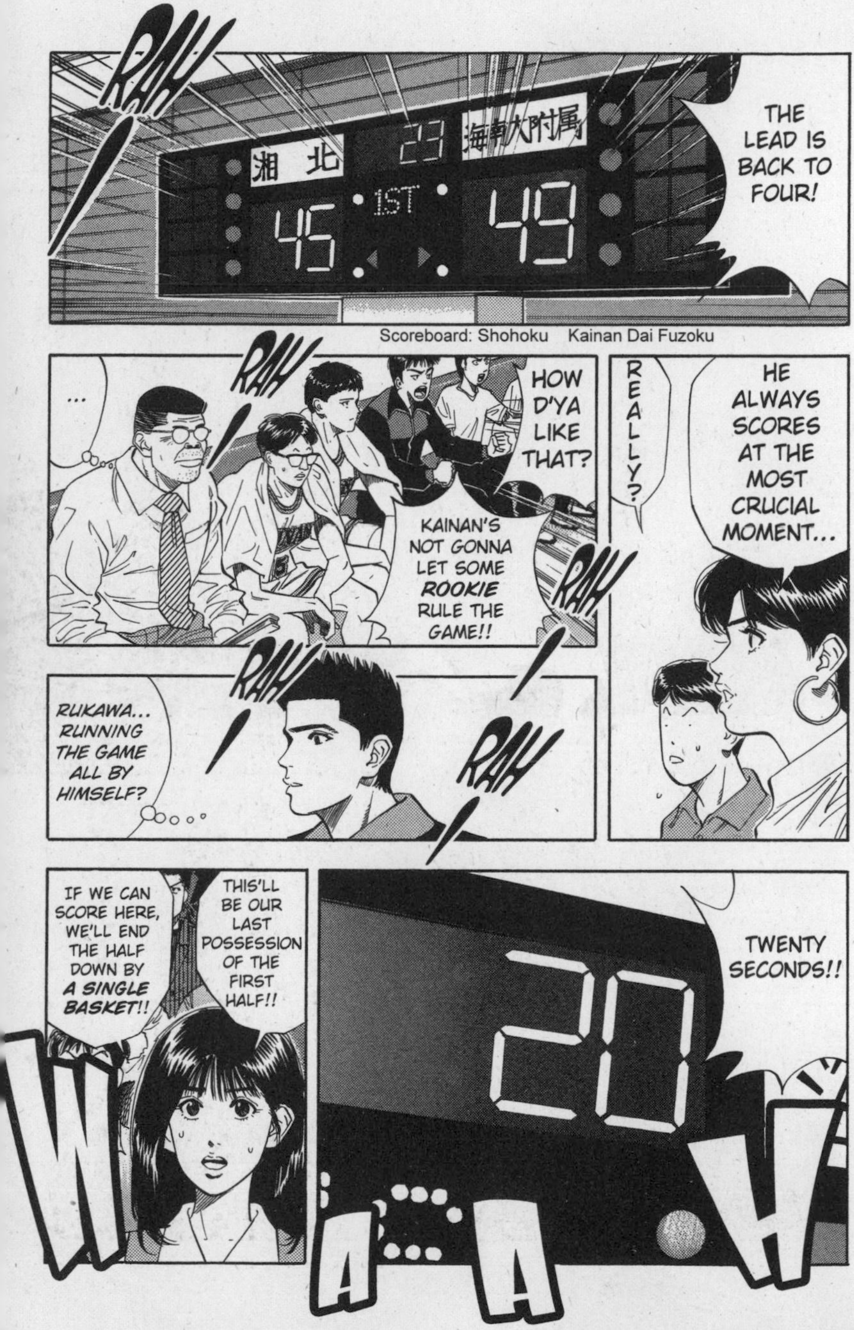
RAH
湘北
23
海南大附属
1ST
45
49
THE LEAD IS BACK TO FOUR!
Scoreboard: Shohoku Kainan Dai Fuzoku
HE ALWAYS SCORES AT THE MOST CRUCIAL MOMENT...
REALLY?
RAH
RAH
HOW D'YA LIKE THAT?
RAH
KAINAN'S NOT GONNA LET SOME ROOKIE RULE THE GAME!!
...
RAH
RUKAWA... RUNNING THE GAME ALL BY HIMSELF?
TWENTY SECONDS!!
20
THIS'LL BE OUR LAST POSSESSION OF THE FIRST HALF!!
IF WE CAN SCORE HERE, WE'LL END THE HALF DOWN BY A SINGLE BASKET!!
WAAAH

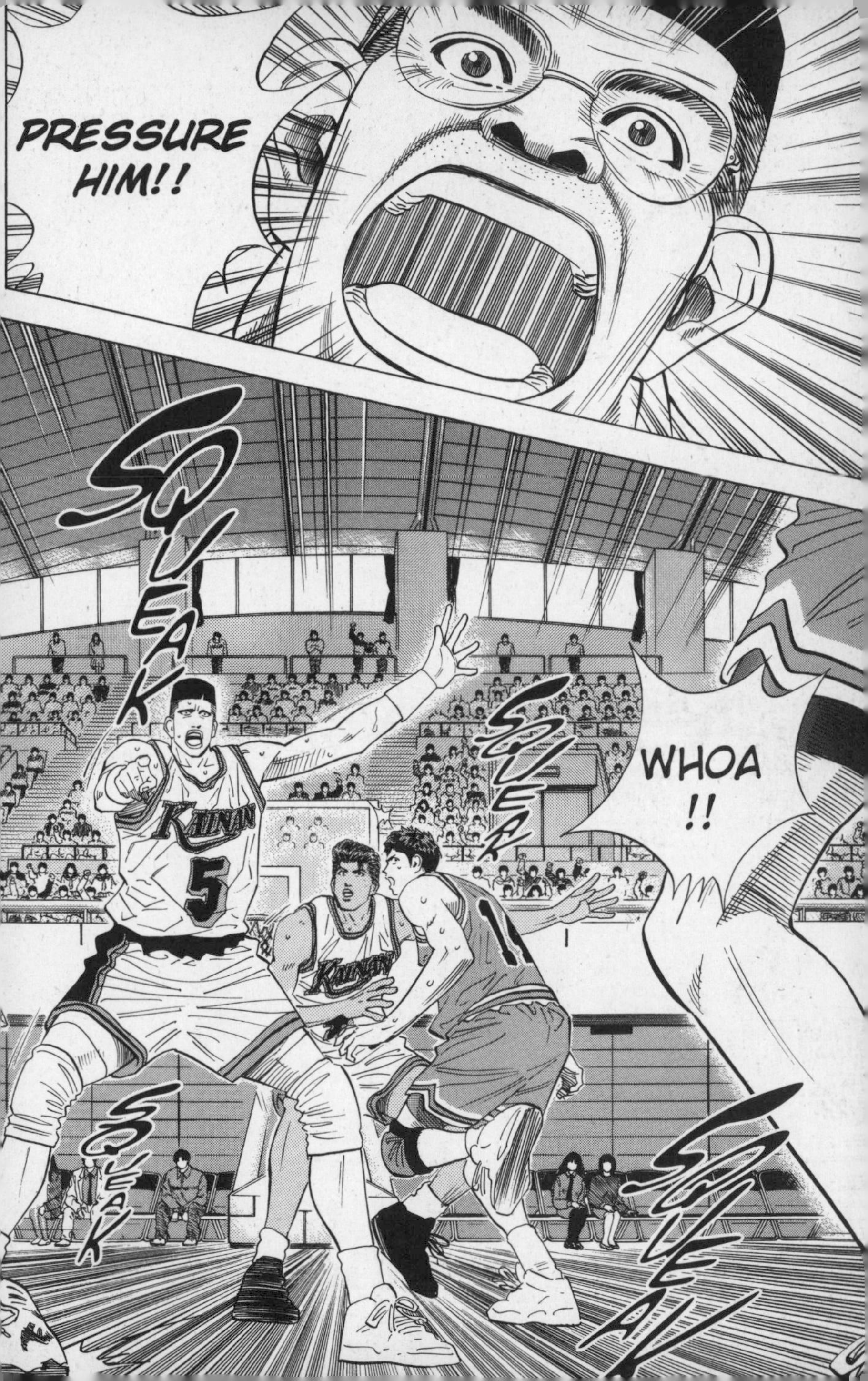
PRESSURE HIM!!
WHOA!!
SQUEAK
SQUEAK
SQUEAK
SQUEAK

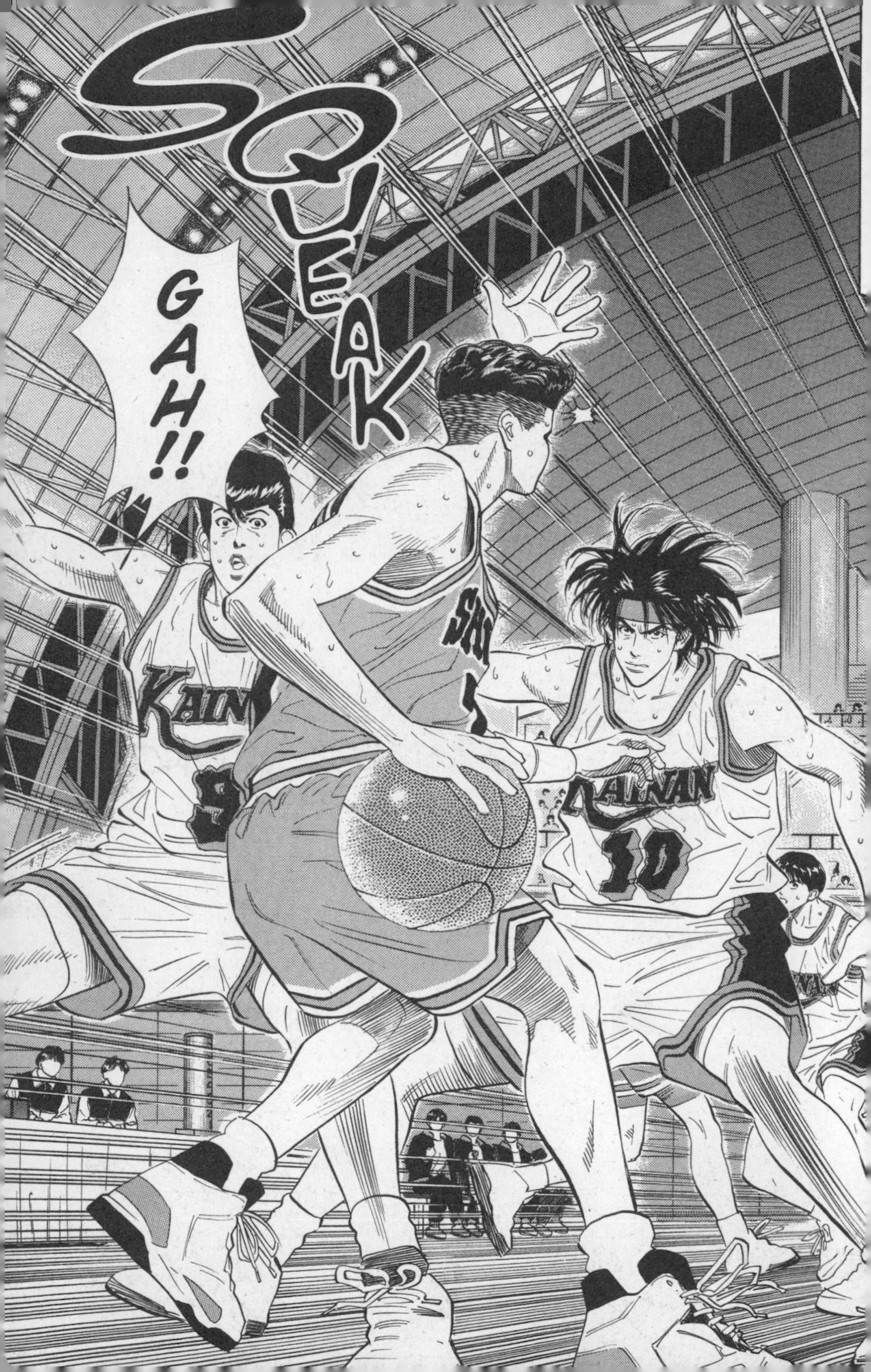
SQUEAK
GAH!!

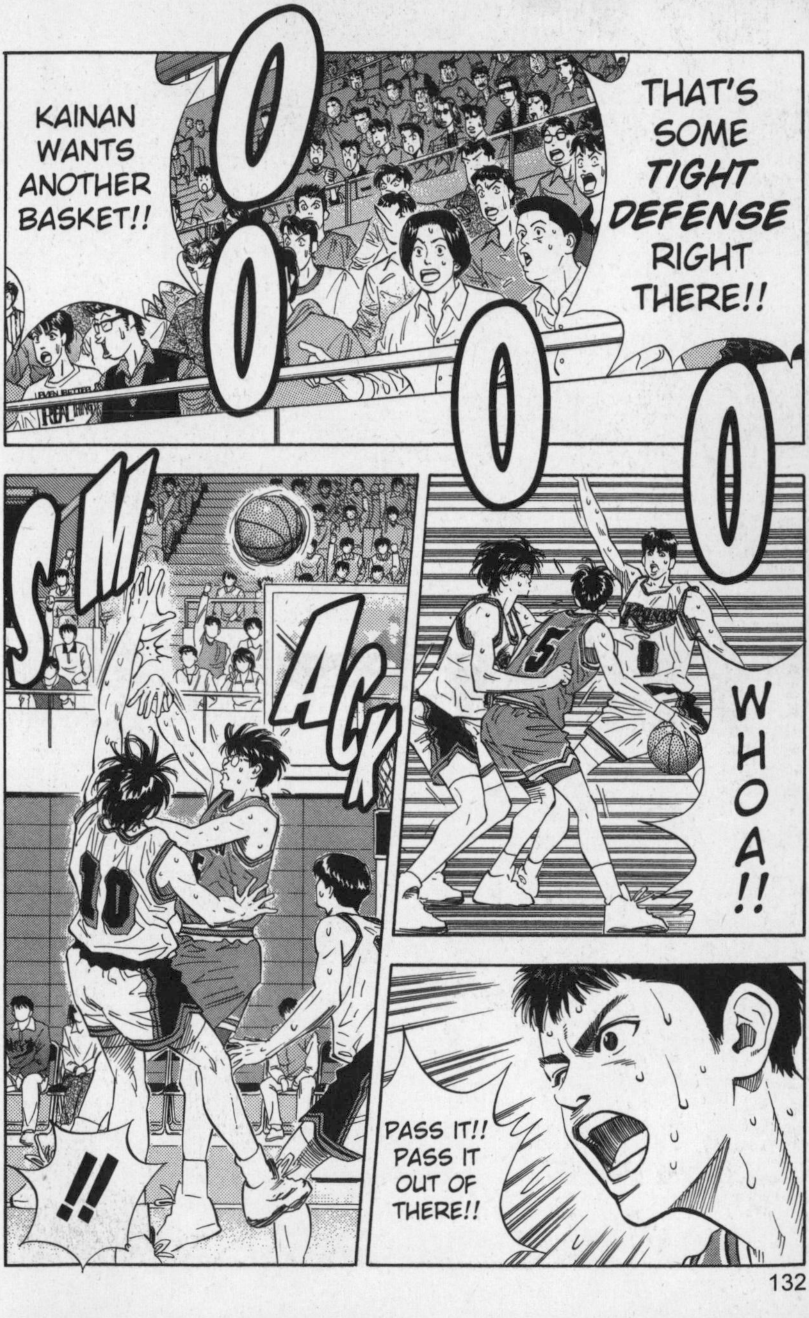
THAT'S SOME *TIGHT DEFENSE* RIGHT THERE!!
KAINAN WANTS ANOTHER BASKET!!
OOOO
WHOA!!
PASS IT!! PASS IT OUT OF THERE!!
SMACK
!!

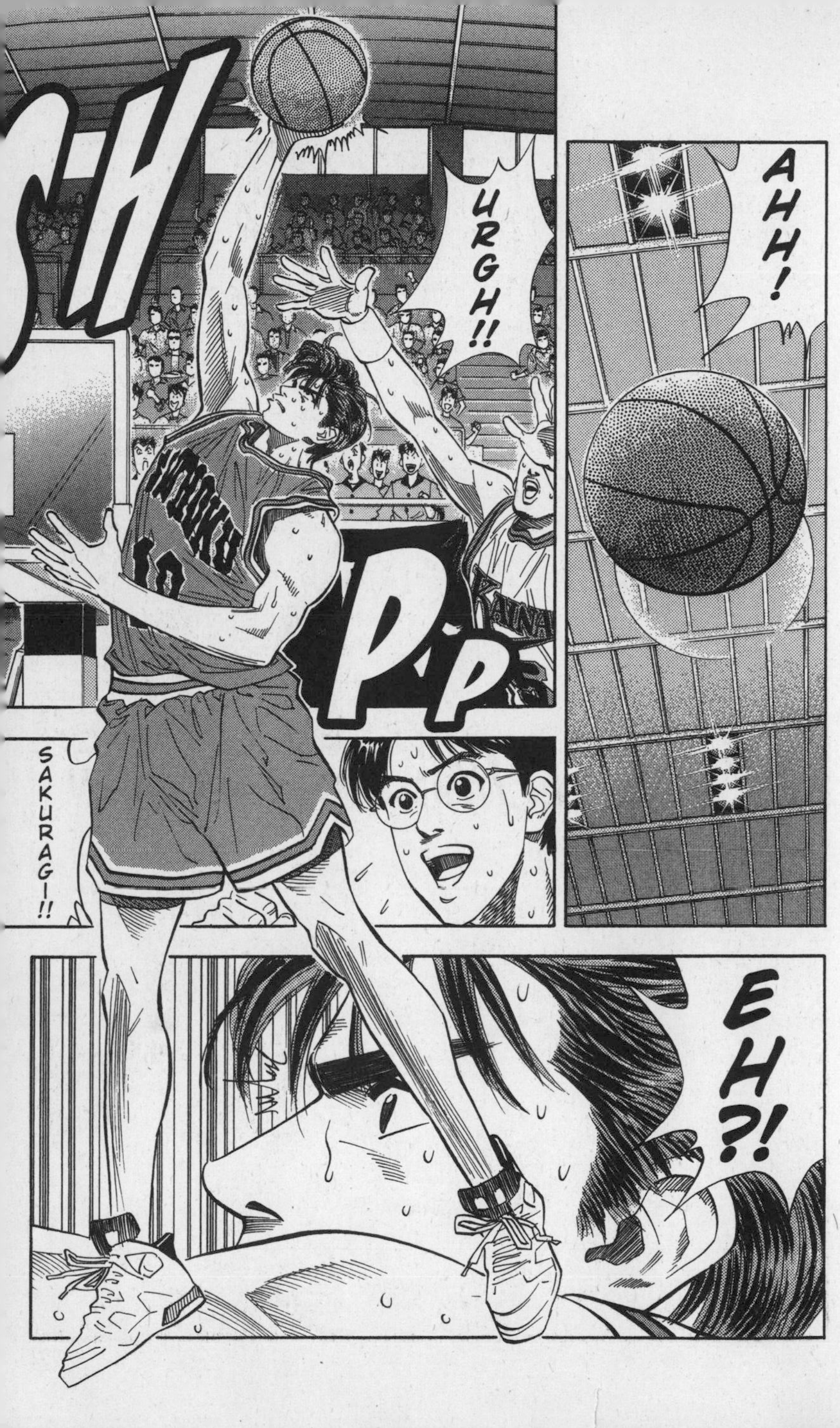
AHH!
SH
URGH!!
PiP
SAKURAGI!!
EH?!

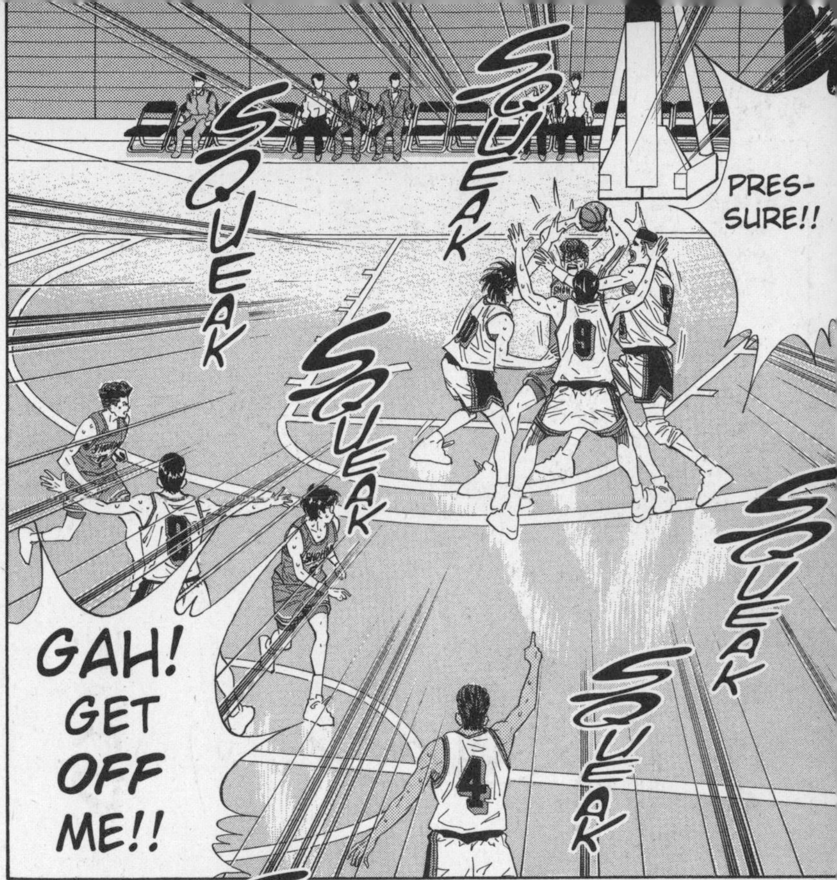
PRES-SURE!!
SQUEAK
SQUEAK
SQUEAK
SQUEAK
SQUEAK
GAH! GET OFF ME!!

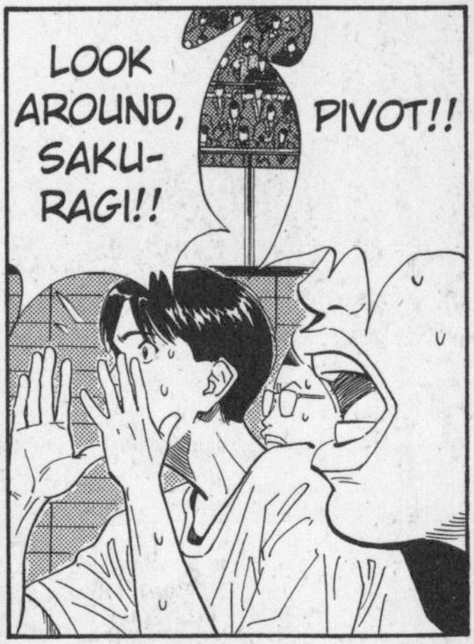
PIVOT!!
LOOK AROUND, SAKU-RAGI!!

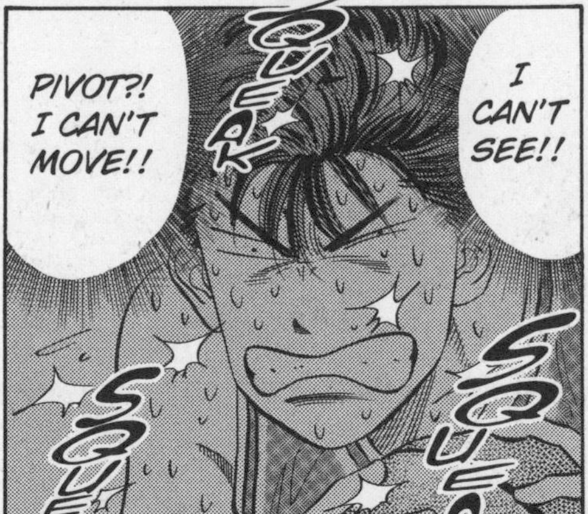
SQUEAK
I CAN'T SEE!!
PIVOT?! I CAN'T MOVE!!
SQUEAK
SQUEAK

READ THIS WAY

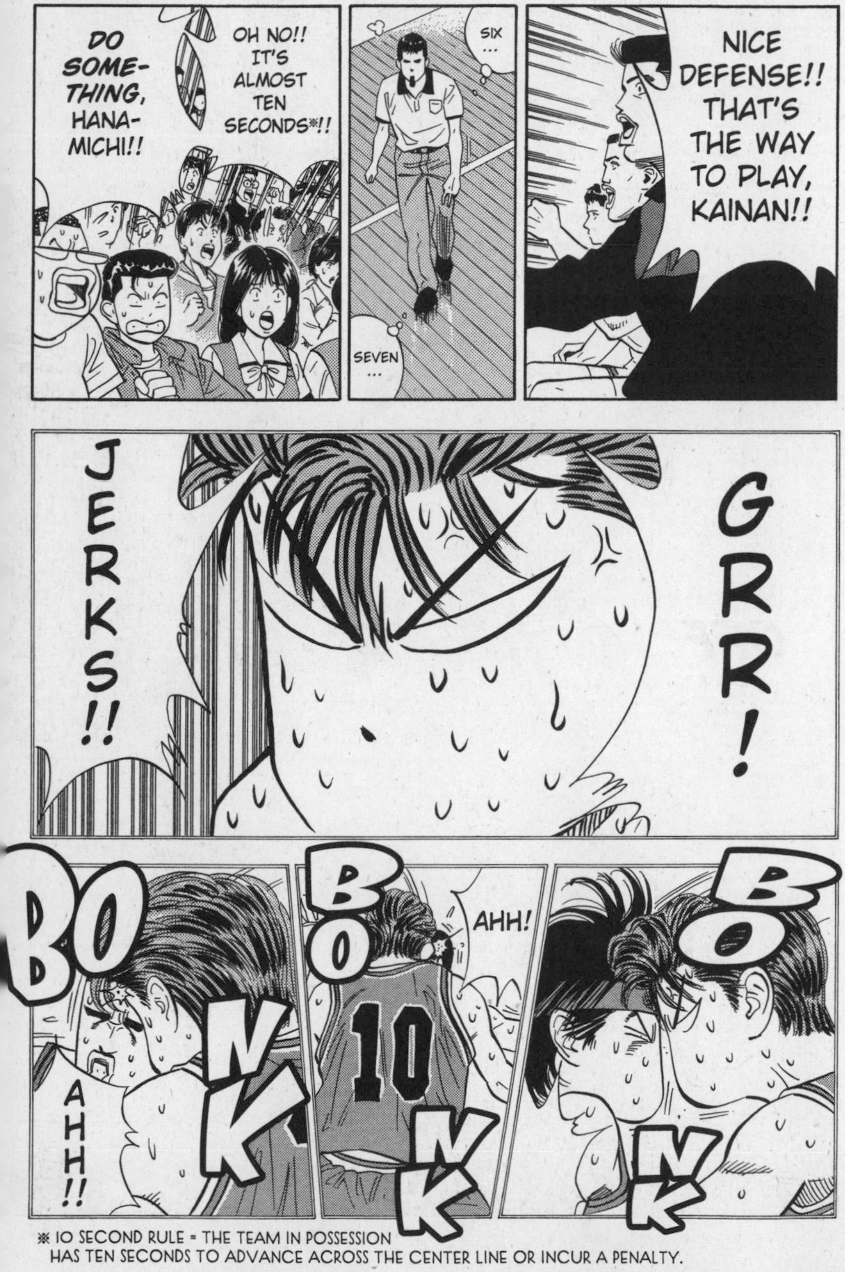
NICE DEFENSE!! THAT'S THE WAY TO PLAY, KAINAN!!
SIX ...
SEVEN ...
OH NO!! IT'S ALMOST TEN SECONDS※!!
DO SOMETHING, HANAMICHI!!
GRR!
JERKS!!
BO
NK
BO
AHH!
NK
BO
NK
AHH!!

※ 10 SECOND RULE = THE TEAM IN POSSESSION HAS TEN SECONDS TO ADVANCE ACROSS THE CENTER LINE OR INCUR A PENALTY.

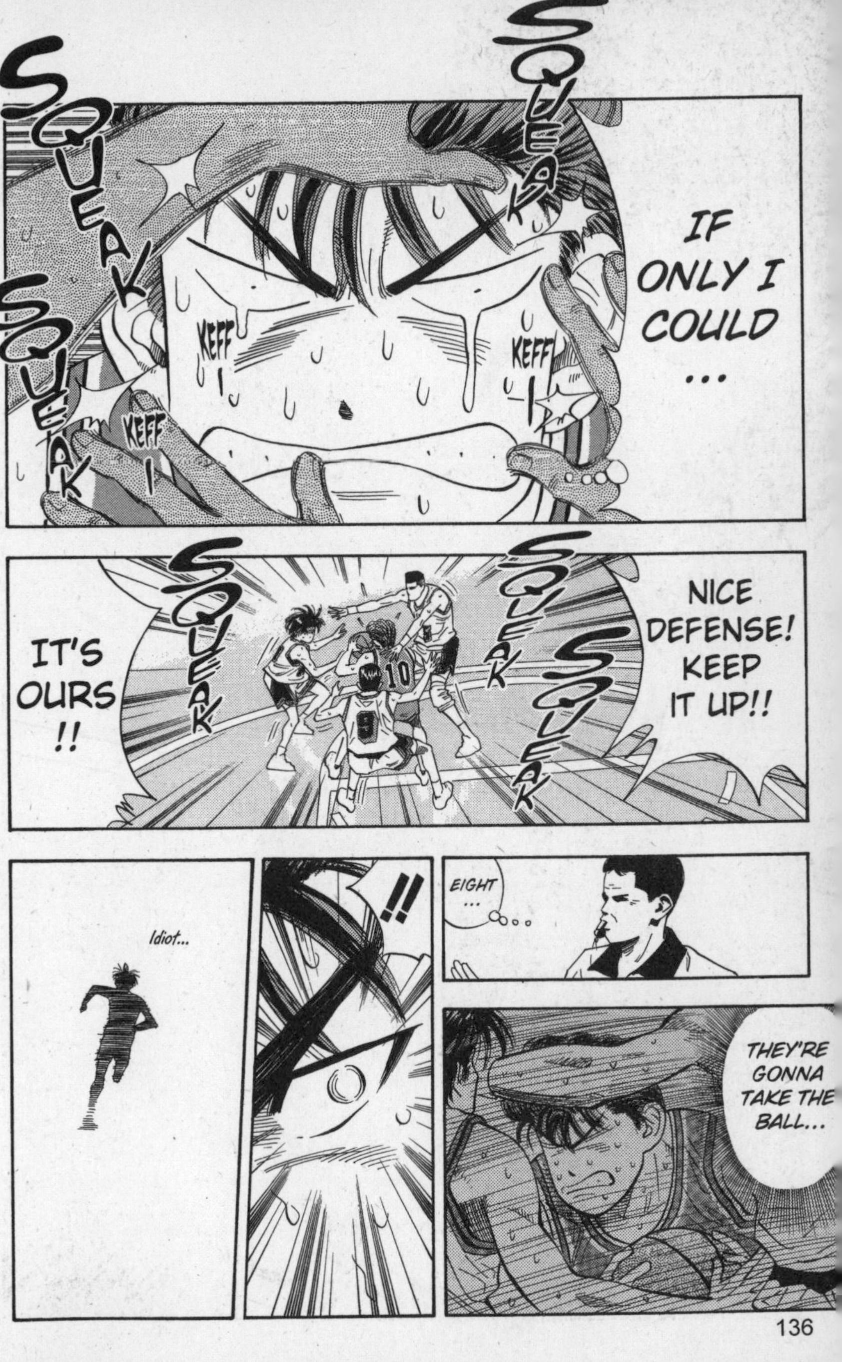
IF ONLY I COULD ...
SQUEAK
SQUEAK
KEFF
KEFF
SQUEAK
KEFF
NICE DEFENSE! KEEP IT UP!!
SQUEAK
SQUEAK
SQUEAK
IT'S OURS !!
EIGHT ...
THEY'RE GONNA TAKE THE BALL...
!!
Idiot...

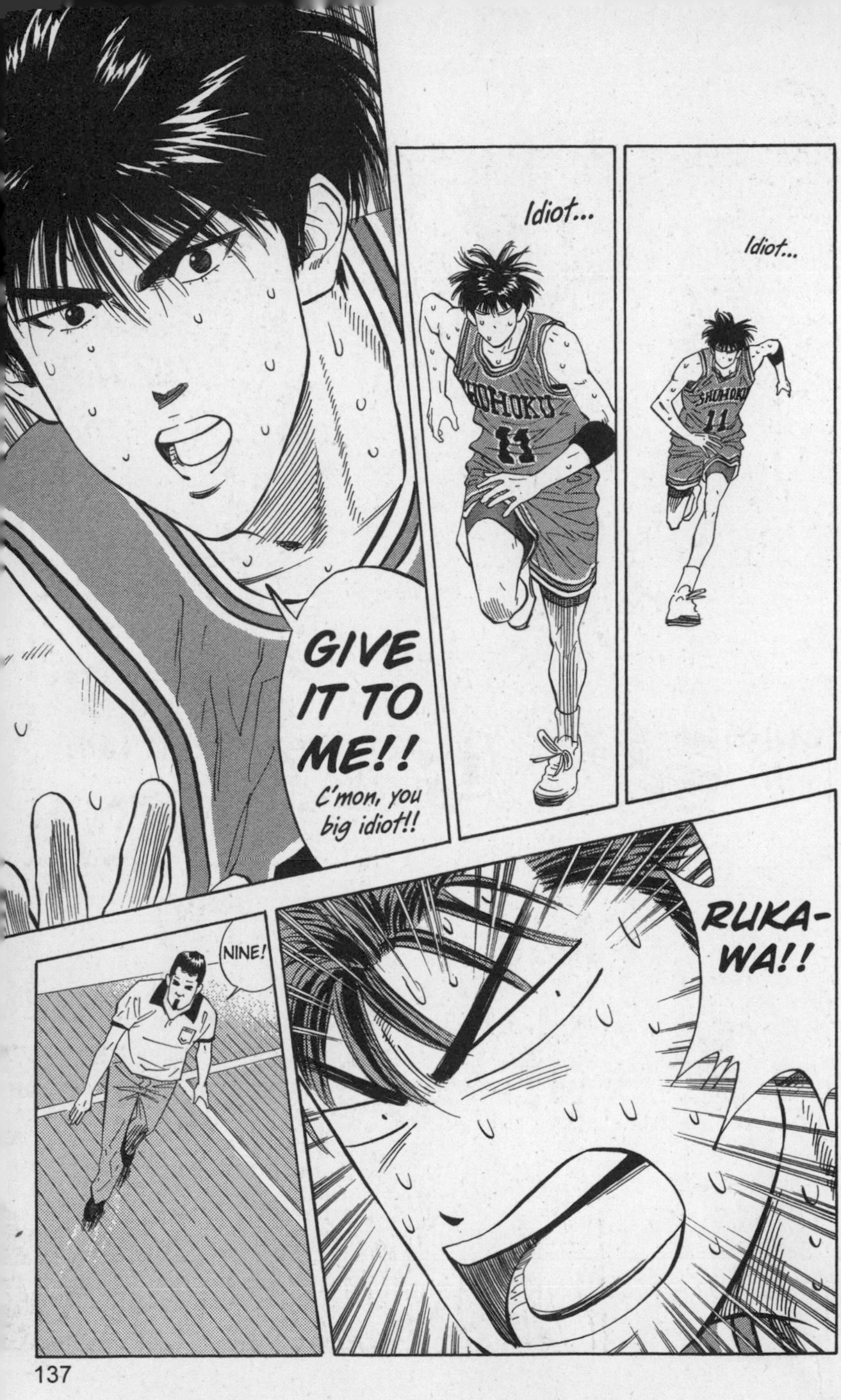
Idiot...
Idiot...
GIVE IT TO ME!!
C'mon, you big idiot!!
RUKA-WA!!
NINE!

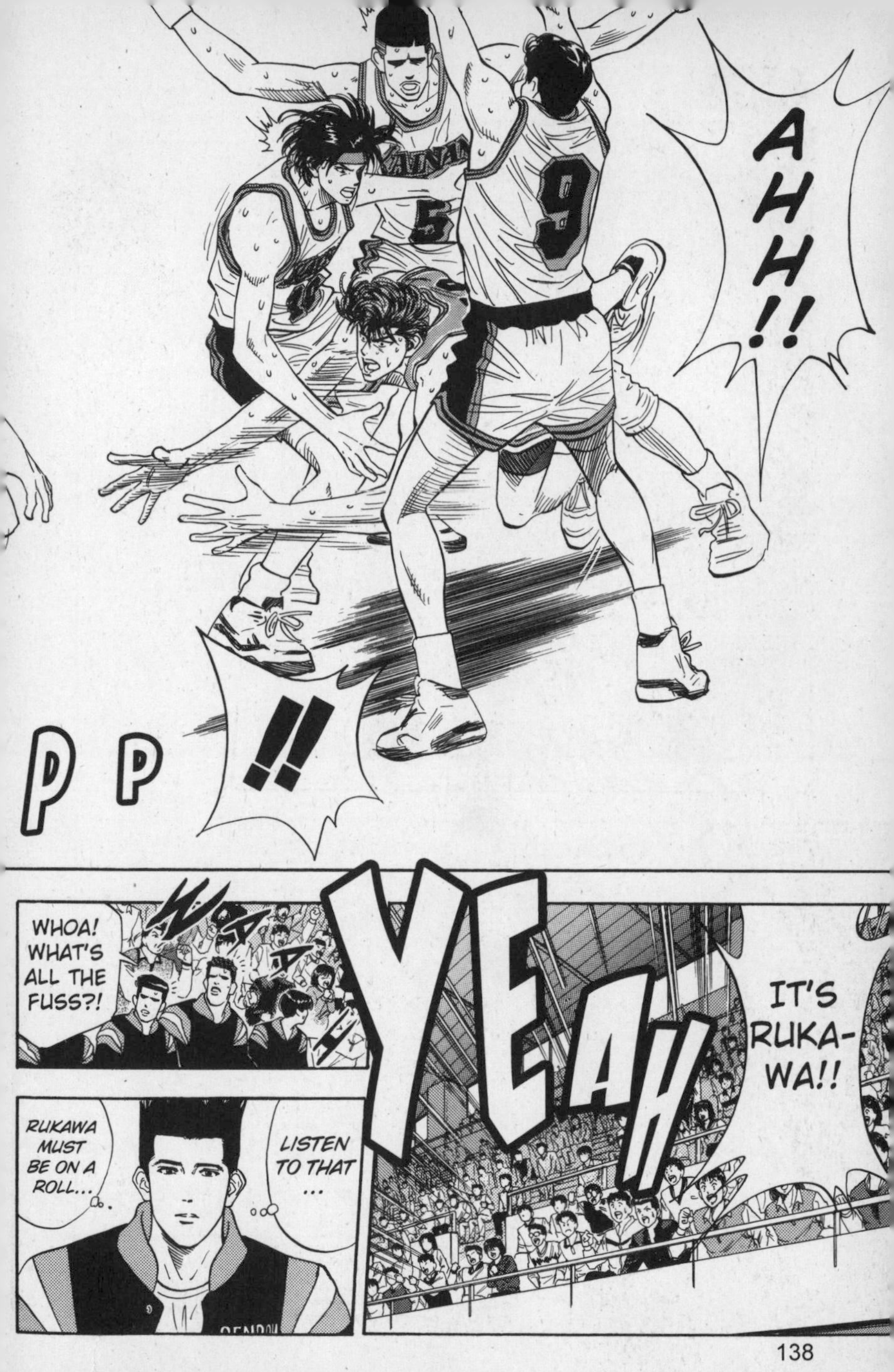
AHH!!
P P !!
YEAH
IT'S RUKAWA!!
WHOA! WHAT'S ALL THE FUSS?!
LISTEN TO THAT ...
RUKAWA MUST BE ON A ROLL...

READ THIS WAY

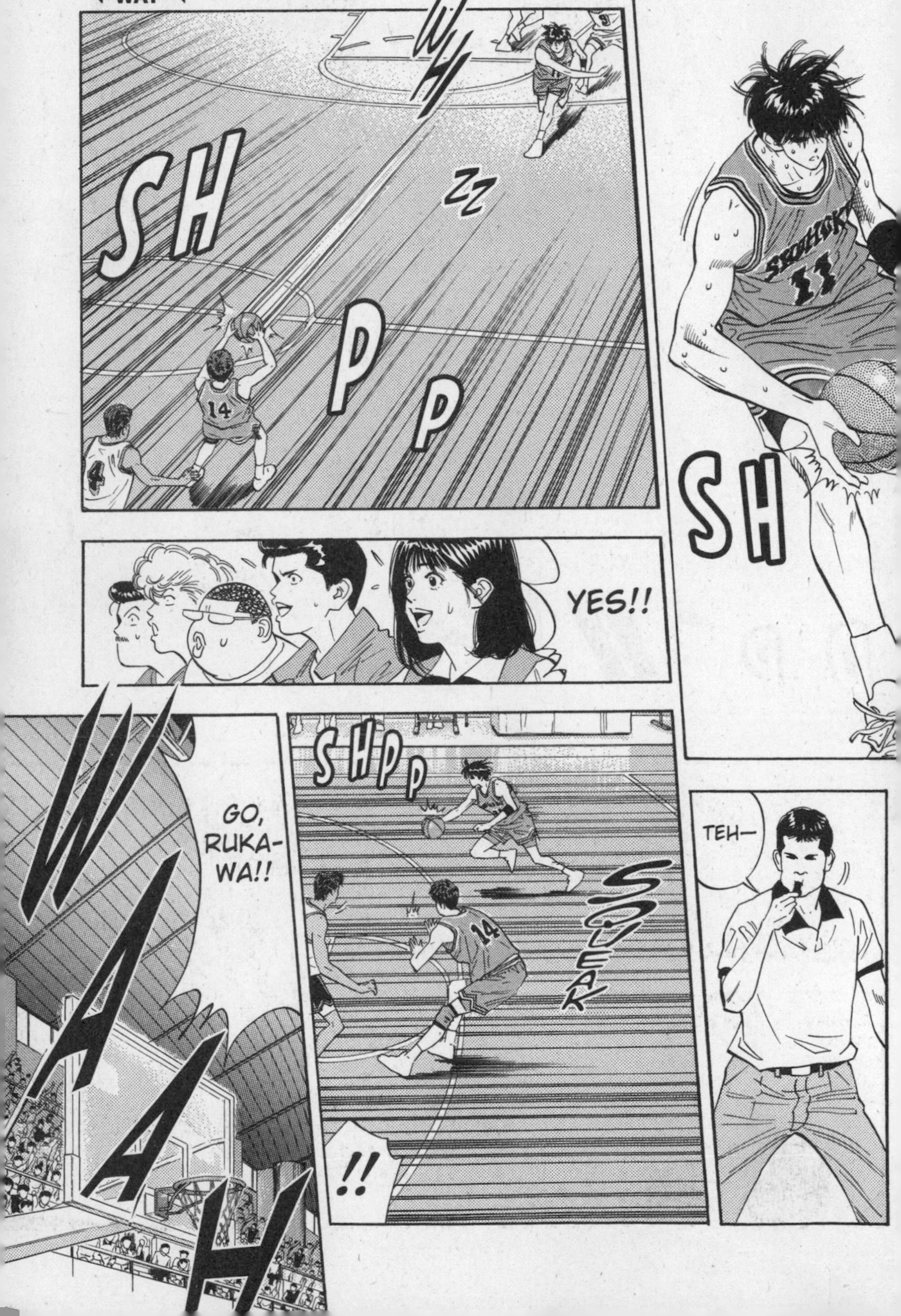
SH
WH
SH
ZZ
P
P
YES!!
TEH—
SHPP
SQUEAK
!!
GO, RUKAWA!!
WAAH

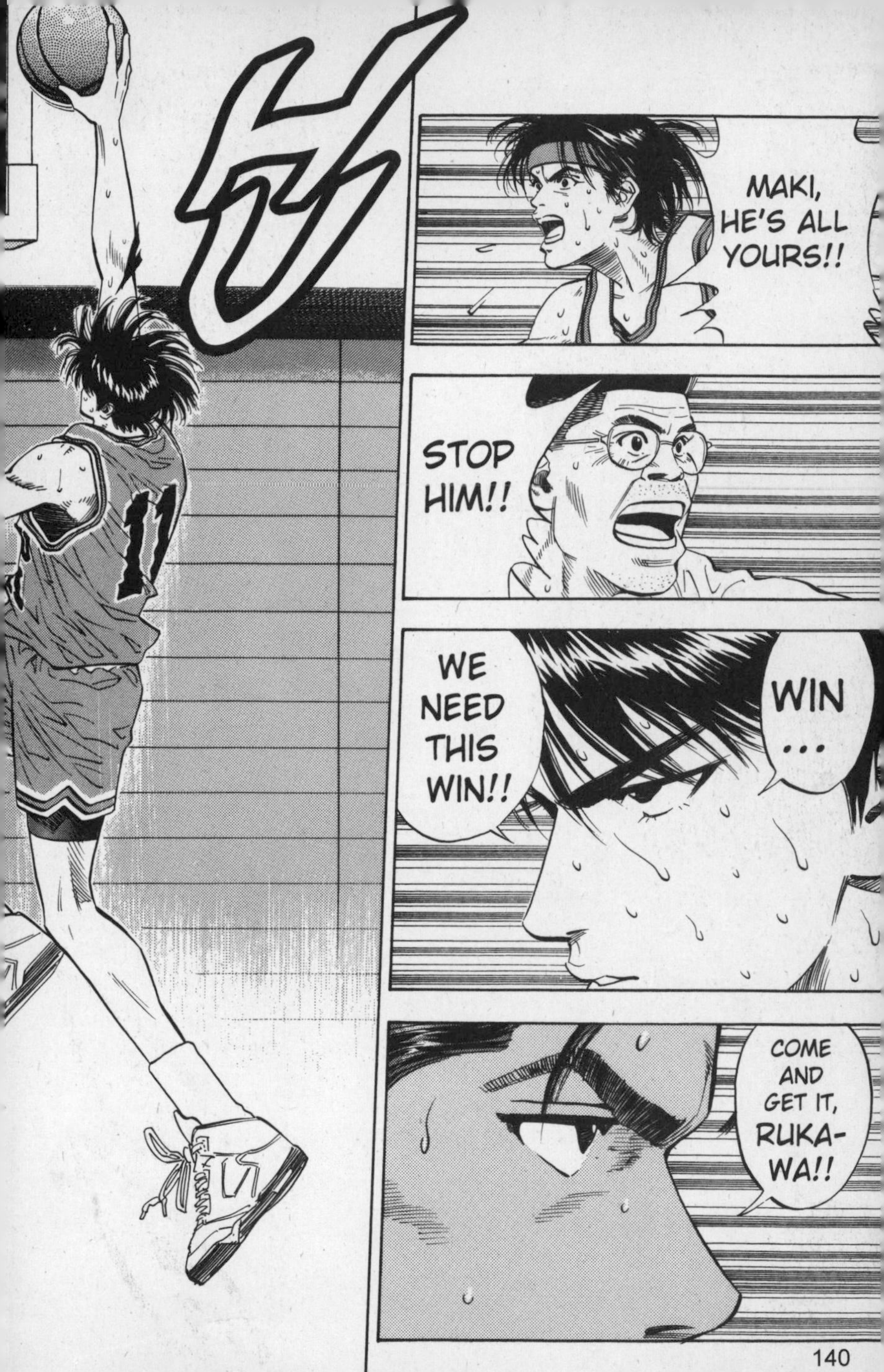
MAKI, HE'S ALL YOURS!!
STOP HIM!!
WIN...
WE NEED THIS WIN!!
COME AND GET IT, RUKA-WA!!

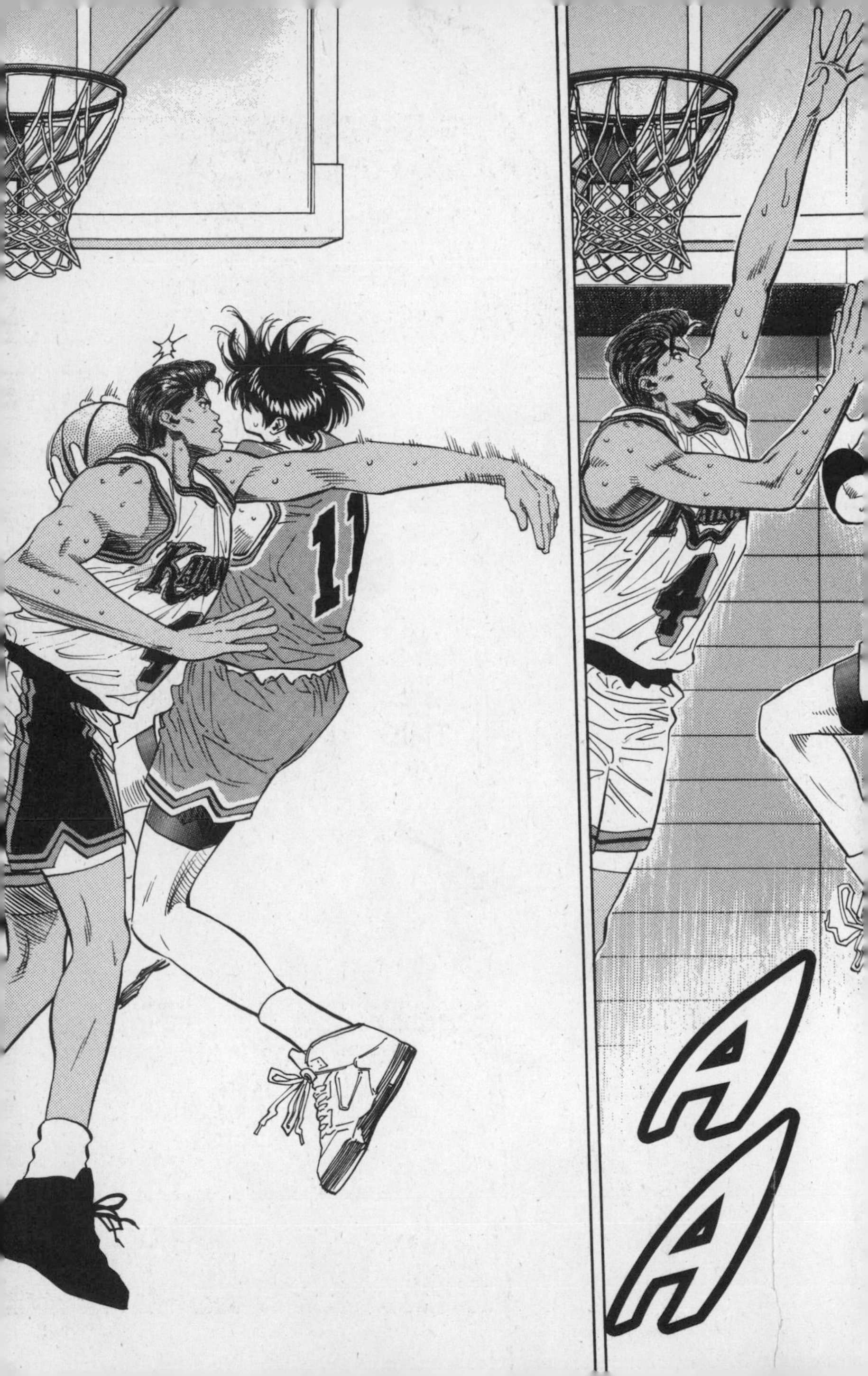
AA

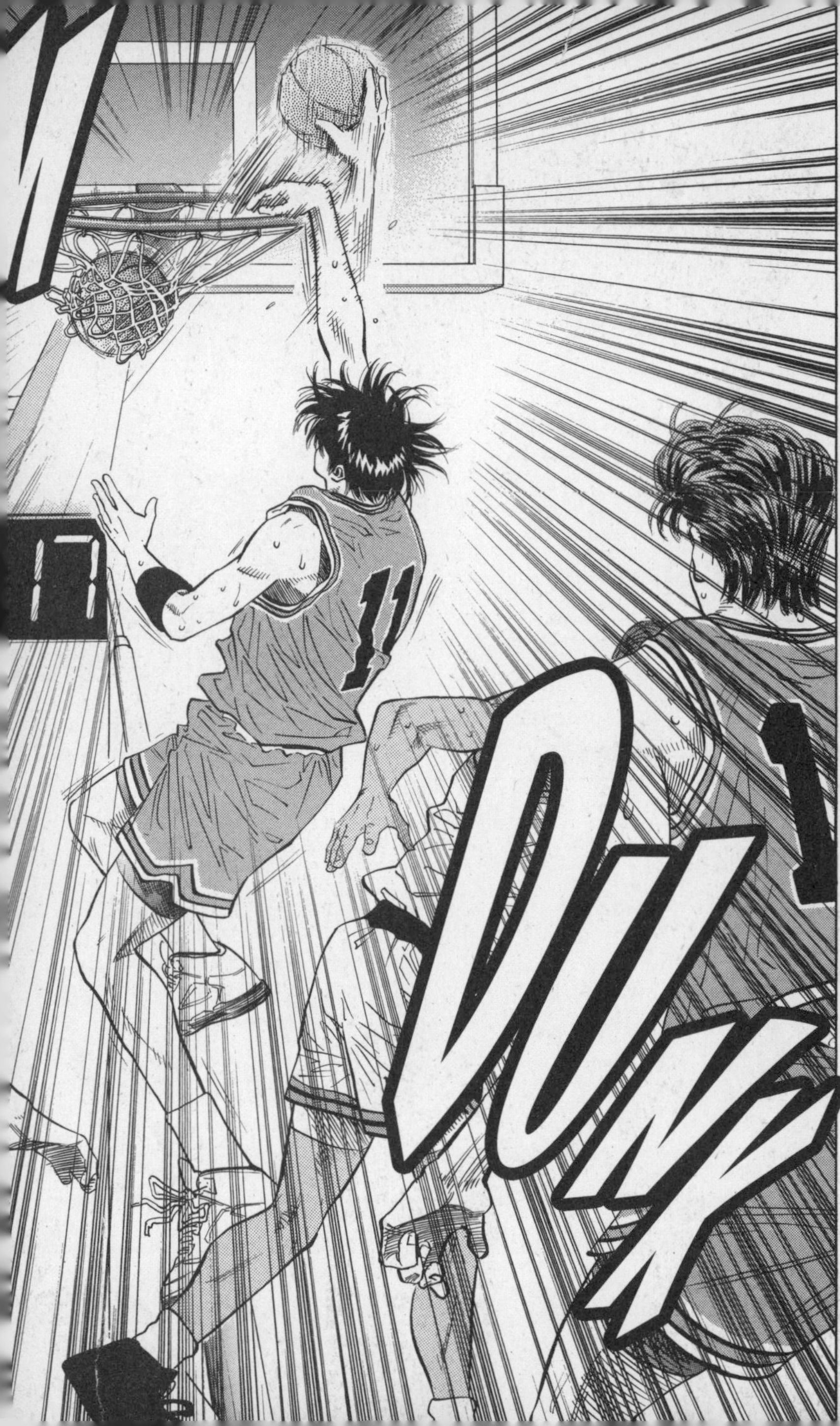
DUNK

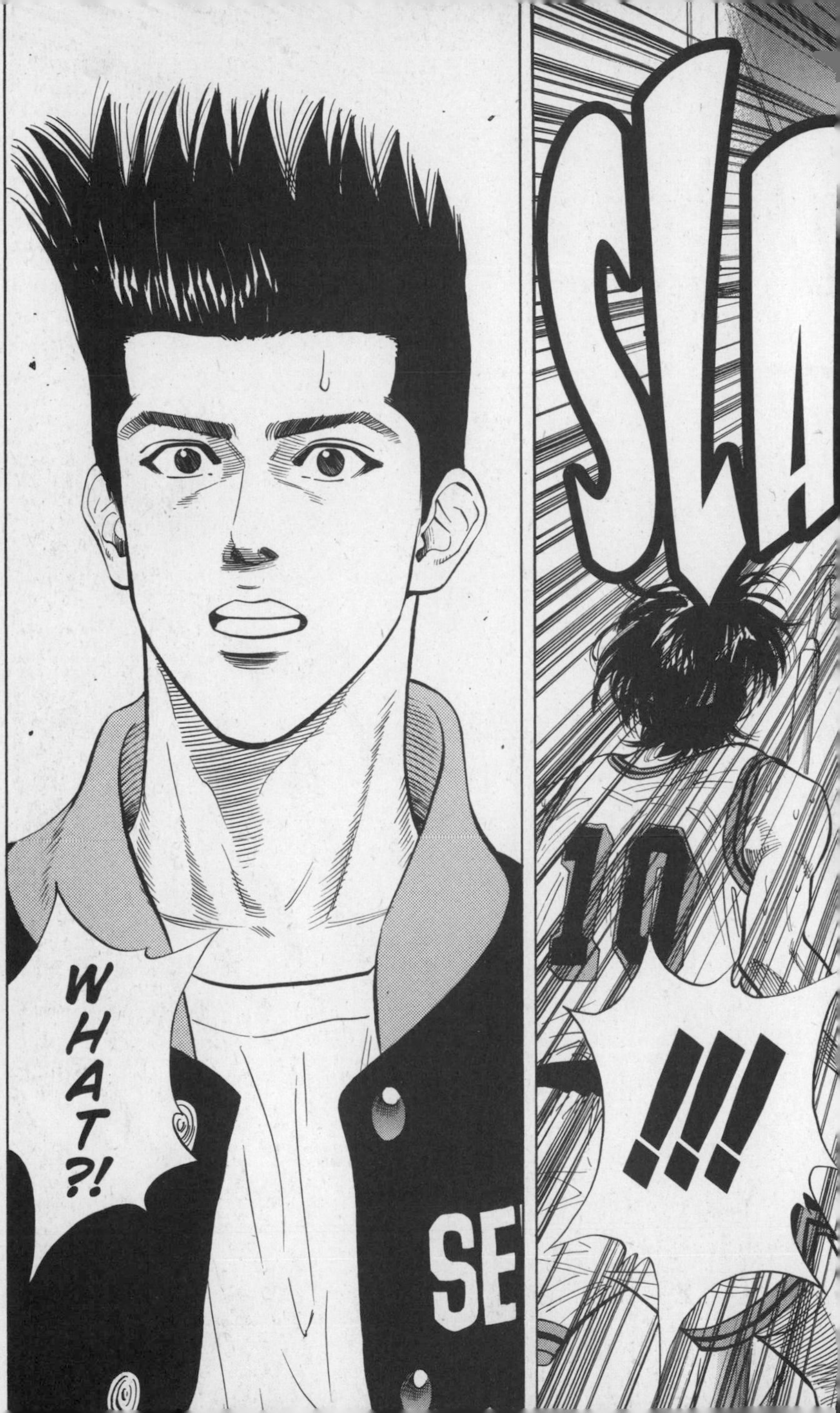
SLA
!!!
WHAT?!
SE

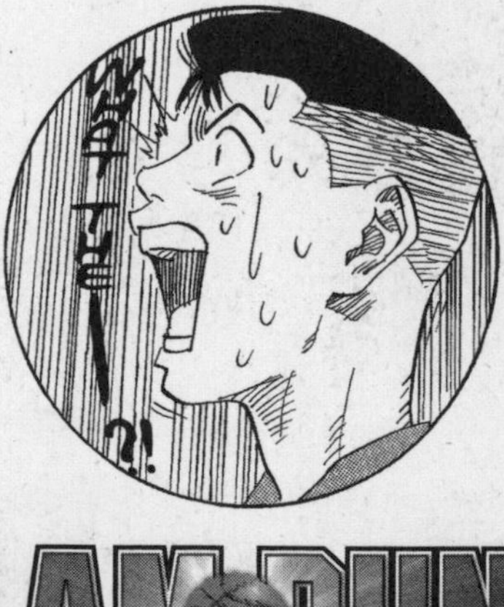

SLAM DUNK

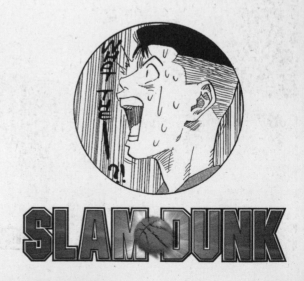

READ THIS WAY

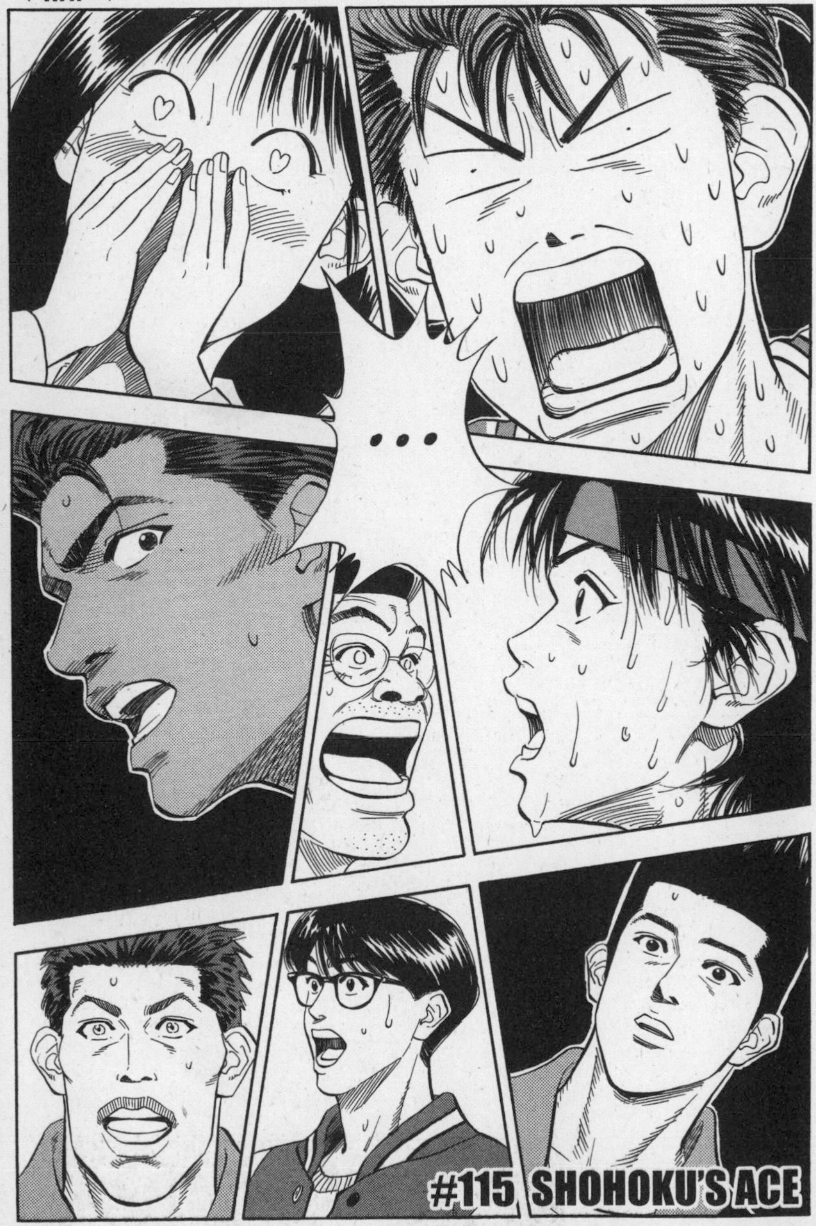
...
#115 SHOHOKU'S ACE

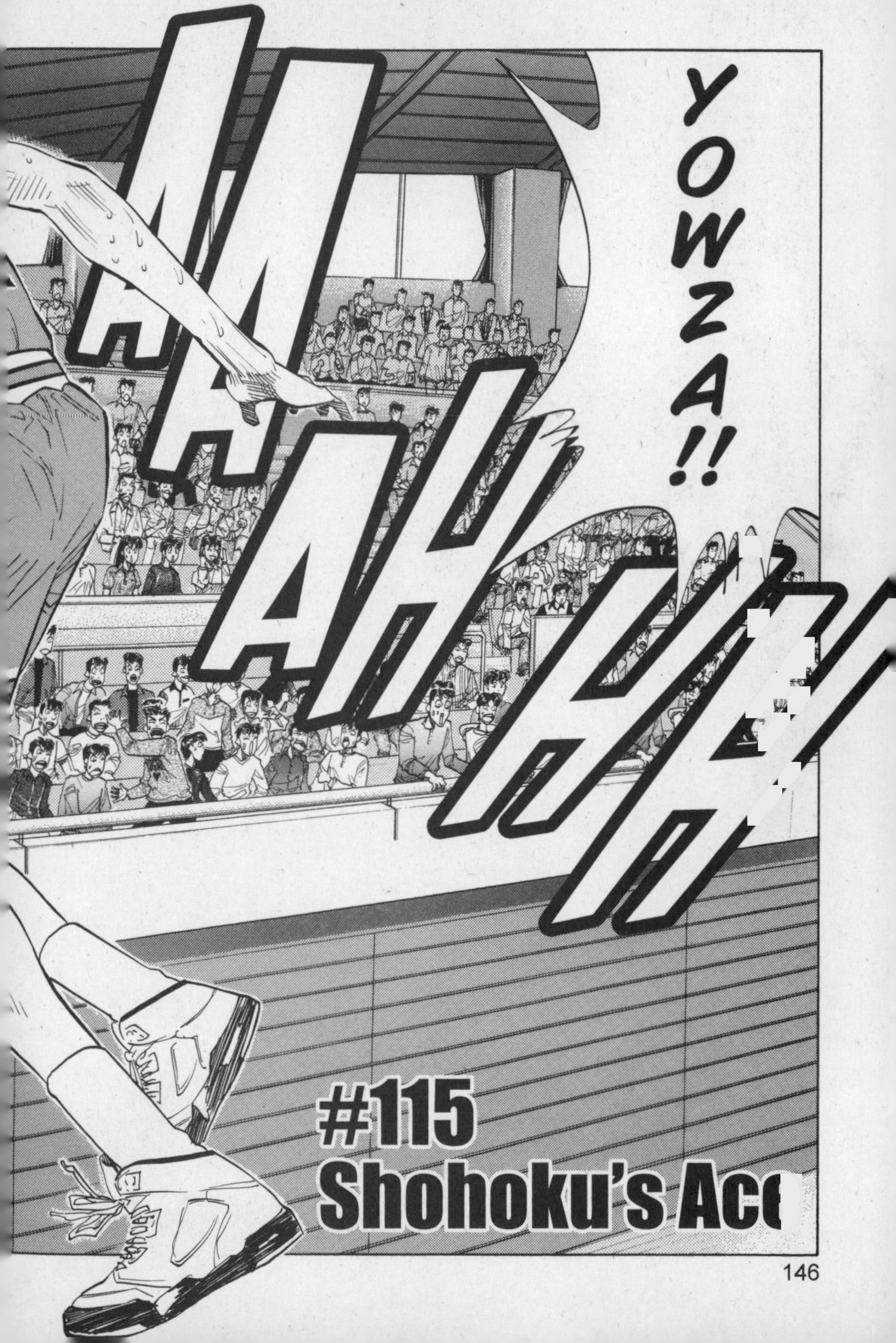
YOWZA!!

#115 Shohoku's Ace

READ THIS WAY

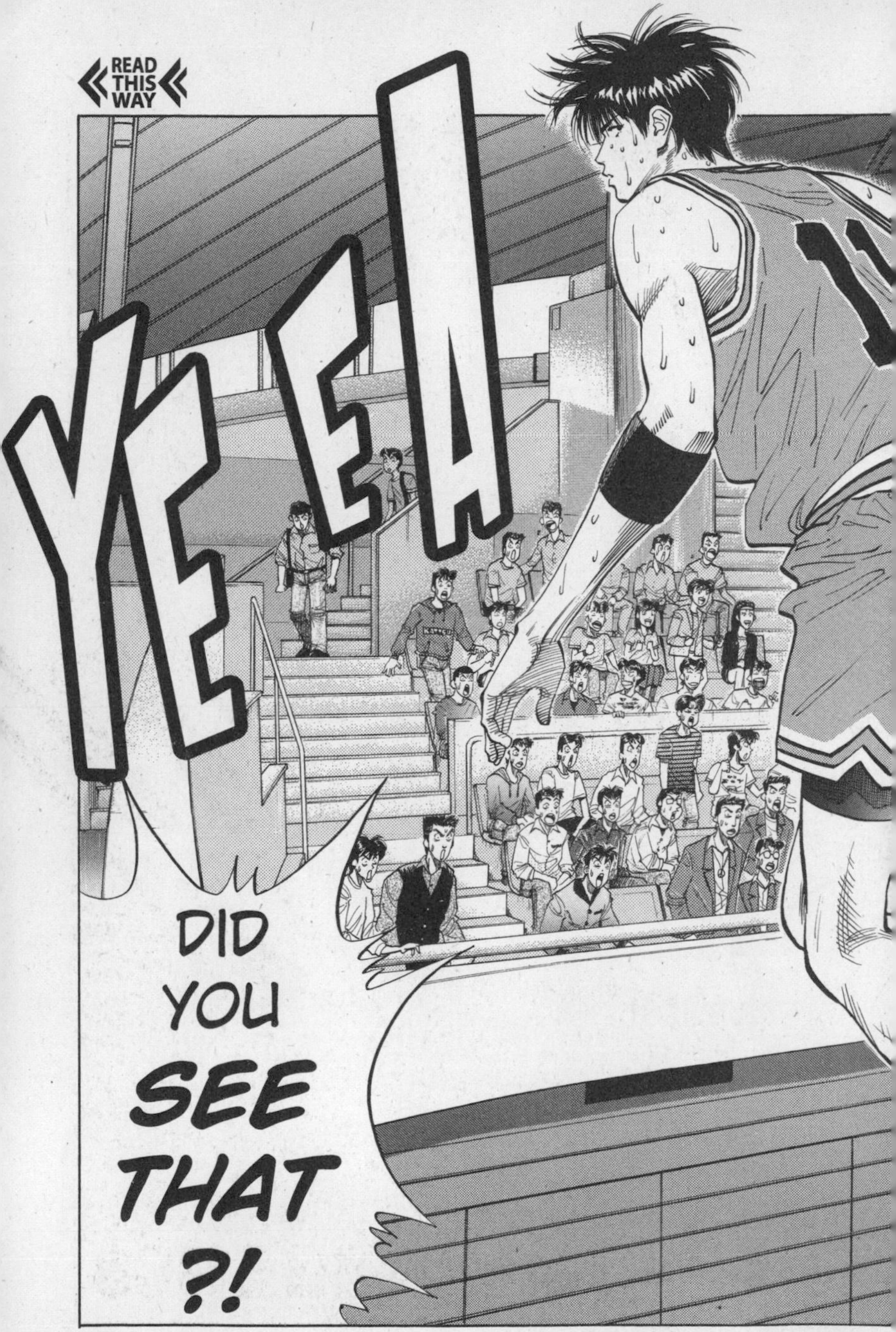
YEA
DID YOU SEE THAT?!

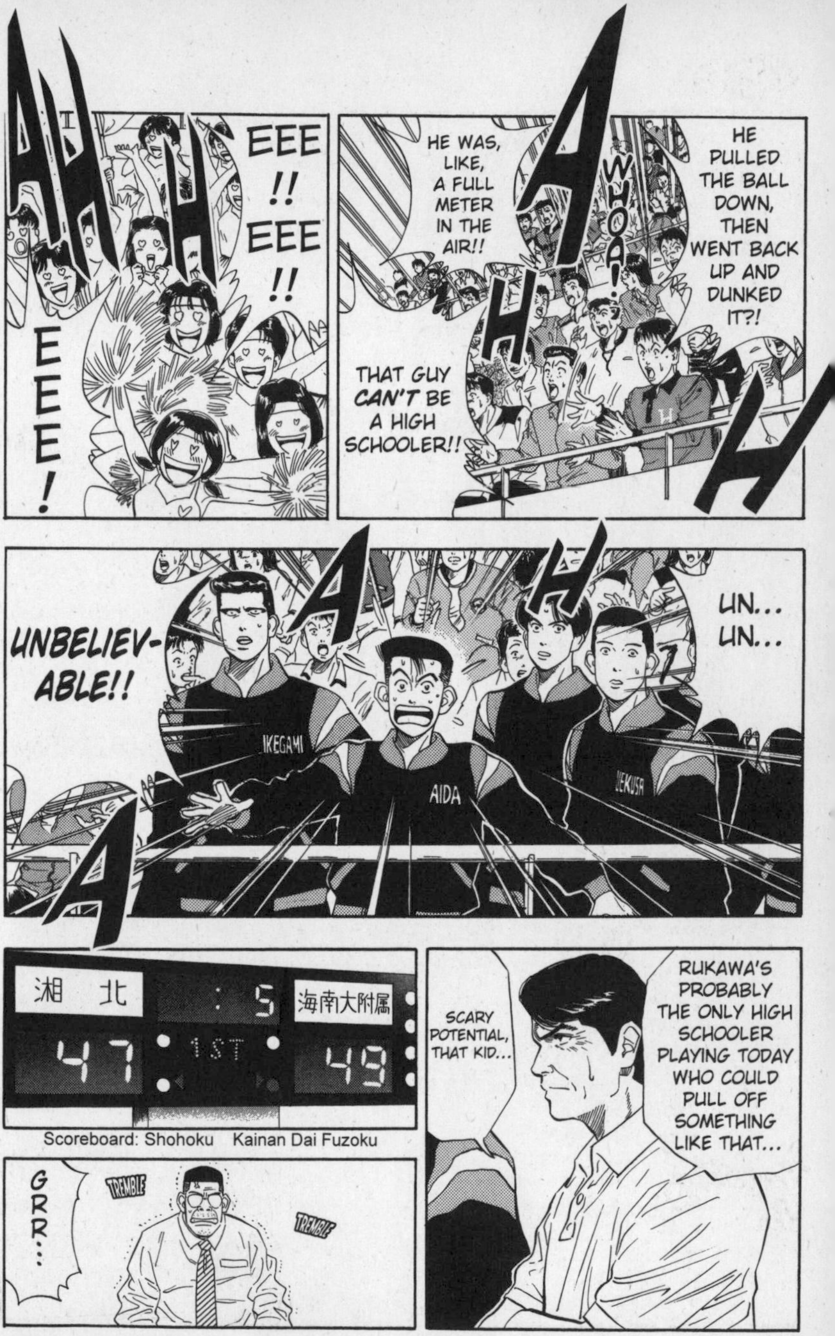
HE PULLED THE BALL DOWN, THEN WENT BACK UP AND DUNKED IT?!
WHOA!
AHH
HE WAS, LIKE, A FULL METER IN THE AIR!!
THAT GUY CAN'T BE A HIGH SCHOOLER!!
AHH
EEE!! EEE!!
EEEE!
UN... UN...
AHH
UNBELIEV-ABLE!!
A
RUKAWA'S PROBABLY THE ONLY HIGH SCHOOLER PLAYING TODAY WHO COULD PULL OFF SOMETHING LIKE THAT...
SCARY POTENTIAL, THAT KID...
湘北
5
海南大附属
47
1ST
49
Scoreboard: Shohoku Kainan Dai Fuzoku
GRR...
TREMBLE
TREMBLE

READ THIS WAY

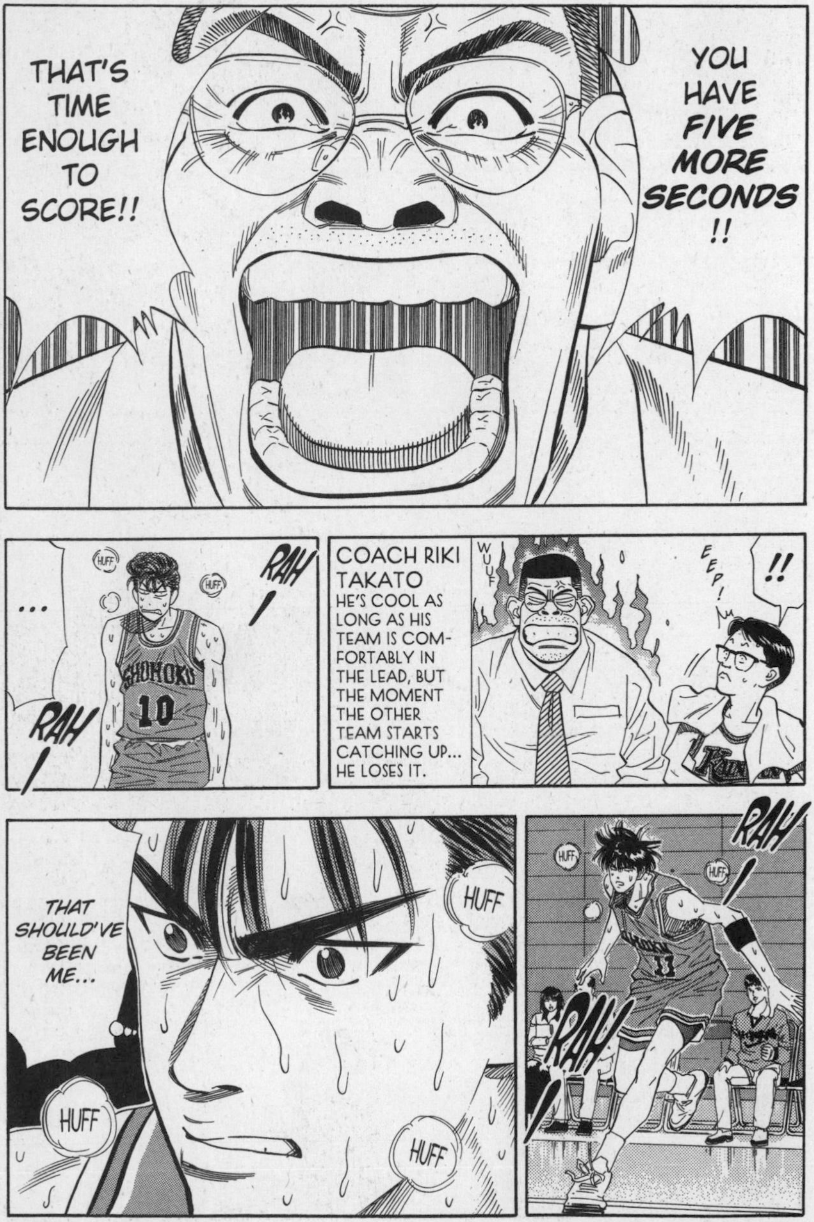

YOU HAVE FIVE MORE SECONDS!!
THAT'S TIME ENOUGH TO SCORE!!
!!
EEP!
WUUF
COACH RIKI TAKATO
HE'S COOL AS LONG AS HIS TEAM IS COMFORTABLY IN THE LEAD, BUT THE MOMENT THE OTHER TEAM STARTS CATCHING UP... HE LOSES IT.
RAH!
...
HUFF
HUFF
RAH!
RAH!
HUFF
HUFF
RAH!
HUFF
THAT SHOULD'VE BEEN ME...
HUFF
HUFF

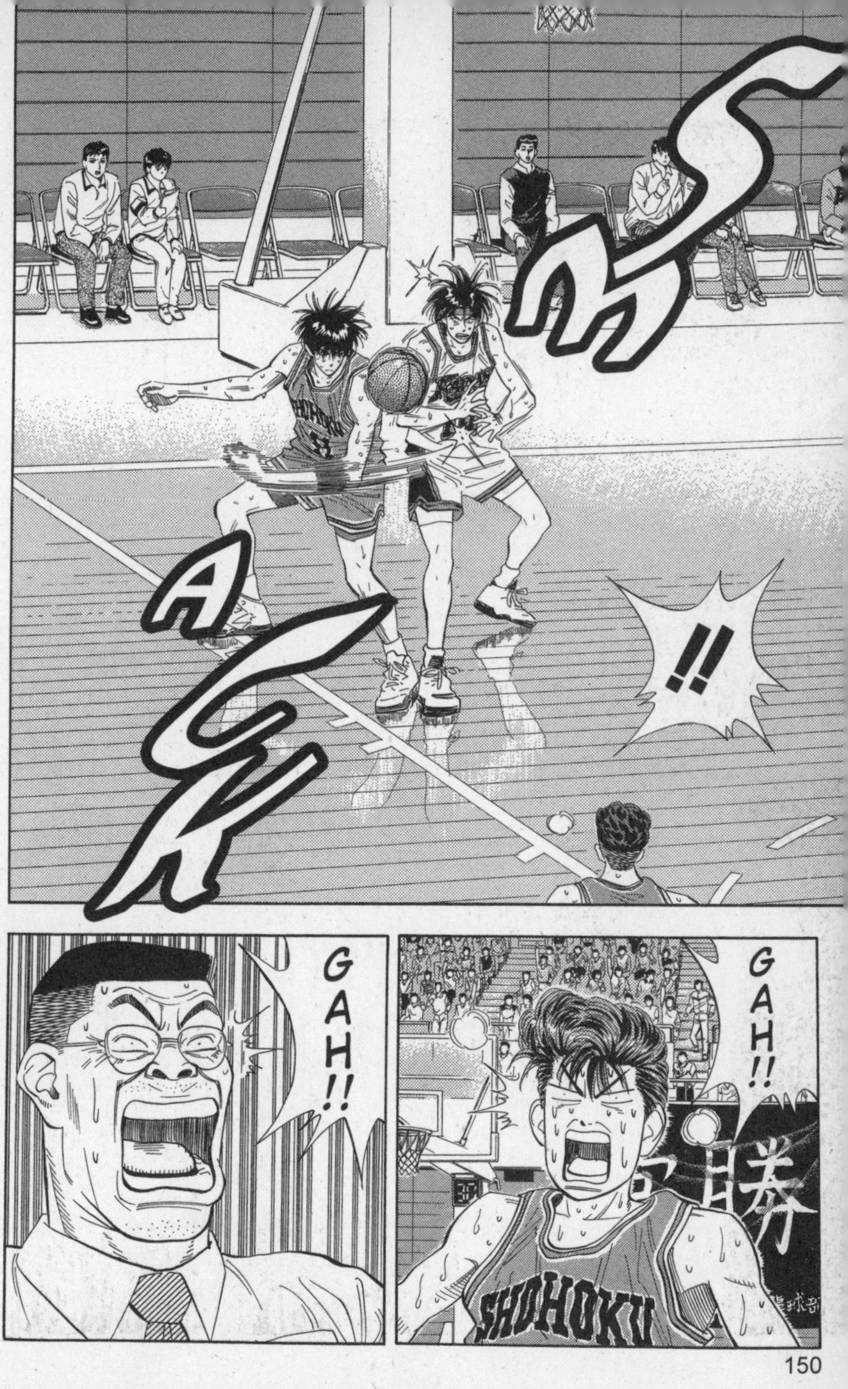
SMACK
!!
GAH!!
GAH!!

READ THIS WAY

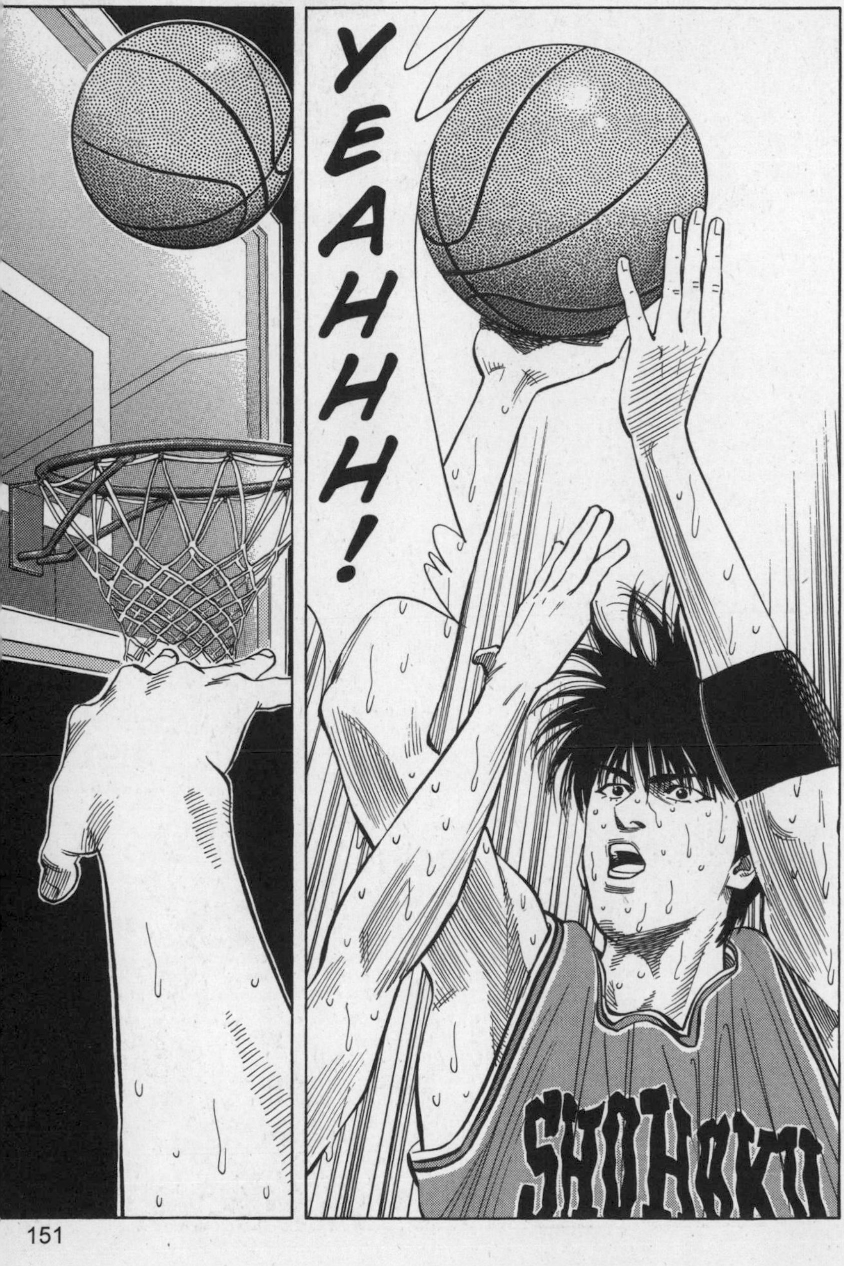
YEAHHHH!
SHOHOKU

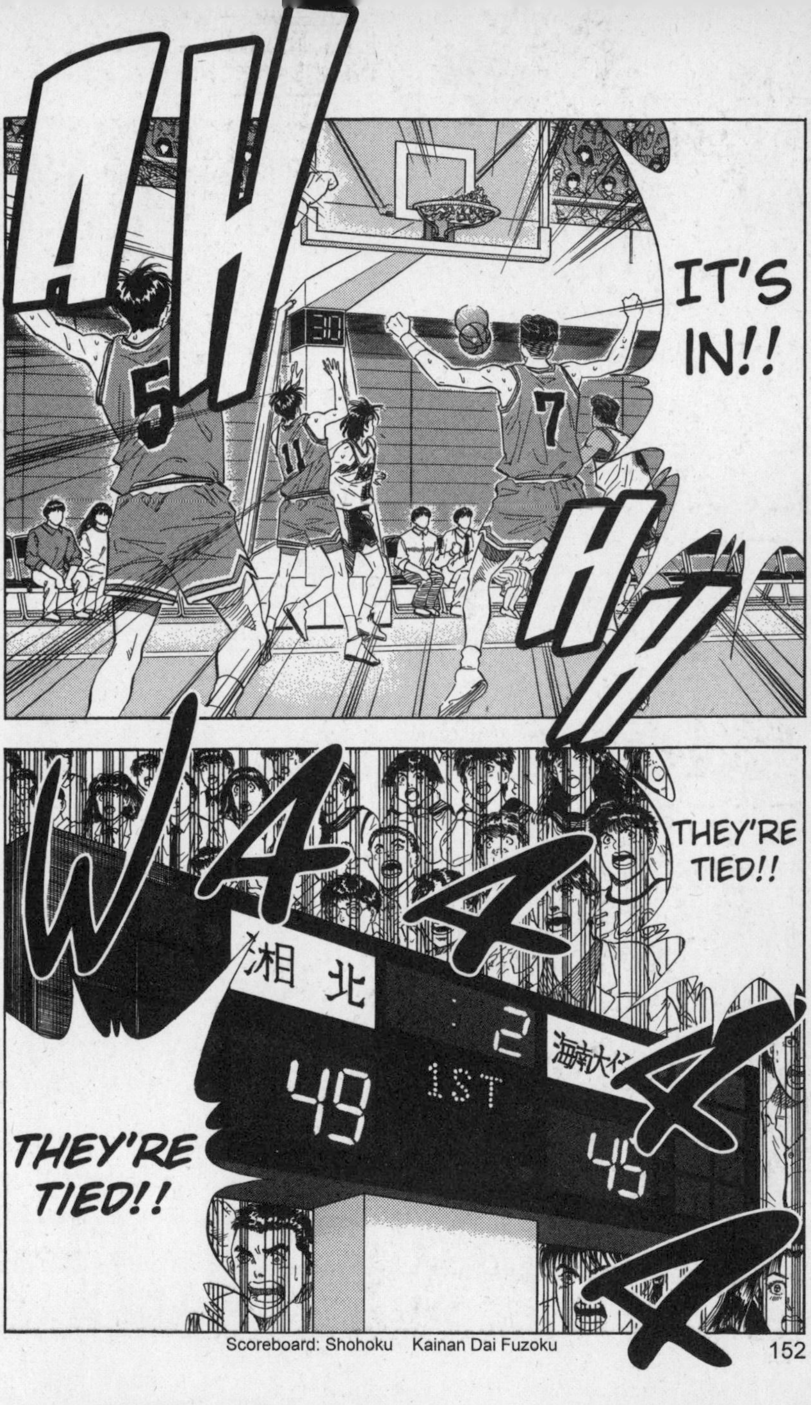
IT'S IN!!
AHHH
WAAAA
THEY'RE TIED!!
湘北
2
1ST
49
45
THEY'RE TIED!!
Scoreboard: Shohoku Kainan Dai Fuzoku

READ THIS WAY

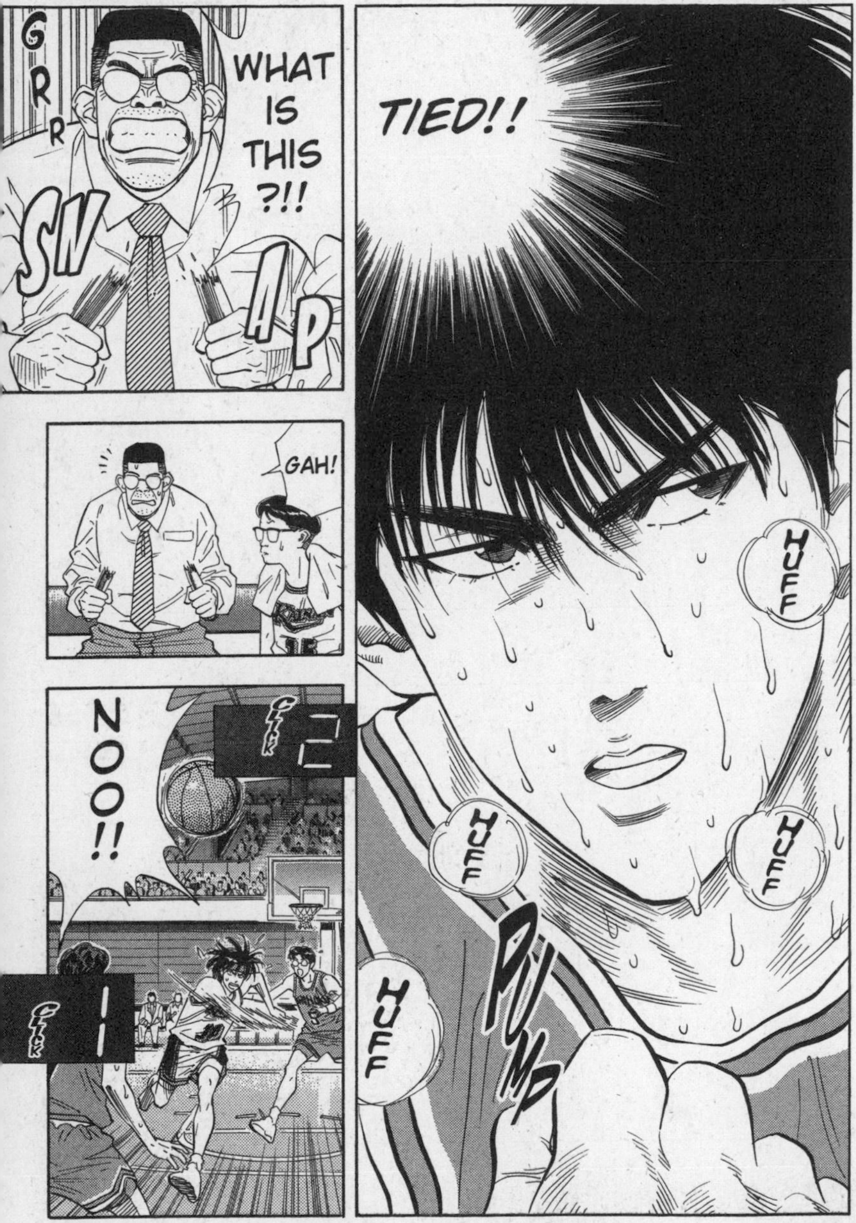
TIED!!
HUFF
HUFF
HUFF
HUFF
PUMP
WHAT IS THIS ?!!
SNAP
GRR
GAH!
2
CLICK
NOOO!!
1
CLICK

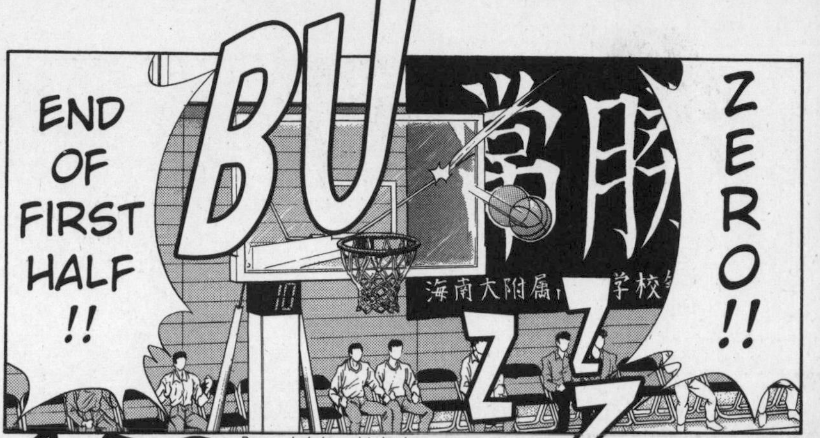
ZERO!!
BUZZZ
END OF FIRST HALF!!
海南大附属 学校

Banner: *Josho*(ever victorious)
Kainan Dai Fuzoku High School Basketball Team

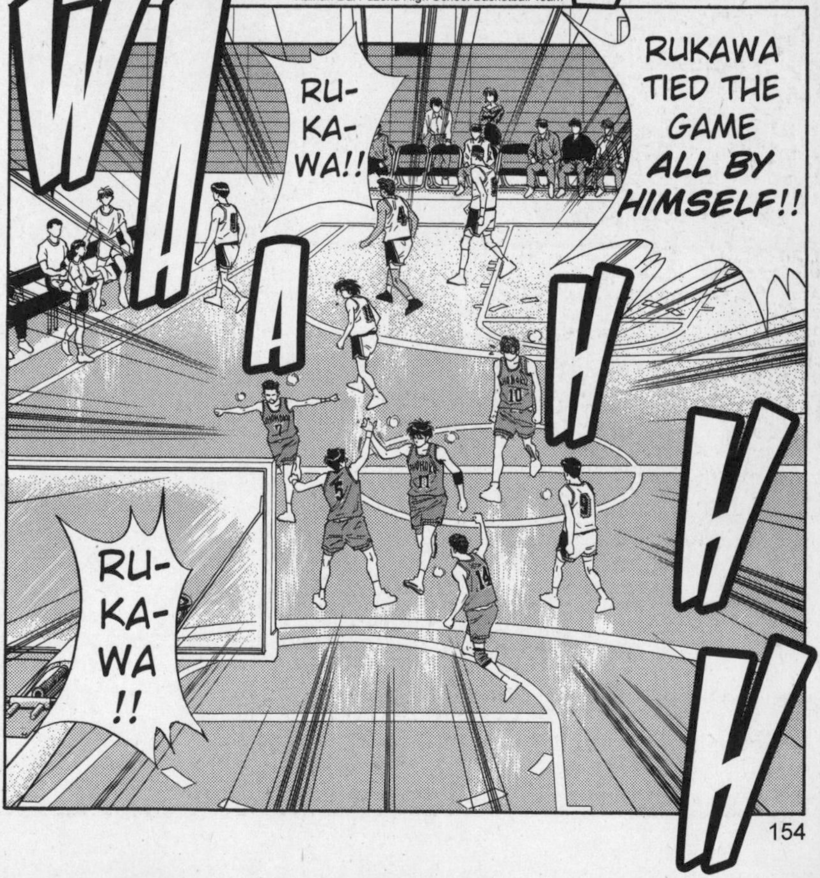
RUKAWA TIED THE GAME **ALL BY HIMSELF!!**
RU-KA-WA!!
WAAHHHH
RU-KA-WA!!

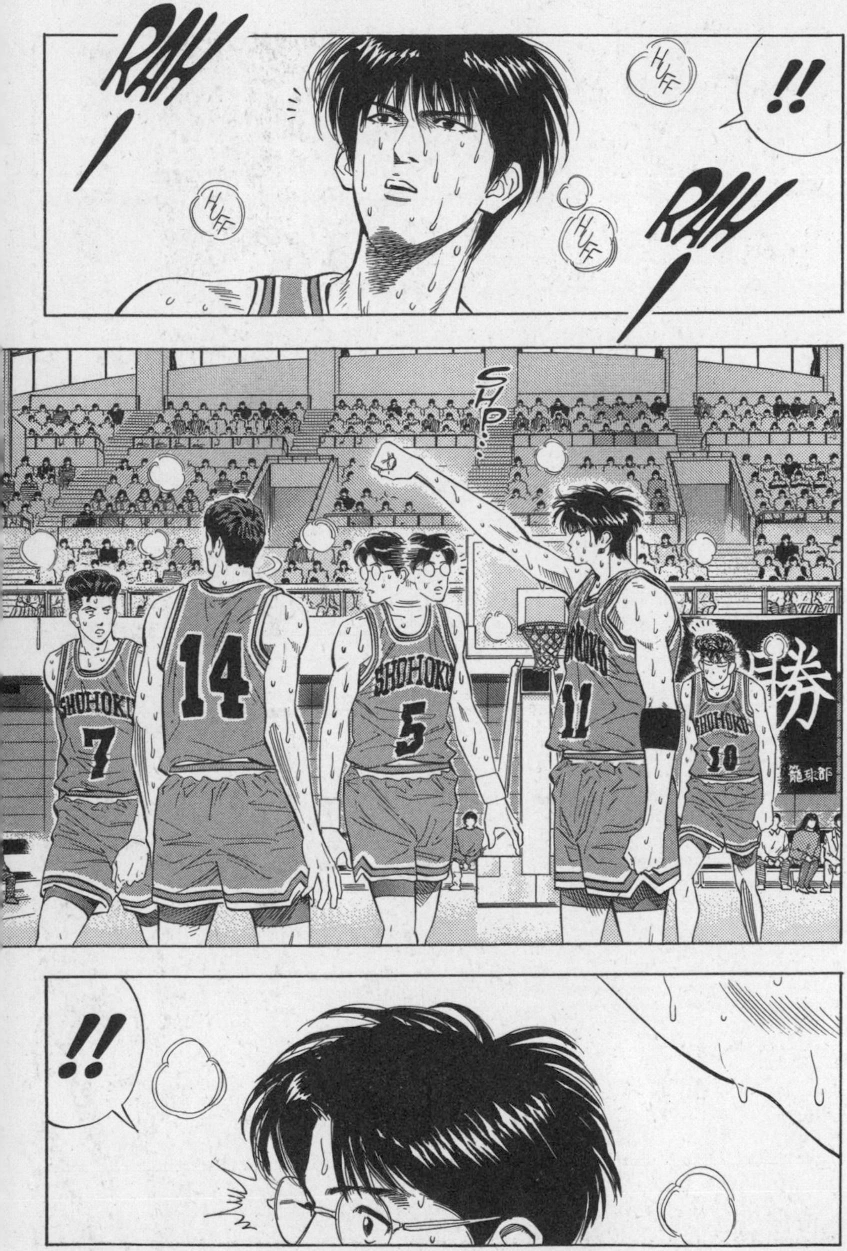
!!
HUFF
RAH!
HUFF
HUFF
RAH!
SHP...
勝
籠球部
!!

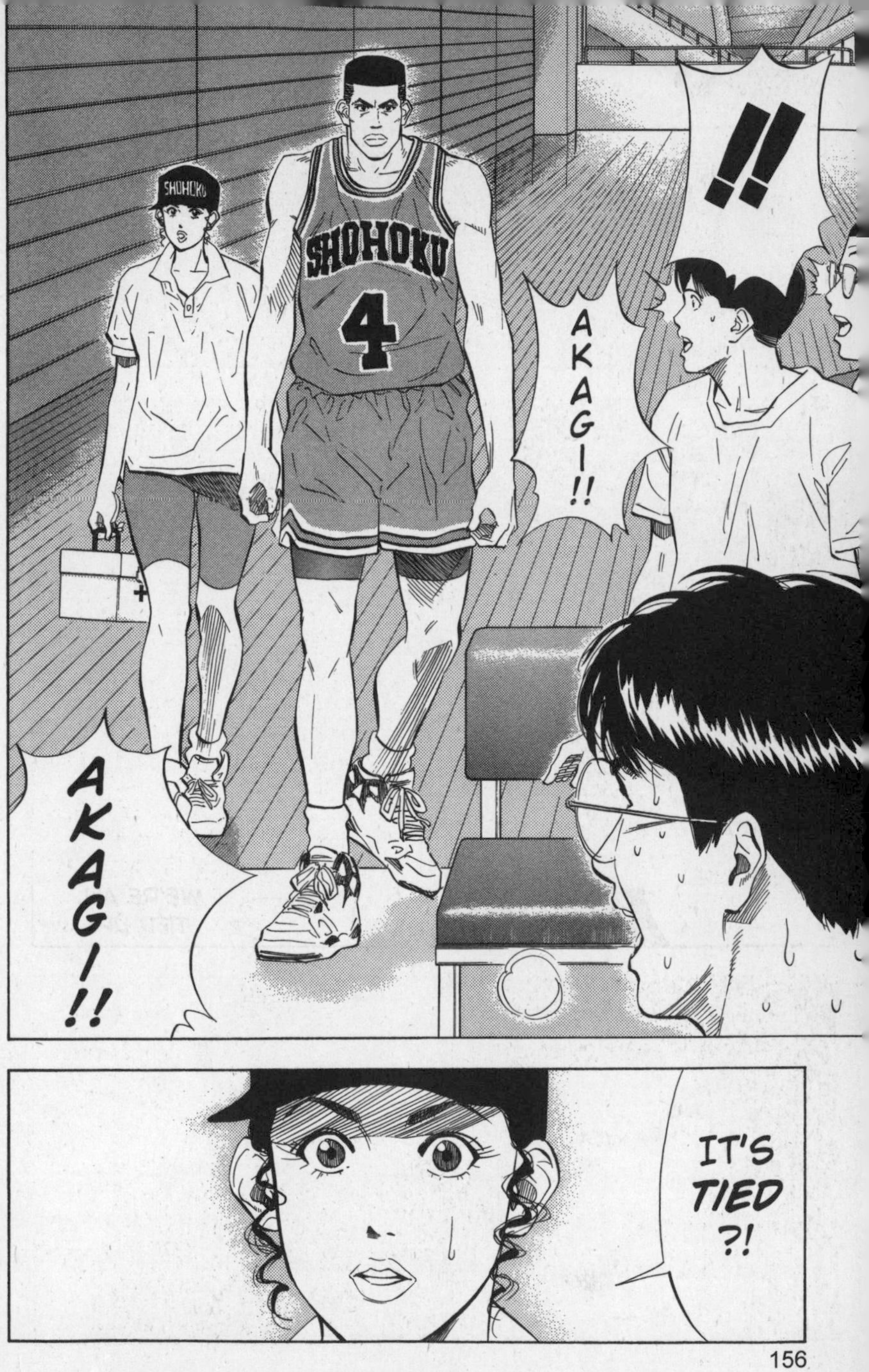
!!
AKAGI!!
AKAGI!!
IT'S TIED ?!

READ THIS WAY

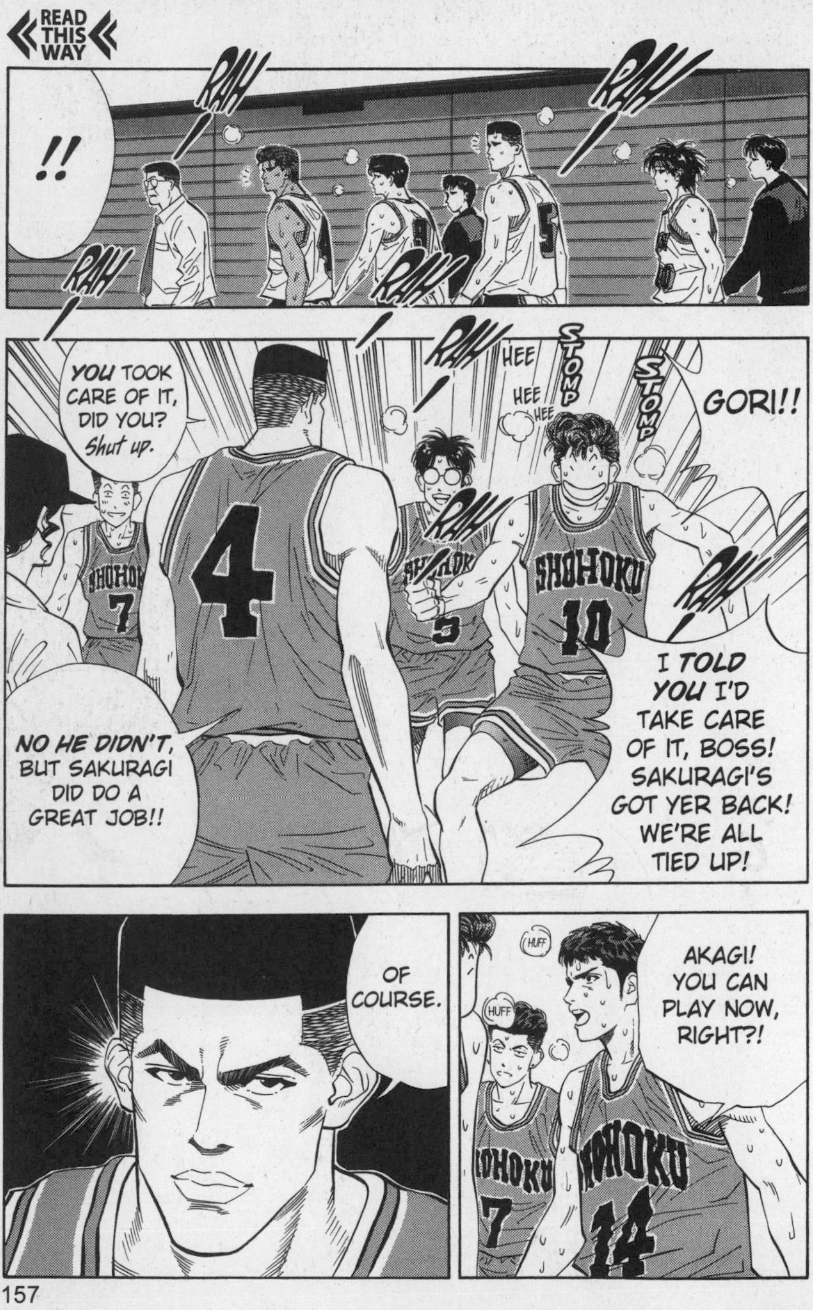
RAH
RAH
!!
RAH
RAH
GORI!!
STOMP
STOMP
HEE
HEE
HEE
RAH
RAH
RAH
I TOLD YOU I'D TAKE CARE OF IT, BOSS! SAKURAGI'S GOT YER BACK! WE'RE ALL TIED UP!
YOU TOOK CARE OF IT, DID YOU? Shut up.
NO HE DIDN'T, BUT SAKURAGI DID DO A GREAT JOB!!
AKAGI! YOU CAN PLAY NOW, RIGHT?!
HUFF
HUFF
OF COURSE.

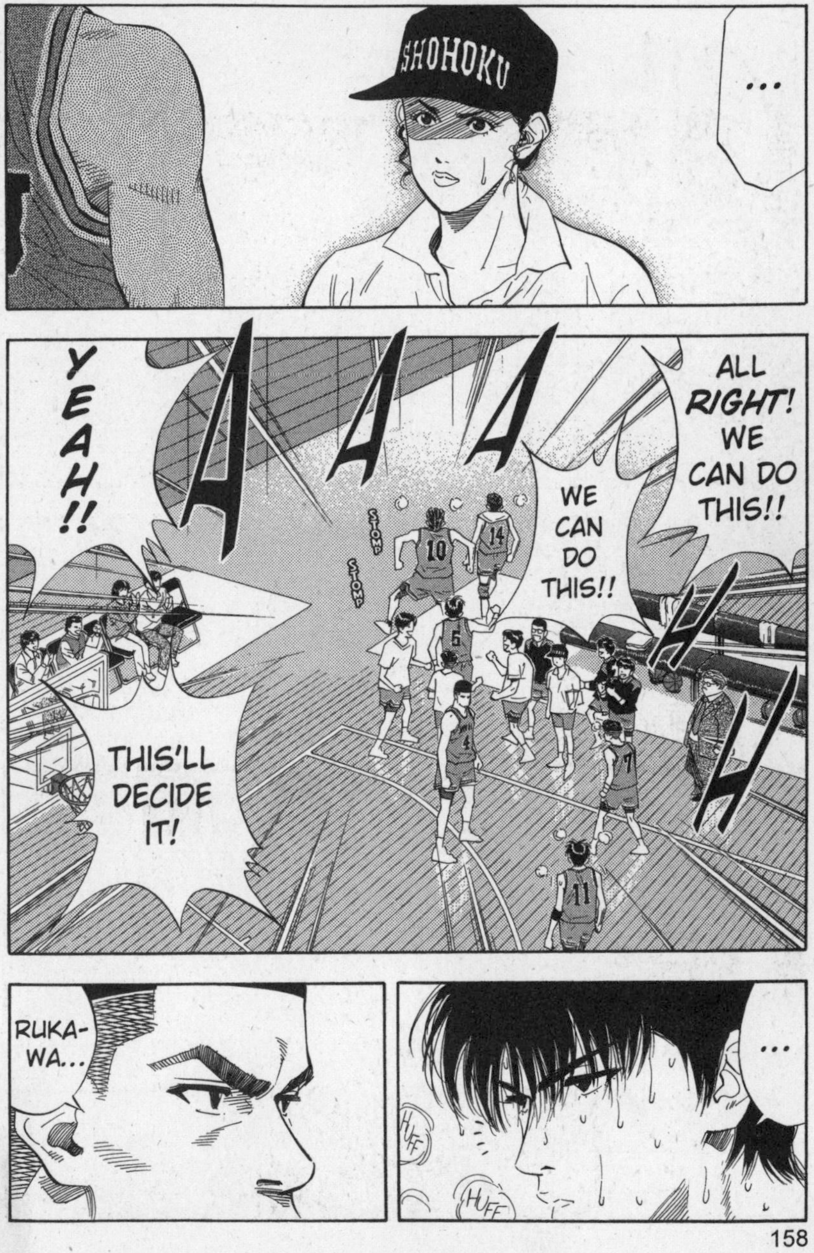
...
ALL RIGHT! WE CAN DO THIS!!
AAAHHH
WE CAN DO THIS!!
STOMP
STOMP
YEAH!!
THIS'LL DECIDE IT!
...
HUFF
HUFF
RUKA-WA...

READ THIS WAY

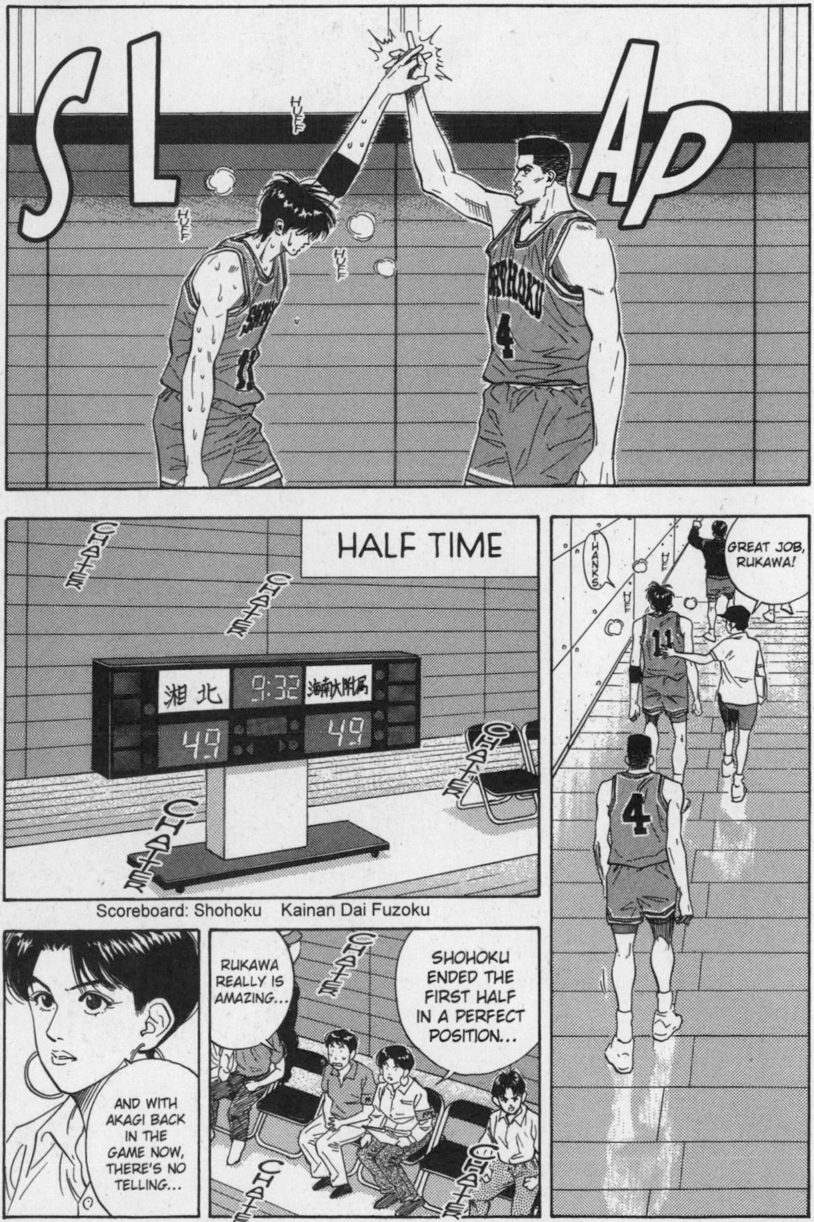
SLAP
HUFF
HUFF
HUFF
GREAT JOB, RUKAWA!
THANKS.
HUFF
HUFF
HALF TIME
CHATTER
CHATTER
CHATTER
CHATTER
湘北
9:32
海南大附属
49
49
SHOHOKU ENDED THE FIRST HALF IN A PERFECT POSITION...
RUKAWA REALLY IS AMAZING...
CHATTER
CHATTER
CHATTER
AND WITH AKAGI BACK IN THE GAME NOW, THERE'S NO TELLING...
Scoreboard: Shohoku Kainan Dai Fuzoku

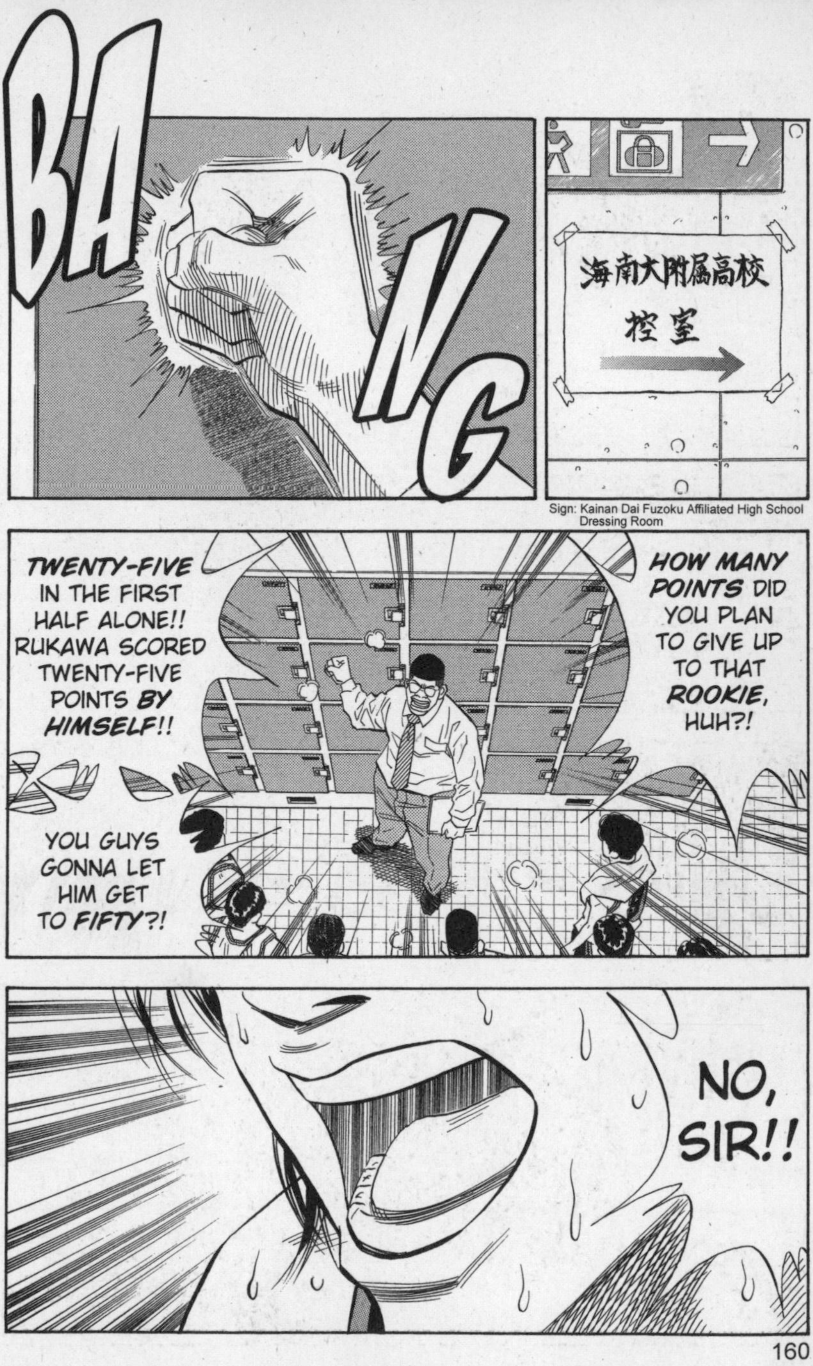
海南大附属高校
控室
Sign: Kainan Dai Fuzoku Affiliated High School Dressing Room
BANG
HOW MANY POINTS DID YOU PLAN TO GIVE UP TO THAT ROOKIE, HUH?!
TWENTY-FIVE IN THE FIRST HALF ALONE!! RUKAWA SCORED TWENTY-FIVE POINTS BY HIMSELF!!
YOU GUYS GONNA LET HIM GET TO FIFTY?!
NO, SIR!!

READ THIS WAY

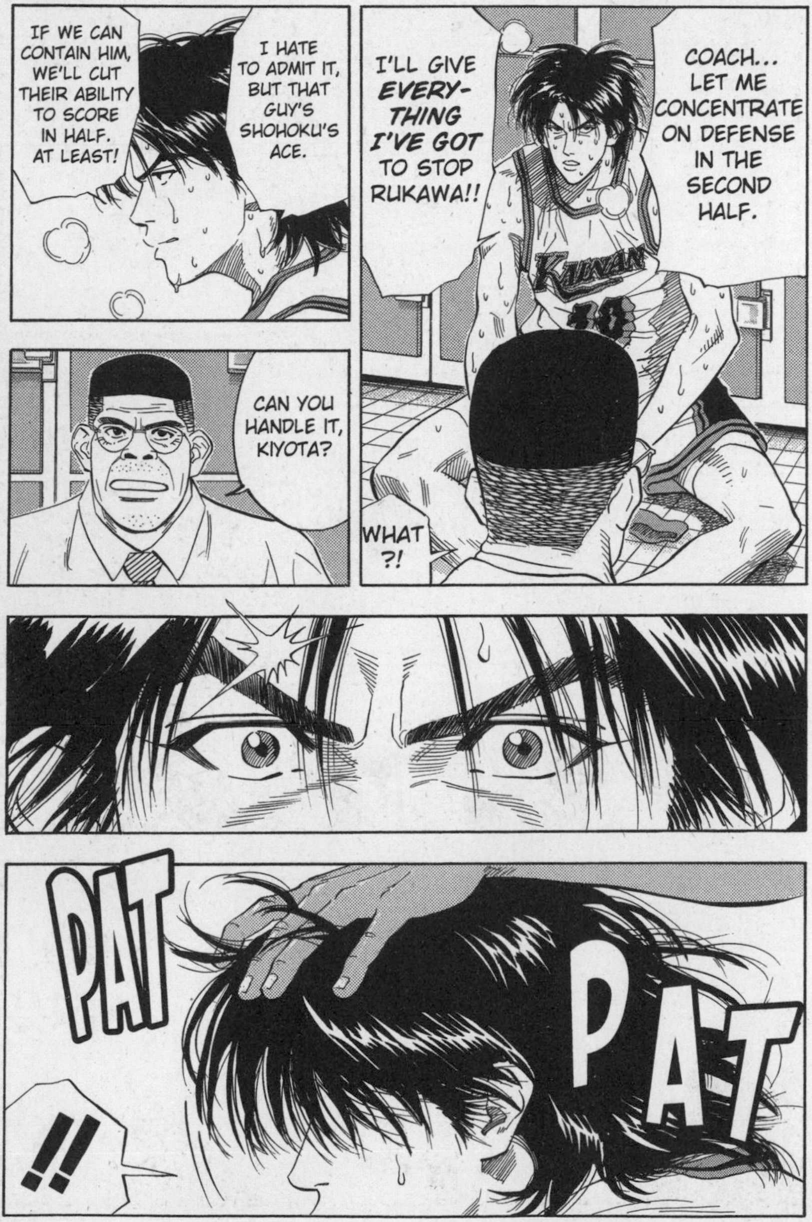
COACH... LET ME CONCENTRATE ON DEFENSE IN THE SECOND HALF.
I'LL GIVE EVERYTHING I'VE GOT TO STOP RUKAWA!!
WHAT?!
I HATE TO ADMIT IT, BUT THAT GUY'S SHOHOKU'S ACE.
IF WE CAN CONTAIN HIM, WE'LL CUT THEIR ABILITY TO SCORE IN HALF. AT LEAST!
CAN YOU HANDLE IT, KIYOTA?
PAT
PAT
!!

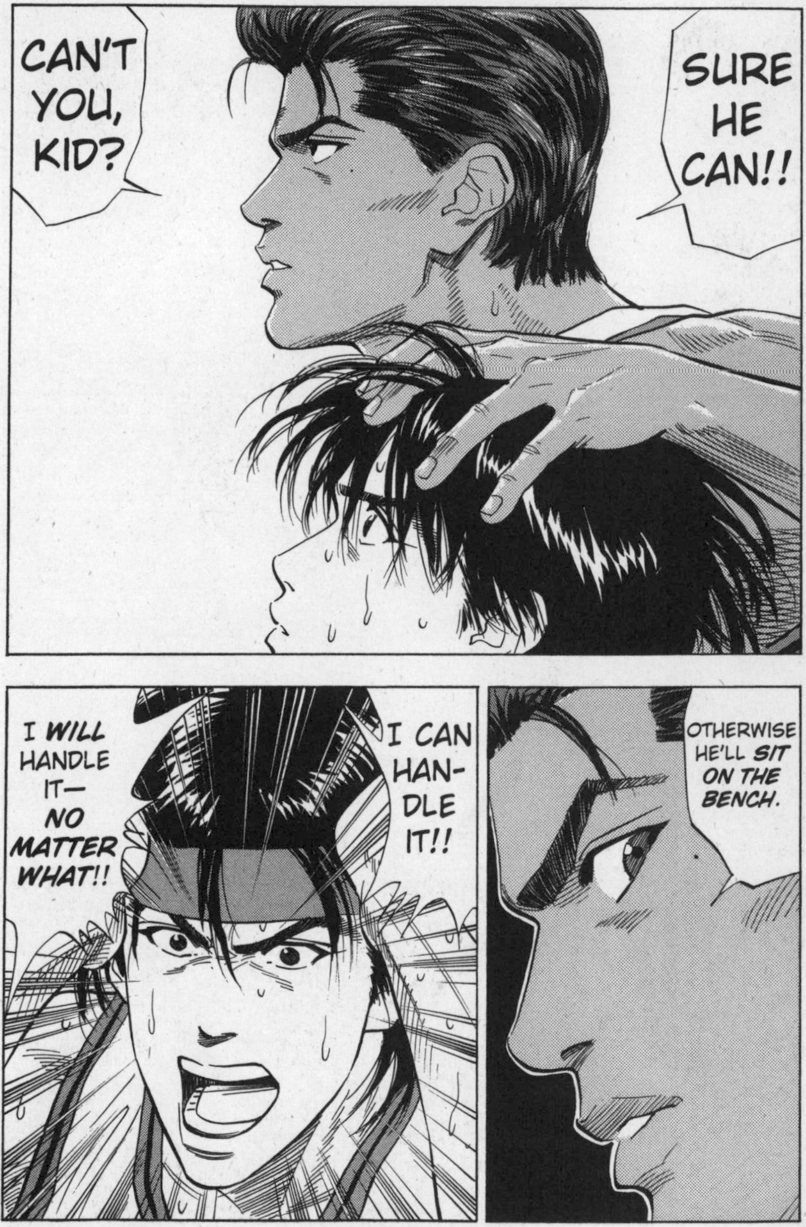
SURE HE CAN!!
CAN'T YOU, KID?
OTHERWISE HE'LL SIT ON THE BENCH.
I CAN HAN-DLE IT!!
I WILL HANDLE IT— NO MATTER WHAT!!

READ THIS WAY

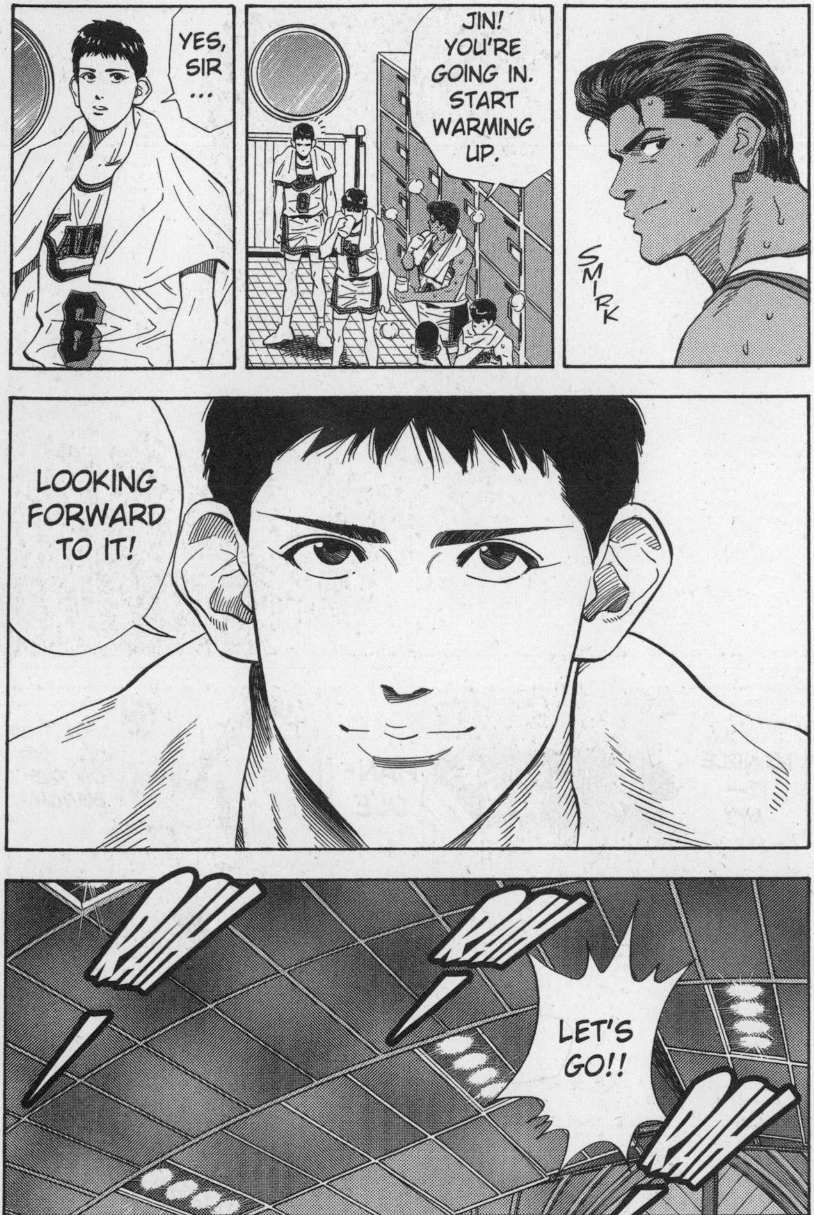

SMIRK
JIN! YOU'RE GOING IN. START WARMING UP.
YES, SIR ...
LOOKING FORWARD TO IT!
RAH
LET'S GO!!
RAH
RAH

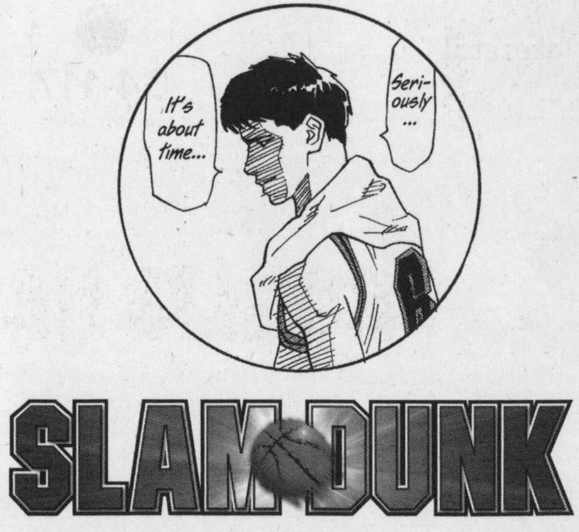
Seri-ously...
It's about time...

SLAM DUNK

#116

	Kai	Sho	Ryo	Take	Win-Losses
Kainan		☆			
Shohoku	☆				
Ryonan				◯ 117-64	1-0
Takezato			● 64-117		0-1

GORI IS BACK

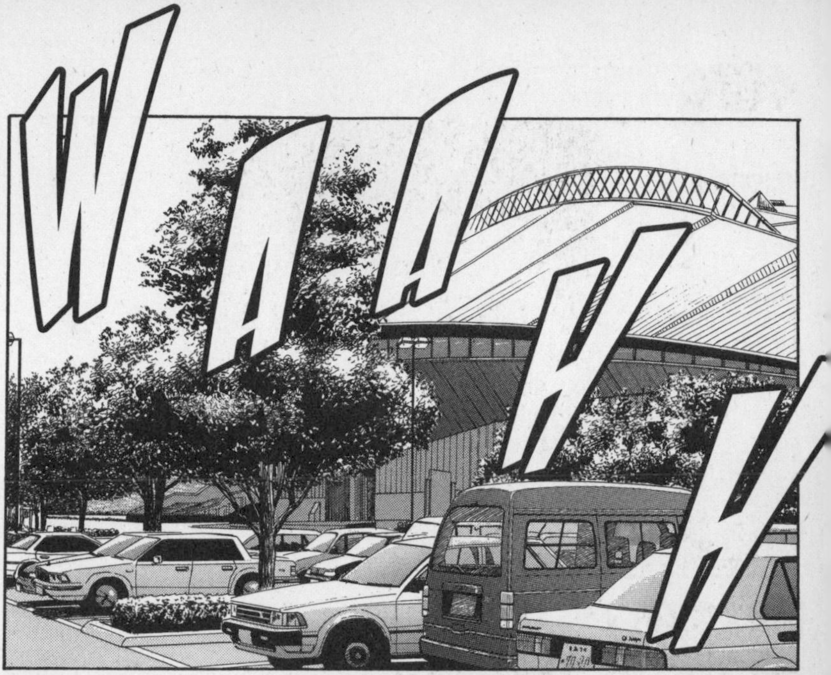
WAAHH

Scoreboard: Shohoku Kainan Dai Fuzoku

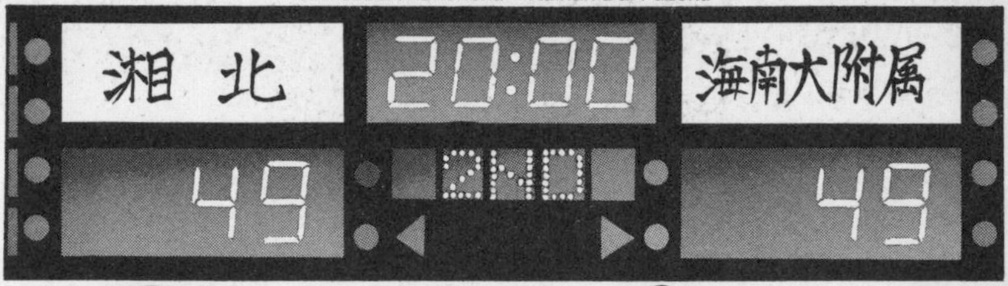
湘 北
20:00
海南大附属
49
2ND
49

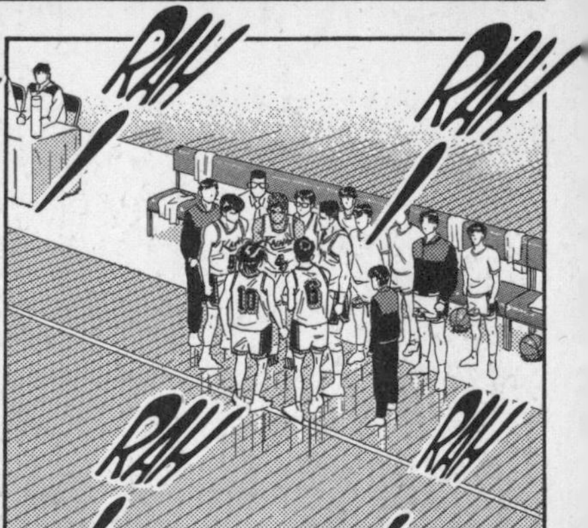
RAH!
RAH!
RAH!
RAH!

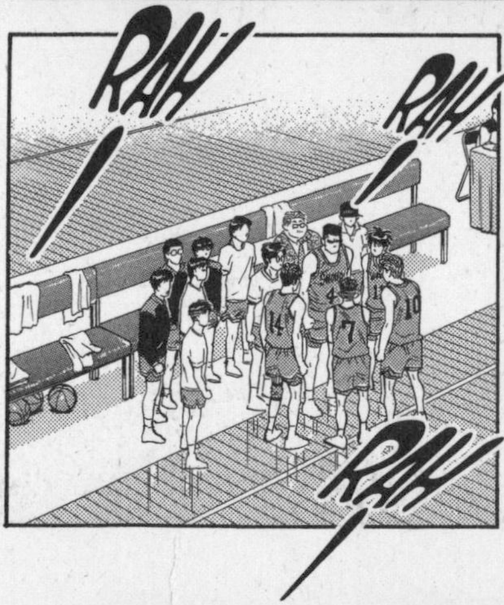
RAH!
RAH!
RAH!

READ THIS WAY

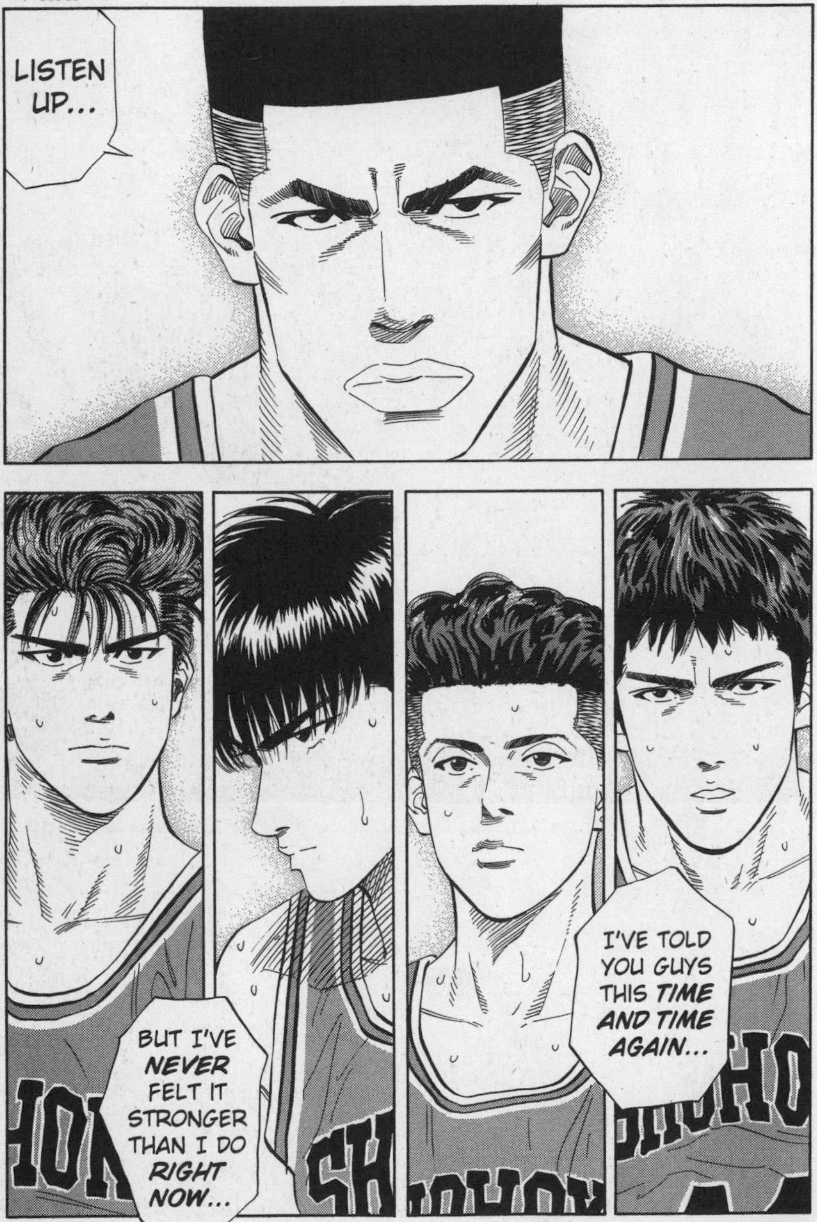
LISTEN UP...
I'VE TOLD YOU GUYS THIS TIME AND TIME AGAIN...
BUT I'VE NEVER FELT IT STRONGER THAN I DO RIGHT NOW...

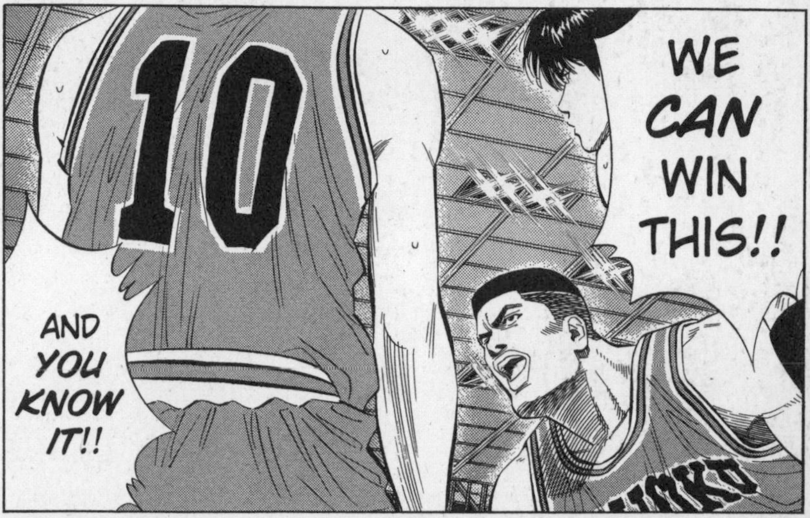
WE CAN WIN THIS!!
AND YOU KNOW IT!!
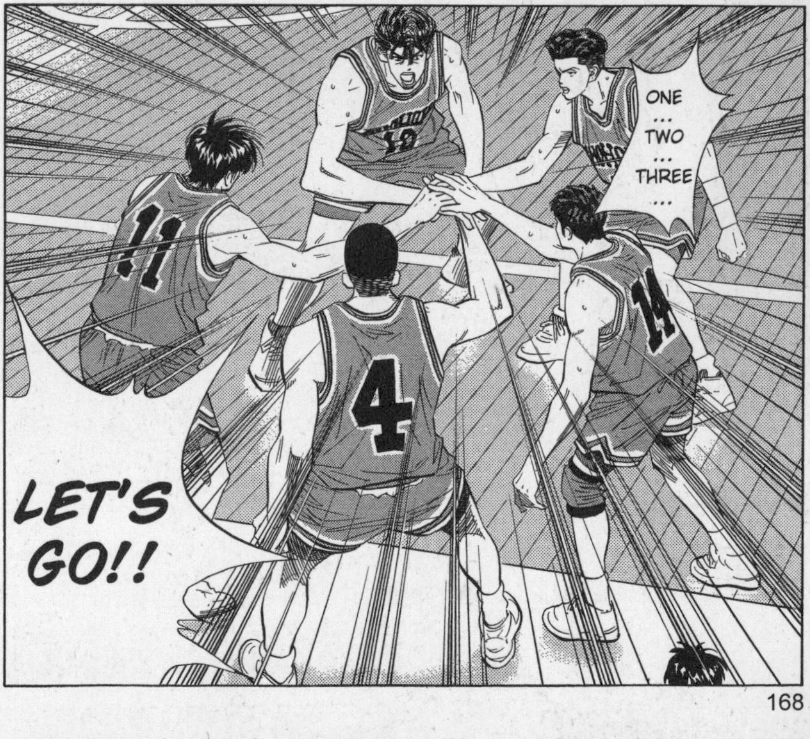
ONE ... TWO ... THREE ...
LET'S GO!!

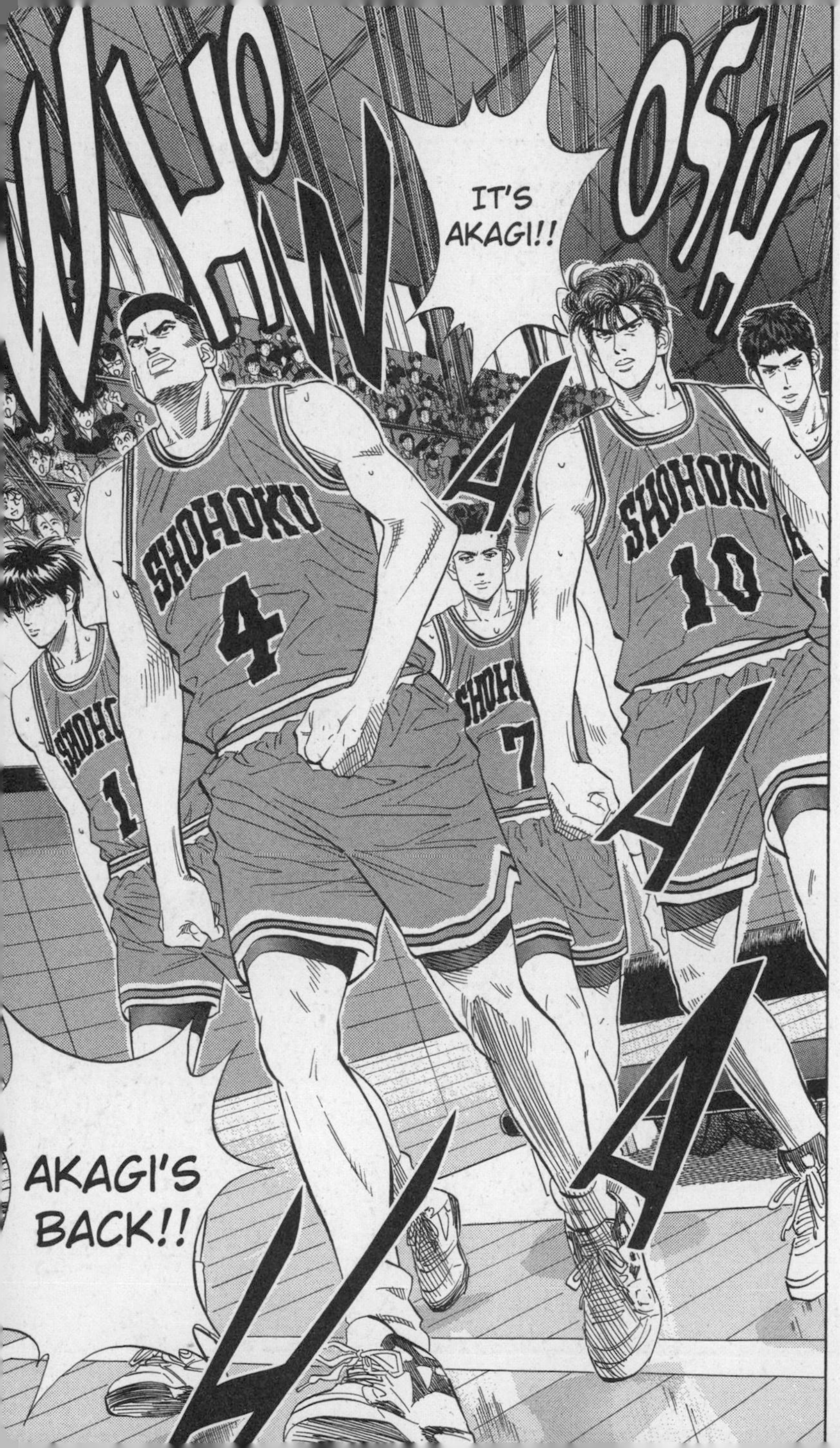
IT'S AKAGI!!
AKAGI'S BACK!!

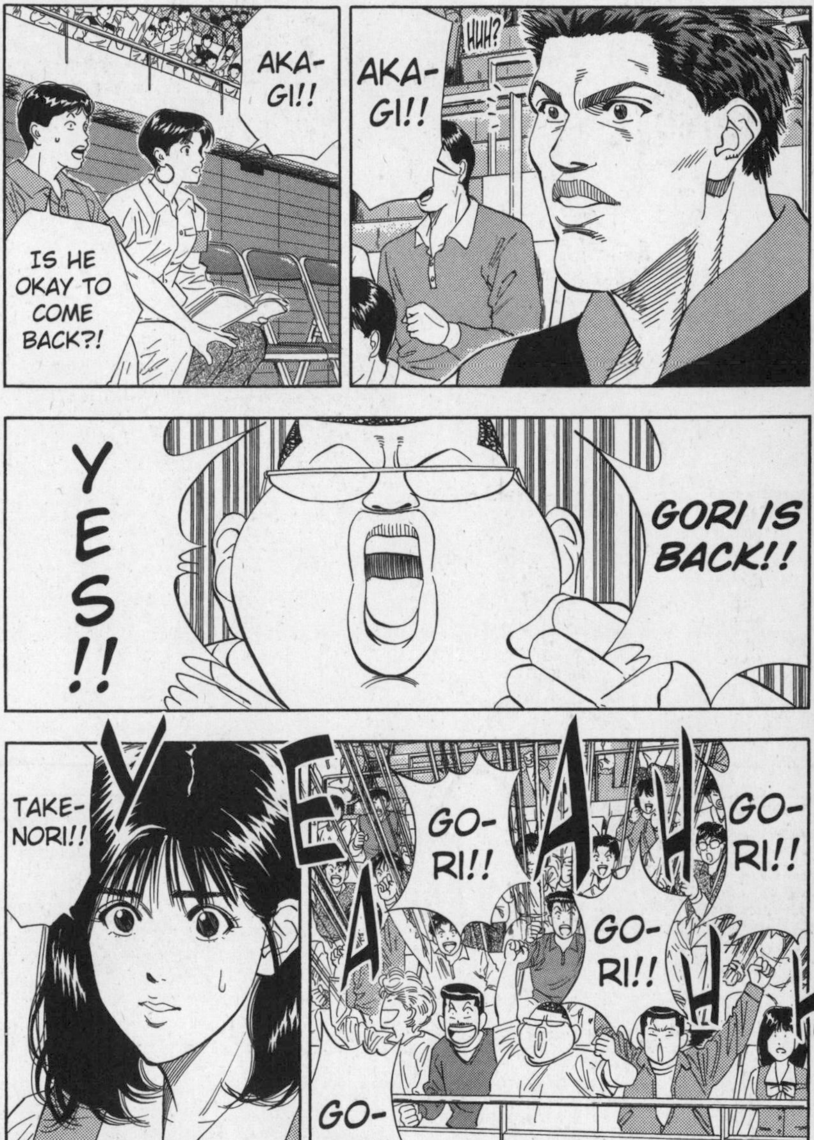
HUH?
AKA-GI!!
AKA-GI!!
IS HE OKAY TO COME BACK?!
GORI IS BACK!!
YES!!
GO-RI!!
GO-RI!!
GO-RI!!
GO-RI!!
YEAAHHH
TAKE-NORI!!

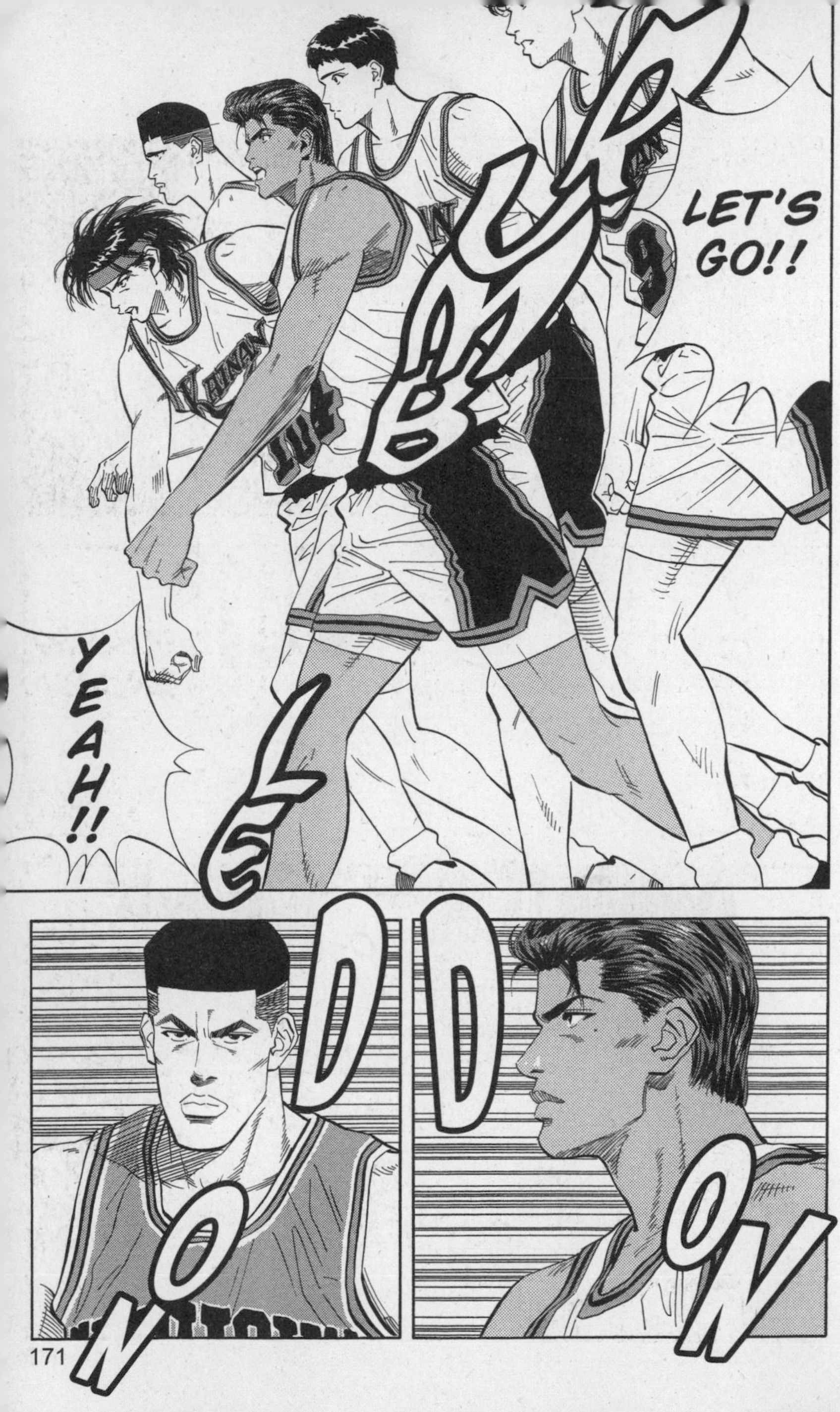
LET'S GO!!
YEAH!!

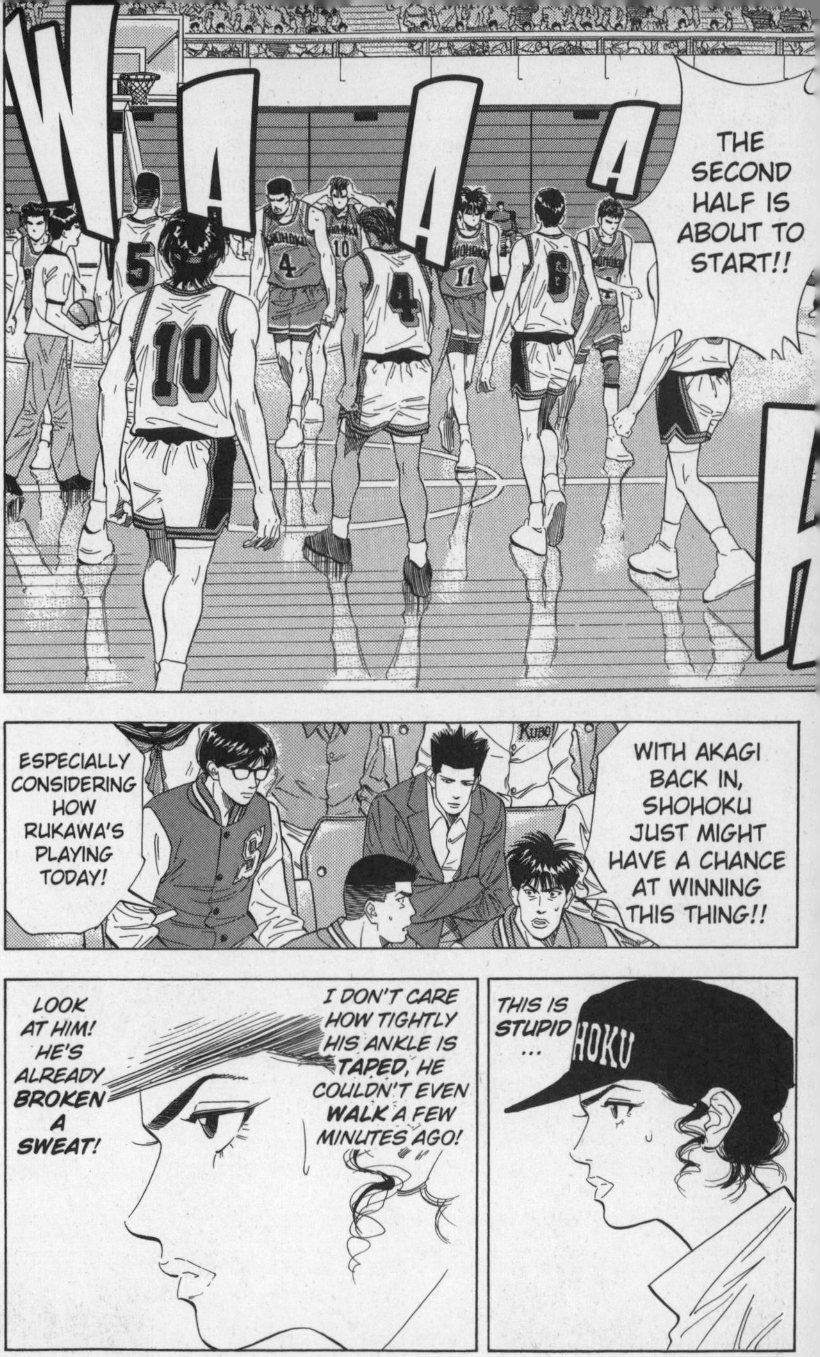
WAAA
THE SECOND HALF IS ABOUT TO START!!
WITH AKAGI BACK IN, SHOHOKU JUST MIGHT HAVE A CHANCE AT WINNING THIS THING!!
ESPECIALLY CONSIDERING HOW RUKAWA'S PLAYING TODAY!
THIS IS STUPID ...
I DON'T CARE HOW TIGHTLY HIS ANKLE IS TAPED, HE COULDN'T EVEN WALK A FEW MINUTES AGO!
LOOK AT HIM! HE'S ALREADY BROKEN A SWEAT!

READ THIS WAY

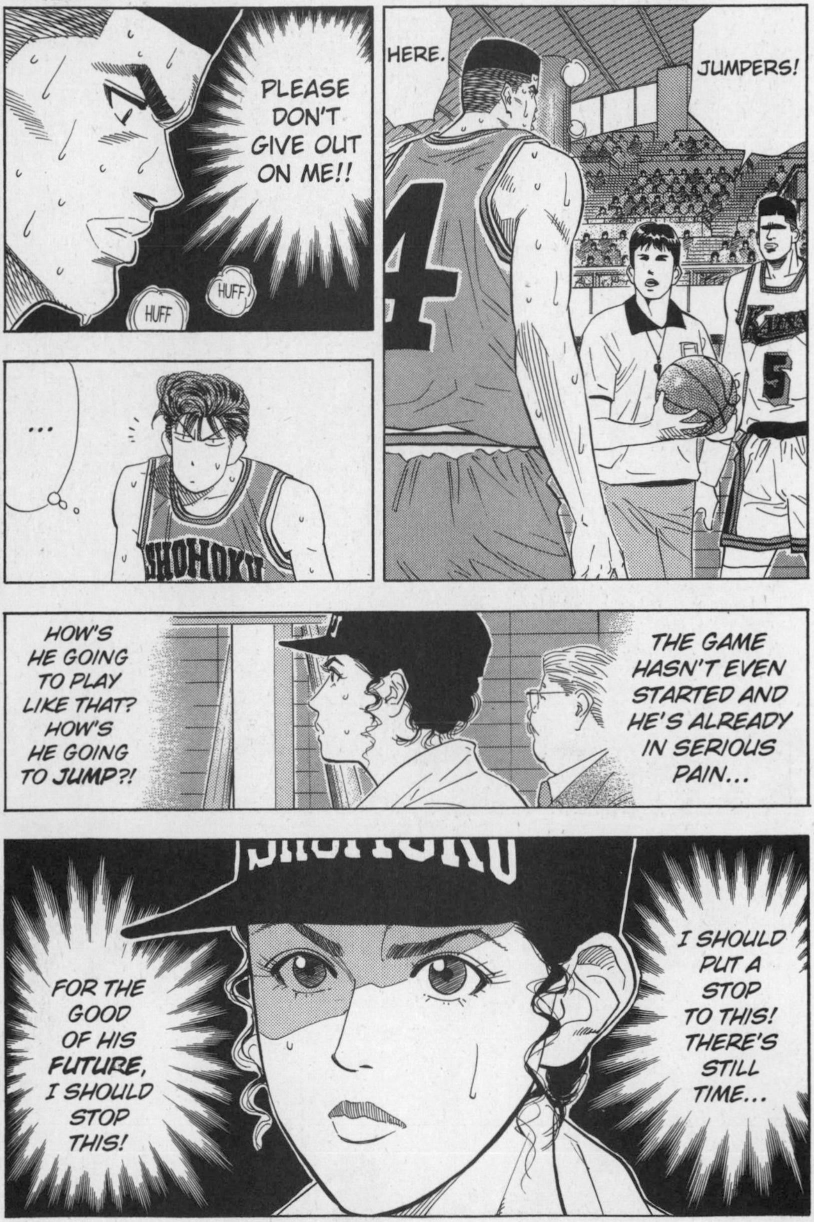

JUMPERS!
HERE.
PLEASE DON'T GIVE OUT ON ME!!
HUFF
HUFF
...
THE GAME HASN'T EVEN STARTED AND HE'S ALREADY IN SERIOUS PAIN...
HOW'S HE GOING TO PLAY LIKE THAT? HOW'S HE GOING TO JUMP?!
I SHOULD PUT A STOP TO THIS! THERE'S STILL TIME...
FOR THE GOOD OF HIS FUTURE, I SHOULD STOP THIS!

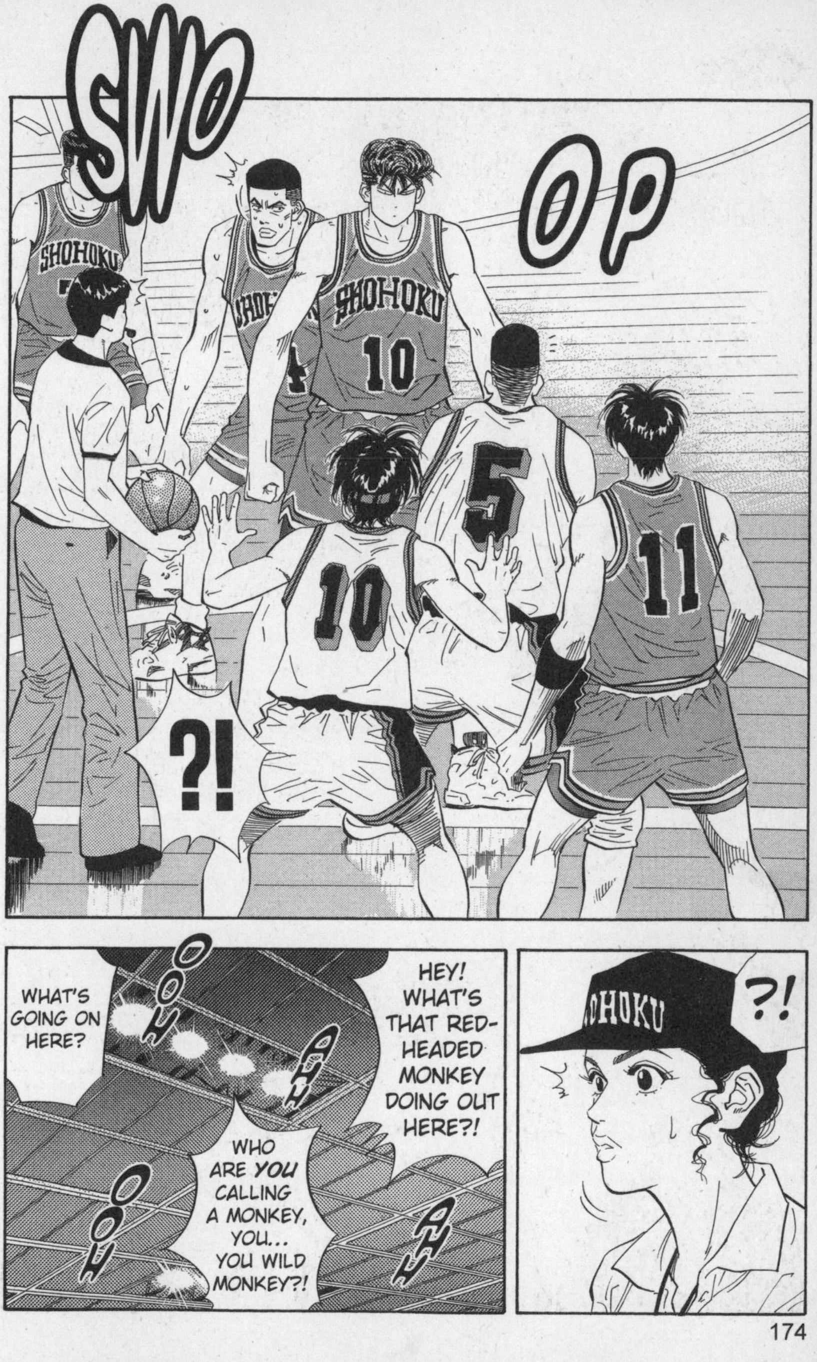
SWOOP
?!
?!
HEY! WHAT'S THAT RED-HEADED MONKEY DOING OUT HERE?!
WHAT'S GOING ON HERE?
OOOH
AHH
WHO ARE YOU CALLING A MONKEY, YOU... YOU WILD MONKEY?!
OOOH
AHH

READ THIS WAY

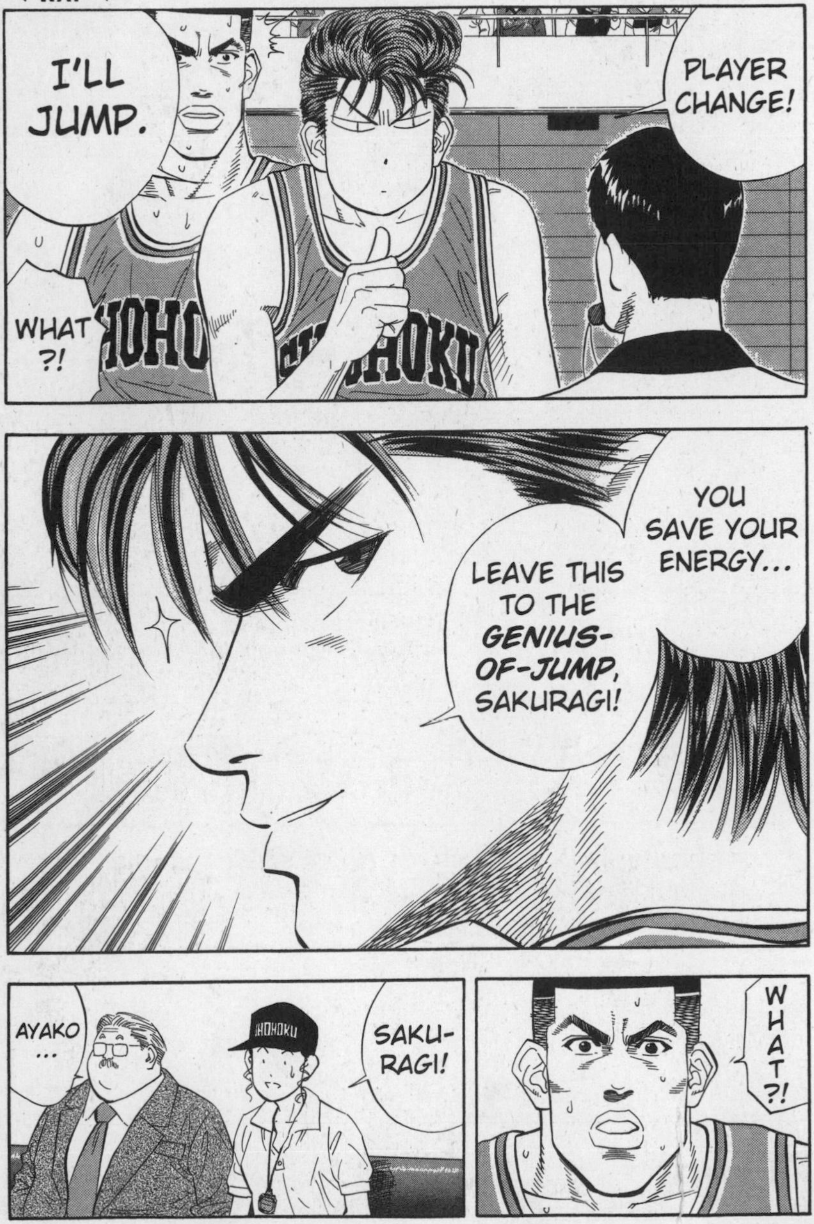
PLAYER CHANGE!
I'LL JUMP.
WHAT?!
YOU SAVE YOUR ENERGY...
LEAVE THIS TO THE *GENIUS-OF-JUMP*, SAKURAGI!
WHAT?!
SAKU-RAGI!
AYAKO ...

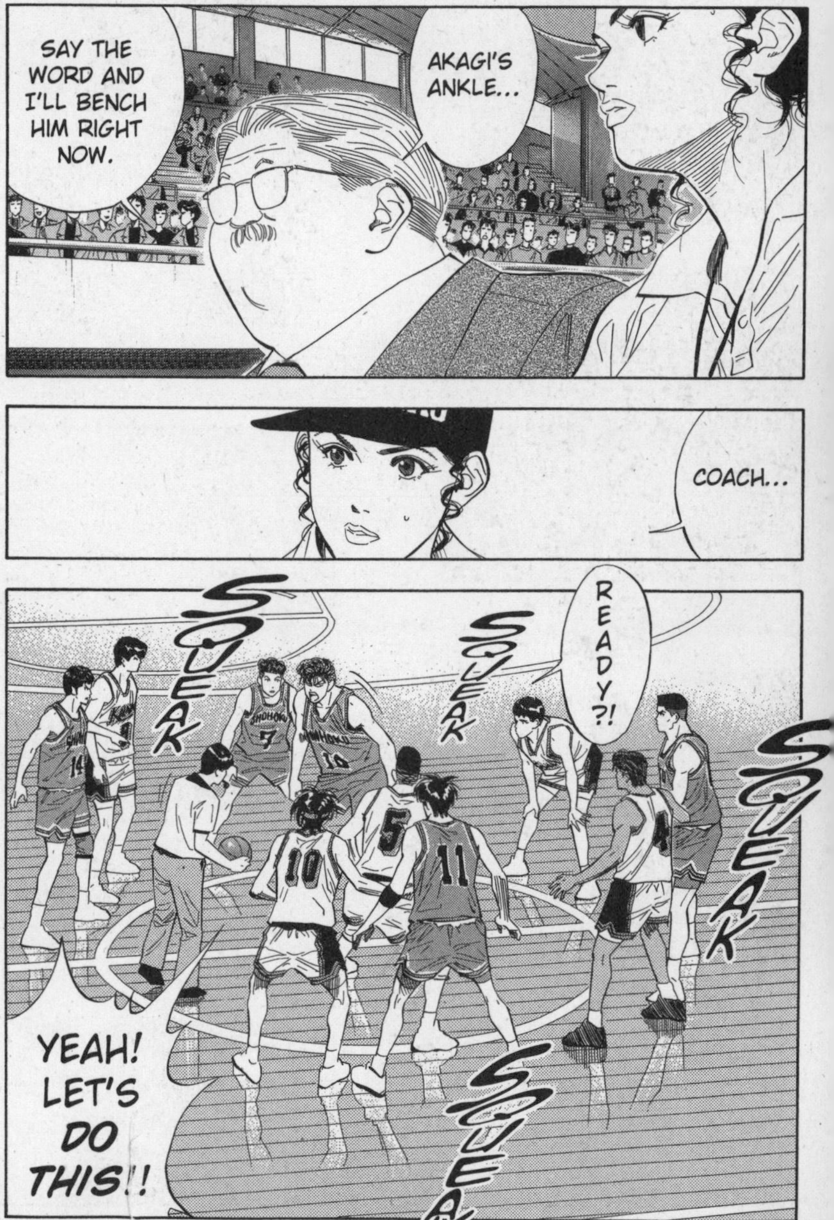
AKAGI'S ANKLE...
SAY THE WORD AND I'LL BENCH HIM RIGHT NOW.
COACH...
SQUEAK
READY?!
SQUEAK
SQUEAK
YEAH! LET'S DO THIS!!
SQUEAK

READ THIS WAY

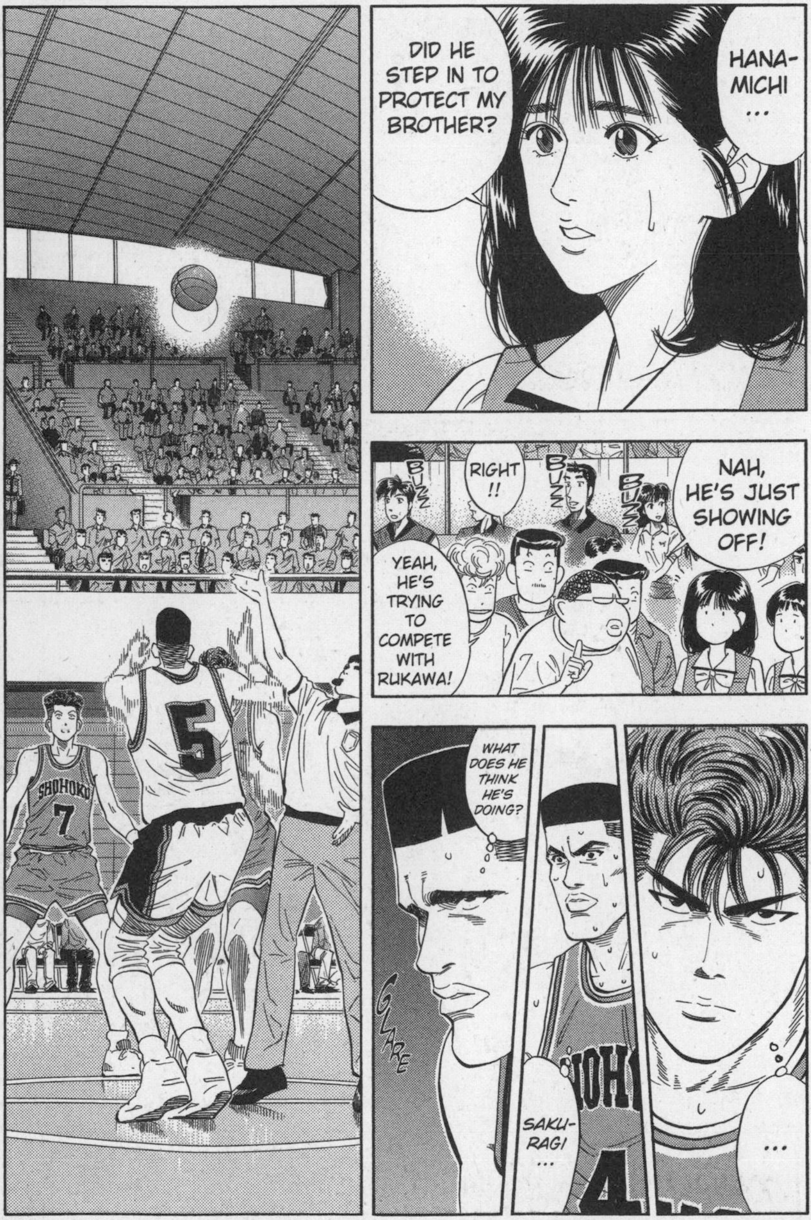
HANA-MICHI ...
DID HE STEP IN TO PROTECT MY BROTHER?
NAH, HE'S JUST SHOWING OFF!
BUZZ
RIGHT !!
BUZZ
BUZZ
YEAH, HE'S TRYING TO COMPETE WITH RUKAWA!
...
SAKU-RAGI ...
WHAT DOES HE THINK HE'S DOING?
GLARE

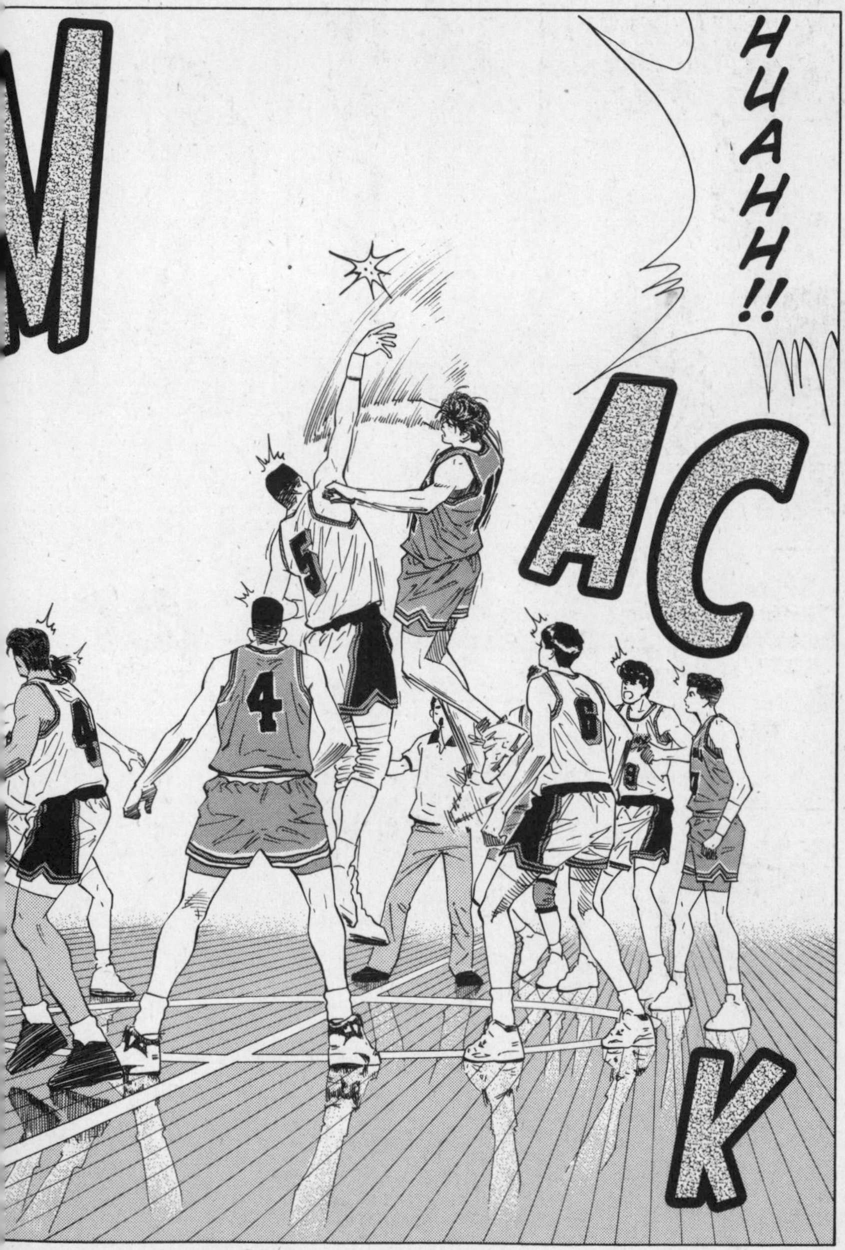
HUAHH!!
M
AC
K

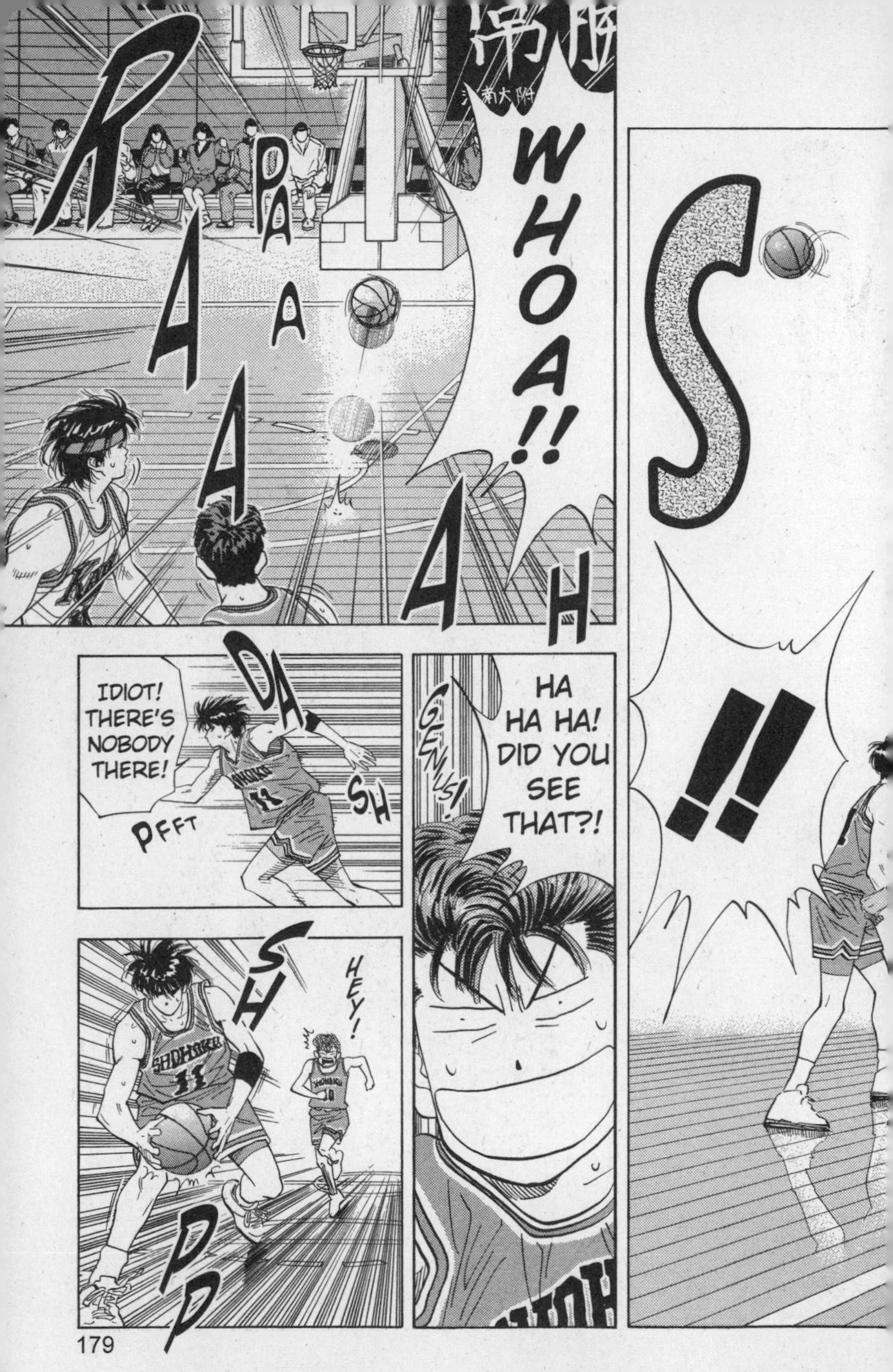
S
!!
WHOA!!
AH
PAA
RAA
GENIUS!
HA HA HA! DID YOU SEE THAT?!
IDIOT! THERE'S NOBODY THERE!
DA
SH
PFFT
SH
HEY!
DD

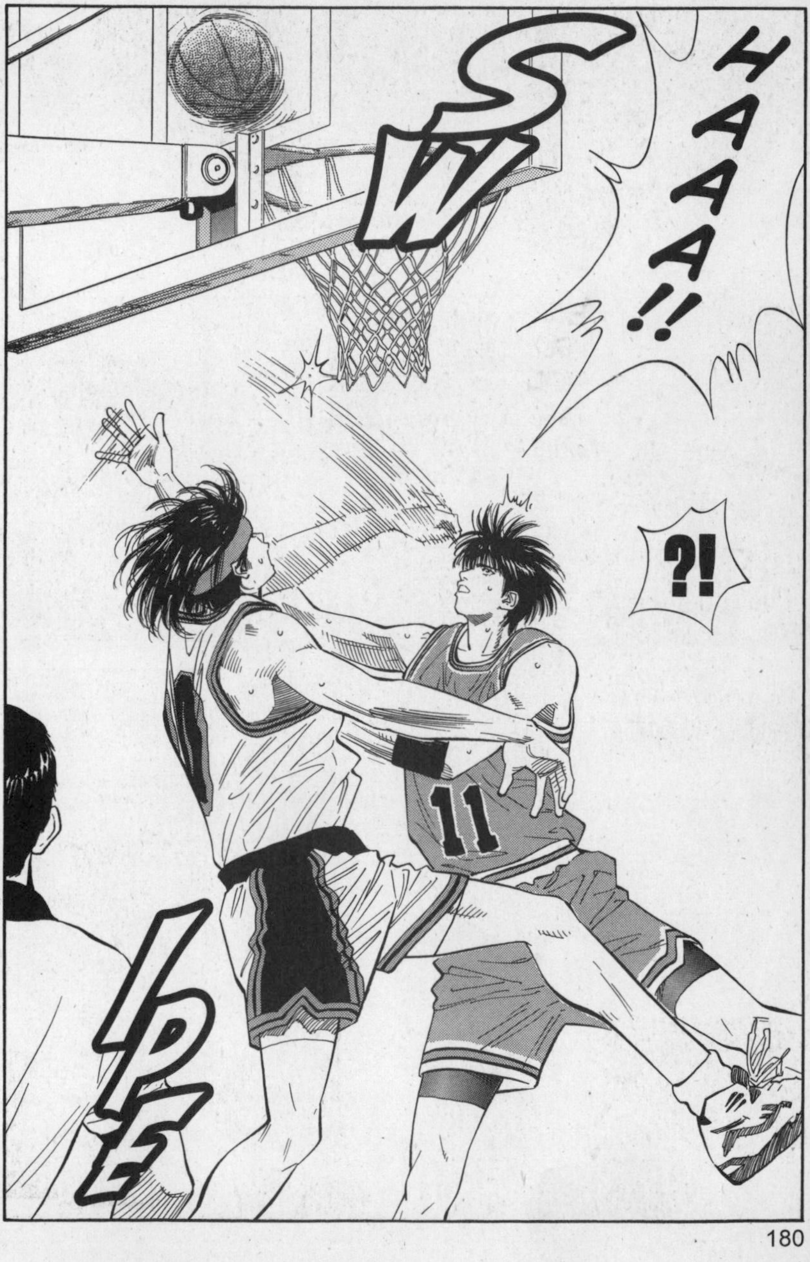
HAAA!!
SW
?!
IPE

READ THIS WAY

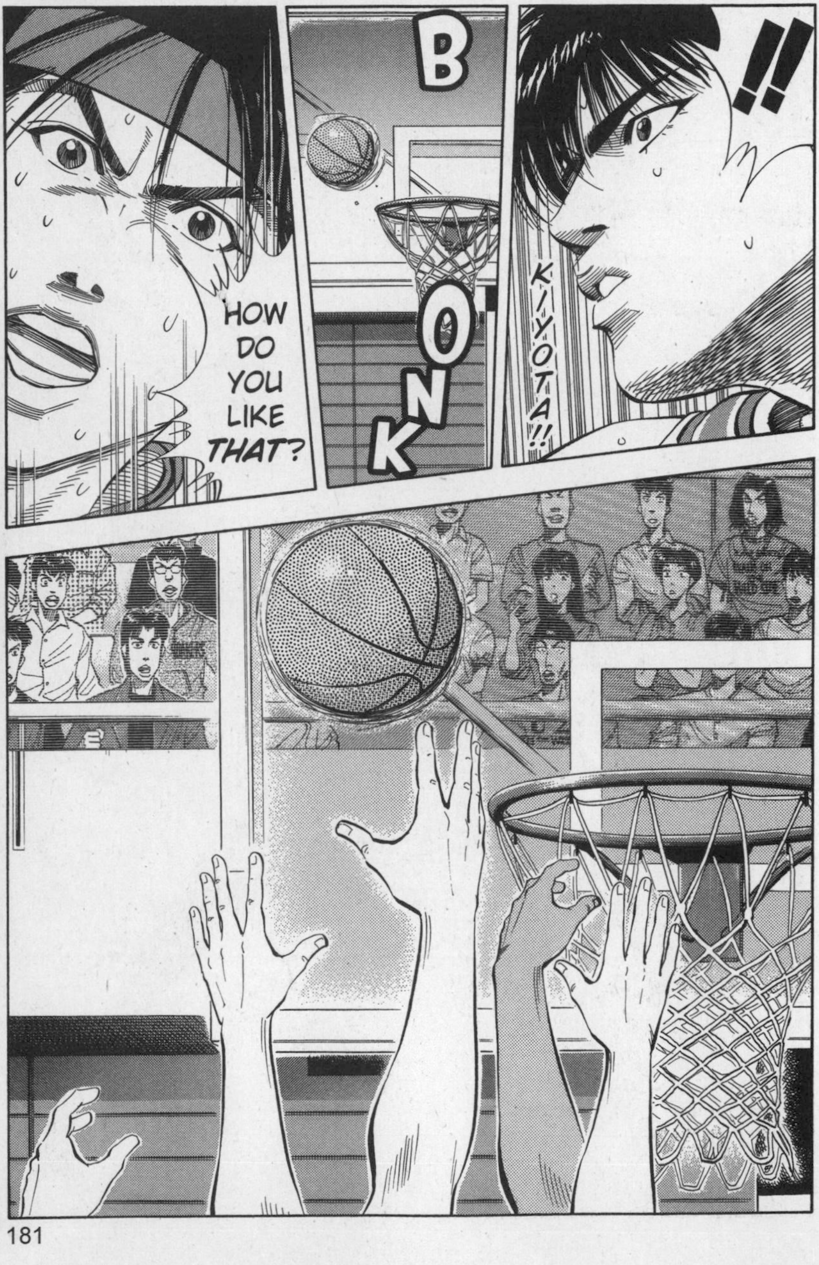
!!
KIYOTA!!
BONK
HOW DO YOU LIKE THAT?

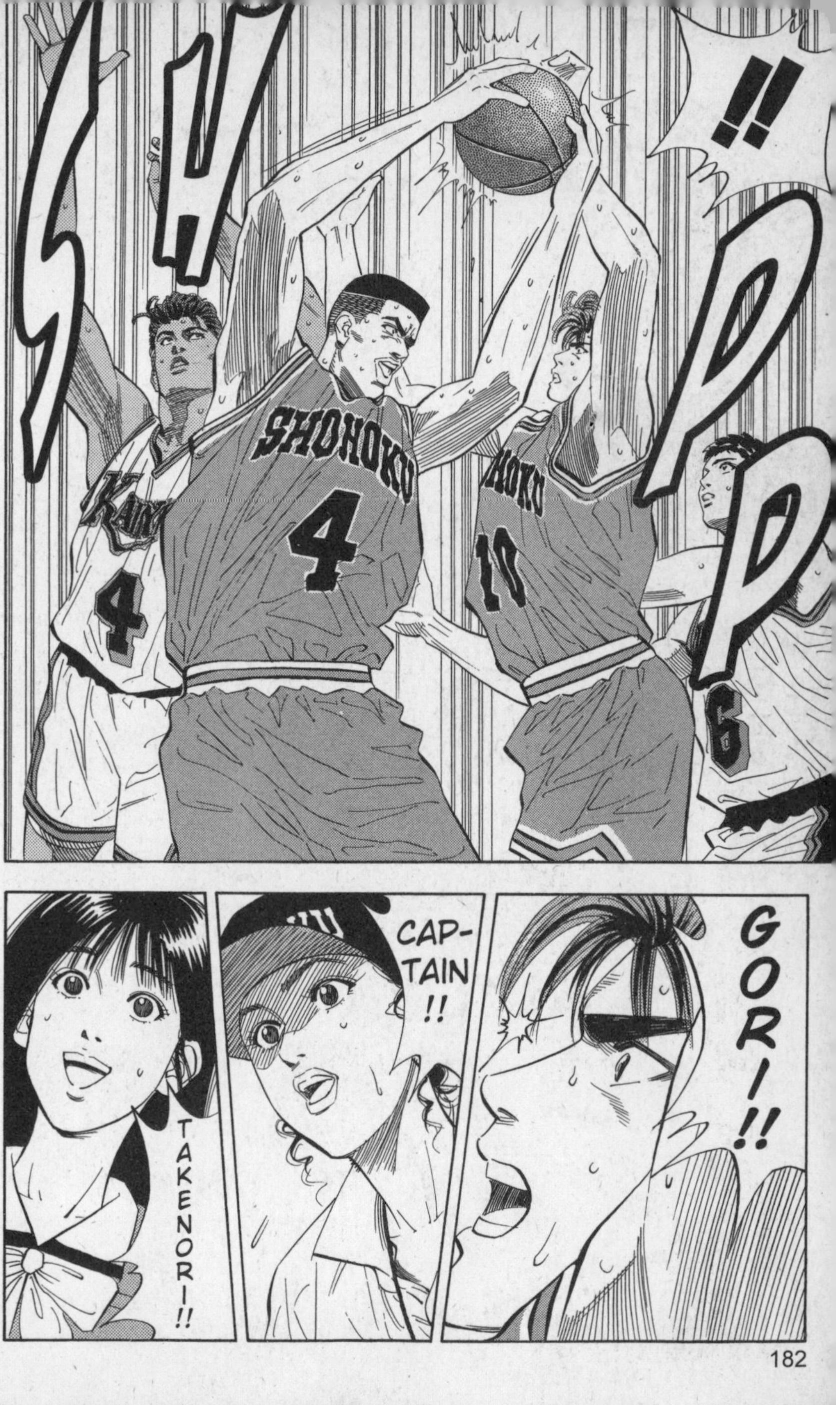
!!
SHPPP
GORI!!
CAP-
TAIN
!!
TAKENORI!!

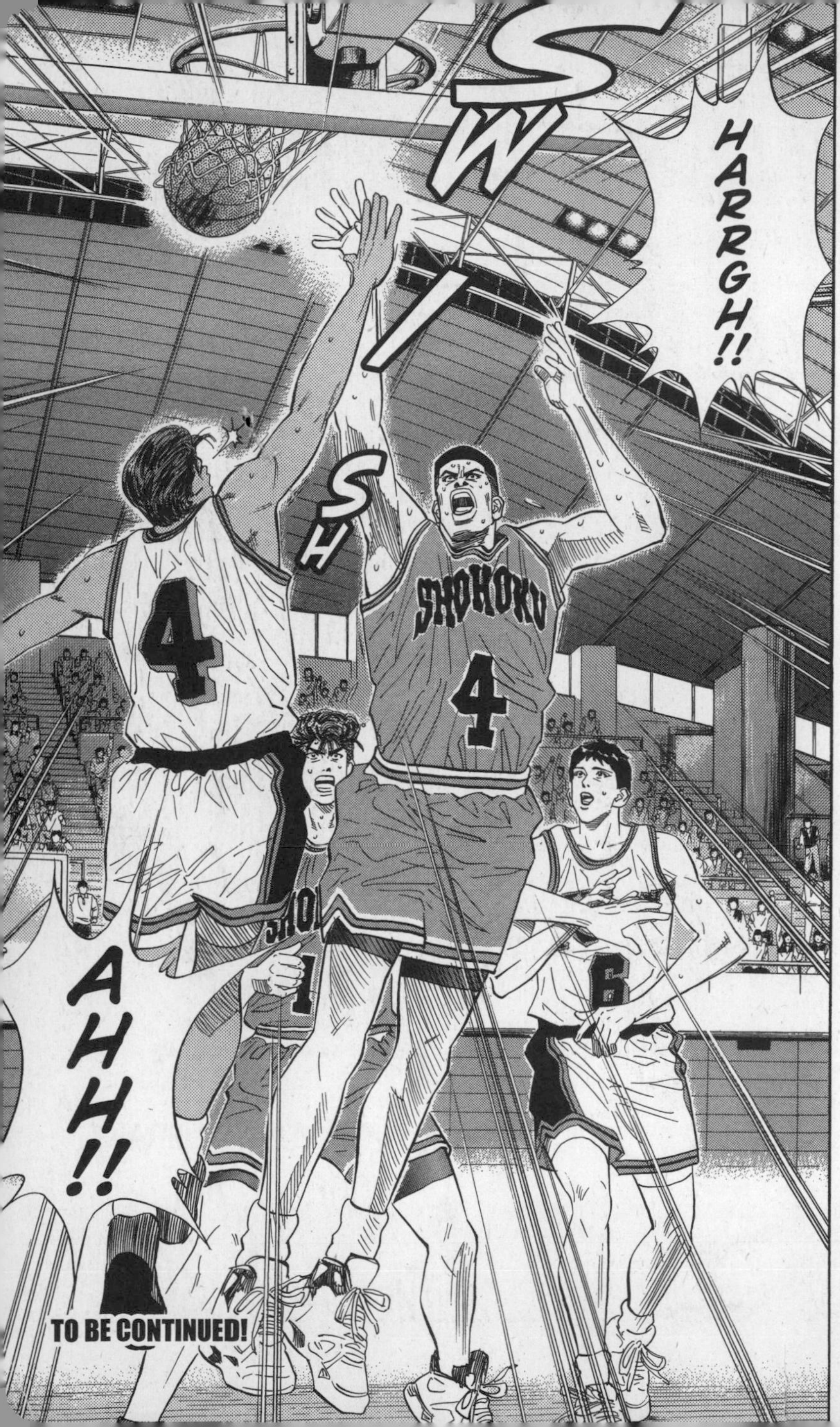
HARRGH!!
SWISH
AHH!!
TO BE CONTINUED!

Coming Next Volume

Captain Akagi is back in the game, but he now has a nagging injury that will certainly make it harder for his team to seal up a win. As expected, the Kings continue to show the squad from Shohoku absolutely no mercy. Shohoku tries desperately to stay in the game, but at this point Kainan seems to be able to simply score at will. Does Coach Anzai have a super-secret tactic up his sleeve, or are his boys about to be dealt a crushing defeat?

ON SALE FEBRUARY 2011